& Running a
Successful
Research
Business

A Guide for the Independent Information Professional

Second Edition

Mary Ellen Bates

CyberAge Books

 Information Today, Inc.

Medford, New Jersey

First Printing, 2010

Building & Running a Successful Research Business, Second Edition:
A Guide for the Independent Information Professional

Library of Congress Cataloging-in-Publication Data

Bates, Mary Ellen.
    Building & running a successful research business : a guide for the independent information professional / Mary Ellen Bates -- 2nd ed.
      p. cm.
    Rev. ed. of: Building & running a successful research business : a guide for the independent information professional. 2003.
    Includes index.
    ISBN 978-0-910965-85-9
    1. Information services industry. 2. Information services. 3. Information consultants. 4. New business enterprises. I. Title.
    HD9999.I492B38 2009
    025.5'2068--dc22

                                  2010001419

Printed and bound in the United States of America

President and CEO: Thomas H. Hogan, Sr.
Editor-in-Chief and Publisher: John B. Bryans
Managing Editor: Amy M. Reeve
VP Graphics and Production: M. Heide Dengler
Book Designer: Kara Mia Jalkowski
Cover Designer: Danielle Nicotra

www.infotoday.com

Building & Running a

Successful
Research
Business

Second Edition

Also by Mary Ellen Bates

Building & Running a Successful Research Business, 1st Edition
(Information Today, Inc., 2003)

*Super Searchers Cover the World: The Online Secrets of Global Business
Researchers* (Information Today, Inc., 2001)

Mining for Gold on the Internet (McGraw-Hill, 2000)

Researching Online For Dummies, 2nd Edition, co-authored with Reva
Basch (IDG Books Worldwide, 2000)

*Super Searchers Do Business: The Online Secrets of Top Business
Researchers* (Information Today, Inc., 1999)

The Online Deskbook (Information Today, Inc., 1996)

To the memory of my parents, Flo and Pete Bates, who taught me
to believe in myself and to take risks, and to Lin, who so enriches my life

Contents

Section One: Getting Started

Section Two: Running the Business

Section Three: Marketing

Section Four: Researching

Foreword

Mary Ellen Bates' first edition of *Building & Running a Successful Research Business* was published in 2003. Since then, a staggering explosion of content, sources, and tools have become available on the internet, and the development and growth of Web 2.0 blogging, wikis, RSS feeds, and podcasts are a sign of the times. In 2009, many more information professionals—individually or as part of their professional and trade associations—turned to social networking and the likes of Twitter, LinkedIn, Facebook, and others to collaborate, communicate, conduct research, or market themselves as name brands, a result of the growth and development of social media. Web 3.0 and the implementation of semantic web applications are on the horizon. In fact, by the time this book goes to press, they will be in the forefront of online life.

Apart from the massive growth of the internet, other major changes facing society and individuals emerged. The U.S. and the world experienced the worst recession since the Great Depression and almost everyone has been affected in some way. During economic downturns such as the one that began in December 2007, the bursting of the dot-com bubble that resulted in dot-gone at the turn of the 20th century, and the 1980s and 1990s recessions, more people consider starting businesses than during average times and more settled economic periods. Information professionals in particular are often well-positioned to succeed because employers continue to require the skills that their former employees possess. As such, some info businesses get their start by negotiating contracts with a previous employer, and colleagues and contacts from past environments become excellent referral sources. Nevertheless, starting a business can be daunting, and feeling fear and trepidation about change is a common emotion. Still, there are great opportunities for earning a satisfying and satisfactory income by applying one's creative energy to difficult times, and knowledge—such as the material presented in this book—overcomes fear.

Adding to vast changes in the information industry and broader socioeconomic trends are changing demographics among library and information science professionals. There has always been a wide range of expertise among independent information professionals, but today, there are even more business choices than ever. In particular, evidence of changing demographics is apparent, and the next generation of information entrepreneurs has materialized as professional colleagues within the Association of Independent Information Professionals (AIIP). Their business vision is quite different from my early introduction to information brokering in 1981. I was visiting the exhibit hall at a California Library Association conference when I first met pioneer information broker Sue Rugge and learned of her research and document delivery company, Information on Demand. The moment I met Sue, I realized that I too could start a business using these modern late-20th century inventions, if I were to hone my skills and learn how to operate a business. I set out to research the information brokerage industry—talking to several information brokers and digging up the articles and one book available at the time. Over the next year or two, I enrolled in business planning, marketing, and sales courses and workshops to learn about business. I began networking locally with business groups face-to-face and set the wheels of my business marketing in motion.

Many who start a research business today continue to come from the field of library science as I did, and their business visions are similar to mine; they work from a traditional information brokering model, conducting primarily secondary research using a wide range of resources. Others have embarked on their new business ventures with different ideas and individual and unique skill sets, experience, and knowledge. An information business today may offer services about or for many different industries or use business models that differ from my experience. Whereas some of the earlier information business pioneers primarily started out by conducting online research, those in today's world are all over the map with web and content management skills; publishing, writing, and internet development expertise; or knowledge of marketing and market research. Furthermore, and significantly, today's independent research professionals focus on value-added services. The products and services I offered in the 1980s included added value but today, value-adding means much more. Essentially, independent information professionals (IIPs) provide a specialty or expertise and save their clients time, while incorporating analysis over and beyond performing online, telephone, or primary research. Organized, synthesized, and analytical deliverables are required by clients and expected of IIPs today.

Many with library science education and experience, especially those from the public or academic sector, need more grounding and training in business development and marketing, whereas those who have worked in the business world often need additional instruction about how information is organized, how to conduct research using fee-based databases, what types of research methods there are, and how to better formulate research questions and apply advanced search techniques.

No matter what one's background, the detailed information about all aspects of building and running an information business that Mary Ellen provides in this book is indispensable. Classic business and marketing strategies rarely change, although ideas such as viral marketing have evolved. Technology, on the other hand, is in constant flux. The latest technologies have created a plethora of both opportunities and distribution channels for information business products and services. Mary Ellen lays the foundation needed to build and grow your business by putting into words her vast business experience and incorporating both the new and traditional. Whether one hails from library science, primary market research, private investigation, public records, nonprofit organizations, computer science, the hard sciences, or another business or consulting field, this book is the perfect starting place for finding answers to all the essential questions relevant to constructing a successful information business. Whether beginning a start-up or wanting to refresh your knowledge and expand, it's extremely fortunate that Mary Ellen has given us this second edition as a guide. Prospective and current information entrepreneurs will want to read the book a first time and then go back to it again and again to double check your ideas and experiences against the wisdom that Mary Ellen's insight and recommendations provide. *Building & Running a Successful Research Business* should be a required text for everyone in the business or thinking about it.

Amelia Kassel
MarketingBase
amelia@marketingbase.com

Acknowledgments

Sue Rugge, a pioneer independent information professional, is the person who inspired me to even consider writing this book. Sue started her first research business, Information Unlimited, back in 1971, and went on to found two more successful information businesses. She wrote *The Information Broker's Handbook* (now out of print), and many of us independent info pros depended on it when we started our businesses. Sue gave seminars on starting and running an information business and provided advice, encouragement, and friendship to thousands of people. She passed away in 1999, at the young age of 58. I feel enriched to have known her, and I still catch myself wanting to pick up the phone or email her to ask her advice. The Association of Independent Information Professionals (AIIP) established the Sue Rugge Memorial Award to recognize an AIIP member who, through mentoring, has significantly helped others establish their businesses. I was honored beyond words to be the first recipient of that award in 2000.

I especially want to thank a small group of friends and colleagues who let me pick their brains as I wrote the second edition of this book—Jan Davis, Marjorie Desgrosseilliers, Kim Dority, Jane John, Amelia Kassel, Alex Kramer, Marcy Phelps, Risa Sacks, and Cynthia Shamel. Their insights have enriched this book, and I have credited them whenever I could. More than that, though, they gave me valuable insights into how they have successfully run their information businesses. They are all successful business owners, and each of their businesses reflects the owner's unique talents and interests. I have tried to include their perspectives throughout this book.

And of this amazing group, I have to separately thank Marcy Phelps and Kim Dority. Your insight, friendship, and compassion have been a real gift in my life, and I always enjoy our SSW meetings.

I owe many thanks to John Bryans, my publisher at Information Today, Inc. He has been supportive of and enthusiastic about this book throughout the process of seeing it into print, as he has been with the four other titles of mine that he's published. John is always a joy to work with.

As anyone who works from home knows, a supportive family can make all the difference. I have been extraordinarily blessed with a partner who always has my back and whose love and support I cherish, and parents who always believed in me. Thank you, Lin (and Dad and Mom).

And finally, I owe a special debt, which I'll never be able to repay, to Scott Smith, a dear friend and extraordinary person who, in the year I knew him before his death, taught me so much about living mindfully and listening carefully.

Mary Ellen Bates
Niwot, Colorado

Introduction

When I wrote the first edition of this book, blogs were a novelty; Google's ad server was cranking out ads so fast that it ran out of "inventory" (not enough advertisers for the space available); and "knowledge management" was the hot new job title. What I find most exciting about what has happened since the early 2000s is that what was then only available to the big players is probably now just an app you can download to your phone.

When I first considered writing a second edition of *Building & Running a Successful Research Business*, I was daunted by the amount of work involved. So much has changed that I wasn't sure I could even use the same format for a second edition. Fortunately, many of the core principles and practices haven't changed that much. In fact, there are some basics that apply to info-entrepreneurs across the board. We still have to find ways to find and communicate with our clients. We still have to provide high-end services beyond "merely" providing high-quality research. And we still have the challenges inherent in this type of business, such as marketing effectively, pricing ourselves appropriately, and ensuring that we have happy, long-term clients.

That said, I found a lot of areas that, er, had been overtaken by events, and some of the brilliant marketing strategies I mentioned in the first edition are no longer all that innovative. I wound up rewriting about half of Section One: Getting Started (including a new chapter on You.com), about a third of Section Two: Running the Business, much of Section Three: Marketing, and a fair bit of Section Four: Researching. This edition also has three more chapters and about 20 percent more content.

Another big change from the first edition is that, back in 2007, I began offering strategic coaching services to new and long-time info-entrepreneurs. This is by far the most rewarding aspect of my business, and it keeps my perspective fresh in terms of knowing how it feels to be at the very beginning of your business. At least once a month, I hear one of my clients say, "I have all these good ideas but I have no idea where to start," and I am reminded of how it felt when I started my business. One of the most heartening aspects of coaching is that I continue to see people succeed in this business, and I get the opportunity to help people who have been in business for five or 10 years look at their business with new eyes and a new perspective. I continue to be very optimistic about the future for independent information professionals. We offer what clients need more and more of every year: assistance in making strategic decisions based on the best information and analysis available.

And now, back to my original introduction, with minor updates.

I'll never forget when I met my first independent information professional. It was 1979, and I was taking the Friday afternoon ferry from San Francisco back home to Berkeley. This was the party ferry—everyone brought wine or snacks—and we would hold a floating happy hour as we watched the sun set over the Golden Gate Bridge and marveled at our good fortune of living in the most beautiful place in the world. I was chatting with my boss, a law firm librarian, and she introduced me to Georgia Finnigan, who had recently dissolved a partnership with Sue Rugge and launched her own information business, The Information Store. I'm not sure what amazed me more—that Georgia had just up and started a new company or that she read the *Wall Street Journal* because she found it thought-provoking. (This was back when we counter-culturalists simply didn't read the publications of "capitalist pigs.") I remember thinking that Georgia had the most exciting job I had ever heard of, but also that I couldn't imagine how there would be more than two people in the world who could run this sort of business and that she and Sue must have the market locked up.

Years went by, and I continued working in specialized libraries of one sort or another. I am not quite sure how it happened; it may have been on the exhibit floor at a librarians' conference, when I stumbled onto the booth of the Association of Independent Information Professionals (AIIP). There they were, in the flesh—normal-looking people who had walked away from a regular job in an office with a steady paycheck and were now running their own information businesses. I couldn't believe that there was an entire association of people like Sue Rugge and Georgia Finnigan, and that they actually got together, talked with each other, referred work to each other, and were friends.

Intrigued, I sidled up to the booth and struck up a conversation with the AIIP member who was staffing the booth at the time—Reva Basch. She encouraged me to join AIIP, even if I wasn't ready to start my own business yet. I nodded doubtfully, took the membership application, and scurried off to the more "normal" booths of information vendors and bookshelf manufacturers. "Whew," I thought, "close call!"

Well, I kept thinking about this independent info pro thing, and somewhere along the line, I decided that if all these other people could do it, I could, too. As

Reva suggested, I joined AIIP, I listened in on the private AIIP electronic discussion board, and I got to know a number of established info pros. I realized that it wasn't all sitting around in your bunny slippers waiting for clients to call, but I also figured out that it was the type of work that I enjoyed doing and that I would find challenging, not just at first but over the course of years. After a year or two of thinking about it, saving up enough money to pay for my first six months' of expenses, and screwing up the courage to abandon the safety net of steady employment, I finally did it—on April 1, 1991, I started Bates Information Services.

I loved being an information entrepreneur from day one. I was able to try anything I wanted—no committees to run proposals by, no boss to sign off on a new strategy—and, as my business grew, I had the satisfaction of knowing that it was because my clients wanted *me* to do work for them. Yes, I have had my share of days when I longed for the relative simplicity of a regular job, where I didn't have to juggle the responsibilities of CEO, financial planner, sales staff, marketing director, file clerk, and researcher. But I have also never had as much fun in any other job. In fact, when I entered the second decade of my business, I realized that I had been an independent info pro longer than I had held any other job in my life, and I never cease to marvel that I managed to stumble into what is, for me, the perfect career.

As I watch the economy go through its inevitable growth and contraction cycles, I am reminded that running my own business actually gives me more job stability than if I were working for someone else. How's that? If you are an employee, you get all your income from one source—your employer. If you lose your job, your income immediately drops to $0/year, and you can spend the next few months at that same (non)salary until you find another job. On the other hand, if I lose a client, I see a temporary drop in my revenue, but that was only one client among many. I always have other sources of income, so the loss of any one client is never devastating. Now that no employer offers lifetime employment, the steadiest job is often one you make yourself.

Where Independent Info Pros Come From

When I first learned about independent info professionals, most of the existing businesses were run by librarians and researchers—people who had already spent years finding information in physical libraries, in online databases, through telephone interviews, and by going to courthouses and government agencies to dig around in files. These days, though, AIIP is full of people who come to this profession from other fields, having worked as marketing specialists, engineers, or lawyers. Lynn Peterson, owner of PFC Information Services, previously owned a business that offered recruitment and placement services for nannies and housekeepers. Tom Culbert, president of Aviation Information Research, served 21 years in the U.S. Air Force, as a pilot and then a staff officer. Alex Kramer, owner of Kramer Research, worked for PI firms. Not a librarian among them.

Successful independent info pros may launch their companies without all the business, entrepreneurial, research, and people skills they need, but they've figured out how to acquire the expertise they don't have or outsource the aspects of the business that they can't do themselves and that are not mission-critical. This book will show you what you need to know, give you the tools to help you succeed, and teach you where to go to fill in the gaps in your knowledge.

Getting Started as an Independent Info Pro

The comment I hear the most from aspiring independent info pros is, "I've always been an info junkie, but I never realized that I could make money from it." Well, maybe you can, but it's not as simple as that. Running a successful business means not only having the research skills but also being able to think and act like an entrepreneur—to know how to price your services, anticipate changes in the economy and the information environment, market yourself and your business constantly, and develop new skills as your clients' needs change.

Running an information business also requires courage and determination. You're it; there is no one else to help you make the tough decisions, to handle the difficult client, or to tell you that you need to work on your financial planning skills, for example. Your income fluctuates from month to month, and at times it seems like all your marketing efforts are failing and no client will ever call you again. That's when you pick up the phone or go online to get a reality check with your colleagues. We have all gone through similar difficulties; we have all weathered the same kinds of crises.

The first section of this book introduces you to what is involved in info-entrepreneurship—what kinds of work you can do, what kinds of clients you can market to, and what kinds of resources you will need. I talk about how to plan your business launch, how to mentally prepare yourself for your new life as a business owner, what you need to set up your office, and how to make time for life outside of work.

Now That I've Started, Where Do I Go?

Once you have hung out your shingle, virtually if not physically, what do you do next? Section Two, Running the Business, gets into the nitty-gritty of being a business owner. You will learn about writing proposals and presenting project estimates, about finding the money to start your business and keep it going, about running a business ethically, managing (and firing!) clients, and about functioning as your own private brain trust to provide yourself with a strategic vision. You will also learn how to establish rates and fees that will sustain your business, send the right message to your clients (that you're an expert and worth your fee), and enable you to pay yourself the salary you want. I also cover the topic of subcontracting—taking advantage of the web of relationships we independent info pros build among ourselves to ensure that we can all provide high-quality research services to our clients.

While you may read the first section of this book just once, when you are planning and starting your business, you will be consulting Section Three, Marketing, for as long as you are in operation. Marketing is a constant in most businesses, and independent info pros are no exception. This section will tell you about establishing your business image, about low-cost and low-effort marketing efforts that you can start now and sustain over the years, and about high-impact marketing techniques that will get your clients to pay attention to you and what you offer to them.

When I started my business, I didn't realize how much I would need to market myself, not just at first, but even after my business had been growing for a few years. Fortunately, I started out, like the early U.S. space program, with the attitude that failure was not an option. So, when I decided that I needed to do some public speaking to get my face and name in front of potential clients, I didn't immediately reject the idea, even though my first reaction was to recoil in horror. Yes, the first four or five speeches I gave turned my knees to jelly and tied my stomach into knots, but I did them anyway, because my business was *not* going to fail. After a while, public speaking got easier, and I learned how to harness the nervous energy I would get before my talk and direct it into the focus and enthusiasm I needed to get my points across.

There are probably some aspects of marketing that you will tell yourself you simply cannot do. At that point, remind yourself that the worst that can happen is that it won't work, and you will have to try something else. You only spend as much money as you can afford to lose. If that's all that is at stake, why not try it? Perhaps, like me, you will learn that you have skills you didn't suspect you had, and you will discover that you actually enjoy doing something that at first seemed impossible.

Getting Down to Research

Section Four, Researching, comes after the discussions about running and marketing your business for a reason. I assume you are already interested in research; that's why you are reading this book. What many new independent info pros forget, though, is that your research skills alone won't bring in the clients and revenue. You must first think through the practicalities of how you will actually make money at it.

The section on researching covers the client information needs assessment, known in librarian circles as the reference interview. It also includes a template for developing your mental road map for research and discusses which information resources are best for different types of research. Then you'll get an overview of the various kinds of research that independent info pros provide: research on the web and the fee-based online services, telephone research and in-depth interviewing, public records research using government agencies and courthouses, and other types of services independent info pros can offer. I also describe tools and techniques for highlighting the value of the information you provide to clients, presenting your research results in ways that your clients will find most useful, and becoming a strategic member of your client's team.

One final caveat: I have quoted a number of experienced info pros throughout this book and, whenever possible, have included the perspective of as many information entrepreneurs as possible. But I accept responsibility for any opinions, conclusions, or recommendations that I don't attribute to others, as well as any errors.

For new ideas on searching and on marketing your business, you might be interested in subscribing to my free email newsletters. You can sign up on my website at www.BatesInfo.com. Good luck with your new business! I trust that you will find this profession as challenging, satisfying, and fun as I have over the years.

Getting
Started

Chapter 1

What's an Independent Info Pro?

What's This Business All About?

I assume that you have some notion of what the independent information profession covers—finding, organizing, and managing information—or you wouldn't have picked up this book. But different people define this profession differently, and it is a common misconception that most research can be done on the web. While the internet *has* radically changed how independent info pros operate, much of our work involves research outside the portion of the web that most people are familiar with—that is, beyond what you can find by typing a few words into your favorite search engine.

In the most general terms, independent information professionals work for themselves or as partners in a two- or three-person business; they provide information services, such as research, analysis, information management, or consulting services, and they charge their clients for their services, either per project or on an hourly or daily basis. Many independent info pros worked as librarians or researchers before launching their own businesses; they may have spent years honing their research skills within large corporations or research centers. Others started out as professionals in other fields—lawyers, engineers, or marketing consultants, for example—then shifted their focus to providing research support to others within their profession. What all successful independent info pros have in common are strong entrepreneurial skills. They enjoy the challenge of building a business, they excel at managing their clients, and they are self-motivated. They didn't all start out as natural entrepreneurs, but they were willing to hone their business skills in order to succeed.

The independent information profession is a wide-open field; there are far more potential clients out there than people providing research and analysis services to them. No one has accurate numbers on the total number of independent info pros in the marketplace. The Association of Independent Information Professionals (AIIP; www.aiip.org), the trade association of the profession, has about 700 members. But this total does not accurately reflect the total number of independent info pros in business at any point in time; probably 10 times as many exist who aren't AIIP members. A fairly high turnover rate prevails among independent info businesses, reflecting the entrepreneurial world as a whole, in which, according to many studies, more than half of all small businesses fail within the first year and 80 or 90 percent of all businesses close within five years.

People who leave the independent info pro field usually cite one of the following reasons:

- They miss the daily stimulation of a more traditional office environment.

- They have difficulty dealing with the dramatically fluctuating cash flow.

- They don't enjoy the amount of administrative and marketing work required.

- They no longer have the passion and energy for the business that they had initially.

I have been an independent info pro for nearly 30 years, and I have watched a number of colleagues' businesses start up and then shut down. Often the closing of the business results in unexpected successes—formerly independent info pros re-enter the more traditional work force with newly acquired business skills and often find that they are much more valuable to employers because of their experience running a small business.

So What Do You Do, Anyway?

The independent information profession encompasses a wide variety of services. This section includes brief descriptions of many of the most common types of services offered by info-entrepreneurs. Most independent info pros specialize in a particular kind of research and focus on a specific industry or vertical market. Many of us have a wide range of clients—mine include consultants, engineers, ad agencies, executives from *Fortune* 100 firms, lawyers, and web entrepreneurs, among others— but most of us focus on a specific market or niche. What all my clients have in common is that they call me for strategic business information. Other independent info pros may target the healthcare industry, architectural firms, the pharmaceutical market, or the IT industry. While many of us also have clients outside our primary market, we tend to target our marketing efforts on a specific subject area or industry. Note that some of the information services described here, particularly document delivery, are more likely than others to serve clients across vertical markets.

Web Research

With the prevalence of databases on the web, most independent info pros who provide research services of any sort include at least some web-based research in their portfolios. That may include locating government statistics on international trade, analyzing company filings at the U.S. Securities and Exchange Commission, or scanning blogs for discussion of a consumer product. Info-entrepreneurs use social networking sites such as LinkedIn or Facebook to identify experts to interview as well as to build their network. They mine email discussion groups and online forums to identify key opinion leaders.

The key element is that info-entrepreneurs don't just throw a few words into a search engine and retrieve exactly what their clients want. While being a good web searcher is essential to just about any research business, that alone will not provide the skills needed to provide high-end, high-value research to clients. But even projects that do not appear to focus on web research usually require some web aspect:

- A client wanted a strategic overview on the iced tea market in the U.K. As I expected, most of this work required identifying in-depth market research reports and searching the fee-based online services. However, as I was creating a table with the key features of each of the beverage companies, I realized that I had to analyze the messages of each brand. That required drilling deep into each company's website to see how each positioned its brand.

- I was asked to gather information on the vacuum-insulated panel (VIP) industry; VIPs are what keep refrigerated trucks cold, medical coolers cool, and your house warm. Part of my research involved identifying the major players in this field, and one of my approaches included searching in the

U.S. Patent & Trademark Office's database of patents, on the assumption that companies with multiple patents in this field are probably big players in the VIP industry.

- An entrepreneur who wanted to create a network of highly influential executives asked me to identify the 10 most influential chiropractors in 15 cities. While much of the work for this project was telephone research, I used an add-on for Google Maps to show where each of the chiropractors was located and the relative population density and household income of each location—something that added substantial value to the results of the telephone work.

Online Research

While the depth of information on the web can sometimes feel overwhelming, the professional online services described in Chapter 34 are even richer sources of information than the free or public web. These databases include material that never appears on the web, and they provide sophisticated search tools and value-added features that enable users to conduct in-depth research in ways not possible on the web.

Using the professional online services can be an expensive proposition. These services charge by the search, by the document, by the amount of time you spend connected to them, or by various other pricing algorithms. As an independent info pro, you pass along the online expenses to your clients, and these costs can sometimes add up to a third or more of the total project cost. Note that there is very little demand in the marketplace for independent info pros who only provide web research without in-depth analysis and other added value. The public perception, whether or not it's correct, is that it takes no great skill to search the web. We set ourselves apart by offering access to online research sources not generally available to our clients and by using uncommon, lesser-known, and complex web-based sources.

Public Records Research

Although much consternation has arisen recently about supposedly easy access to personal information on the web, a great deal of information about individuals has always been available in court clerks' and county recorders' offices and other government agencies. Some of these records are now available on the web, but many still reside only in print files. Public records research includes:

- Reviewing bankruptcy filings to determine what assets are held by a corporation

- Conducting a pre-employment check of a school bus driver to make sure he has no criminal record or driving offenses

- Looking through articles of incorporation to identify the executives of a privately held company

- Finding prior court testimony given by an expert witness to determine how she is likely to testify for an upcoming case

Public records research is not for the faint of heart. It often requires a private investigator's license, it requires a good understanding of the ins and outs of various government agencies, and it takes a gut sense to know when you have found all the pieces of the puzzle. See Chapter 36, Public Records Research, for more information.

Telephone Research

Despite the much-talked-about "information explosion," a lot of information never appears in print or in any electronic format. Sometimes, the fastest way to obtain such information is simply to call an expert in the field and ask. Telephone research is an art form, and many independent info pros—myself included—don't have the necessary combination of charm, patience, persistence, and chutzpah, and the ability to talk to anyone about anything. This type of work tends to involve more hours per project and a longer turnaround time than other types of research because of its very nature. Merely identifying the person who can answer your question might involve 10 or 15 calls. When you factor in the inevitable delays brought on by voice-mail tag and varying business schedules and time zones, it means that very few telephone research projects can be completed in less than a week, even if the total amount of time spent on the phone is only a fraction of that time.

The kind of telephone research I am talking about here requires more sophisticated research techniques than just running through a list of survey questions with a preselected list of contacts. Usually, you will get an assignment to find out about a specific topic, and you will have to develop your own leads. That means some preliminary web, online, or library research to identify likely sources for the information, as well as deciding on the best way to approach the project and exactly what questions to ask.

Telephone researchers get much of their work from researchers within organizations and in the form of referrals from other independent info pros. From a marketing point of view, networking is particularly important in order to develop a large client base of subcontracting sources. Chapter 35 goes into more detail about what is involved in telephone research.

Library Research

When the independent information profession began, much of our research involved going to libraries on behalf of clients. Some projects still call for library research or, similarly, contacting information centers or other brick-and-mortar collections of material. An info pro might travel to a government agency's information center to search a database not available on the web, email a university library in Sweden to find a copy of a doctoral thesis, arrange to visit a trade association's library to use its specialized collection, or review records in the U.S. National Archives to determine how a particular site was used by the U.S. Army 50 years ago, in order to determine what hazardous materials may still be lurking in the soil and groundwater.

As more government agencies, embassies, associations, and other resources make their information available on the web, demand for hands-on library research has diminished. On the other hand, library research can sometimes unearth information not available anywhere in electronic format. I recently browsed through the membership directory of AIIP, looking at the listings for "unique collections" that members could access. Entries ranged from the Cornell University library of veterinary medicine to the Public Relations Society of America library, the Italian Patent and Trademark Office, the Georgia state archives, and the World Bank.

One of the difficulties in offering library research is that it requires a fair amount of overhead time going to and from the library away from your office. Chapter 15, Setting Rates and Fees, discusses how to set a price for your time; keep in mind that it can be difficult to find clients willing to pay your professional hourly rate.

Document Delivery

Tracking down obscure citations and obtaining copies or originals of articles, reports, and books is the job of document delivery (doc del) firms. Unlike most other types of independent information businesses, doc del firms may employ a number of people, due to the amount of clerical and paraprofessional work involved. A doc del company acts, in a sense, as a librarian's—or researcher's—librarian. Once an info pro has identified the white paper, academic treatise, industrial standard, conference paper, 20-year-old annual report, or obscure article from a Polish medical journal that the client needs, the doc del firm's job is to get a copy of the item. Sometimes that means searching online library catalogs to find an institution that subscribes to the journal or maintains an archive of old corporate annual reports, and arranging to send someone to that library to photocopy or scan the material. Sometimes it involves contacting the publisher and negotiating an appropriate royalty payment for a copy. Sometimes it means tracking down the original author or conference speaker to see if he is willing to supply a copy of his paper or presentation.

Many doc del clients are librarians looking for material they don't have in their own collections and may not have been able to find through their own network of sources. That means that doc del firms often get difficult, incomplete, or incorrect citations. So part of the job of a good doc del researcher is to think like a detective. To an extent, doc del firms are threatened by the perception that "it's all available on the web." People are sometimes not willing to wait a week for an article when they are accustomed to getting material at the click of a mouse. And customers often balk at the price for document delivery; an article can easily cost $25 or $50, once the publisher's royalty fee is included in the invoice. Document delivery is a specialized niche for people who are detail-oriented, able to generate and manage large volumes of orders, and can identify clients willing to pay the often substantial fees.

Competitive Intelligence

Despite rumors to the contrary, competitive intelligence (CI) doesn't require industrial espionage or diving into dumpsters and digging up a company's strategic plans from the trash. What CI *does* involve is using a variety of research and analytical skills to gather information on a company or industry and to figure out what it means and identify risks and opportunities. CI research may tackle questions such as "Why are my competitors pulling back from Asia?" "How should we interpret a competitor's price cuts?" or "What are our threats from new entrants or new product launches?" Some of this information is available via in-depth online research—in market research reports, industry newsletters, published interviews with executives, and so on. But much of this type of intelligence resides in more obscure sources, so CI research may involve, for example, researching public records to find factory blue-prints filed with construction permits, monitoring company websites to see what jobs are being advertised or what new offices or divisions have been opened, or conducting telephone interviews with a target company's vendors, customers, and competitors.

CI often includes analyzing research findings and developing conclusions regarding a company's strategies. CI researchers find it challenging to dig up hidden information without compromising the confidentiality of their clients and without misrepresenting themselves. In fact, this is one reason why CI research may be outsourced to independent information professionals; the CI department within a company doesn't want its employees associated with the research and prefers to have an independent researcher (with an independent perspective and set of assumptions) making those probing phone calls. Good CI researchers are able to think creatively, question all their assumptions about the industry and marketplace, recognize significant outliers, see the big picture as well as the details, and provide high-end analysis of a situation.

The principal professional association for this type of research is the Society of Competitive Intelligence Professionals (SCIP; www.scip.org). SCIP members include CI researchers and analysts within organizations, CI consulting firms, and academicians in business and related disciplines. The Special Libraries Association (SLA; www.sla.org) also has a Competitive Intelligence Division, which is a particularly good resource for the research aspects of CI.

Nonprofits/Prospect Research

When you hear the word "nonprofit," what do you think?

- Hey, that describes my business right now!

- "Nonprofit" means "no money."

- Don't they just rely on volunteers for everything?

While that first thought may feel accurate, nonprofits are a great source of business for some info-entrepreneurs. Although their goals aren't to make a profit, that does not mean that nonprofit organizations are poorly funded; they may well be willing to pay market rates for your services. Yes, the local gardening club is a nonprofit without much of a budget, but the American Red Cross is also a nonprofit, and it has a multibillion-dollar budget. And while the local animal shelter relies on volunteers for most of its services, the World Wildlife Fund spends $2 million a year on professional fees.

Also within the nonprofit world are professional and trade associations, many of which are well-funded. The Institute of Electrical and Electronics Engineers (IEEE) sponsors almost a thousand conferences a year for its 400,000 members, and it is involved in developing industry standards and in publishing hundreds of journals and annual conference proceedings. Nongovernmental organizations (NGOs) also fall within the realm of nonprofits. NGOs, often funded by governmental organizations, include NATO, the United Nations, and the World Bank. With budgets in the billions, NGOs can be sources of significant business to info pros who are able to identify the points at which their services would be most valued.

Nonprofits have the same concerns any for-profit company has: They need to bring money into the organization, they spend money on products or services, and they produce something, either tangible or intangible. For example, Samsung Electronics brings in money through sales of its products; it spends money in developing, producing, and selling its products as well as marketing to its customers; and it produces electronic devices. Médecins Sans Frontières (Doctors Without Borders) is funded primarily by charitable foundations and wealthy individuals; it spends money providing its medical services, lobbying, and attracting and maintaining donors. It also provides medical aid and advocates on behalf of those it serves. Both organizations need to bring money in, spend it, and create something of value to others.

The services that info-entrepreneurs provide to nonprofits are similar to those they offer other clients, but the focus is often different. Priorities for nonprofits include identifying sources for funding, building membership, developing the skills of their board members, staff, and volunteers, and communicating with their various stakeholders. Info-entrepreneurs provide services to nonprofits such as:

- Prospect research: This involves researching major donors to identify their capacity for and propensity to giving and opportunities for a major gift program. What other organizations have these individuals given to recently? What is the individual donor's estimated net worth? What grants has this foundation made to groups similar to ours? What corporate giving programs could we tap into?

- Grant writing: Many nonprofits depend on grants for much or all of their funding. They need info pros to identify likely donors, research the organization, and identify its funding priorities and frequent grant recipients, and write the grant proposal in a way that is compelling to the funding organization.

- Consulting services: Nonprofits are notoriously strong in their own area of expertise and dismally weak in the area of management and administration. Info-entrepreneurs offer training services to help the staff conduct better prospect research. They help identify prospective advisory board members and executives. They even help the organization develop information services for its members.

Information Management

While most independent info pros specialize in particular types of research, some provide more general consulting services related to the acquisition, organization, management, and distribution of information within organizations. These consultants may provide "information audits"—in-depth surveys and analyses of an organization's information needs and resources. They may offer recommendations on what information sources should be acquired, how these sources should be distributed within the organization through intranets or other technologies, and how to teach employees how best to use the information. Information consultants also help set up information resource centers and libraries, develop websites and databases to organize and disseminate internal and external information, and offer workshops and training sessions on information-related topics. Most information consultants come from a library or information services background. Since most of their clients are in the information field, having a deep familiarity with information resources is key to providing information management consulting services.

Library Staffing

Libraries within organizations, sometimes called "special libraries," need occasional assistance and guidance in recruiting new staff or finding temporary help during a busy period or while a staff member is on leave. In fact, some organizations want the entire library function handled by a third party, preferring to pay a set fee to have all the staffing responsibilities managed by someone who understands the information profession, rather than trying to build and staff the library internally.

Library staffing companies usually focus on a single geographic region or a vertical market—government libraries or engineering firm libraries, for example—because it is difficult to maintain staffing quality when the client libraries are all over the country or all over the map in terms of specializations. With the exception of firms that only do library personnel recruitment, most staffing companies consist of the principal(s) and a number of information professionals. Thus, one of the skills that these types of independent info pros need is the ability to manage and motivate employees. This is one skill that those of us who are one-person businesses do not have to develop. Note that many of the issues related to outsourced personnel management services go beyond the scope of this book. If you are considering this type of business, be sure to expand your reading to include material on these other concerns as well.

Training and Seminars

Finally, a number of independent info pros offer training, workshops, or seminars on research-related topics, in addition to other information services. They often find that these are good vehicles for marketing their expertise, expanding their client base, and keeping their information skills sharp. (There's nothing like knowing you will be speaking in front of a room full of people to encourage you to stay up-to-date on whatever topic you're speaking on.) Some independent info pros work their seminar schedule around trips they have already planned—to professional conferences, meetings with clients, and the like—and they handle all the marketing, registration, and administrative tasks involved in organizing and promoting their sessions.

Others work with the organizers of existing professional conferences to present their workshop as pre- or post-conference sessions. They piggyback on the attendance and marketing effort of a larger conference, but they give up a portion of their income in exchange for having someone else handle all the marketing. In fact, info pros who give pre- and post-conference workshops are usually just paid a flat fee, regardless of the number of people attending the session. The stand-alone route works best if you already have some name recognition and/or a large base of contacts you can market to; generating interest in your workshops from scratch is difficult, time-consuming, and expensive. Another option that some info-entrepreneurs take is to provide customized workshops to large organizations or professional associations, offering to travel to various offices or locations or, alternatively, to develop digital learning products such as webinars, distance-learning seminars, online meetings, and tutorials.

However you decide to approach it, workshops and seminars can be a source of supplemental income if you are a lively speaker and can develop presentations that pique people's interest. And don't worry that you are giving away the store by teaching others your research techniques. The skills that got you to this point will keep you ahead of the pack. More importantly, most of your clients will be calling you for work because they know you have years of expertise that can't be acquired or taught overnight. Teaching others about research helps to build their appreciation of what is involved in your work and enables them to do simple research themselves.

Focus, Focus, Focus

It can be rather daunting to think about all the kinds of information services that independent info pros can provide. However, I don't think anyone offers *all* the services I just described. The late Sue Rugge, one of the founders of the independent information profession, was well-known for her advice to "do what you do best, and hire the rest." Many independent info pros put this in practice every day as they subcontract work to fellow info pros. For example, I focus primarily on online research, and I use a small network of colleagues for all of my telephone research and document delivery work. Several public records researchers call me when they need online searches to supplement what they can do themselves. When I get calls for information audits or knowledge management consulting, I refer them to a couple of people I know who are experts in that area. This informal network ensures that all of us are able to offer a wide range of high-quality research to our clients by tapping into the skills of other info pros who can provide what we do not. This is, I believe, the best reason to join AIIP; the contacts I have made there have enabled me to provide a much deeper, richer range of services to my clients than I could possibly do on my own. See Chapter 16, Subcontracting, or I'll Scratch Your Back If You Scratch Mine, for more discussion of how these relationships work, how subcontractors get paid, and who gets to keep the client at the end of the day.

Where Will I Find My Clients?

I am oversimplifying a bit, but your clients will probably be some combination of the following:

- Information-hungry professionals, such as CI researchers, marketing professionals, and product managers

- Intermediaries such as other consultants who will pass your work along to their clients

- Organizations that do not have an in-house library but need professional research support

- Librarians who need to outsource some of their research

- Individual professionals with more money than time and a specific research need

You might find these people in advertising and public relations agencies; research, strategic planning, and marketing departments of large corporations; nonprofit organizations, private investigation firms, engineering companies, hospitals and medical research facilities; and among upper-level executives who need outside research on their competitors and the industry.

Real-Life Examples

So, what does an actual research project look like? I asked several colleagues to describe a project they had done, and the following are their examples. These are quite extensive in their scope; any part of one of these projects might constitute a separate research job. And each example shows a different type of research—online, public records research, or a combination of information sources. Some of the details have been changed to protect the confidentiality of the clients.

Color Printer Market

Objective: A client needed to learn what business consumers thought about the quality of their desktop color printers. Did they expect the same quality as traditional photographic film processing? Did they generally just use color printers to add pizzazz to a marketing brochure or sales chart? What did they like and dislike in color inkjet printers?

Research: I searched a number of online databases to see what was written in the trade press about color printers and about consumer purchases and use of digital cameras. I also searched market research report databases to find consulting reports on the color printer market. I searched the web for product specifications for various color printers and for discussions of these printers in various web-based forums and online bulletin boards. I monitored several bloggers who follow this industry closely. After I had pulled all the material together—more than 300 pages of information—I wrote an analysis of the major concerns of consumers and an executive summary for my client to provide to her vice president.

Total time: 40 hours

Finding Funding

Objective: My client, a public/private consortium, needed to identify potential sources of grants and funding in order to expand its efforts in recruiting information technology (IT) companies as tenants for a new "technology village" office complex as well as to train IT workers directly.

Research: I started with a general web search and identified a model program in another state. On its website, I found program descriptions and contact information so my client could talk with them directly. I searched the U.S. Department of Education's website and found two federal funding initiatives. I also found information on a new bill in Congress that would have a direct impact on my client's program and looked up information on the chief sponsor of the bill. It turned out that one of my client's senators is very interested in this issue, so I called her office and obtained further details. I also searched the Foundation Center's database and identified a number of relevant grant programs. I ended with an in-depth search in one of the professional online services for success stories of companies announcing funding they had received for on-the-job training of IT workers.

Total time: 25 hours

Automobile Aftermarket

Objective: A client that manufactures automobile accessories—hubcaps, chrome wheels, fog lights, and so on—is considering acquiring a privately held competitor. It needs as much information as possible on the competitor.

Research: I went to the state Department of Corporations and looked up the company records to get information on the officers and directors. Then I went to the courthouses in three local jurisdictions and looked up court documents to see if I could find any litigation involving the company or its officers. I found a suit filed by a former employee regarding an alleged breach of an employment contract, and contacted the ex-employee to find out what she had to say about the company. I also found a divorce suit involving an officer of the company; the settlement agreement listed company assets and gave me additional details on the spouse's involvement in the company. Finally, since this industry uses a lot of plastics and paints, I contacted the state environmental protection agency and got the permits the company had filed for its manufacturing plants. This gave me information on the number of employees at the plants and the type of equipment used. I wrote all this up and gave the client the information I had gathered, along with suggestions on other sources of information we might be able to pursue.

Total time: 16 hours

Frequently Asked Questions

I speak and write frequently about the independent info pro business, and some questions seem to come up all the time, either from people who are considering this line of work or those who are thinking about hiring an independent info pro.

"How can you sell me someone else's information?"

Most independent info pros don't specialize in original research; that is, they don't spend all their time conducting surveys, studying trends, and writing their own market research reports. Instead, they gather information from a number of sources, including the web, trade and professional journals, newspapers, magazines, government agencies, associations, blogs, social network groups, and other sources. What they are charging for is not the information per se but their time and skill in *finding* the information, in knowing where to go to find it, and in making sense of the information after they find it.

That's why an independent info pro still charges even if he didn't find the information that exactly answered the client's question—the client is paying for the info pro's time and expertise, not just for the information retrieved. Compare it to going to a doctor for an illness; you pay the doctor for her time regardless of whether you were eventually cured. Unlike real estate agents and personal injury lawyers, few independent info pros work on a contingency basis, hoping to cash in big if their client finds the information particularly useful.

"Why do you charge me when it's all free on the web?"

Three words: Time Is Money. Well, that's the smart-aleck answer, anyway. And, indeed, an independent info pro should be able to find useful, accurate, and relevant information in less time than her client can. But more to the point, most information is *not* available on the free web. It's hidden in databases that don't show up in search engines. It appears in articles and white papers that never make their way to the web. It's found in government and association reports that are hidden deep within websites. It's buried in a book chapter or periodical article housed only in a library somewhere, or in a document filed in a county courthouse. Or it's unearthed by doing telephone research, interviewing experts to get their take on a given situation.

In addition to finding information that simply never shows up in a web search engine, independent info pros also add value by analyzing and synthesizing the results—by providing not just information but answers.

"What if you don't find any information?"

There are really very few research projects for which no information exists. You might not be able to find the exact answer. My guess, for example, is that no one knows the exact value of all the personal property of U.S. residents—and yes, this was a real research question. However, a good researcher can often find enough information to deduce or extrapolate an answer. To use the example just mentioned, useful statistics from insurance industry associations and from the U.S. Census Bureau enabled the client to make an educated guess.

And sometimes finding no information is just what the client wants to hear. If a client has invented a new infrared, hands-free potato peeler, he would be delighted to hear that I can find no existing patents for similar inventions. If a company is considering marketing its new children's pager to parents in western Canada, it will be pleased to learn that no Canadian newspapers or parents' magazines have mentioned a similar product in the past five years.

As I mentioned in the answer to "How can you sell me someone else's information?" independent info pros charge for their time and research skills rather than for the quantity of information retrieved. Of course, if you find, partway into a project, that you aren't uncovering anything useful, it makes sense to stop and consult with the client about expanding or changing the focus of the research.

"What training or education is required?"

Many longtime independent info pros have master's degrees in library or information science and years of experience as professional librarians. A number of graduate library schools are developing new programs that cater to the entrepreneurial interests of their students, some of whom have no interest in working within a traditional library after graduation. Some of the best programs also offer distance-learning options, which enable students to get the skills they need without leaving home.

However, a library background isn't required, provided you have other experience as a researcher or you are willing to outsource the actual research to others. Perhaps most important is the ability to use a wide variety of information sources, including the professional services described in Chapter 34, and to think creatively about how to find the information needed.

Another option is to outsource the complex research and analysis to subcontractors, and to focus your time and energy in marketing your business and cultivating your clients. Sue Rugge, the owner of three successful independent information companies, focused all her energy on marketing and relied on a group of employees and subcontractors to do the research for her clients.

In addition to research skills, you have to be able to run a business. That means marketing yourself; developing and implementing a strategic business plan and a yearly marketing plan; handling the day-to-day operations of a small business including invoicing, collections, accounts payable, and cash flow; continually upgrading your information skills through professional development; and managing your clients. You need good communication skills because you will be talking with clients face to face, over the telephone, or via email, and you will be writing analyses, summaries, and reports.

You can subcontract some of these duties, but one thing you can't easily subcontract is marketing. No one knows your skills, abilities, and talents as well as you do, and no one can establish clients' confidence in your abilities better than you. If marketing isn't your strong suit, consider finding a business coach who can work with you to develop a marketing strategy that is comfortable for you. I had no background in marketing when I started my business, but I developed the attitude that this was simply part of the job, and I could either figure out how to find an enjoyable way to market myself or I could choose to be miserable. Fortunately, I picked the former option. I go into detail about marketing techniques in Section Three.

"Will you hire me? Can I intern for you?"

Many aspiring independent info pros hope to hone their skills by working for established information businesses. Unfortunately, very few independents can absorb the overhead required to train new info pros and, more importantly, the inevitable cost of their "learning experiences"—known to clients as mistakes. We have to stand behind the work that goes out under our name, and that means we need to have complete confidence in the research. It is difficult to develop that level of trust with someone we haven't known for period of time or who hasn't developed an expertise in the resources used.

Most of us work from our homes or in one-room offices outside the home and don't have the room and equipment to accommodate a new employee or intern. Most importantly, we are already busy providing information services to clients, as well as marketing and handling the administrative end of the business, and we just don't have the time to guide and train someone who isn't already an experienced information professional.

The one exception to this rule is public records research. It is labor-intensive, and experienced independent info pros sometimes take on new employees or interns to provide an additional set of eyes and ears. Note, though, that this usually requires that you are located near the info pro you want to work with; this is hands-on research, and it is hard to train someone remotely.

In general, if you want to get into the independent info profession, your best bet is to read the rest of this book, evaluate your own strengths and weaknesses, take the necessary steps to enhance your skill sets, then—as that sporting goods company admonishes—just do it, and start your own business.

"Can I do this part time?"

Yes and no. Most, if not all, of the work you get will come from word of mouth, and it takes time to generate that initial buzz. The more hours, energy, and creativity you can devote to marketing at the beginning, the faster your network of contacts will grow. The strongest argument for holding down a paid part-time job is that it provides a source of steady income while you are building your business. However, trying to start an independent info pro business while working full time is almost always doomed to failure. This is simply not the kind of business that can be done evenings and weekends.

The disadvantages of working part time while running your business are that you are unavailable to talk to your clients during part of the day, you have less time to generate business, and your focus is split between your two jobs. If you decide to work part time, make a firm commitment to yourself that you will only do so for a specific amount of time—say, six months or a year—during which you will focus on making your business self-sustaining. Note that some kinds of research really cannot be done part time or during off-hours, particularly phone research (you have to be in your office during business hours to make and receive calls), public records research (you have to be available to travel to another county at the drop of a hat, and you are limited to the hours that the public records offices are open), and library staffing (you have to be there when your clients want you in the library). Some beginning independent info pros handle such conflicts by finding part-time jobs that involve evening hours only.

"How much will I earn?"

This depends on several factors—how much time you can devote to marketing your business, who your clients are, how established your business is, how many professional contacts you start out with, and whether this is a full-time or part-time business for you. During your first year, assuming you're working at it full time, you can expect to make anywhere from $15,000 to $50,000. Once you have been marketing for a year or two, and your clients have begun recommending you to colleagues, the sky's the limit. Net income (after expenses but before income taxes) can range from $40,000 to $200,000, or more. How much *you* make depends on your ability to find clients that you can charge $150 to $200 an hour and on your willingness and ability to work at least 40 hours a week. See Chapter 15 for more discussion on setting your rates.

"What was the hardest part of starting a research business?"

Everyone has his or her own pain points and areas of insecurity. That said, there are some challenges that most independent info pros face during their first year. A discussion among AIIP members yielded the following as the most common issues:

- "Consistently communicating to everyone I met that this business is real, viable, and will be around for the duration. It is not a hobby, a part-time diversion or a stepping stone to becoming a corporate employee." (Cynthia Shamel, Shamel Information Services)

- "Developing a clear vision of what I wanted my business to look like. How do I want my customers to see my business and exactly who are my target customers?" (Michelle Fennimore, Competitive Insights)

- "Getting up the courage to just take the leap of faith and DO it, after planning, and planning, and planning …" (Liga Greenfield, BioMedPharmIS)

- "The hardest part of starting was like the hardest part of a swim—jumping into the cold water; i.e., deciding to leave steady employment, and believing that I could make a go of it." (Judy Koren, ResearchWise Associates)

- "I found it hard to charge enough. I got lots of work early on, but I didn't charge enough for it, so I was very busy but not profitable. One of my early clients took pity on me and told me to double my fees (his company was paying, not him personally)." (Lorna Dean, Bedford Research Consultants)

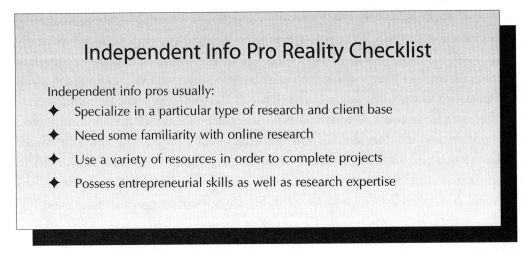

Independent Info Pro Reality Checklist

Independent info pros usually:

✦ Specialize in a particular type of research and client base

✦ Need some familiarity with online research

✦ Use a variety of resources in order to complete projects

✦ Possess entrepreneurial skills as well as research expertise

Chapter 2

A Day in the Life
of an Independent Info Pro

Before I started my business, I didn't really know what to expect on a day-to-day basis. What would I spend my day *doing*? Since my prior work experience was as a corporate librarian, I knew what a day of research felt like, but I also suspected that working as an independent info pro had its own unique pace and feel.

Although I had heard this before, I did not really believe that a third to half of my day would be spent doing nonbillable work. But then I thought about it—almost every company has a sales department, a marketing staff, strategic planners, some administrative support people, an accounting department, *and* the employees who actually produce the goods or provide the services that the company's customers buy. In a one-person business, all those jobs have to be done by—you guessed it—you. Certainly, some efficiencies are achieved when you work solo, but you still have to bring in customers, keep them happy, and bill them—as well as provide the information services that those customers are paying for.

My Typical Day

So, what does a typical working day look like? There is probably no such thing as an average day; in fact, I would be happy if any given day were 100 percent predictable. But here is a composite diary of one of my days:

After an early morning walk with the dogs, a quick breakfast, and a scan of the newspapers (the local paper, the big regional paper, and the *Wall Street Journal*), I braced myself for the 25-foot commute to my home office on the second floor of my house. I spent the first hour going through email and reading postings from the seven or eight email discussion lists I subscribe to. I replied to a query from a program planner who wanted to know my availability and fee to speak at a conference in six months, giving her a flier I had composed of possible topics. I sent a prewritten reply to someone who asked about starting an information business from home and deleted the inevitable spam messages offering me free satellite TV service, porn, and enhancements to body parts I don't even have.

I then spent time monitoring a number of blogs and RSS feeds, as well as several professional groups on LinkedIn and Facebook. I planned to spend lunch in front of my computer, catching up on my contacts on Facebook. My goal is to check these sources at least once every couple of days, and I set aside time every Friday to get caught up. I usually open my RSS feed reader whenever I'm stuck on hold or just have a short amount of time free—those interstitial periods when I am waiting for a webinar to start, killing time before an appointment, or taking a break from billable work.

Then I settled down to the work of the day. I was in the middle of a project to identify the major buyers, manufacturers, and uses of optical amplifiers, a job commissioned by a corporate librarian who didn't have the time to do it himself. I had already looked through websites of the major manufacturers, so now I headed to the professional online services to see what I could find in the industry press, technical journals, and market research reports. I often start with Factiva (global.factiva.com) because of its favorable pricing, but this project struck me as one that required the wide variety and power search tools offered by Dialog (www.dialogweb.com). If you are not familiar with these resources, take a look at Chapter 34, Professional Online Services. I found more information than I had expected, so I refined the search to get just what I thought the client would want, and I had the results sent to my email account so that they would be nicely formatted.

While waiting for the email to arrive, I ran a quick search on the U.S. Patent & Trademark Office's website for recent patents on optical amplifiers and wrote up an analysis for my client, listing the number of recent patents granted to the major industry players. Then I headed for some sources that specialize in in-depth market research and downloaded tables of contents of the reports I thought my client might want.

By now, the results of my Dialog search had arrived in my email inbox, so I downloaded the files and started going through the material. I deleted a few articles that were not as useful as they first appeared, organized the rest, and did some simple formatting to generate a table of contents and make the material easier for my client to read. I noticed that two interesting articles were not available online in full text, so I sent an email with the bibliographic citations to a document delivery company, which could arrange to have the articles scanned, the royalties paid, and the material emailed to me by the end of the day. (Note that I did not do this portion of the research myself; it is more cost-effective for me to outsource this kind of work to a company that specializes in it and has someone stationed on-site at a library that has the journals I need, rather than it would be for me to drop what I was doing and to try to find the materials during my visit to a local library. The doc del company also handles copyright fees so that I don't have to try to figure out who gets paid what.)

I made note of several websites mentioned in the articles and followed through on the ones that looked as though they might be useful. Then I put the project aside until later in the day. I like to let my work percolate in my head for a few hours to make sure I haven't forgotten anything. Besides, I had to wait for the two articles to arrive from the doc del company.

Since it was the end of the month, I sat down to do my monthly invoices and pay my bills. I sent out reminder notices to two clients who were late in paying, and sent a thank-you note to a new client. Just as I was backing up my accounting file, I got a call from a colleague, a researcher in California. She told me that she was digging up information on a scoundrel who, it seemed, was bent on defrauding half the state of Florida. She wanted me to run an online search to see if he or his wife were mentioned in any Florida newspapers in the past five years. We agreed on a not-to-exceed budget and deadline, and I thought to myself that my clients often send me interesting work, but rarely do they ask me to track down real estate crooks. And thank goodness that I can keep comfortably away from the crooks while doing my research.

By now, the dogs had gotten restless, so I took them on a quick walk around the neighborhood. I saw the real estate appraiser walking his dogs; he lives up the street and also works from home. There must be some mysterious canine schedule that requires walking at 11 AM.

The dogs quieted, I called a researcher in Boston who was working on a phone project I'd subcontracted (obtaining standards for electrical power systems on ships) to see how the work was going and to find out if she needed any additional information from the client. As I expected, she had the project completely under control. She told me that she would have a report written, using my electronic memo format, and ready for me to send to the client by the end of the next day.

I had hoped to put in a couple of hours on the web for a project involving marketing to the Millennial generation. I had just found some good sites to check next when a client called about a job I'd done for her last week. I had pulled together several study reports on a topic of interest for her, and she wanted me to get the survey instruments used in the studies. Dang, just when I thought I had finished with that job! I put aside my Millennial generation job, pulled up my notes from last week's report, and spent time hoping I would be lucky and find the surveys online. I sent her what I found, sent emails to two authors and a fax to a contact in South Africa, made notes for myself to follow up in a couple of days, and reviewed where I was in my day.

I checked my email and, sure enough, there were the two articles I'd ordered earlier in the day from the doc del company. I incorporated those into the collection of material I have and then sat back to think for a moment about what I learned, what would be of most interest to my client, and how I could present it most compellingly. First, I realized that I needed a few charts and graphs, so I pulled together a table with the key players in the optical amplifier industry, gathering the data points from the material I had compiled and from the companies' websites. I then copied a few salient paragraphs from each of the articles, pulled them together into coherent text, and finished the writing of the report itself. (See Chapter 37 for thoughts on providing added value to your research.)

It was getting close to the end of the day, so I picked up the phone and called a new independent info pro I am coaching. We spent an hour talking about her marketing strategy and how she was going to measure its effectiveness, how she was going to handle a difficult client situation, and a seminar she was planning to teach in a few months. I followed up with a quick email with links to some additional sources she might find useful and thought once again how much I enjoy watching people become successful entrepreneurs.

By now, the dogs had started nudging my elbow; it was time for dinner, and they were getting impatient. I breathed a sigh of relief that they had refrained from barking during any of my phone calls during the day; they aren't always so well-mannered.

I put my laptop in its tote, tossed in some professional reading that I might or might not get to that evening, and steeled myself for the 25-foot commute back down the stairs.

Your Typical Day

Everyone's day is going to have its own rhythm. Info-entrepreneurs with children at home will have to factor in the interruptions of caring for them; young ones can have a serious impact on the amount of time you are able to put into your business. Info pros who provide public records or other hands-on research will probably spend much of their time out of their offices—in government agencies, court houses, libraries, archives, or other repositories of hard-copy information. Telephone researchers generally have much less freedom to leave the office in order to walk the dog or meet a friend for a lunch or an afternoon walk because they're often waiting for contacts to return phone calls.

And my day reflects the fact that I have been in business for many years, and I have clients who call me regularly. Your day may be less filled with multiple clients and more occupied with building up the word of mouth that will be your most effective marketing strategy.

What you will find is that you will get interrupted during the day, and you will have to be able to drop and return to projects smoothly and pick up where you left off. Yes, you can let the phone calls go to voice mail or keep your email program closed all day, but if you don't respond to your clients and prospects promptly, they will find someone else who does. So interruptions are a necessary evil in this business.

But at the beginning of your business, you will probably welcome those distractions. I remember when I sat in my office, wondering why my phone wasn't ringing and why no one was emailing me with inquiries about my services. I confess that I would pick up the phone and call someone every so often, just to see if my phone was working. ("That *must* be why they're not calling … my phone's dead, right?") And I can tell when a friend is in that situation when I see that she changed her Facebook photo five times yesterday. It's frustrating when the phone doesn't ring; now when I notice that it's been too quiet, I make a note to start up my short-term marketing efforts again.

One of the benefits *and* drawbacks of being independent is that we can set our own hours. The advantages, of course, include flexibility to attend to family matters, the ability to work when we're at our sharpest (which for me is often 10 PM), and the freedom to take a day off just because the weather is perfect and we want to enjoy it. The downsides are that our clients often expect us to be available from early morning until early evening, we run the risk of allowing our work to take over all our available time ("I work part time … just 12 hours a day!"), and we only get paid for the hours we bill to clients, which means that in a slow month, we can be working a lot and making very little.

Issues We All Face

Regardless of the type of information service you provide, some basic issues will remain the same. You'll have to figure out how to make the best use of every hour of the day. You'll spend a significant portion of your day doing work that can't be billed to a client, such as marketing, staying in touch with colleagues, and handling administrative chores. All of that is essential work, but it doesn't contribute to your bottom line, at least not directly. You will be juggling a lot of different responsibilities, some of which you will probably enjoy and some of which you won't. The chances are slim that you will have an entire day uninterrupted by phone calls, the noisy neighbor who thinks that, because you are working at home, you aren't really busy, or other unexpected disruptions.

Even if you don't do online research, you will be using various software applications during the course of the day. You will be writing up summaries of your research in a word-processing program; you will probably be using a financial management software package such as QuickBooks for basic accounting; you'll be checking and managing your email, and I trust that you will be using a backup system for all your business-critical files. I recommend a web-based service to ensure that, should anything happen to your office, you would still recover your files. If you aren't comfortable having your information held by someone else, you can back up your files to some external device and keep it separate from your computer. Chapter 11, Business Apps for Info-Entrepreneurs, goes into more detail about what you will need.

The consequence of relying on software, as virtually all businesses do today, is that you are responsible for providing at least the first line of defense when your PC goes down. As an independent info pro, you have no in-house help desk and no friendly computer geek down the hall who can wander by and figure out what's wrong. If your printer experiences a meltdown, your phone line goes dead, or your

PC suddenly develops dementia, you're on your own. Most of us develop a good relationship with a local computer pro who is reliable, willing to make home/office calls, and who understands that if our PC is down, our business is shut down, too.

Many independent info pros are introverts by nature and find it difficult to market themselves and their businesses successfully. It feels awkward at first; I remember feeling like what I was really saying was, "Oh, I'm so great, hire me, blah blah blah." Then I realized that I wasn't really talking about myself—I was telling someone about the company I own, that can help that person make better business decisions. Even when it becomes less difficult, marketing still has to be done in busy times and slow, when you are feeling really excited and passionate and when you are not feeling very energized.

Perhaps not surprisingly, another challenge many info-entrepreneurs face is how to price their services. For many, it feels unbelievable to say they are worth $175 an hour, without remembering all the hours that went into getting that project. We tend to think that projects shouldn't cost more than a few hundred dollars, even when their value to the client could be in the millions.

One of the advantages of belonging to the Association of Independent Information Professionals (AIIP) is that it offers a private email discussion group where members talk about these issues and how they resolve them. Having a virtual community of entrepreneurs who understand what it's like to run an information business can mean the difference between effectively solving a problem and crying in desperation.

Eternal Verities in the Life of an Independent Info Pro

◆ Time management is essential. If you are not reporting to a boss or working on a regular 9-to-5 (or whatever) schedule, it is easy to let time get away from you.

◆ You switch hats constantly. You need to be able to mentally put one job on hold while you deal with other projects or concerns, then pick up the first job where you left off.

◆ It is critical to set aside time to get some exercise or otherwise refresh yourself. Work can easily take over your life, and that's no way to live.

◆ There is a lot of overhead and administrative time in running your own business.

◆ No matter how busy you are, you never stop marketing. Even after many years in business, some time must be spent every week on marketing efforts.

Chapter 3

The Joys and Frustrations of Being an Independent Info Pro

Way back when I was considering whether being an independent info pro would be right for me, I talked to a number of people who had been in business for a while, and I lurked on the email discussion group of the Association of Independent Information Professionals (AIIP; www.aiip.org). What I really wanted was to get a sense of the highs and lows of this business—what made this such a rewarding profession and what caused people the most aggravation.

As you are reading this chapter, think about how important each of these aspects of the business is to you. Some of the negatives almost everyone experiences, such as isolation, the lack of a steady paycheck, and the constant need to market yourself and your business. Likewise, some features of the entrepreneurial life almost all independent info pros find rewarding—the ability to work from home, the relationships we establish with clients, and the personal satisfaction of knowing that we have built a business ourselves. If, as you read this chapter, you discover that what we find rewarding doesn't resonate with you, then this may not be the best choice of profession for you. On the other hand, if you read through this chapter and think, "Wow, that sounds like so much more fun than what I'm doing now," then you know you are cut out for this business.

Keep in mind that very few of us info-entrepreneurs started our businesses because we relished the idea of marketing and making collections calls. You can tell they are good entrepreneurs not by what innate skills and abilities they have but by whether they are willing and able to build the skills they need. When I started, I had no idea how much I had to plan for quarterly tax payments, for example, and it took me a year to establish a good system for managing my cash flow. It can be challenging to be responsible for recognizing your weaknesses, but just about every aspect of entrepreneurship can be learned, and I address all the aspects that are specific to being an independent info pro in the rest of this book.

The Thrills of Being an Independent Info Pro

For many of us independent info pros, one of the biggest thrills is knowing that, single-handedly, we have built solid, successful businesses. Except for the lucky few who were already luminaries in their field when they started out, most of us didn't have clients flocking to our door on our first day of business. But gradually, we learned the best ways to attract customers, keep them happy, and build our revenue year after year. We know that we always have competitors, but our clients want to call us and that can be very satisfying.

One of the often-mentioned benefits of being an independent info pro is the ability to manage your workload and have a more family-friendly schedule. I'm not persuaded that this is always a realistic expectation, but it is possible to build more flexibility into your schedule than can be done in a traditional work setting. As you can see from reading Chapter 2, A Day in the Life of an Independent Info Pro, I value the ability to take breaks during the day for nonwork activities such as walking the dogs. I have also been responsible for eldercare, and I really appreciated the flexibility I had to work around doctors' schedules and clinic hours. While it meant that I worked late some nights and may have had a less focused day, I cannot imagine how I could have combined my home and work responsibilities without being able to juggle my work schedule as much as I did.

Other info-entrepreneurs find advantages in being able to choose what kind of work environment works best for them. Some like being able to share office space with someone else. Some enjoy working in coffee shops or other places where there is a lot of background activity. Some info-entrepreneurs rent office space so that they can get away from home every day; they find it much easier and more efficient to have an office in which to spread out and bring in other workers when needed.

Although it's not always feasible and it takes a lot of cooperation on the part of one's family, some independent info pros are able to build their schedules around their children's school schedules—by starting their workday before the kids get up, enforcing the "no talking to me while I'm on the phone" rule, tackling administrative work in the evening, and building a client base that doesn't expect them to be available in the afternoon when school gets out. If you have children who are too young to be in school or daycare, you will probably need to plan on having someone else responsible for childcare while you are working. Trying to juggle marketing, talking with clients, writing reports, and keeping up on your administrative responsibilities is challenging enough, without adding to it the responsibility of caring for a child at the same time.

To Be Online or Not To Be

A friend and colleague of mine, Alex Kramer, is a public records researcher. Until recently, almost all of her work involved going to courts and other government offices and conducting research in document files. I, on the other hand, almost never need to leave my home office and do most of my research online. Alex would often tell me that she thought she had the better deal, since she has to stop work at the end of the day when government offices and courthouses close. She never got stuck working far into the night; knowing that she could only work during normal business hours meant that she stayed particularly focused during the day.

I responded to her by saying that I had the better deal because I could take time off in the middle of the day and make up the time in the evening or during the weekend. "Think of how much more flexibility I have," I would tell her. "Look at how many nights and weekends you work," she said.

As it turns out, Alex is now using online resources in her business, so she isn't able to close up shop at 5 PM anymore. Most info-entrepreneurs whose work is not primarily online—public records researchers like Alex, telephone researchers, and library management, for example—are finding that they need to hone their online searching skills for their business. Even if you aren't interested in being a web researcher, you will probably find it necessary to use the web and online databases in your work.

Although I will mention this later as a drawback of being independent, I consider the opportunity to work from home one of the joys of this business. My commute is 30 seconds, if I encounter a congestion of dogs on my way up the stairs to my home office. I can throw a load of laundry in the washer while waiting for a document to print. I can take a coffee break and water the yard. In good weather, I can open the door and windows of my office and hear the birds singing and the neighbor's ducks gossiping among themselves. This type of environment would spell disaster for some people; for them, a shared office space or generous use of a neighborhood hangout is much more attractive. In any event, we all agree that one of the benefits of being an independent info pro is the ability to create the work environment that works for us.

Have Laptop, Will Travel

Many independent info pros value the freedom to travel and to work from any location. If they have a phone and a Wi-Fi connection, they're in business. In fact, on my last vacation to a mountain cabin with my family, I speculated on whether I could run my office from the ranger's look-out station at the top of a nearby mountain peak. A wireless modem and a cell phone could keep me connected to the world. My only problem was that the nearest post office and FedEx drop-off location were several hours away; as wired as I am, I still need to receive hard-copy material every few days. There are plenty of road-warrior consultants who revel in serving their clients while they are sitting on a beach in Spain and who have figured out how to operate wirelessly. While I won't go that far, I was able to move my business from Washington, D.C., to Colorado with virtually no disruption for my clients. I had the same toll-free phone number and email address; the biggest challenge I had was teaching my clients that it was two hours earlier where I lived now, and I didn't really want calls at 6:30 AM.

Related to this is the opportunity to see more of the world as an independent info pro. I was never attracted to jobs that required frequent travel; I'm a homebody at heart. But I love the chance to see the world, at least in short visits. I decided to look for speaking opportunities outside the U.S., in order to meet info pros in other countries and find out how the information industry in other places differed from the U.S. I began sending proposals to conference program committees in countries that I wanted to visit, and I have been fortunate enough to have made it to a number of them. Even if you don't like travel and would prefer to stay put, marketing your services internationally—and, yes, that takes some creativity—allows you to meet and interact with clients throughout the world without leaving your neighborhood. It also can serve to diversify your business and buffer the impact of a weak economy in one region.

Of course, the advent of global wireless access has its disadvantages for the mobile info pro. We now feel obligated to travel with phone and laptop, because our clients expect us to remain in touch even when we're out of the office. On the other hand, we are the ultimate telecommuter. We can work from home. We can use voicemail, email, VoIP (voice over internet protocol), and chats to stay in touch while we're traveling. As long as we are willing to stay tied to our electronic leashes, we can look like we are hard at work in the office while we are working on our tans on Maui or taking the grandchildren to the zoo.

I Love My Boss

You don't hear most employees saying how much they enjoy their job, their co-workers, and their boss. Independent info pros, on the other hand, have a good working relationship with their bosses, whom they look at in the mirror every morning. While I jokingly complain about how much my boss makes me work sometimes, I still find her fairly reasonable.

One of the most frustrating aspects of working in a traditional job, at least for me, was the bureaucracy that inevitably slowed innovation and change. If I wanted to introduce a new service, it required meetings, proposals, focus groups, and approvals. A certain amount of structural inertia is built into almost any organization. While that provides stability, it also means that change takes time. As a one- or two-person business, you can turn on a dime. Want to offer a new service to your clients? Institute an email newsletter? Refocus your marketing to a different client base? No problem! You can be fearless in your approach, because you know that you can regroup if you see that something doesn't work. Such flexibility is particularly valuable during economic downturns. If you find that one group of clients has been hit hard by a slowdown in that industry or niche, you can re-evaluate your strategy and target another market. If you notice a sudden interest in a particular type of research—monitoring of regulatory changes, for example, or the ability to analyze and read between the lines of company web pages—you can retool and refocus your marketing efforts much more quickly than a larger competitor could.

Perhaps even more fun than being the boss is that we get paid for doing what we love. We get paid to learn stuff for our clients. We can get into the thrill of the chase as we try to track down an elusive bit of information. And for those of us who do not subcontract out most of the research, we get the satisfaction of seeing through an entire project from start to finish and of being the person responsible for making sense out of information.

Oh, the People You'll Meet

One joy of being an independent info pro is the opportunity to meet so many inter-esting people. My clients come from a wide variety of industries, backgrounds, and countries. Some are fellow entrepreneurs; some are CEOs of large companies; some are well-known in their fields. I would not have met any of them if I were not run-ning my own business. We independent info pros are often brought in (virtually, if not physically) as part of a team for a specific project. The client benefits from an outside perspective, and we benefit from learning how that organization perceives a problem or addresses an industry issue. Seeing the world from the points of view of many diverse clients gives us a depth of perspective that most employees do not have an opportunity to develop.

An entrepreneur does not get an annual review (or pay raise) from the boss, and the lack of formal feedback and reinforcement can be difficult for some people. On the other hand, you get a lot of satisfaction from knowing that your clients keep coming back because they really like what you do and they are willing to pay you to do it. A related benefit is the supportive note that comes when you least expect it. I publish several free electronic newsletters and, as I was writing this chapter, I received a message from someone on my distribution list telling me how much she appreciates the newsletter and how grateful she is that I take the time to write it. That kind of response makes my day. I believe that info-entrepreneurs hear more genuine thank you's than traditional employees do; our clients are far more aware of what value we bring to them than employers are since they are paying directly for that value.

Independent info pros also tend to develop strong bonds with other independ-ents. Although we always maintain client confidentiality, we often bounce ideas and questions off each other and get advice and support from colleagues who have addressed similar problems. As a community, independent info pros are remarkably supportive; we understand the challenges of running a business, and we know how important encouragement is. We also recognize the need for plenty of other independent info pros in the marketplace—for subcontracting and as referral sources—so we are all invested in the success of each other's businesses.

One of the less-tangible benefits of running your own business is the ability to turn down projects or clients that you just don't want to work with ... within reason, of course. Sooner or later, everyone runs into the Client From Hell—someone who makes unreasonable demands, is consistently rude or abrasive, or represents an organization or cause that you would rather not work with for whatever reason. Since you are running the show, you can decide that you simply won't do business with that person. (See Chapter 13, Managing Your Clients, for more discussion on this topic.) By the same token, you can decide to discount your rate or donate your services to a nonprofit or charitable organization that you do support. Being able to incorporate your personal values into your business can be a gratifying aspect of entrepreneurship.

The Chills of Being an Independent Info Pro

The thrills of running your own business sound great, don't they? Generally, it is great—otherwise, we wouldn't keep doing it. But there are some less appealing aspects of this profession. A lot depends on your own tolerance for risk and uncertainty, whether you need external structure to work most efficiently, and whether you can ride out the highs and lows of running a business. But talk to any independent info pro long enough, and you'll probably hear most of these challenges.

Perhaps the hardest part of being independent is that fact that you're *it*. You *are* the company. You have to do the strategic planning, the marketing, the client management, and the administrative work, as well as providing the actual information services. You have to take responsibility for all the difficult decisions and for the occasional really bad error in judgment (yes, it happens to all of us sooner or later). There will be times when no work has come in for a week or two, and you start wondering if this whole information-business thing was just a horrible mistake. There will be times when you wish you had someone else with whom to share the responsibilities and decisions. And there will be times when you suffer burnout, when you are sick of what you do, tired of always having to hustle for new clients, and longing for the security of a steady paycheck. It happens to all of us—usually not for long periods, but it can feel crippling when it hits. As I mentioned earlier, your info pro colleagues will offer sympathy and encouragement; that is what has always kept me going. But you have to be willing to reach out for help, which is hard for some people to do. While being an independent info pro requires that you work well alone, you will find that asking for suggestions and ideas from colleagues will make your first few years much smoother.

Should You Hire Someone or Do It Yourself?

Running your own business means conducting a fearless self-evaluation at least once a year to assess your strengths and weaknesses and to figure out how to take advantage of the former and either address or work around the latter. You're not expected to be perfect, but you must know yourself well enough to recognize what you don't do well and then either improve or outsource those responsibilities.

Some portions of our business do not lend themselves to being outsourced, regardless of how poorly we might initially do the job ourselves. High-contact, high-visibility responsibilities such as talking with clients, estimating and selling projects, and marketing yourself and your services usually cannot be handed off to a third party. These activities go to the very heart of what you do, and no proxy can replace your personal attention to clients.

I have seen a number of beginning info-entrepreneurs contract with a marketing expert to handle their promotion and communications with their prospective clients, for example. Unfortunately, I have yet to see this arrangement succeed, for a few reasons. First, you are selling an intangible—your expertise and commitment to your clients—and no one else can convey that confidence the way you can yourself. And most of the marketing consultants I have seen info-entrepreneurs use do not understand how unusual our market is. We get most of our business from word of mouth, which means that the focus of our marketing is in building that word of mouth through speaking, writing, and networking. Those all require your own voice and presence; they are not the sorts of activities most marketing pros are familiar with, and the strategies they offer are usually not a good fit for our line of work.

More importantly, this is the type of business that is "high-touch." Your clients are hiring *you*, and they want to know that you care about them, that you are committed to providing them with the best services possible, and that you are working as their partner as much as their vendor. Clients want to talk with you, not someone else, when they are discussing what their research needs are, what the budget will be, and what you anticipate finding. Likewise, new clients will learn about you—and gain confidence in your ability to solve their information needs—by hearing about you from colleagues or by hearing or meeting with you directly.

If you feel that you're weak in one of these areas, focus on developing your skills by taking a professional development course, reading up on the subject, or working with a job coach. For example, there are many options for marketing yourself, and Section Three goes into depth about the kinds of marketing strategies that not only work for info-entrepreneurs but that are relatively painless to put into practice. See also the checklist "With a Little Help From My Friends" for a list of what can and cannot easily be delegated to someone outside your business.

With a Little Help From My Friends

Nobody's perfect at all aspects of running an info pro business. Some tasks can be contracted out fairly easily; others are more difficult to delegate.

What's easy to contract out:

- Accounting

- Collections

- Design and writing of marketing material

- Webpage design

- Computer maintenance and purchasing

- Specific types of research at which you are not expert

What's difficult to contract out:

- Strategic planning

- Marketing

- Client contact

- Estimating cost and time for projects

"Where Did My Money Go?"

Two of the challenges that almost every independent info pro faces are cash flow and pricing. (I address these in detail in Chapter 14, Money, Money, Money, and in Chapter 15, Setting Rates and Fees.) Even after many years in business, you will probably find that some months you are flush with cash, and some months (usually, it seems, just before you have to pay your taxes) you are running low. Besides the obvious need to bank surplus income in anticipation of the lean times, it takes a strong stomach to ride out those periods when you have sent invoices out but none of the checks have come in.

Pricing your services is the other financial-related aspect of the business that many info pros find difficult. Quoting a four- or five-figure estimate for a job can be hard, particularly when you have no idea what your competitors are charging or offering. In general, we info pros tend to undercharge, relative to what clients pay for other high-value professional services such as attorneys or strategic planning consultants. Knowing how much to charge, accurately estimating what the market will bear, and setting a price that appropriately reflects the expertise and value we offer is difficult for many of us.

Related to pricing and cash flow is the issue of marketing. Independent info pros always need to market. When you start out, you will probably spend 90 percent of your time marketing yourself and your business. For some people, this is the most difficult part of running a business: "How can I tell people how great I am without sounding conceited or pompous?" Section Three goes into marketing issues in depth; the short answer here is that running an independent info pro business means being able to look at yourself as a brand, a product, a business. This never stops. Even after you have been in business for five or 10 years, you still need to market yourself—although the amount of time you spend on marketing will drop to 20 or 30 percent.

Vacation? What Vacation?

Vacation and business-related travel pose problems for independent info pros. For starters, there is no such thing as a paid vacation for the self-employed. (That's not quite true; I have sometimes arranged to subcontract jobs to others when I go on vacation, so I do earn the difference between what the subcontractor charges me and what I bill the client. But most vacations mean zero income.) A bigger challenge is what you do with your clients while you're away. Yes, you can try to stay in touch while you are on the road. With call forwarding, cell phones, pagers, and email, you can respond fairly quickly if a client wants to get in touch with you. But is that any way to enjoy your vacation? One of the things I value most about a vacation is being able to leave my job behind, which is why vacations to locations with spotty internet access are so appealing.

In addition to vacations, there are the inevitable doctor appointments, sick time, the morning you have to take off to renew your auto registration, and the time you spend waiting for the plumber. Employees are usually paid for a certain amount of personal time off; we independent info pros don't have that option. Generally, if we're not working, we aren't earning anything. And this is why it is useful to develop information products, such as podcasts or white papers, that provide passive income.

For those times when you are out of your office and not able to respond quickly to clients' information needs, what do you do? There is no perfect solution, and it is inevitable that some clients will be dissatisfied, particularly those who are accustomed to having researchers available on-call, 24 hours a day. Some independent info pros develop relationships with colleagues, then forward their phones or leave outgoing voicemail messages directing callers to call "my associate" or "my colleague." Others use their travel plans as an opportunity to contact all their regular clients, tell them that the office will be closed, and suggest that they take care of their anticipated information requests right away. And some hardy souls attempt to give the impression that they are in the office, even when they aren't. But, as hard as you try, you can't offer the same degree of service that a large company can; sometimes you just can't get back to the client immediately. And that means you will lose clients who expect their info pros to be available 24/7/365. I cover the issue of travel in more detail in Chapter 12, Work and the Rest of Your Life.

The Best and Worst of Being an Independent Info Pro

Before you launch your own business, think about whether, for you, the "bests" outweigh the "worsts."

BEST:

✦ Pride of ownership; taking credit for the success of your business

✦ Flexibility about where, when, and how you work

✦ Meeting and developing relationships with a wide variety of clients and colleagues

✦ Freedom from bureaucracy

WORST:

✦ Stress of ownership; being responsible for the success of your business

✦ Needing to be available whenever your clients need you

✦ Cash flow fluctuations

✦ Constant need to market yourself and your business

Chapter 4

Are You a Potential Independent Info Pro?

I am often asked why there aren't more independent info pros out there in the marketplace. It seems like the perfect job—sit at home all day, find information for people on all kinds of fascinating subjects, and send out invoices for thousands of dollars. What's not to like about that?

If only it were that easy! The curious thing about this profession is that, in fact, it requires an unusual set of skills that are not innate in most people. Fortunately, you can fill in the gaps in your skill set by reading this book, hiring experts, and focusing your business in areas that take advantage of your strengths. But before you get too far into the planning process, let's look at exactly what it takes to be a successful independent info pro.

The People Skills

Running an information business requires great people skills—getting along with a wide variety of personality types; being able to talk with an irate client without becoming defensive, belligerent, or tongue-tied; and being able to talk enthusiastically about your business to prospective clients. Most independent info pros have clients all over the country, not to mention the world. So you need to come across well on the telephone and via email because it may be the only contact most clients will have with you. (I have clients I've worked with for many years whom I have never met face to face. Sometimes they ask me to send them a picture just so they have an image of the person they have been talking to all these years.) Conveying your winning personality and professional competence via email or other written medium can be challenging; depending on the client, you need to develop some combination of professionalism and informality that comes across well in text. You need to have a good command of English (or your clients' language), both written and spoken. You have to write clearly, concisely, and engagingly.

Beyond client management, being an independent info pro means having client *attraction* skills. You need to be the kind of person that people enjoy working with. Information services are an expense that clients choose to incur. And your clients will call you rather than calling someone else or choosing to do the work themselves because they know you will deliver results cost-effectively, on time, and with a minimum of aggravation and effort. If you are someone they enjoy working with, someone who is personable, professional, and friendly, and who cares about your clients' success, your clients will be more likely to want to contact you when they need your services.

You also need the ability to evaluate people and to trust your instincts. Is this caller a legitimate potential client or just a tire-kicker, someone who loves to talk but is never going to send you a real job? Does this person have budget authority to approve the purchase, or is he just shopping around for his boss and not the person authorized to contract for your services? You do not want to waste your valuable time with someone who will never become a client or a good referral source, nor do you want to alienate a good prospect who is simply shy or vague about what she needs or who spends some time asking intelligent questions before deciding to engage your services.

Then there are some clients who aren't worth keeping. They demand unreasonable deadlines, have low budgets, are abusive, or otherwise cause you to cringe when you see their call coming in. Those clients don't deserve your love and devotion; Chapter 13 tells you how to fire a client gracefully. However, all your other clients, including those who are challenging but worth the aggravation, need to be treated as if they are your one and only focus and concern. You may not actually love them, but you will need to find ways to work with difficult clients.

To keep our clients happy, we are often asked to accommodate what might feel like unreasonable requests. Rather than defaulting to saying "no" to these requests, we have to at least consider them; a vendor who frequently declines to meet a client's specific requests soon becomes an ex-vendor. How would you handle each of these situations?

- Your contract requires that you submit your report using your client's template. This requires that you learn a feature of your word-processing software that you have never seen before.

- Your client insists that you submit your invoice through a web-based portal, using his or her expense categories rather than your own.

- Your client wants you to send a summary of your findings in a presentation slide deck, using his company's template. You can use no more than five slides of three bullet points each.

- Your client calls you every day to get a status report of the project.

- Your client calls halfway through the project and tells you to drop everything and take a different approach.

- Your client asks you to write down every step you took during the research process.

Can you handle these situations gracefully? Can you meet these requests? If not, how skilled are you at redirecting your client to an alternative that you feel is less of an imposition?

The Entrepreneurial Skills

New independent info pros often underestimate the need for entrepreneurial skills. You may be great at finding information for your friends or family, but can you develop a business in which people will pay you $100, $150, or more per hour for your research? How comfortable are you in producing a report that will be used by an executive to make a strategic decision?

What's your tolerance for risk and uncertainty? It's a scary thing to move from knowing that you will be getting a paycheck every two weeks to realizing that you are going to have to hustle for every dollar you earn. You will be trading the security of knowing that someone is paying you regularly for the freedom to create your own job. You will be making decisions about the direction of your business, how you will

What About the Home Front?

In addition to having people skills, a successful info-entrepreneur needs a supportive home life to come home to, even if that shift is more attitude than distance. No two households are alike, and no single household is unchanging from year to year. That said, these are a few of the personal questions that many of us ask ourselves as we have built and grown our businesses:

- Is my spouse or partner fully supportive of this venture? Does he or she understand the changes that this will necessitate in terms of financial uncertainties, insurance coverage, expenses, schedules and chores, availability to run errands, and so on?

- Does my spouse or partner respect the time I spend on my business? Does he or she understand that I have regular hours that I work and that I won't just be sitting around surfing the web?

- What household chores can we outsource? Can we pay for a house cleaner every week or two? Can a neighborhood kid run some of our errands?

- Can I set boundaries for myself and my family so that I pay attention to work when I need to and my family when I want to do so? Can I enforce those boundaries? Can my family members learn to keep interruptions to a minimum during my workday? If my door is closed, will they simply stand outside and ask questions through the door?

- If I am working from home, who else will be home during the day? Will that be distracting for me?

- Am I able to compartmentalize enough to keep my work life from impinging on my home life? Can I stop working in the evening and put energy into the care and feeding of my home life?

- If I am working from home, will I let my business take over my entire house? If so, will that be acceptable to my spouse or partner?

market your services to clients, and when to invest in new technology. How well do you make decisions? How comfortable are you in unfamiliar situations? You don't need to be the kind of person who rappels off cliffs without a second thought, but you should be able to tolerate ambiguity and to assess new situations quickly and pick a course of action.

As any entrepreneur knows, running your own business means that you have to market—and that means marketing yourself as well as your company. You must be able to evaluate your marketing efforts as your business grows and the business environment changes, decide what works now and what doesn't, and modify your strategies to reflect a changing client base and economic environment. Marketing never ever goes away, even after you have been in business for years.

I am often asked whether it is possible to subcontract the marketing to someone who specializes in promoting businesses. Although I suppose it can be done, it does not seem to be a workable option for many of my colleagues; what your client is paying for is *you*—your skills, experience, and ability. It is difficult for someone else to project the air of authority and expertise that comes naturally to you—or will. On the other hand, a number of independent info pros have worked successfully with business coaches or marketing consultants to build up their marketing skills. Because promoting your business is a never-ending task, it is wise to invest in learning how to do this as painlessly as possible, and yes, it can become painless over time.

Entrepreneurs tend to have a drive to succeed and the self-discipline to keep going when business slumps. You are going to be discouraged sometimes. The phone doesn't ring, a client yells at you, even your dog won't wag her tail when you walk by. At such times, you'll want to take advantage of one of the biggest benefits of membership in the Association of Independent Information Professionals (AIIP; www.aiip.org)—a ready network of fellow independent info pros who can give you suggestions on new approaches to your business or simply offer a sympathetic ear.

Successful entrepreneurs are self-starting, persistent (some might say to a fault), energetic, and full of ideas. They realize that they have to work for each of their clients, and they seldom wait passively for something to happen or someone else to take care of a problem. They are willing to go outside their comfort zone on a regular basis. They do not give up when an idea fails.

I was the librarian at MCI, an early and very entrepreneurial telecom company, back in the 1980s, when its founder, Bill McGowan, was still at the helm. The entire company (then about 500 people) lived by Bill's commandment: "Don't be afraid to make mistakes, because if you're not making mistakes, you're not taking risks. If you aren't taking risks, you aren't valuable to us. Just don't make the same mistake twice." I have lived by that rule ever since and have found it particularly valuable since I started my information business. I have made some bad decisions, but I have also taken risks and expanded my business in new areas. As long as I don't make the same bad decision twice, I know I am doing alright.

I have found that most successful independent info pros tend to be detail-oriented. They can see the big picture, but they also focus on the little things that make that big picture happen. Being a one-person operation means that there is no one else to catch your mistakes, cover for you, or take the blame if you miss something. If you are the type of person who is careful about details, thinks through all the aspects of a project, and follows through on everything that has to be done, you will have a much better chance of succeeding in this business.

Time management is a critical entrepreneurial skill. How well do you function in a work setting with very little structure? Will you be tempted to spend the day gardening, watching TV, or working in the garage instead of focusing on your business? Alternatively, will you be able to close the door (figuratively if not literally) on your business at the end of the day, or will it wind up taking over every waking hour of your life?

How much do you enjoy working alone? Do you need the excitement of an office to get fired up, or do you find the hustle and bustle of an office exhausting? Do you need input and recognition from others in order to feel that your work is meaningful and valuable? If so, can you get that from your clients, or do you need the more immediate feedback of co-workers and a boss?

Finally, a successful entrepreneur is someone who not only has a vision but is able to implement it. What is your track record of implementing your ideas? Can you think through what is involved in bringing an idea to fruition and then take all the steps required to do it on your own initiative? Do you think creatively? Do you have the ability to think of new ways of doing things and new ways to build a business?

The Business Skills

In addition to entrepreneurial skills, independent info pros need to master the basics of business management. You are the CEO, CFO, Marketing Director, Sales Manager, IT guru, Strategic Planning VP, and Head Analyst, all in one, and although you don't have to have advanced degrees in all these areas, you will need to develop some skills in management, finance, sales and marketing, and so on.

You have to be able to set up a business infrastructure and operate as a professional entity, even if you are just doing it from your kitchen table. You must keep accounting records, manage your cash flow, and comply with tax rules regarding periodic reports and payments. If you are not a detail-oriented person, hire an accountant or bookkeeper to take care of this part of your business. You can be fairly casual about some things, but you do not want to tell the tax man, "Oops! I forgot to pay my taxes. Sorry about that."

You should feel comfortable projecting a professional image to everyone you deal with. This may take some practice. Some independent info pros find it hard to sound professional when they are talking on the phone in their bathrobe and bunny slippers, or when they're doing business with a client who is also a friend. You have to be able to see yourself as a business owner, regardless of whom you are talking with or what setting you are in. Even if your office consists of a corner of your living room, you must be able to view it as the corner office of an executive suite.

You have to be able to close a sale. When someone asks you for an estimate on a project, you have to feel comfortable and self-confident talking about budgets, what you charge per hour or per project, and your payment terms.

It's Not Personal, It's Just Business

One of the most difficult parts of running a business is collections. Yes, we would like to think that all our clients will pay us promptly, but that doesn't always happen. See Chapter 14, Money, Money, Money, for a discussion of how to accept credit cards and other finance-related topics. The bottom line is whether you are able to pick up the phone and say, "Hello, Ms. Smith. I notice that my invoice dated January 15 is past due. What can we do to get this invoice processed by Friday?"

I sometimes think of independent info pros as information pitbulls. We are the people who won't take "no" for an answer and who keep digging for what our client has asked us to find, hour after hour. Persistence is an admirable trait in a researcher, but it can get in your way if you are running your own business. You only earn money for the time that you can bill to a client. If your client is not willing to pay you for more than three hours of research, you have to stop at that point, even though you may have identified lots of other avenues to explore. If you do not stop working, you will be giving away your time for free and will be training your client to expect bonus time from you on every project. It is hard to walk away when you are involved in research, but if a client is not willing to pay for an extensive effort, you cannot survive as a profitable business if you only charge your client for a portion of the time you spent on the project. And you certainly cannot bill a client for more than the authorized budget. Your client may pay that invoice, but you can bet she will not call you again if you prove that your word cannot be trusted.

One of the most common mistakes that new info-entrepreneurs make is to bill for only a fraction of the hours they spend on a project, with the excuse that "I can't charge my client for my learning curve!" Keep in mind that clients are not hiring you because you know all the answers; they are hiring you because you can find the information and provide the analysis and synthesis they need. Your learning curve is often a necessary part of that process. Would you have spent the time learning all you need to know about Chinese tungsten or the ins and outs of the European Union's antitrust commission if a client were not paying for you? I suspect not, and if you are doing work that is required to get a project done, then it is billable time.

Thinking Strategically

Part of running a business is the ability to watch your competition and predict what is going to happen in your market. Can you make the time to think strategically about where your business is going and what your clients will want a year from now? You are not expected to have psychic powers, but you do have to be able to hazard a guess on the future direction of your business and your clients' needs, and then take appropriate action. No one else can tell you where your market is going to be a year from now; you have to decide for yourself where you want your business to go. One way of ensuring that you make the best decisions in terms of your strategic direction is to monitor the news of your key clients' industries. When you hear rumblings of significant challenges or threats to that industry, think about what your clients will need to respond to these new threats. Contact them individually and offer a service that would directly address their concerns. Do they want a company overview of their newly emerged competition? Would your clients like a monthly enewsletter alerting them to developments in their clients' industries?

Every business owner knows—or quickly learns—about money management and cash flow. If you live in the U.S., you will be writing a check to the IRS every three months for a portion of your income tax for the past quarter. If you have already spent that money, too bad. How do you handle cash? Do you have the discipline to set a substantial percentage of your revenue aside to pay for things like taxes or that big invoice from an online service provider or a subcontractor?

Finally, everyone who owns a business needs the ability to recognize hype and oversell. I am amazed at the number of people who have approached me over the years, offering me the chance to partner with them for an "amazing opportunity" or who wanted to pay my invoices in equity in their company instead of cash. Although your experience may be different, I have found that people who really do have sustainable business opportunities are willing to pay their vendors (that would be you and me) in cash. Independent info pros are usually independent for a reason—we like having control over our own destiny. And that serves us well when we are approached by people who would love to let us in on the next big thing in exchange for a substantial discount on our rates or part-ownership of their business. Until you figure out a way to pay your phone bill with a start-up company's stock options, stick to payment in cash.

The Information Skills

You may have started reading this book because you just love finding things out, or you're the one everyone comes to for help in gathering information. That passion for finding information is essential, but turning your avocation into a business means developing a whole new level of research expertise. Independent info pros don't just surf the web for information, nor do they typically just head down to the library and bury their heads in books all day. They usually use a variety of resources, including the web; fee-based online services such as LexisNexis, Factiva, or Dialog; government databases; telephone interviews; and court records. If the only information source you know is the web, it will be very difficult to differentiate yourself from anyone else with an internet connection, not to mention that some of the most useful information cannot be found through a web search engine. (See Chapter 32, Web Research 101, for more discussion of the invisible web.)

In order to succeed in this business, you need to have experience as a researcher or be willing to subcontract out any project involving types of research in which you aren't already an expert. (See Chapter 16, Subcontracting, or I'll Scratch Your Back If You Scratch Mine, for a discussion of how you can build a business around subcontracting.) The bottom line is that you generally cannot get your clients to pay for your learning curve as an online researcher. And it is a steep curve if you do not have a foundation in research skills to build on. It takes a surprising amount of time and money to learn how to search the professional online services, how to find court documents, how to conduct effective telephone research, and so on.

You can, of course, pick up those skills by taking the long view—a year or two—and structure your business so that you can subcontract out the work you are not yet able to do, until you can build the research skills you need.

Many independent info pros come from a library background, complete with masters' degrees in library science and years behind the reference desk. Librarians have the advantage of knowing where to look for information, how to find it quickly, how to organize it, how to interview clients to make sure they're looking for the *right* information in the first place, and countless other research-related skills. You don't need to get a graduate degree in information science, but consider taking some continuing education courses in information organization, reference skills, and online research. A number of university graduate programs offer distance-learning courses so you can attend classes on your own schedule.

A number of successful independent info pros almost stumbled into the profession from another field, after deciding that what they really enjoy is finding information and then figuring out how to build that passion into a business. For example, Risa Sacks, owner of Risa Sacks Information Services and a top-notch telephone researcher, started out as a speech therapist. "My work involved identifying what a client's speech problem was and how to get that client to where he needed to be," Risa told me. "It was all about figuring out what people need and then finding a solution. From there, I moved into training development and technical writing, which also involve identifying problems and developing solutions. Both training development and technical writing required that I interview experts in order to learn about whatever I had to write about. About 30 percent of my time was spent interviewing, and 70 percent was writing, and I realized that I really wanted to find a profession in which I could spend 70 percent of my time interviewing people and 30 percent of the time writing. And that's how I fell into telephone research!"

Where Can You Get Help?

You've read about the skill sets involved in successfully running an information business. Unless you are a perfect specimen of humanity or are unable to conduct a critical self-evaluation, you have probably identified some areas in which you could use a little help. Congratulations! I have yet to meet anyone who came to this business with all the necessary people skills, entrepreneurial skills, business skills, and research skills—myself included. If you are strong in at least two of these areas and are willing to develop your skills in the others, you can join the ranks of successful independent info pros.

One of the best ways to enhance your CEO-ability is going back to school. Your local college may offer continuing education courses on entrepreneurship or specific business-related subjects such as cash management and financial planning, marketing on the web, and government contracting. In fact, some schools even have courses specifically titled, "Home-Based Business."

The U.S. Small Business Administration (SBA) offers a number of resources through its website (www.sba.gov) including free basic tutorials—the SBA calls them online courses—on writing a business plan, conducting a self-assessment, building your business, and so on. The SBA also sponsors the SCORE (Service Corps of Retired Executives) program. SCORE volunteers provide free counseling and workshops for people considering starting a business. In addition, SCORE offers a number of articles and tutorials on aspects of running a small business. Topics range from transitioning from employee to entrepreneur, managing cash flow, and office management. Go to www.score.org to learn more about SCORE's online and in-person counseling, and check the SBA website to find locations of local SBA offices.

You may also want to check the website of your state or regional government. You are likely to find information not only on business licenses or permits you may need but also on financial assistance programs, help with business planning, and workshops and other continuing education programs.

And what about the necessary information skills? A number of graduate-level library schools offer specific programs on what's often called information brokering. Check with your local university to see if it has a School of Library Studies (some library science programs are eschewing the "L-word" and are calling themselves Information Management Studies or simply the Information School). For a list of the American Library Association (ALA)-accredited library schools in the U.S. and Canada, go to www.ala.org and search for the directory of ALA-accredited master's programs in library and information studies. This site also indicates which accredited schools offer distance-education opportunities, including programs that are 100 percent online—a great way to build your research skills if you don't live near a school that offers a library science degree.

The Imposter Syndrome

"I'm Mary Ellen and I'm faking it."

No, I'm not going to put that on my name badge any time soon, but if I did, I would see a lot of people nodding their heads in sympathy. We are the people who, at one time or another, suffer from what has been called the Imposter Syndrome. Do you worry that people will finally realize that you are not the incredibly smart, capable expert they once thought you were? Do you think that your success is due to luck or a fluke rather than because you are an astute business owner? Do you obsess about making a mistake and interpret any constructive criticism as further proof of your incompetence?

While both men and women experience the imposter syndrome, the groups among women most likely to experience the imposter syndrome are high achievers, those labeled as "gifted" as children, and those who have very specialized skills. From my own experience, it appears that a lot of women info-entrepreneurs fit that profile. In fact, one of the appealing factors of being our own boss is that we don't have to worry about co-workers finally discovering that we're frauds.

The mere fact that you are—or are considering—starting your own business belies the belief that you are a fraud. The process of shifting from the expectation of a steady paycheck to the adventure of entrepreneurship isn't for wimps. Here are some tools for dealing with the imposter syndrome:

- Take constructive feedback gently. If someone suggests things you could change, it means he sees you as having higher abilities than what you are currently showing.

- Imagine talking with someone who has your qualifications, skills, and abilities. Would you really call her incompetent?

- Learn to appreciate your own accomplishments and successes. The ability to reward yourself rather than waiting for external feedback is a critical skill for any info-entrepreneur.

- Let go of the need to know everything about everything. Our clients hire us because we know how to apply our skills to their need.

- And finally, the best suggestion: Fake it 'til you make it.

Before you go into a networking event, find someplace quiet and create a narrative in your head that describes your experience, expressed in the past tense, after the fact. I sometimes tell myself, before I walk into the room, "I was surprised at how much I enjoyed this event. I just walked up to several people and asked them about their work. It was a lot easier than I had thought it would be." Take a deep breath, and then go in there and pretend that narrative is true.

The same technique works for negotiating the parameters of a project with a client, giving a presentation, pitching a proposal, or just about any other "performance" in your life. Take a different view of faking it and remind yourself that this is, in fact, a skill. You are creating confidence by your actions, which is a pretty amazing thing.

Checklist of Key Independent Info Pro Skills

✦ Ability to deal with a wide range of personalities.

✦ Self-motivation: The flip side of never having to endure a job performance evaluation is that no one tells you that you are doing a great job.

✦ Knowing when to stop: You only make money on the time you can bill a client.

✦ Ability to market yourself and your business: This is one area where it does not pay to be shy or self-effacing.

✦ The skills to develop a strategic plan and direction, and then take the steps necessary to implement that plan.

✦ Basic money-management skills and a strong stomach for fluctuating cash flow.

✦ A drive to succeed and to make your business grow.

✦ Excellent information skills or the willingness to subcontract to other experts.

Chapter 5

Who You Are and What You Do

Who Needs You?

The first question to ask yourself is, "Who are my potential clients? To whom should I be marketing?" There are a number of factors to take into account as you decide on the clientele you will be targeting.

What subject(s) do you know best? If you have experience in a subject area—patents, biotechnology, advertising, chemistry, architecture—professionals in that field represent a natural client base for you. You speak their language. You understand their concerns. You know the subject matter, and you know the information sources. You have instant credibility. Of course, most independent info pros eventually expand from their core expertise. When I began my business, I focused on research in the telecommunications field because that was my background, and I knew that there weren't many other independent telecom researchers. Pretty soon, though, my clients started asking me for research on other business-related topics, and I was happy to tackle those projects, too. Note, however, that there's a fine line between taking on projects that go beyond your core expertise and accepting jobs for which you just aren't qualified.

Who is willing to pay for information? You may be an expert in a particular field, but unless you can find clients who are willing to pay you for your expertise, all your knowledge won't pay the mortgage. Your neighbors may appreciate your ability to help them with their genealogy research, but they would be shocked, most likely, if you started charging them your professional rate for your time and expertise. Instead, you need to focus on a client base that is not particularly price-sensitive and that puts a high value on information—people who have more money than time, who need on-point intelligence to do their jobs, and who are willing to pay for the insights you provide. That means that your local grocer or hardware store owner is probably not a likely prospect, but a new product manager, consultant, marketing professional, or strategic planning director would be a good target.

Who doesn't already have easy access to free research? Because I had worked in law libraries earlier in my career, when I first launched my business I considered marketing to small law firms without in-house libraries. But after some conversations with colleagues and a few lawyers, I realized that this wasn't the best market for me. Many small law firms and sole practitioners view research on the professional legal services such as Lexis or Westlaw as a profit center. They mark up the online costs and make money from each search, and they can't easily do that if an independent info pro does the research. (Note, however, that law firms do use independent info pros for specialized nonlegal research, particularly in connection with litigation and business development.) Medical researchers tell me that marketing to physicians is also very difficult. Most medical professionals have access to librarians at their local hospital or through their professional medical association, and they are reluctant to use a for-profit researcher when they can get the research done for free or at cost. This is not to say that you should cross law and medicine off your list of possible market niches, especially if you have expertise in either area. Litigation support is a varied and potentially lucrative research area, and an independent info pro who can market successfully to law firms (either directly or indirectly) can dip into a significant revenue stream. And doctors aren't the only people who require medical research. Although the web has empowered consumers seeking medical information to an incredible degree, healthcare industry consultants are often in need of detailed, authoritative journal articles that only a researcher familiar with the ins and outs of the specialized medical databases can effectively provide.

Who will be a consistent source of referrals and/or repeat business? John Levis, retired owner of John E. Levis Associates, initially specialized in providing medical information to consumers. But he changed the direction of his business when he realized that most individuals who need medical information aren't the kind of clients who can sustain a business. Why? For starters, they generally used John just once—unless they had multiple diseases, which isn't something you would wish on your clients!—so he couldn't count on their repeat business. He also found that an adequate answer to even the simplest question involved fairly extensive research. Because most consumers wanted the work done for a set price rather than at an

Information-Hungry Professions

What kinds of people are likely to need and value information and be willing to pay for it? The following job titles and functions represent likely prospects:

- Marketing director

- Analyst

- Strategic planner

- Corporate development director

- Market researcher

- Consultant

- Research and development director

- Advertising professional

- Public relations officer

- Competitive intelligence director

- Product development manager

- Librarians (yes, librarians need expert researchers, too, as I explain in Chapter 27, Starting the Word of Mouth)

hourly rate, John would either have to charge more than the client wanted to pay or perform work for which he couldn't bill.

It costs far more to get a new client than it does to keep an existing one. And the best—and least expensive—way to get new clients is by word of mouth from your existing clients and colleagues. That is why successful independent info pros focus their marketing time and attention on people who they think will use them repeatedly, and why they stay in touch with "influencers"—people whom others go to for advice, suggestions, and referrals. Concentrating on prospects like those can increase the scope of your marketing immensely.

Offering What the Client Needs

It's easy to think about what services you can provide. You offer online research, you locate public records for law firms, and you conduct primary research through telephone interviews. But that's not enough to make a prospect turn into a client. The crucial step that some independent info pros forget is to think beyond what you do to what your clients *need*. Your most powerful marketing approach is to offer something that your client didn't even realize he needed until he talked to you.

When you are talking with a prospective client about what strategic information needs he has, describe yourself not in terms of what you do but in terms of how you are an essential part of your clients' strategic decision-making processes. By changing your definition of your role in your clients' professional life, you enable yourself to think more expansively about what expertise and perspective you bring to the table. What can you do with your unique skill set? Where are your clients' informational pain points? What role can you play when your clients face key decision points?

You know you have identified the right kind of added value when you describe your services to a prospect and she responds not with, "That sounds great," but "I have to have that *now*!" The former response is enthusiastic, but I also think that winning the lottery jackpot sounds great. When you hear, "I must have this now," then you know that you have identified something that your clients will pay you well for and that makes you competition-proof. What your clients are paying you for is not simply your ability to gather the most relevant information but also your perspective and analysis.

Developing these kinds of can't-live-without services requires more upfront effort on your part; you have to think of yourself as a member of your client's team and focus on what information services your client needs and would be willing to pay for. Of course, this is a challenge if you don't have any clients yet. As I suggest in Chapter 19, Strategic Planning, consider joining your clients'—or potential clients'—major industry associations and read the trade publications they read to keep up on their key issues. And see Chapter 8, Before You Launch, for a discussion of how to conduct "informational interviews" to identify their information needs.

The advantage of this can't-live-without-you approach is that it makes you virtually invulnerable to competition. You have demonstrated to your client that you are focused on her business needs rather than on your own set of stock information services, and it's clear from the research and interviews that you've conducted that you understand her business and industry. It also enables you to charge a higher hourly rate; your client isn't going to shop around for the cheapest information service when you have already demonstrated that you want and value her business.

Think Globally, Not Locally

When you first ponder where your clients will come from, it's natural to think locally—the corporations headquartered or with large offices in your town, the local chamber of commerce, and even your friends and neighbors. That's great; you might get some business from nearby people and organizations. But it's a very limited field. Even if you live in the middle of Chicago, there are only so many companies in the area for you to market to. You are vulnerable to any economic slump that hits your region particularly hard. And if you live in a small town, your chances of supporting yourself on local businesses alone are pretty slim. Besides, why restrict your horizons in such an arbitrary way? Defining your market in geographical terms is, generally speaking, an obsolete and income-limiting assumption.

Another factor to keep in mind is that it is usually much easier to target a vertical market (e.g., pharmaceutical companies, labor organizations, architects) than it is to focus on all prospects within a geographic region. Why? Vertical markets have well-established communication tools—industry publications to write for; professional associations to join (and, more importantly, volunteer with); email discussion lists to participate in; conferences and trade shows at which to network, speak, or exhibit; and so on. You can reach prospects around the country or around the world by taking advantage of the opportunities provided by such channels of communication. Oddly enough, it's much harder to market cost-effectively to a local audience. Very few independent info pros have successfully built a local business using time-intensive marketing efforts such as in-person sales visits or cold calling or broad strategies such as direct mail. By going deep and narrow, you get a much greater return for your marketing efforts.

Tips for Defining Your Services and Clients

✦   Target professionals with a high need for strategic intelligence.

✦   Focus on clients who will provide repeat business.

✦   Get to know your prospective clients before you define your services.

✦   Offer something that your clients immediately see the value of.

✦   Don't limit your geographic range unnecessarily.

Chapter 6

Understanding Your Competition

One of the strange aspects of being an independent info pro is that our competition is generally invisible. We don't have a storefront, so we don't see the Discount Info Supermarket down the street with "50% off all information this week only" signs in the window. In fact, you will probably find that you spend far more time thinking about how to attract new clients than you do worrying about what your competitors are up to. It's a big market out there, and it is far from saturated. However, you may find it useful to stroll down the virtual sidewalk every so often to see where else your clients could be shopping.

Who Am I Up Against?

As you begin marketing your services, one of the first questions to ask yourself is, "Where are my clients going *now* for the services I want to provide them?" The most likely answer will be the web; although it is not always the most efficient or cost-effective way to find in-depth information, it sure is fast, easy, and cheap. When you present yourself to prospective clients, you will have to address the perception that it is all on the web, for free, and anyone can find it. See the sidebar, "Can You Find That on the Web?" for some thoughts about talking with your clients about what *can't* be found by searching the web. You will also want to evaluate specific aspects of the services you offer and the value you add that differentiate your deliverable from what your clients can find on the web. This shouldn't be hard, but sometimes you do have to spell it out.

"I Can Just Google This"

Search engines and other web finding tools understand that one of the ways to attract visitors (and, hence, ad revenue) is to offer *answers* instead of just a list of URLs. Most of the major search engines offer a customized display of search results, based on your prior search activity. Search engines also have a boggling number of prepared answers to simple questions. For example, if you type *weather Mumbai* in the Google search box, the first item in the search results list is a box with the current weather and daily forecast for Mumbai, India. Type in *150 GBP in USD*, and the first search result will be the converted value of British pounds in U.S. dollars. As search engines get smarter, people are lured into believing that they can find the answer to anything on the web.

Another challenge (and opportunity—see Chapter 24, Marketing on the Web) is the ease of asking a question to a large network of people and getting responses. With any social media site, I can post a query about virtually anything—who to talk to about widgets, whether Megatron Corp. is a good company to work with, even competitive intelligence queries to find former employers of a target company. Of course, depending on your network, these responses can range from useful to useless to downright misleading.

One of the ways that info-entrepreneurs can respond is to participate in the Q&A features of social media sites. While we cannot offer to provide high-quality research at no charge, we can point them to some good basic sources and remind them about the additional resources that aren't on the web.

In-House Libraries

Your clients may have the option of using an in-house library or information center. Most large companies, government agencies, nonprofits, and associations have specialized internal-use-only information centers that serve that organization's employees. Why should your clients pay you when they can get the information for free? Good question, and it has to be answered carefully. I have always viewed in-house librarians (also known as special librarians) as colleagues and partners, not competitors, and I will usually ask my clients if they have checked with their internal library before I start working on a project. Am I crazy? No, I want to make sure that I stay in the librarian's good graces. Special librarians are great referral sources; when they get a request that goes beyond the scope of what they can handle, they want to refer their client to someone who can do the work, and you will be on their short list if you play your cards right.

Likewise, I refer clients to their own library for simple projects that aren't profitable for me to work on but that their librarian can answer quickly. And special librarians may have access to high-priced information sources that you can't afford. So, working with your client's librarian on a complex research project usually benefits everyone—your client gets your expertise as well as the specialized information that only the librarian can find, the librarian sees you as a partner rather than a competitor, and you keep your client happy.

Information on the Desktop

Large organizations often provide external information resources through an intranet, distributing news stories, market research, and articles from trade publications directly to employees' desktops. Such arrangements can be difficult to compete against—you don't know exactly what your client has access to internally, but he probably thinks that everything he'd ever need is right there on his desktop. You can respond that you have access to a broader range of publications, you can conduct primary research (telephone interviews, surveys, and so on), you provide customized analysis rather than just collections of news and general industry information, and you can dig deeper than the preselected material that pops up on the client's desktop. Keep in mind that the client probably does have access to some material that you won't be able to get, particularly high-priced industry analysis and consulting reports. Work with the client to ensure that he taps into his internal information sources and that you focus on resources that his intranet can't deliver.

Joe Down the Hall

Some of your "competitors" are harder to pin down. Some potential clients rely on interns or younger staff to do in-depth research; some ask the colleague down the hall who always seems to have the information they need; and some people just do without necessary information. Such prospects are hard to attract—they don't know what they're missing, so they are not inclined to seek out an info pro to help them find it. On the other hand, they are relatively easy to impress because they are accustomed to minimal added value. When you are talking to someone who relies on "Joe down the hall," be sure to describe the services you provide that go beyond what Joe could find on the web, such as research in sources that don't exist online, confidential calls to industry sources, analysis of results, and so on.

Public and Academic Libraries

Public and university libraries sometimes compete with independent info pros, at least indirectly. A few libraries actually operate fee-based services of their own. The hourly rates for these services are usually comparable to what independent info pros charge. They're attractive to clients because they usually have several people on staff, so someone is always available to handle calls, and they have direct access to a wide variety of information sources.

As an independent info pro, you can compete successfully if you focus on what sets you apart from fee-based library services:

- You offer consistency—the client always works with the same info pro.

- You provide services that the library can't, such as telephone or public records research.

- Because you own your own business, you might be more responsive to your client's needs than an overworked librarian.

Can You Find That on the Web?

We've all been encouraged to believe that all you have to do to find information on the web is type a few words into a search engine. And search engines are taking a wide range of approaches to finding out about as much web content as they can. There are semi-acceptable automated speech-to-text features in some multimedia search engines, and the major search engines are putting a good deal of focus into interpreting and making sense out of images. Books that are in the public domain are being scanned into enormous digital libraries. And speaking of libraries, you can now even search within the card catalogs of thousands of libraries around the world.

All that said, most of the useful information on the web can't be found through search engines—at least not through the search engines you have come to know and love. This "invisible web" includes material that search engines can't get to, such as articles within databases or websites that require registration; material that most search engines can't read, such as images, audio clips, and other multimedia content; material that search engines don't even try to capture, such as an archive of real-time stock quotes; and material that search engines simply miss, such as pages buried deep within a website or information on a new website they haven't gotten around to indexing.

When you are talking with a prospect who thinks she can find everything she needs from a web search engine, you might want to tell her:

- The information on the invisible web is often more useful than what a search engine could find.

- The publishers of much of the most useful industry press never put their content on their website; you have to use one of the professional online services to retrieve it.

- Websites that look authoritative may be misleading or just plain wrong.

- Some information never shows up online at all. Sometimes a recent book or a phone conversation is your best bet.

- For research that requires using search engines, you can search the web more efficiently, and your client can spend her valuable time doing something else.

You'll want to state your case gracefully so you don't inadvertently insult your client; many people believe that they are expert web researchers. Develop a couple of examples showing how you found something important in the invisible web or that wasn't on the web at all.

In addition to the specialized research services that some libraries offer, most public and academic libraries offer a wide range of in-depth databases, comparable in coverage to what is available in the fee-based services. The main distinction is that the public library versions are much easier to use and, well, you can't beat free—

at least for library card holders. If you want to conduct some quick research, these are good resources. But the user interfaces on these services are generally targeted to noninfo pros, so most of the sophisticated searches that high-end researchers would want to run simply can't be done through the public library services.

Working With Your Competition

You might have noticed that I haven't yet mentioned other independent info pros as competitors. That's because they virtually never compete with you. In the two decades I've been in business, I can think of only two situations in which I found myself directly competing with another info pro for a client's business. Instead, we see each other as colleagues and partners. Other independent info pros will be your subcontractors when you get a job you can't or don't have time to do; they will hire you as a subcontractor when they need your expertise; and you will find yourself referring clients to a colleague who is the best in his subject area.

One of the biggest reasons why I renew my membership in the Association of Independent Information Professionals (AIIP; www.aiip.org) every year is because I value the network of fellow info entrepreneurs that I can tap into. Members use AIIP's private email discussion list to ask for help with a tricky research project, the name of a good online searcher in Hong Kong, suggestions on how to use a website for marketing, or advice on how to keep clients happy while on vacation or traveling on business. These people aren't my competitors—they're my secret weapon! They are what enable me, a one-person business, to provide a wide variety of services to a broad spectrum of clients.

Every once in a while, I get a call from a prospective client who explains in painful detail just why he is so very unhappy with his current independent info pro. While it's gratifying that he is calling me—and I hope I'll be able to keep him happy—I also make sure that I never criticize a colleague. It's a small world, and if you bad-mouth a fellow info pro, you can bet that word will get out. In this situation, my response to the unhappy prospect is something like, "I'm so sorry that you're not happy with so-and-so. Sometimes it just doesn't work out." See Chapter 13, Managing Your Clients, for a sobering reminder of the fact that each of us will eventually experience a project that blows up in our faces. Sooner or later, you will probably learn first-hand that, indeed, sometimes it just doesn't work out between an independent info pro and a client.

Looking for Competition

When you are considering your market and deciding whom to target, look at how many other independent info pros are in that market and how long they have been in business. Check the membership directory of AIIP to get a general sense of who's out there doing what you want to do. Then mull over the following questions:

- Is your potential market niche full of people who have been in business for less than a couple of years? Is that because it's a really new market or because it isn't a sustainable market?

- Is the niche full of established businesses that have been around a long time? If so, can you break into it? Do you have a proven track record in that industry? Do you have contacts in the industry who could serve as referrals for new clients?

- If nobody seems to be doing the kind of work you have in mind, is it because there's no market for it, no one else has the expertise, or because you're the first to think of it? Can you conduct some brief market research interviews with prospective clients to get an idea of whether you are leading edge or totally off the page?

- Do clients in this market have ready access to in-house research centers, libraries, or other in-depth internal information resources? Do they need and value the information services you can provide? Are they willing to pay what you plan to charge for your services?

Making Yourself Competition-Proof

The best way to deal with competition is to eliminate it. Easier said than done? The secret is to develop a business that provides a unique set of services and that features the irreplaceable *you*. Sell a service that doesn't lend itself to price comparisons—that way, your clients aren't going to leave you for someone who charges 10 percent less.

How do you develop this kind of competition-proof business?

- Provide "frictionless service." Make sure that getting you started on a project is as easy as using a search engine. Think about what you can do to make it easier for your clients to work with you. Get a toll-free phone number. Have an easy-to-remember email address. Return phone calls as quickly as you can.

- Invest in your clients. Keep an eye out for articles they might be interested in. Subscribe to their leading industry publication. Attend the major trade conference that your clients attend and make sure they know you're there. (Offer to send them a report of the conference when you return home, for example.)

- Provide analysis as well as research services; move your services up the value chain. Find out what your client intends to do with the information you provide, and see what you can do to make the information easier to use, more valuable, more irreplaceable. If your client is pulling together material for a PowerPoint presentation, for example, deliver your research results in simple bullet-point form.

- Notify your most valuable clients before you leave town on a business trip or vacation; let them know who will be covering your phone. Make sure that your clients have someone they can call while you're gone—and that whoever is taking those calls knows that these clients are to be given the red-carpet treatment.

- Take your best clients to lunch once in a while. If they aren't local, let them know if you're going to be visiting their city. Even if a client doesn't have time for lunch, you can stop by, say hello, and drop off a small gift—a fruit basket or other specialty food item, a book, or a similar token to indicate that you appreciate working with them.

Lessons Learned About Competition

✦ Most independent info pros have very little direct competition. Fellow info pros are more often referral sources and subcontractors than competitors.

✦ Competition can take the form of prospective clients' attitudes that they can find everything they need themselves.

✦ Check how many other info pros are already in the sector you plan to enter. Does their presence, or absence, indicate a strong potential market or a weak, unprofitable niche?

✦ Look for ways to make yourself competition-proof. Establish long-term relationships with clients.

Chapter 7

Structuring Your Business

Most independent info pros start out as one-person operations, and many find that this works just fine, thank you very much. Others begin their entrepreneurial life with a business partner, on the assumption that two heads are better than one. Some people build their businesses by hiring employees or using subcontractors extensively; others prefer to limit their growth to what they can handle themselves. You will have to make some decisions about how to structure your business before you open up shop, but you can also restructure later, as your needs and goals change.

Of course, this book cannot take the place of advice from your lawyer and your accountant. And before you even consult with your advisors, you will have to consider the following factors:

- Legal restrictions within your industry: Many states and entire countries regulate access to public records, for example, and may require special licenses.

- Liabilities in the type of work you will do: Intellectual property research, for example, inherently involves more risk than many other types of research.

- Type of business: This depends on whether you will be providing a service that requires a permanent staff of employees, for example.

- Tax advantages or disadvantages: The financial situation of your household is something that only you can assess; your accountant can help you identify the most important tax issues to consider for you, your family, and your business.

Note that the material in this chapter applies specifically to U.S. businesses, but most of the considerations for structuring a business are universal. For those of us in the U.S., the most efficient place to find information on the legal requirements of starting a business is at the U.S. Small Business Administration's website (SBA; www.sba.gov). Go directly to www.sba.gov/smallbusinessplanner to walk through the SBA's "Small Business Planner: Manage your business from start to finish."

For more information on the legal requirements for businesses in the U.K., and other information you need to consider when starting your U.K. business, see HM Revenue & Customs' "Starting in Business" guide (www.hmrc.gov.uk/startingup).

For information on Canadian business forms, see Revenue Canada's "Guide for Canadian Small Businesses," which walks you through setting up a business and explains the tax liability in detail. This publication is available on Revenue Canada's website; start at www.cra-arc.gc.ca and use the "Search" feature to find the guide by title.

Protecting Your Social Security Number

As a sole proprietor in the U.S., you will be asked for your Social Security number (SSN) by just about every client. They need your "Taxpayer Identification Number," which in your case is usually your SSN, in order to file an IRS Form 1099 on which they report how much they paid you during the year. (Remember, 1099s must be filed by anyone who pays an individual at least $600 annually, supposedly to ensure that you don't cheat by under-reporting your income as a sole proprietor.) Since a loose SSN can be used by criminals to commit all kinds of fraud, some independent info pros are reluctant to give out that number left and right.

You can get around this remote but real possibility by requesting an Employer Identification Number from the IRS. You don't have to be an employer; you don't even have to be incorporated. You just have to fill out IRS Form SS-4, Application for Employer Identification Number (EIN), which you can download from www.irs.gov; your EIN will be mailed to you. Then you can provide your EIN to clients instead of your Social Security number. Your clients will still have to fill out a Form 1099 on the payments they made to you, but at least your SSN will remain secure.

Incorporating or Keeping It Simple

Independent info pros in the U.S. have the following four primary choices of business structure, and most other countries offer similar structures:

- Sole proprietorship

- Partnership

- Limited liability company

- Corporation

Each of these forms of business has its advantages and drawbacks, some of which will vary depending on where you live. To grossly oversimplify, here is a quick description of each form.

Sole proprietorship: You and your business are essentially one; you are personally responsible for the profits and expenses of your business; you report your business income and expense through your personal income tax return. The vast majority of info-entrepreneurs are sole proprietors.

Partnership: Two or more people share the responsibilities, profits, and liabilities of the company; just as with sole proprietors, partners are not distinct from their businesses; you each report your business income and expenses through your personal income tax return.

Limited liability company: This more structured version of a partnership functions more like a corporation; the owner(s) are not personally responsible for corporate debts; business income and expenses are passed directly to your personal income tax return.

Corporation: This is a formal entity, legally independent of its owner(s) and able to enter into legally binding contracts; income is routinely distributed to you in the form of a salary; there are tax benefits after your income rises to a certain point; there is more recordkeeping and accounting required, and more filing requirements with various government agencies.

We will go into more detail about the advantages and disadvantages of each form of business organization later in this chapter. But before we can get to the nitty-gritty aspects of limited liability companies versus Subchapter S corporations, you will need to pause for a more strategic view of your business. Table 7.1 looks at five strategic issues to consider, along with an indication of what factors suggest choosing an

Table 7.1 Incorporate or Go Solo

	Choose to incorporate/LLC if you:	Choose a partnership or to be solo if you:
Strategic Concern		
Your vision of the size and nature of your business, presently and in five years	Anticipate substantial year-to-year growth Expect to sell your interest in the business within a few years	Expect to earn a good salary but not to grow substantially beyond your (healthy/generous) salary goal
The level of control you want	Want to share responsibility, risk, rewards with partner(s) or employee(s)	Want to make all decisions Are comfortable identifying and taking strategic risks
How much formal structure you want or need	Want to have an entity that is entirely separate from your household Don't mind additional accounting and recordkeeping expense	Want to have a simple structure that allows for easy monitoring of financial situation Want to do your own routine accounting and recordkeeping
Your potential liability	Are conducting research in an area with high liability, such as in some intellectual property, legal, or medical areas	Are comfortable with the usual risks of any business enterprise
Your exit strategy	Expect to build a brand-based (versus personal-based) business that can be sold successfully to another owner for your retirement income	See your business more as a consultancy than a "company" and do not expect to derive income from the business when you close it

incorporated structure (limited liability company or corporation) or a sole proprietor or partnership set-up. There are, of course, no correct answers; if you don't have a clear idea of any of the strategic concerns listed here, count that as another "vote" toward the sole proprietor route for its simplicity and flexibility.

Should You Partner With Your Partner or Your Pal?

As those of us in marriages or other life partnerships know, our spouses are involved in our business in some level, whether we want it or not. They usually live in our office space (er, we have our office at home), they experience the impact of cash flow fluctuations along with us, they help trouble-shoot our tech problems, they are invariably gracious when we answer a client call during dinner, and we force them to listen to our stories of the thrill of victory and the agony of defeat.

Some couples set up their businesses as joint partners simply for the tax or liability issues; if that's the only contribution that one of the two partners makes, then these cautions won't apply to you. But for the rest of us, it may be tempting to bring our partner—or a personal friend—in as a kind of buffer or back-up:

- "He answers my phone when I'm out anyway, so why not bring him in to the business?"

- "We have really different skills, so we'll complement each other."

- "We make big decisions jointly anyway, so I might as well formalize it."

- "We've known each other through a professional association, and we have a similar idea. Why not do it together?"

Do any of those statements sound familiar? If so, think twice about your motivations for bringing in a partner. If what you really want is support, either focus more on your professional colleagues for a sounding board (one reason I am such a proponent of the Association of Independent Information Professionals) or negotiate with your spouse as to how much input you want regarding your business.

Perhaps you hatched a great business plan with two close friends. You're all excited about it, and you can't wait to get started. Two of you are dating, and you knew each other all through college, so you figure there's no reason why this can't work. Or perhaps you are both refugees from the "traditional" library world, looking for new options; you've known each other for years and figure that two heads are better than one.

Marge King, of InfoRich Group, Inc., has some useful advice for spouses or close friends who are considering forming a business partnership, based on personal experience and a course she teaches on small business start-ups:

> In one of my business classes, I brought in an attorney, a banker, an accountant, and an insurance agent to talk about real-world issues. When asked about going into business with a family member or a close friend, the surprisingly strong and universal reaction from the panel was "do NOT do

it!" No one on the panel could think of a successful company formed of family members or close friends, with the exception of some husband/wife teams. I am sad to say that my experience is in line with this.

That said, here are some of the issues I encourage my students to consider regarding a partnership with a spouse or close friend.

First, have a well-defined exit strategy developed before you start the business. Make sure that you agree on the answers to questions such as:

- If one person calls it quits, will the business survive?

- Will it be bought by the other owners? If so, how will you value it?

- Can a partner sell his/her stake to an outsider?

- Will the person leaving the business accept payments over time for his/her share of the partnership?

- What will happen if someone dies? Will the person's heirs suddenly become your business "partner"? Will they be involved in the day-to-day activities?

Do not operate it as an "equal" partnership or stock ownership; someone needs to be the boss and make the final decision.

Everyone needs to write down their expectations of how they anticipate benefiting from the business and how they expect to see it run. Who will decide issues such as salaries, expenses, operations, company policies, and so on?

Looking at all these areas before forming a partnership will help everyone gain insight into where problems may arise and will allow the group to address these in advance. Once you have agreement on these issues, develop a business plan that includes this information and make sure everyone agrees to it. Then you can refer back to it when there are disputes or issues. And, yes, there will be disputes and issues.

Personal chemistry is one aspect of successful partnerships among friends that is difficult to assess ahead of time. How do your personalities mesh when things get stressful? Does one person want to make quick decisions and another need time to ponder the possibilities? Carol Lee-Roark, of Hyalite Environmental, LLP, has found a way to successfully maintain a business partnership with two close friends. In fact, as she says, "We couldn't be happier." I asked her to what she attributed her success:

This may work because none of us is overtaxed with ambition—we each have as our goal "to make enough money to pay my bills and support my hobbies," with the emphasis being on quality of life. One of our starting concepts was that we never wanted to hear the phrase "grow the company" again, having been "growed" to death, and merged and acquired and sold too often in our previous careers. And we agreed that we never want to have payroll and employees. We have three home offices, electronically connected, and we try to do the best work in our field with the best quality of life as well. Personality-wise, we are totally compatible—mellow and easygoing about relationships, but Type-A about doing things right.

What I think was key is that we already knew each other in a working relationship; the other two were on a team I managed. We knew each other's work-related strengths and weaknesses, and we had enough years together to have built a shared collection of experiences and insights. As a result of working together, we became friends, and eventually we became business partners. We know who shouldn't be called before 10 in the morning, who needs to be reined in from doing too much research, and who is chronically over-scheduled.

Our partnership agreement pretty much sets us up as cooperating individual consultants—we can contribute time, effort, and so on as we wish, and anyone can take their ball and go home whenever they wish. On the other hand, we are not proprietary about clients and projects, which I've seen in other partnerships and which seems really difficult and hostile to me. We figure that we each should be able to take over and do any job, and to make the difference among the three of us invisible and seamless to our clients. We share all projects—none of us thinks that any project or client would be better off without input from the other partners. We do have arguments about technical issues, but these are debates in which we are discussing a specific issue, and more often than not we each end up switching opinions a few times and eventually beating out the most appropriate solution.

What Kind of Entity Are You?

As you read through the following section on different business structures and formats, consider which would make sense for you, whether you expect to be in a partnership or operating solo. If you want to work with others, you can create a partnership, a limited liability company (LLC) or a corporation. In fact, you could even structure a group in which some members are employees and others are owners. Likewise, if you want to work alone, you could form a sole proprietorship, a corporation (with you as the sole employee), or a single-person LLC. What matters most is not the number of people involved as much as what you want to accomplish with your business structure.

As I have said elsewhere, remember to talk with your lawyer and accountant before you form your business. Your personal situation may dictate one corporate entity over another.

Sole Proprietorship

This is the simplest way to start your business and the one that most independent info pros opt for, at least at the beginning. In essence, you and your business are the same entity—you can operate under a trade name but your clients and vendors are dealing with you as an individual. The legal agreements you enter into and the contracts you sign obligate you personally. The biggest advantage of a sole proprietorship is simplicity. In the U.S., you report your income to the IRS on the familiar personal income tax Form 1040, using Schedule C to itemize your business expenses. Bookkeeping is relatively simple, and the only midyear filings required are the quarterly payments of your estimated income tax.

One of the main reasons why some info pros eventually change their business structure is that sole proprietors are legally liable for all the debts of the company. Companies to which you owe money can go after your personal assets (yes, that's your house we're talking about) if you don't pay your bills. In addition, some business expenses cannot be fully deducted from your income, such as health insurance payments. You may also find it more difficult to obtain a business loan or line of credit from a bank as a sole proprietor than you would as an independent company. You cannot sell a sole proprietorship business because you and the business are one, so if you plan on eventually selling your business, you will need to incorporate. And finally, once your business is successful and you are earning a substantial income, you run a higher risk of being audited by the IRS as a sole proprietor than you would as a corporation or LLC.

The equivalent of a sole proprietorship in the U.K. is a "sole trader," and the concerns are much the same as in the U.S. You are personally liable for any debts incurred by your company, and you report your income directly to the Inland Revenue. Canadian sole proprietors operate similarly; you report your business income and expenses on Form T2125.

Partnership

You can form a partnership with someone who will take an active role in the business or with someone who provides some or all of the funding but will not participate in day-to-day operations. Partnerships are easy to set up, although you should plan to spend a good deal of time working through the partnership agreement. As with a sole proprietorship, the income of the business is reported on the partners' individual tax returns, simplifying the accounting and bookkeeping burden. A couple of the downsides of partnerships are that you and your partner are personally liable for the debts of the company, and you are each liable for the actions of the other. And if one of you wants to leave the partnership, the business itself has to be re-formed.

In the U.K. and Canada, partnerships are structured similarly; you are jointly liable for all debts of the company, and you report your income individually.

Limited Liability Company

LLCs are fairly new entities, designed to provide both the tax benefits of incorporation and the flexibility of a sole proprietorship or partnership. A limited liability company exists for a specified amount of time, although the partners can extend the time limit as desired. LLCs offer limited protection from personal liability, which makes it an attractive alternative to a partnership. However, like corporations, LLCs have some additional filing requirements and less operational flexibility than sole proprietorships or partnerships.

Beginning in 2001, the U.K. introduced the option of limited liability partnerships, similar to LLCs. The LLP is a separate legal entity and the members of the partnership are somewhat protected from individual liability. As an LLP, you have more flexibility in terms of how you structure and run your business than you would as a private limited company.

My Newly Incorporated Life

I was a sole proprietor for the first 10 years of my business, on the advice of my accountant and my lawyer. It kept my life simple. I could manage both my personal and business finances through QuickBooks. Preparing my own tax returns was relatively simple, but then, I do have a mathematical bent.

However, after 10 years, I decided to revisit the question of the form my business should take. I consulted with a CPA and, on his advice, finally incorporated at the end of 2001. The process itself was pretty straightforward and doing it at the end of the year made the transition fairly simple. I continue to handle the day-to-day activities myself; I do all the accounts payable and receivable myself. I email my QuickBooks file to a bookkeeper once a month, and she handles all the reports, filings, and deductions. At the end of the year, I send my balance sheet and profit and loss statements to my accountant, who handles my income tax filing.

The advantages for me at this point include:

- I can put more money into a tax-free retirement fund.

- I have reduced my personal liability.

- I have reduced my chances of being audited by the IRS (knock wood).

- I can write off some expenses that I couldn't as a sole proprietor.

The downsides of incorporating include:

- I can't do all of my tax filings myself (I know … most people wouldn't see this as a disadvantage, but I can't help it—I'm a math nerd).

- I have to be extra careful about not mingling my business and personal accounts.

- I have to pay a bookkeeper to handle my monthly filings, whereas as a sole proprietor I could do most of the accounting myself.

The bottom line is that I am glad I incorporated when I did. It saves me money and gives me a sense of security that I am keeping my business and my personal accounts entirely separate. I recommend that you have a heart-to-heart talk with your accountant before you start your business and then

every few years thereafter. Your financial situation will change, your life situation may change and, heaven knows, the tax laws will change, so it makes
sense to get a reality check periodically.

Corporation

Several types of corporations can be formed, but the one most relevant to independent info pros is the "Subchapter S" corporation—a specific type of corporation
best suited for most small companies in the U.S.. Corporations have the advantage
of existing separate from their owners or partners. This means that the assets of the
owner—that's you—are at least somewhat protected from the debts of the corporation. That doesn't mean you can spend like there's no tomorrow and escape the consequences when the bills come due, but it does help shield you if, heaven forbid,
your company goes into bankruptcy. If you plan on doing the kind of research that
involves higher risk—trademark searching or litigation, for example—you may want
to incorporate for an extra layer of liability protection, in addition to carrying errors-
and-omissions (E&O) insurance. E&O policies cover claims by clients who might sue
you because you either failed to find crucial information, or you provided incorrect
information. See Chapter 17, Ethics and Legalities, for a discussion of how to avoid
such lawsuits.

Unlike a sole proprietorship or partnership, a corporation can be transferred to a
partner or sold outright, which can be an important consideration if you think you
might someday sell your business. There are also some tax benefits to incorporating,
and if your revenue is high enough, you somewhat reduce the risk of an audit if you
are operating as a corporation rather than a sole proprietorship. If you plan on hiring employees, you may want to be incorporated for liability and tax reasons.

In the U.K., the most common incorporation form is the private limited company,
indicated by Ltd. in the name. You are required to be registered at Companies House
(www.companieshouse.gov.uk) and complete an Annual Return (Form 363) with
basic information about the company.

For Canadian entrepreneurs, the limited company is the most common form for
corporations, and it offers the same benefits as previously described. The company
must file annual income tax returns on the business accounts.

Hired Help or Ad Hoc Subcontracting

Very few independent info pros hire employees. On the other hand, many use sub-contractors on an occasional or regular basis to handle overflow work or projects that go beyond the info pro's area of expertise, or they use them simply to free up some time to focus on building the business.

I suspect that if you asked most independent info pros, they would say that they have intentionally chosen not to have employees, even though that decision usually restricts their income potential somewhat. Both practical and less tangible reasons are cited for choosing not to build a business with employees:

- Employee salaries are fixed expenses, whereas an independent info pro's revenue and work flow can fluctuate dramatically from month to month.

- Hiring and training employees can be difficult and time-consuming, particularly for a small business.

- Paying for an employee's learning curve (and inevitable mistakes) can be expensive.

- Many independent info pros enjoy the hands-on aspects of the business— doing the research, visiting a client's site, and so on. With employees, the business owner usually gives up some of the day-to-day work, which can often be done less expensively by a research assistant or paraprofessional employee.

- An independent info pro may not be a good manager of people; in fact, he may have left traditional employment to get away from the aggravation or stress of supervising others.

One situation in which you might consider hiring employees is if you don't have a research background and are willing to focus all your energy on marketing. In that case, you can hire or subcontract expert researchers and spend your time bringing in business. The late Sue Rugge, one of the first independent info pros, successfully built several businesses using this model. Doing so requires that you find and manage excellent researchers who enjoy working in a small business, that you dedicate yourself to generating enough work to keep your researchers busy, and that you find clients who are willing to pay the relatively high hourly rates that you must charge to cover the costs of your employees plus your profit.

Another instance of strategic hiring is when you want to expand your business and need to free up time in order to accomplish that goal. Jane John, of On Point Research, described how she decided to bring in part-time help: "I brought in two part-time subcontractors before I truly needed them, but that was a strategic choice. I was committed to bringing in the work to keep them busy, and having them gave me the freedom to focus on getting new clients."

If you decide that hiring employees isn't for you, you can do what most independent info pros do and subcontract with colleagues as the work demands. See Chapter 16, Subcontracting, or I'll Scratch Your Back If You Scratch Mine, for a discussion of how subcontracting works and how to be a successful contractor and subcontractor.

Deciding on the Structure of Your Business

✦ Want to keep the accounting and paperwork simple? Try sole proprietorship.

✦ Expect to have a business partner who either contributes financially or works with you day to day? Choose a partnership or LLC.

✦ Think you'll want to sell your business? Think corporation.

✦ Plan to hire employees? Decide on a corporation.

✦ Concerned about personal liability? Go with an LLC or corporation.

Chapter 8

Before You Launch

In the first seven chapters of this section, we've looked at what it is like to be an independent info pro, the upsides and the downsides, the skills you need to succeed, and how you might structure your business. This chapter helps you think through what you want for your business and how you can get there. It looks at the essence of what your business is all about.

Note that, in addition to the preparations described in this chapter, you will want to have a marketing plan that you revise every year. The marketing plan is, in essence, the operating instructions that bring your business plan to life. Since this is a recurring event, I have devoted a separate chapter to this subject, Chapter 22, Your Marketing Plan. After you have completed the steps described in Section One: Getting Started, head over to Chapter 22 to create the first of your annual marketing plans.

If you don't have a background in business, you might want to take a course on how to start a small or home-based business through your local community college or university extension program. Many schools offer continuing education courses that are just a few weeks long that cover the basics of business accounting, sales and marketing, cash management, and so on. If you are more of the autodidact approach, find a clearly written book that covers the basics of business finance and accounting; even with accounting software, it is important to understand the fundamentals of the money end of the business.

Business Plans and Other Pipe Dreams

Everyone starting a business is told that it's critical to write a detailed business plan. If you don't have a business plan, how will you know which way you're going and when you've gotten there? How can you ask a potential lender for heaps of cash if you haven't spelled out what you want to do with the money when you get it? I generally don't recommend taking out a loan to finance your start-up expenses, much less your day-to-day operations; however, this may the only option you have. If you do decide to borrow money, include in your business plan how you expect to pay back the loan and what you will use the money for. Needless to say, borrow only as much as you need and only what you can pay back within a reasonable amount of time. You will certainly need a business plan—complete with financial projections—to apply for money from a bank or credit union or from family or friends. (For more information on financing your business, see Chapter 14, Money, Money, Money.)

Even if you aren't planning to borrow money, writing a business plan can be a useful reality check. If you're going to leave that $80,000/year job, with its insurance benefits, retirement fund, and paid vacation, what will it take to generate $80,000 in *profit* (not just revenue) from your new business? You'll use your business plan to set goals for how much income you intend to bring in, how much you need to pay yourself as a salary, how much overhead you'll have, where and how you'll find clients, and so on. You'll want to write a business plan that is aggressive but realistic—there's no sense aiming low just to make your goal, nor is it wise to plan on earning $100,000 the first year.

Another reason for writing a business plan is that the process of putting your ideas into writing helps you make that vision a reality. It's a tangible commitment—to yourself if no one else—that you take this new business seriously, that you intend to make this enterprise thrive. It also enables you to think through what you need to do and how you intend to accomplish your goals. One of the characteristics of most successful independent info pros is the ability to see not only the big picture but also the details, and to pay attention to all the little things that have to happen in order for the business to succeed.

Of course, at some point down the road as your business grows and matures, you will probably notice that real life has overtaken your well-designed plan, and your business has moved into areas that you hadn't foreseen. That's OK—it's an indication that you are able to recognize changes in the marketplace and your client base, and adapt to new situations. That original business plan helped you organize your thoughts, plan your actions, anticipate challenges and opportunities, and get started.

There's no single way to go about writing a business plan. In fact, unless you intend to use it to apply for a loan, the only people who will see it are you and your business advisor, typically an accountant and/or a lawyer, or your business coach. Don't sweat the format; focus on thinking through what is involved in getting your business going.

Plenty of websites give pointers about writing business plans. To begin, the U.S. Small Business Administration (SBA; www.sba.gov) has a "small business planner" that includes a number of short articles on business plans. You can also find lots of websites with sample business plans; the SBA has a pointer to some resources, and you can find large collections of materials at SCORE (Service Corps of Retired Executives; www.score.org), the Center for Business Planning (www.businessplans. org), and the Ewing Marion Kauffman Foundation (www.entrepreneurship.org).

Be careful, however, in relying on these templates. Most small businesses are very tangible operations, usually providing a distinct product or service. A coffee shop, a janitorial service, an accounting company, or a dentistry practice each have pretty standard concerns, so a business plan template for any of those enterprises could be fairly useful. But you will be hard-pressed to find a template for the kind of businesses that independent info pros build.

A number of companies sell software to help write business plans, which you may find useful if you prefer to work from a template. But be careful of invalid assumptions built into the software; as noted earlier, an independent information business isn't a typical small business like a real estate agency or hardware store. Your local library and bookstore will have plenty of books specifically on writing business plans that you can choose from as well.

Who Are Your Clients?

Both your business plan and your marketing plan presuppose that you have some idea of who your clients will be. As I discuss in Chapter 13, Managing Your Clients, assume that you will be marketing far beyond your local area, unless you expect to offer a specialized on-site service that cannot be provided remotely. If you're like most independent info pros, you will probably start with a prospective client base of former employers and colleagues who know your work, other contacts in the industry you've come from, and people in industries or professions that are information-hungry and not overly price-sensitive.

Business Plan Checklist

Your business plan may be polished and formal, or a simple write-up of how you envision your company and its first year. In either case, you should answer—or at least think carefully about—each of the following questions:

- Why am I starting this business?

- What service am I providing to clients?

- What tangible benefits do I offer my clients?

- Who are my potential clients?

- How will I attract clients?

- How many repeat clients do I expect by the end of my first year?

- Who are my competitors?

- How will I price my services?

- What will my overhead be for the first year?

- What is my expected revenue the first year? And after that?

- How will I cover all my living expenses for my first six months?

- What are my personal strengths and weaknesses as a business owner?

- What are my strengths and weaknesses in this market?

Of course, the industry or niche you are most familiar with may not be adequate to support your business long term. Before I started my business, I thought I would get lots of business from local firms, from writers who needed background research, and from law firms that didn't have a library staff of their own. I found that I was wrong on all counts. As it turns out, all of these groups are very price-sensitive—they consider $400 a large expenditure for something as intangible as information, and they generally want to do their own research rather than pay someone else to do it for them. The lesson I learned was to look for clients with an established research budget or that can pass my charges on directly to *their* clients. So I focused my marketing toward companies with revenue of at least $100 million that needed business research and to consulting firms and advertising agencies that would bill their clients for the cost of my research. If, after some initial research, you realize that the group you initially thought would be your market won't be profitable, shift to another group. It's tempting to keep plugging away simply because this was how you planned on creating your business. If you don't immediately start seeing some evidence of interest among the people you talk with, it's time to re-evaluate your assumptions about your client base.

Expect to Expand

Before I started my business, I worked for a number of years as the librarian at a telecommunications company. Once I got Bates Information Services going, I focused on people in the communications industry—large corporate marketing and strategic planning departments, industry consultants, and fellow telecom librarians. I emphasized my expertise in the telecommunications industry, and that gave me instant credibility. As it turned out, the focus of my business broadened within a year or two to other forms of business research. What's important is that my clients drove that shift. People who had come to me originally for telecom research started asking for more general research, and then they referred me to colleagues and friends who needed nontelecom research, too. But the reason my clients called me in the first place was that I had made myself memorable for a specialty. If I had started by telling prospects that I could find any information they needed on any topic at all, they would have been less likely to remember to call me. There's no "hook" there—why should potential clients think of *me* whenever they're looking for information? But once they've associated me with industry-specific research, they think of me for other and more general information needs as well.

The Informational Interview

I was fortunate when I started my business, in that I had already developed a network of contacts within my chosen field. All I had to do was start sending out brochures, newsletters, and postcards to my colleagues and former co-workers; they knew who I was, and I knew the kind of information they needed. If you don't already have a virtual stack of business cards from people you can market to, it's time to do some hands-on research. (It's also time to start building your online social networks. See Chapter 23, Your Business Image, for more about creating and building networks.)

First, you are going to identify some people to interview. The goal here is to get inside the brains of people who might be your target market, to learn how information figures into their work flow, and to identify the services they would not just think were "nice to have" but for which they would be willing to pay you well. I sometimes liken this process to a wildlife photographer. You want to know where the elk will be congregating so that you can be where they are. You will need to learn their habits, their preferences, and what alerts them. Once you understand how an elk thinks, you can anticipate what it will do, and where it will go. Likewise, you are going to learn about your clients' habits, needs, and concerns. Where do they usually go to graze for information? What gets them worried? What would they find immediately valuable if you offered it to them?

Select a few likely companies within your target industry, and check their websites for an organization chart, annual report, or a page that profiles their executives. Look for information-hungry people, such as the directors of marketing, strategic planning, corporate development, competitive intelligence, and product development. Be sure to also check your own network on LinkedIn, Facebook, or whatever social networking sites you call home. You may be surprised at who you know or with whom you share a common friend or colleague.

Once you've identified a few key executives in each company, either email or snail mail them a letter. No, you're not going to send them marketing material—you're going to ask them if you can conduct an "informational interview" to find out how people find information, what frustrates them about doing their own research, what they'd pay for, and what their biggest challenge is, informationally speaking. Ask for a 15-minute interview at their convenience. Reiterate that this is not a sales call, but that you are contacting them to learn how [marketing/competitive intelligence/you fill in the blank] professionals find and use information. What you learn from these interviews will help you identify the most likely prospects and understand what kinds of research services you can provide to them. As Amelia Kassel of MarketingBase says, "Find an information need and think of how you can fill it." These informational interviews should help you do just that.

You will need to prepare some open-ended questions that are clear, free of info-jargon, and that look at the world from your clients' perspective. The point here is to find out what your clients' pain points are. Your questions might be similar to these:

- What will be the biggest challenge in your industry within the next six months?

- How do you maintain a competitive edge—both you personally and your company within the industry?

- What do you wish you knew about your competition?

- How do you stay on top of industry news and opportunities?

- When you need to make a strategic decision, what information do you use? What information are you missing?

- If I sent you a weekly package of information, what would you find most useful?

- What keeps you awake at night?

Note that none of these are yes/no questions; they are all open-ended and encourage your contacts to think about what they need but don't even know they need. During your short interview, remember that your job is to ask questions and then just listen. You aren't marketing to them, and you aren't talking about the fabulous services you provide. You are just listening and asking follow-up questions to learn enough so that you can later design a product or service they would find immediately beneficial. You are creating a business around your clients' needs, and that means you have to learn about their needs before you can create your business.

Once you have conducted several of these in-depth interviews, you will have a much better idea of what your market's biggest concerns are and in what situations they would be willing to pay well for what your company does. And keep the people you interviewed in the loop about your business. They have already proven that they are engaged enough to share a bit of time with you; while you never want to market directly to them, send them personalized notes every quarter, letting them know how your business is going. They may turn into clients; at the least, they can offer feedback as you go forward.

Follow Your Heart

What if you don't have many ideas on where to start? What if you don't know a lot of prospective clients? Perhaps your last job didn't give you much contact with colleagues. Maybe you worked in an industry that doesn't do much research or rely on outside expertise. You might be re-entering the marketplace after a long period away from employment. In any case, follow the money and follow your heart. No, those two aren't mutually exclusive. Think about what kind of work you enjoy doing and at which you're fairly proficient. I'm not talking about the web surfing you do for friends or neighbors—unless they're willing to pay you market rates for research, that experience counts as fun, not an indicator of a market for your business services. Instead, think about who would want to pay you for your expertise or familiarity with an area and what you would really enjoy doing all day long.

Are you proficient in Spanish? Perhaps you could focus on working with Latin American companies that are exploring international business opportunities. If you live in Los Angeles and find the entertainment industry fascinating, look into providing background research services to film writers and television companies. If you worked for the marketing department of an oil company, maybe you can use the contacts you have and focus on providing services to the petroleum or energy industry. If your passion is working with disadvantaged populations, design a business around serving the prospect development needs of nonprofit service agencies—not just locally but the headquarters of the organizations whose goals you support. If you know the pharmaceutical industry, figure out what companies and organizations need your services and which people within those organizations need information and don't have the time to get it themselves. If your background is in political science, identify think tanks and consulting companies that need your expertise on an ad hoc basis. That's your client base. Remember Amelia Kassel's advice: Find a need and fill it.

What About My Steady Paycheck?

One of the first considerations when planning to open an independent info pro business is whether to quit your regular job before you launch. There are two schools of thought about this: Some independent info pros say that the only way you can survive financially the first year is to run your new business on the side, and others say that the only way to get traction is to focus totally on your business on a full-time basis. Eventually, most successful independent info pros wind up working full time (and then some). The question is whether you start out full time or not. Here are some of the advantages and disadvantages of each choice.

Full-Time Entrepreneur

This is certainly the scariest option. You go from a steady income and employee benefits like health insurance and paid vacations to zero—or rather, to put it in a more positive light, to a full focus on your new business. This option works best if:

- Someone else in your household is bringing in a steady income.

- You have set aside enough money to live on for six to nine months.

- You already have at least one regular client, such as your last employer.

On the positive side, going full time means that word-of-mouth referrals get started that much faster. Also, you can devote more time to marketing, which takes time to show results. The more time you can spend on marketing at the beginning of your business, the sooner those clients will start calling you.

Speaking of calling, one of the underappreciated competitive advantages of devoting full time to your business is that clients can reach you during normal business hours. Think of how much more likely you are to do business with someone you can speak with when you call, rather than having to resort to voicemail messages and telephone tag.

As a full-time entrepreneur, you have the ability to take on short turnaround projects and large projects that need to be done quickly. Unlike someone who must somehow squeeze in the time during nonwork hours, you have eight (or more) hours a day that you can throw at a project. Also, some kinds of information work, such as telephone research and going to government offices to research public records, have to be done during normal working hours. You limit your service options if you can't work full time during regular business hours. You also have the flexibility to attend conferences and speak at meetings your prospective clients are likely to attend. Starting your word-of-mouth referral network requires work and time, and you are much more able to devote the necessary time to marketing during that first year if you are doing this full time.

One advantage of taking the plunge and working full time for yourself is less tangible but just as important as the others I've mentioned. By devoting yourself full time to your business, you demonstrate both to yourself and to your clients that you really take it seriously. You're committed to making your business work and to providing high-quality professional information services to your clients. Granted, part-timers can be just as committed, but it's substantially harder to maintain that level of enthusiasm, creativity, and persistence if you're juggling your new business, an existing job, and at least a minimal personal life.

As for the downsides of going full time, the most obvious one is financial. Unless you already have clients lined up, don't expect to be able to pay yourself a salary for at least a few months. The first year will be lean; there's no getting around that. Before I quit my job and started my (full-time) information business, I spent a year focused on lowering my living expenses. I got into the habit of not eating out as frequently, not practicing "shopping therapy," and generally learning that a lot of my discretionary spending really was unnecessary. This made my first year in business easier to handle, as I could get by with substantially less income than I had been earning in my last job. I also figured out ahead of time how much money I needed per month just to pay the bills, and banked six months' worth of living expenses, which I drew upon when I didn't have many clients yet still had to pay my overhead expenses.

Moonlighting Employee

This approach, working full time at a job and running your business only on weekends and evenings, has very little chance of success, or at least of ever growing beyond a weekend-and-evening enterprise. Almost by definition, most of your energy and time will be focused on your regular job, even if it's a job you don't enjoy. In fact, it probably takes even more of your energy to continue to work in a job that doesn't make you happy. You cannot ethically take business calls during the workday, so your clients will find it difficult to talk with you directly. Your employer deserves your full attention while you're on the clock, and returning client calls during your lunch break is simply not feasible on a regular basis.

So this leaves you trying to stay in touch with clients via email and with the limitation that you cannot reply promptly to any email or voicemail queries. Most clients will be put off by your lack of availability; they are accustomed to dealing with vendors who are accessible during normal business hours and who can respond to their information needs promptly. Working full time pretty much precludes all this.

It is extremely difficult to market your business while holding down a full-time job. You don't have the flexibility to give presentations at client groups, take a prospect to lunch, or attend the professional events that your clients attend. In my experience, businesses that are started as evening/weekend enterprises never grow beyond that level.

Part-Time Entrepreneur

Actually, there are two kinds of part-time business owners: people who have another part-time job, and people who choose to work only part time. Some people have childcare or eldercare obligations or health limitations that prevent them from working full time. It's possible to start and run an information business part time, but it takes discipline and flexibility.

If you're juggling care for others with running your business, consider hiring someone to help with your home responsibilities during the day. You'll still be available for emergencies, but you'll be freed up to make phone calls, focus on research, and plan your marketing strategies. Taking a client's call while the kids are trying to put doll clothes on the cat is doomed to failure. Although clients are much more understanding about people who work part time and from home than they were five or 10 years ago, they still want to deal with someone who is professional and focused. One of the essential tasks of someone with others in the house during the day is to teach them that when your office door is closed, you can be interrupted only if someone has severed a limb or the house is on fire.

I've talked about the downside of continuing to work full time while starting your business. As you can tell, I don't recommend it. But what about working at a regular job part time and running your business part time? It's difficult but do-able. The steady income and benefits are a nice safety net while you're growing your business. However, it's easy to fall into the trap of seeing your part-time job as your *real* job. Will you think of your employment as supplementing your independent info pro business or vice versa? The first few years of a new business require a lot of attention and energy without a lot of payback. Being able to devote only part of your working day to your baby means drawing out its Terrible Twos that much longer. It may be necessary, but it can be tiring and difficult.

One option is to find a part-time job with evening and weekend hours. That leaves you free during the day to speak with clients, conduct telephone research, and get out to meet clients and colleagues. Of course, this choice takes a toll, since most of us are accustomed to viewing our evenings and weekends as the time to relax, run errands, and get on with the rest of our lives. On the other hand, it does offer the advantage of freeing you up all day for your clients. In essence, you offer them full-time availability while providing yourself with a part-time salary on the side.

Alex Kramer, owner of Kramer Research, started her business while working an off-hours job. I asked her how she managed to stay focused while working part time, and she said:

> If people think of their start-up company as a serious business and not just something they can do on the side, then I can see how they might make it work. That is to say, they will need regular office hours, work space dedicated for this business, and perhaps a telephone message or website that states their office hours. I don't think it can really happen if someone tries to do this on the sly while working full time, or if they think that business will come to them as if by magic. Constant marketing is essential, especially when you're just starting your business.

Just Do It!

While it's important to think through the ramifications of your choices regarding employment and income, eventually you will probably need to take the leap and become a full-time independent info pro. It involves planning, and it's a risk, but starting any business is a risk. In fact, when you think about it, you have more job stability as an independent than you do as an employee. Your employer is your sole source of income; if you lose your job, your income goes from substantial to zero. If, on the other hand, you're in business for yourself and have a number of clients, the loss of any one client only reduces your income slightly. As long as you continue to market yourself, you will always have other sources of revenue.

It's easy to let all the preliminary tasks—writing a business plan, setting up your office, talking with a lawyer or accountant, identifying your client base, determining your niche—impede you from actually starting your business. I like to compare all this preliminary work to taking up a new sport. For the first few weeks, you're going to be stiff and sore; it seems like all pain and no gain. But once you get your muscles toned, you start seeing dramatic results. Likewise, all these administrative and strategic planning tasks are hard at first—they're new jobs, they're unfamiliar, and they require you to sit down and really think about what you want. But once you've gone through the process, it's a lot easier to continue. You'll always have administrative and high-level management responsibilities; now is the time to learn how to handle them and to start feeling comfortable in your new roles.

A wise friend once told me that starting a business feels like standing on the edge of a cliff, looking down at the ground far below. Then you suddenly realize that what appeared to be empty space is actually a path up, or that it's merely a single step down to the Earth, or that you can fly.

Checklist for Launching Your Business

✦ Write a business plan, even if you don't intend to use it to raise capital.

✦ Identify your market niche and your client base.

✦ Identify the critical information needs of your clients and build your business around that.

✦ Plan ahead of time for a drop in income the first year.

✦ Decide whether you can run your business full time or not.

✦ Take that leap of faith and launch!

Chapter 9

Setting Up Your Business

I remember the time I moved away from home and into my first apartment. What stunned me (besides the price of rent) was how many little things I needed and how fast the cost added up. Bookcases, a desk, stocking the pantry, silverware, cleaning supplies, a vacuum cleaner … I felt like I needed another student loan just to cover the expense of moving into my own apartment!

When you get ready to set up your office, you may suffer similar sticker shock. In addition to the usual office accoutrements such as business cards, stationery, an office desk, an ergonomic office chair, and so on, you'll need to get a business checking account, another phone line, possibly a business license, and so on. This chapter will cover all the practicalities you have to deal with before you open your door for business. And how are you going to pay for all this? See Chapter 14, Money, Money, Money, for some ideas. And if you're serious about starting your own business, set up a separate savings account and start putting money aside now. Think of it as an investment in your future success.

What's Your Name?

For starters, you'll need to figure out how to answer the phone when it rings (and yes, it *will* start ringing). What will you call your business? You have several basic options: You can use your own name (Pat Smith and Associates); you can incorporate your name into your business name (Smith Information Services); you can have a name that describes what you do (Healthcare Research, Inc.); or you can make up a name (InfoSource Solutions). Although it is important to feel comfortable with whatever name you give your company, most info pros find that their clients know them by their personal name as much as by their business name.

Don't count on the company name itself to generate much business just because it is memorable or clever; as I say frequently, most of your business will come from referrals, and a happy client will make just as strong an endorsement whether your company name is Smith Information Services or InfoSource Solutions. Each type of company name has its benefits and drawbacks.

While having a funny or clever name may make you memorable, be careful that it has enough gravitas to convey that you are a professional. "Info Babe" might sound like a catchy name, but consider the experience of Valerie Forrestal, Reference and Research Services Librarian at Stevens Institute of Technology. She started using "Info Babe" as her online persona and user name, but she has since decided to use her real name in all her online identities. As she said:

> Honestly, I had grown tired of the whole "info babe" moniker; I must have thought it was cute at one point, but it just seems silly now, and I don't really think of myself as a "babe." I thought I was too entrenched in my social networks under that username, and I figured I would never get rid of it. But an experience at a professional conference changed my thinking. I was meeting in person people who I had only previously known through online connections, and I found it incredibly awkward to have to follow my introduction with "you might know me as the info babe?" Ick. I'd like to be able to make a more professional impression, so I decided to make the move to use my real name for all my online identities (val_forrestal or vforrestal).

Pat Smith and Associates

Advantages: You are your own brand; you can be reasonably sure that your business name will be unique. You are demonstrating that, when your clients call, they will be working directly with you.

Disadvantages: It is difficult to sell your business when it is so closely identified with you. An "and Associates" name often signifies a one-person business—retired info-entrepreneur Reva Basch once commented, "when I see 'and Associates,' I think 'and cat'"—which may make you less attractive to some clients.

Smith Information Services

Advantages: You can be reasonably sure that your business name will be unique. It may sound somewhat more established than Pat Smith & Associates. Your clients can find your listing in a directory if they remember your last name. The name describes what you do clearly.

Disadvantages: It is difficult to sell your business because your name is part of the business name.

Healthcare Research Inc.

Advantages: Your name makes it clear what you do. Prospective clients know when it is appropriate to call you. You can sell your business without having to change the name.

Disadvantages: You limit your ability to provide a wide range of services because your specialization is part of your business name.

InfoSource Solutions

Advantages: You can design a unique business name. It can be generic enough to allow you to expand the business. You can sell your business without having to change the name.

Disadvantages: Clients may not easily remember your business name. The name may sound dated after a few years.

Note that even if you are a sole proprietor (see Chapter 7, Structuring Your Business, for a discussion of how to set up your business), you should not simply operate under your own name. This sends a clear, if unintended, message to your clients that you aren't really serious about this, that even bothering to set up a business name is too much trouble. Of course, when it comes right down to it, we are our businesses, but it is important to establish an entity separate from your personal identity. In addition, some organizations' accounts payable departments are reluctant to pay an invoice for Jane Doe, preferring to issue payments to business entities.

Will This Name Fly?

Once you have a rough idea of the kind of name you want—You and Associates, The Information Consultancy—it is time to start writing down ideas. It doesn't matter if the first few names you come up with sound dumb—write them all down, and weed 'em out later. Take a few weeks on this, and keep a note pad with you to jot down ideas as they come to you.

After you have some initial food for thought, run through the following considerations, some of which may be more important than others for you:

- Avoid acronyms. Your initials may appeal to you as a business name, but no one else will remember whether "LPB Research" is LPB, LBP, LBB, or LPP.

- Don't make it so generic that it sounds as if it's a tag line. "Research Services for Business" may indeed describe what you do, but it doesn't sound like a unique business.

- Consider how easily you can convert your business name to a URL.

- Have a business name that sparks a conversation.

- Avoid a name that will sound dated in a few years. In 2009, anything Web 2.0 was considered hip. By the time you read this, a company with 2.0 in its name will no doubt just sound silly.

- Unless your long-term strategy is to remain focused on your local geographic area, avoid using geographical names in your company name. If my business were Colorado Research Services, how easy would it be for me to expand outside the state? And what if I move to Hawaii?

- Make your business name easy to spell and find online. A name like "Re:Search Services" might look distinctive when written, but it makes your website virtually unfindable, since most search engines don't handle this kind of internal punctuation well, and it requires that you spell your business name out whenever you tell someone who you are.

One colleague had a practical criterion for naming a business. "The same trick I was taught for naming a child is one to consider when naming a company. When naming my first child, my mother told me to try yelling the name from my back porch. If it isn't easy to yell—and understand—the child will never come when called. When naming the company, make sure it is something that spills readily from your mouth. What's worse than getting tongue-tied when giving out your own name? Say it to yourself in a mirror and to friends and family. If you can't say it with a straight face, or if they don't understand what you said, you may want to rethink it."

In addition to the back-porch test, you can also run a straw poll of friends and colleagues; this can be a great way of getting some quick feedback on something that you will live with for quite a while. In an email message to them, describe in no more than two sentences why clients would come to you, and then present them with three or four options for your business name, along with a line for "Other"—you never know when a random suggestion will turn into inspiration. Not only will people identify ambiguities or difficulties you didn't recognize in one or more of the possible names, but you have just created your first corporate Advisory Panel! They may be a valuable resource as you delve into some of the marketing techniques described in Section Three.

Can I Really Use This Name?

Regardless of which type of business name you choose, make sure it is not already being used by someone else. Here are some simple steps to check for any established businesses with the same name you have selected:

- Search for the name using several web search engines. Try variations of the name; if you have chosen the name InfoSource Solutions, try "Info Source Solutions" and "InfoSourceSolutions" as well.

- Look the name up in an internet domain registry (www.networksolutions. com or www.domaintools.com) to see if the domain has been registered but not yet in use.

- See if the name is being used in social networks such as Facebook or LinkedIn.

- Look up the name in the membership directory of the Association of Independent Information Professionals (AIIP; www.aiip.org) and of any major associations your clients are likely to belong to.

- Look up the name in the appropriate section of the U.S. Patent and Trademark Office (www.uspto.gov), Companies House in the U.K. (www.companieshouse.gov.uk), or the appropriate agency in your country. (Canadians can find information for their provinces or territories through the Business Startup Assistant at Canada Business, www.canadabusiness. ca/eng/125.) Note that a nearly identical name in an entirely different line of business may not necessarily be a conflict, as long as there is no possibility of confusing your business with the existing one. We have Lexis, the online service, and the Toyota Lexus, the luxury car; in fact, Toyota and Lexis once held a joint promotion called "Win a Lexus on Lexis."

- Check one of the many web-based "yellow pages" services that let you search for business listings by city and state. See, for example, www.yellow pages.com for U.S. listings, or the Global Yellow Pages (www.globalyp.net) for links to Yellow Pages sites around the world.

- Search the published literature—general and business news plus trade journals and magazines—for any article that mentions the company name, using one of the professional online services described in Chapter 34, Professional Online Services.

You may also want to consult a lawyer to determine whether you should take additional steps to ensure that you are not infringing on any trademarked names and to establish your right to the name you choose. Some independent info pros register their business name with the trademarks office or registry of their state, province, or country.

"Where'd You Find That Name?"

I have outlined ways to think through a business name for all kinds of strategic reasons. But one of the joys of owning your own business is that you can put your own flair on your business choices.

Michele Bate's business is Archer Van den Broeck Limited. She admits that it's difficult to pronounce, difficult to spell, and doesn't lend itself to a user-friendly URL. But there's a story behind it that I find delightful. According to Michele, "I have always wanted to commemorate the name of my mother, who is no longer with us. She was Belgian and when she married my English father, the poor woman was reduced from Josephine Anna Catherine Van den Broeck to Anne Smith. So I teamed her name with that of my mother-in-law, Archer—who is also no longer with us—as I thought it had a good ring to it ('We at Archer Van den Broeck …')."

Jan Knight, of Bancroft Information Services, has a love-hate relationship with her company name, which had me chuckling and helped make her name memorable to me. (She used Bancroft in her company name because she attended the University of California, Berkeley, where the Bancroft Library is the primary special-collections library.) When asked her thoughts on naming her company, she listed the following:

The Good: I deliberately used "information" and not "research" in my business name as I wanted to allow for business service growth outside of research. That was a good decision, as I've added usability testing/ consulting and other informal information-related services to my offerings.

The Bad: At my very first AIIP conference, someone came up to me after my introduction and asked, "Why did you name your company Bankrupt Information Services?" Obviously, my remaining British accent and lack of annunciation were at fault, but that wasn't the only time someone asked me this, so I have to be careful how I introduce myself now.

The Ugly: I've had more people than you can imagine—people who actually know me pretty well—introduce me as "Jan Bancroft" rather than Jan Knight. [N.B. That includes me, to my unending mortification!]

All that said, I've had plenty of opportunities to explain my company name and, frankly, it's been a good conversation starter. The name has proven to be memorable … obviously, more than my own last name!

Are You My Employer?

Independent info pros, particularly those who work extensively for one client, have to be careful of running afoul of rules regarding taxation of employees as opposed to independent contractors. In most countries, employers are responsible for payment of some or all of their employees' insurance and social benefits taxes; if, during an audit, you are classified by the taxing agency as an employee rather than an independent contractor, your client is liable for back taxes and fines for underpayment.

Obviously, you want to be very careful that no relationship with any client ever becomes so entwined that you could be considered an employee.

In the U.S., in response to the sometime practice of hiring "perma-temps" (contract workers who are for all intents and purposes employees, but who are classified as temporary workers or contractors by their employer), the IRS established a set of criteria for determining whether you are truly an independent business or essentially an employee. Publication 15-A, Employer's Supplemental Tax Guide, is available on the IRS website (www.irs.gov); it spells out the factors that the IRS considers. There are no hard and fast rules, but the key areas of concern include:

- Who controls how you do what is required of the job? Can you decide where and when you want to work and how to do the work, or does your client?

- Who controls how you make money? Are you paid a fixed amount on a regular basis, similar to a salary, or are you paid strictly on the deliverable you produce? Are you maintaining an active presence in the marketplace while you are working for this client?

- What kind of relationship you have with your client? Do you have a written contract specifying that you are a contractor and not an employee? Is what you do a key aspect of your client's regular business activity (i.e., is your position considered essential to your client's business, meaning you are part of the business)? Do you have an open-ended relationship with your client similar to an employee, or have you been engaged for a specific project or period?

In the U.K., the distinction between being self-employed or an employee is also a combination of factors. These include issues such as:

- Whether you have complete control over how, when, and where any particular project is done, or how your day is conducted

- Whether you are paid a fixed price for a project, or a regular weekly or monthly amount regardless of output or deliverable

- Whether you regularly work for a number of different people

- Whether you are responsible for correcting unsatisfactory work in your own time and at your own expense

For those in the U.K., consult the page "Employed or Self-Employed?" at HM Revenue & Customs website (www.hmrc.gov.uk) for more details.

For Canadian info-entrepreneurs, the Canada Revenue Agency has a helpful guide titled "Employee or Self-employed?" (RC 4110, available at www.cra-arc.gc.ca). On the first page, it expresses the distinction succinctly: Did the two parties intend to enter into a contract *of service* (employer-employee relationship) or did they intend to enter into a contract *for services* (business relationship)? For the purposes of independent info pros, the most important factors include:

- Whether your client controls how you do your work and whether you are "subordinate" to your client

- Whether you can accept *or reject* work from the client [emphasis mine]

- Whether your relationship with your client is one of continuity and security

Note that different factors may be applied depending on the province or territory in which the contract was formed.

Of course, the best way to avoid any appearance of being an employee (and the best way to build a robust business) is to ensure that you have a number of clients and that no single client accounts for more than, say, a quarter of your income.

Where Am I?

Most independent info pros work from their home or at least start their businesses at home before moving to an outside office. The decision on where to set up shop will depend on a number of factors:

- Whether you have space at home in which to set up a permanent office

- Whether you are willing to commit to the monthly overhead expense of office rental

- Whether you find working in your home too distracting

- Whether other personal considerations dictate your immediate availability (or your absence) at home

For most people starting a new business, just the thought of having to pay rent every month, regardless of how much money is (or isn't) coming in, is daunting. On the other hand, someone who lives in an efficiency apartment may cringe at the thought of turning essentially her entire home into an office. Who wants to live at work? Look at your own living situation and think realistically about how you can carve out office space separate from your living space, keeping in mind that there are lots of options, including what I call The Way of the [Road] Warrior, which I will cover later in this chapter.

Another factor in deciding whether to start out with a home-based or outside office is how often you expect to meet clients face to face. See Chapter 13, Managing Your Clients, for some thoughts on this issue. You can usually meet at your client's office or at a restaurant over lunch or coffee. You can even sign up with one of the "rental office space" businesses that exist in many cities. They provide you with a street address, a receptionist, and the ability to book a meeting room or office as needed. If, on the other hand, you expect to have other people working with you and sharing your office, both you and your family may prefer renting outside space instead of sharing your house with nonfamily members.

Which Kid Gives Up a Bedroom?

If you decide to set up your office at home, consider where you want to spend the majority of your day. The guest bedroom might be a good option, if you have one, although if you have frequent houseguests, it can get tense when you need to evict them at the start of your business day. Your own bedroom can work as an office, as long as you don't mind sleeping in your office. Some people elect to establish their office in a corner of the living room, dining room, or kitchen, but this can be very difficult. You force your family to co-exist with your office, and you are never able to shut the door on your work—either to leave it at the end of the day or to close yourself *in* to get work done. The basement can be a good solution, as long as you are comfortable with all-artificial lighting and working next to the washing machine. I know of one independent info pro who took her two-car garage and split it in half, turning one car's worth into a nice office. Think creatively about whatever extra space you might have, and how you might turn that area into an office. If you are already considering remodeling or making substantial improvements to your house, consider the feasibility of adding a simple office to your plans.

Wherever you decide to put your office, take note of the natural lighting, ambient noise, ability to control the heating and cooling, the number of electrical outlets, and whether you will need to upgrade your wiring to handle all the devices you will be running. You will live with these features (or lack of them) every day, and most of them are difficult, disruptive, and expensive to change once you have settled in. And yes, this was learned through personal experience.

Your Office Space

Regardless of whether your office is at home or away, there will be some basic requirements for setting up an efficient space in which to work. You will need room for a good-sized desk on which to put not only your computer, keyboard, and mouse but all the other items you reach for during the day. For me, those items include a phone, a coffee cup, pens, a note pad, the files for whatever projects I am currently working on, and my various headsets. As you can tell, regardless of the high-tech hype, I'm not even close to achieving a paperless office. And you will need at least one desk drawer—where else will you put your stamps, paper clips, scissors, and so on?

In addition to a generously proportioned desk, you will need space for your printer and fax machine (or multifunction machine); a filing cabinet; a bookshelf for reference books, manuals and documentation, and the like; charging stations for all your electronic gadgets; and a place to store office supplies (your brochures and marketing materials, printer paper, file folders, stationery and envelopes, note pads, sticky notes, and on and on). A comfortable reading chair is also nice for those times when you want to catch up with professional reading or just take a break.

Were you scratching your head at the mention of a fax machine just now? Yes, I still keep a fax machine with an incoming phone line. (Actually, I share my fax line with my home line, using a little black box that detects incoming faxes, routes those calls to my fax machine, and routes the other calls to my telephone.) While I can easily send a fax with my multifunction printer, there are still times that a client or, more frequently, an accounts payable person needs to send me a fax; perhaps you faxed in an order for this very book. For some clients, sending credit card information via fax feels more secure than through another channel. In any event, it is much simpler for me to simply direct them to my fax line and dedicated machine than to make sure my computer is ready to accept a fax.

The Way of the [Road] Warrior

Most of us work best in some semblance of a structured work environment. We want an ergonomic chair and desk, a peaceful space where we can control the environment, and handy access to all the hard-copy parts of our business.

And there are those us who, by choice or necessity, find themselves away from the home base for significant parts of a day or week. I travel a fair amount, so I have had to learn how to create an office in a hotel room or airport lounge. And a number of independent info pros simply miss the stimulation of being around lots of action and conversations, and prefer to spend much of their day in public spaces such as coffee shops, libraries, or the local community center.

I have learned how to maintain a plug-and-play office, which includes:

- A docking station so that I can quickly disconnect my laptop from all its peripheral devices

- An extra mouse, power adapter, and set of all necessary cords in a carrying case in my briefcase

- Extra charging devices for my electronic stuff, along with a USB hub, in another carrying case in my briefcase

- An automatic remote back-up account, so that I always have access to my files wherever I am

- A file folder of projects I can tackle when I have a few spare minutes

- A printed copy of my key passwords, in case my laptop dies and I have to use a borrowed computer

While I had not initially thought I would find it easy to work on the road, I have learned that the distractions of working outside my office actually help me concentrate. I can plug in my headphones if I need to, and the peripheral action just keeps me focused on the task at hand.

"What's Your Address?"

Some independent info pros who work from home are reluctant to use their street address on their business card. One option is to use a post office box as the business address. Although this solution protects your privacy, its disadvantage is that, at least in some clients' eyes, small businesses look suspect if they don't have a street address. If you live near a storefront business center, you can rent a mailbox and get some of the benefits of a regular office without the high rent. You will have a street address, they will accept packages for you, and you can call to find out if there is any mail in your box before making the trip to the office.

Keep in mind that you do run a risk with storefront rental mailboxes—if you move, your mail may not be properly forwarded. And a worst-case scenario is when the rental mailbox company goes out of business, your address disappears, and you lose contact with clients. One option is to use the service of a business suite or a virtual office. These companies manage office suites that provide a receptionist and live telephone operators who answer your calls with your company name, a street address rather than a post office box, conference rooms available for rent by the hour, and permanent office space if you want it. These facilities are not inexpensive, but they may be a good investment if your clients expect the structure of an office.

Office Equipment Checklist

Here's your shopping list for setting up your office. Make sure your bank account has a healthy balance; this is one area where you don't want to scrimp. You are investing in *you* here, and you will be spending a lot of time living with your choices.

- Desk: Make sure it is at a comfortable height, has plenty of space for all the equipment and supplies you will store on and in it, and convenient drawers for the items you will need to get at all day long. Allow enough space to spread papers out while you are working on a project.

- Chair: Shop carefully for this because you will be spending a lot of time on it. Make sure that, when it is at a comfortable working level relative to your desk, your feet rest on the floor, your armrests are at the right height and angle, your back is supported, and you can shift positions. Many people use an exercise ball, either as their primary chair or as a break from a traditional chair.

- Computer: If you are shopping for a new system, get as much disk space and processing power as you can afford. Choose a separate keyboard that fits you ergonomically. Invest in the latest version of your choice of word processing, presentation, and spreadsheet software, assuming it's not preinstalled on your computer when you buy it. As of 2010, Microsoft continues to be the standard format for business use, so you have to be able to accept and generate files in formats that are fully compatible with Microsoft products. Whatever the standard file formats are in your context, make sure you have the software to work with them seamlessly.

- Large monitor: You will be spending all day staring at a screen, and you want the best technology available for the sake of your eyes. Having a second screen can often be handy when working on a project that requires looking at two windows simultaneously.

- Printer/scanner/fax: Look for speed, reliability, and reasonably priced toner cartridges. See the discussion earlier about the possible need for a separate fax machine.

- Telephone: Make sure that you have a permanent number, that the phone will always be answered professionally, and that you will have access to your voice mail from anywhere you ever expect to be.

- File cabinet: For tax and security reasons, you will need to keep paper copies of your invoices, receipts, project notes, correspondence, and other business documents. Buy a sturdy cabinet with at least two drawers. Lateral file cabinets take up less space than the traditional pull-out kind. Consider also buying a fireproof safe for those papers that you need to keep on hand but that you cannot afford to lose.

- Lights: Depending on your set-up, you may need a good desk lamp as well as a floor lamp and ceiling lighting. I find compact fluorescent lights easy on my eyes; others find these painful. Try several kinds of bulbs until you find what works for you.

- Shelving (or a closet or drawers) for supplies: This is for your extra boxes of stationery, envelopes, invoice forms, brochures, printer paper, file folders, paper clips, and so on.

- Fire extinguisher: If you are lucky, you will never need it. Don't tempt fate; keep one in your office and make sure it stays charged.

How will you pay for all this equipment? The simplest solution is to start setting money aside before you begin your business, so that you can purchase what you need without going into debt. Some entrepreneurs lend their businesses the money, and pay back the loan—with interest—gradually. Look into the possibility of grants for new businesses, particularly those owned by women or minorities, if you fall into one of those categories. If you feel that you have to borrow money for start-up costs, look into low-interest loans through the U.S. Small Business Administration (see the Financial Assistance section at www.sba.gov/financing) or an equivalent government organization.

The one option to avoid is putting all these expenses on a credit card and then paying off the balance gradually. Your first year will be tight enough without having to pay some exorbitant interest rate every month on a substantial balance. If you can't afford to pay cash for it, don't buy it.

Your Phone Number

Your customers can't call you if they can't find your phone number. You will need to arrange for phone lines before you order your stationery and business cards, so you can list your numbers appropriately. Some independent info pros who already have an extra residential phone line simply appropriate that line for their business. Others order an additional residential line. And others order—and pay more for—a separate business line. And still others use their cell phone number. Think carefully about which option you choose because you don't want to have to change your business telephone number once you have printed it and promoted it to clients and prospects.

The advantage of having a business land-line phone number is that your business name will be listed with the online telephone directories and on your Caller ID. If you are using a residential line for your business, you may be identified to the people you call as "Ted & Susan Smith" rather than "Smith Info Services"—not the professional image you want to convey. And keep in mind that cell phone numbers don't usually show up in online phone directories. If your phone number doesn't appear in your local telephone directory, you must make sure that the number is available on your website, your social network profiles, your stationery, and all your marketing material. Make it so easy for your clients to find your phone number that they will never need to discover that you aren't in the online yellow pages.

As with your email address, it is critical to have a permanent telephone number where your clients can reach you. If you can take your cell phone number with you when you change carriers, then your cell phone number is a safe option, even if you move. Another option is to use a virtual number that will forward an incoming call to whatever phone number you want. You can program your number so that it rings on your business line on Monday through Friday from 9 AM to 3 PM and on your cell from 3 PM to 5:30 PM, and takes straight to voice mail all calls outside your normal business hours. In 2009, Google Voice (www.google.com/voice) was one such service.

What about a toll-free number? Surprisingly, this can cost very little and giving out a toll-free number to important clients is a way to show them how much you value their business. Check with several carriers and see how much they will charge you to have a toll-free number go to your existing phone line. Often, the monthly fee is minimal (or waived altogether), and the per-minute charges are usually competitive.

If you have a large number of clients in one metropolitan area and you think it would matter to them, you can arrange for a "virtual" phone line in that city. Some local telephone companies offer this service; VoIP providers allow you to create a local phone number in any city, which will route incoming calls to another phone. Other virtual phone number services provide this service, such as Google Voice.

Your URL

What about a website for your business? See Chapter 24, Marketing on the Web, for details; at this point, you will want to consider reserving a domain name, even if you aren't ready to put up a webpage. Many services will hold or "park" your domain name for you for a small fee. Regardless of whether you have a website, you can use your domain name as an email address—that would be you@yourdomain.com— and have mail automatically forwarded to your regular email account. That way, you can give out an email address that won't change, even if you change internet service providers; email to your personalized address can always be forwarded to your current ISP. See Chapter 10, You.com for more on establishing your web presence.

Paying Your Dues

If you haven't already joined the AIIP, now is the time to do so. AIIP, described in more detail in Appendix A, is the primary association for us independent info pros and can be an invaluable resource for beginning entrepreneurs. Members have access to a lively private email discussion group, a volunteer mentoring program, free members-only webinars, sample forms for subcontracting and confidentiality agreements, and the opportunity to tap into the expertise of hundreds of collegial, friendly, supportive people who have been doing this kind of work for years.

In addition to AIIP, join the major trade or professional association that your clients are likely to belong to. Do you plan to provide research and analysis services for HR departments? Then join the Society for Human Resource Professionals. Are you focusing on product marketing professionals? Join the American Marketing Association or its equivalent in your region. Not only will you hear industry-related news when your clients do, but you will have the opportunity to take on volunteer responsibilities for the organization, which get your name out there to prospective clients.

Now is also the time to look into office (or home office) insurance and professional liability insurance. In addition to general liability coverage, which generally is available through your homeowner's policy to cover incidents like someone falling down your stairs, you might want to consider errors-and-omissions (E&O) insurance. E&O insurance is particularly important if you provide research in situations in which a great deal rides on the results of your work. For example, suppose a patent searcher tells a client that no patents currently exist for the client's new invention. If the client proceeds to market his invention and is later sued for millions of dollars by someone who does, indeed, hold an applicable patent, the client may sue the patent searcher for failing to find the earlier patent. If you are doing research in areas of intellectual property, law, or medicine, you may want to investigate the cost and coverage options of E&O insurance. Also, see Chapter 17, Ethics and Legalities, for a discussion of avoiding liability issues.

Finding affordable health insurance, at least for those of us in the U.S., can be a challenge. Call several of the major insurance companies in your area and find out what options they have for individual coverage. If you are leaving full-time employment, check with your existing health insurance provider to see if the rate and coverage for individuals is affordable. Also, check with any associations you belong to; some larger associations offer at least basic health insurance at a group rate.

And finally, you will need to open accounts with any online information services you expect to use for research. (See Chapter 34, Professional Online Services, for information on these resources.) My approach has always been to subscribe to as many sources as I can, as long as they don't charge a subscription or minimum usage fee. It can be frustrating when I need immediate access to a resource that is only available on an online service I don't subscribe to and find that I have to wait days to get all the paperwork done. Keep in mind that AIIP members are eligible for discounts and special deals with a number of online services, including the waiving of monthly or annual subscription fees.

Final Thoughts on Setting Up Your Business

✦   Expect to spend several thousand dollars setting up your office and your business. Buy the best you can afford, and you will only have to buy it once (with the exception of computers, of course, which you will probably replace every few years).

✦   Do as much of the setup as you can ahead of time. Be prepared to start marketing on your first day in business.

✦   Think five years out. Does your business name and structure give you the flexibility you need?

✦   Be honest with yourself about your ability to work well in whatever setting you have chosen.

Chapter 10

You.com

A business website is one of those necessary-but-not-sufficient parts of your marketing plan. You cannot count on getting new clients just because you have a website—that old saw about people beating a path to the better mousetrap doesn't apply to the web world, if for no other reason than you are competing for attention with approximately 492 gazillion other webpages.

But *not* having a website is tantamount to setting up a storefront business and not having any store hours or front door. Choosing a domain name, building a website, and cultivating your ongoing web presence (even beyond your website) all require thought and planning, as they are the key ways that your prospects can scope you out.

While a website can serve as a static marketing tool, the real action is happening in the interactive area of the web—the collaborative, interactive Web 2.0. There are hundreds of ways that you can contribute to and benefit from Web 2.0. From something as simple as a social network profile or a blog to something as complex as a virtual world presence, a wiki for your market, or an aggregated news feed, there are many options for how to establish a presence—to determine which neighborhood(s) you'll call home. Chapter 24, Marketing on the Web, goes into your Web 2.0 presence; this chapter focuses on the places where you will establish a more static identity.

What's the Purpose of a Website?

Back in the days before the web, businesses had "marketing packages"—nice folders with glossy pages extolling the company's quality and commitment to service, customer testimonials, and perhaps a rate sheet. They were sent out to prospective clients to instill confidence in the firm. A company's website now serves that purpose and more. However, one of the advantages of a print package was that the company could include material of specific interest to each prospect. There's no need to clutter up the folder with services that the prospect doesn't need.

A website, on the other hand, has to serve multiple purposes. Your site will be addressed to your clients, your prospects, your vendors, your colleagues and, peripherally, the random visitor who found your site through a search engine. In order to speak to each of these audiences, your site must be designed to make it simple and straightforward for each visitor to go directly to the most relevant page.

Keep in mind that we independent info pros are most likely to be selling an intangible service rather than a solid product. We need to establish the same credibility that we expect to see when we walk into a lawyer's or business executive's office. We may not expect an extravagant suite of offices, but we expect it to look professional, well-organized, and uncluttered. Likewise, while it isn't necessary to build a website with hundreds of pages, an independent info pro without a web presence or who simply has a placeholder webpage looks like a storefront kiosk with its perceived lack of permanence and credibility. And a URL that isn't your own domain (e.g., bates.home.att.net) looks like a hand-painted sign in your front window. It's funky but not in a good way.

Choosing a Domain Name

There are two competing factors in choosing your domain name: simplicity and memorability. You want a name that is professional, that gives some identity to your business, that is easy to spell and pronounce, that is memorable, and that you will be happy with for a long time, as you don't want to change your "address" once you have established it. Let's look at the pluses and minuses of the simple and the memorable approaches.

Simple Domain Names

If you are more concerned with simplicity, choose a name that is:

- Short: I selected BatesInfo.com as my domain rather than BatesInformationServices.com because it was shorter and thus less likely to be misspelled.

- Unhyphenated: Current web "style" is to run your words together rather than separate them with dashes or underscores. And questbizsolutions.com is certainly easier to type than quest_biz_solutions.com.

- An abbreviated version of your business name: A good example of this is Word Technologies, Inc.; its URL is wordtex.com.

- Easy to pronounce: If your last name is Desgrosseilliers, as is a good friend of mine, you probably shouldn't use it in your domain.

- Unambiguous spelling: Avoid words that are frequently misspelled, such as millennium, threshold, accelerate, or parallel. If you have a number in your domain (info2go), consider registering the spelled-out version (infotogo) as well.

Words of Experience: Choosing a Domain

When Andrea Carrero, president of Word Technologies, Inc., started her business, she found that the domain www.wordtechnologies.com was taken already. Here's what she did next.

I started working my way down from there and ended with wordtex.com. In the end, it turned out to be a good domain name and is a shortened version of my business name. I was disappointed at first, but then I remembered when a former employer had the domain musicboulevard. We had a number of domain names that redirected to the main webpage, including mblvd.com, musicblvd.com, etc. Why? It turns out that a lot of people couldn't spell the word "boulevard!"

Lesson learned: If they can't spell it, they can't find you.

Memorable Domain Names

While simple is good, if your domain is difficult to remember, your prospective clients won't be able to find you. While the initials of my business name are BIS, I have no interest in trying to establish BIS.com as my brand, even if it were available. It's simply not a combination of letters that most people would remember. To ensure that your site is memorable, choose a name that is:

- Clear: The domain IneedInfo.com spells out exactly what a client is feeling at the moment.

- Unusual: Marjorie Desgrosseilliers' business is SmartyPants Research & Marketing, so her domain is SmartyPantsResearch.com. Now *that* is a memorable URL.

- Personal: Since much of our business comes from word of mouth and all of our clients know our name, it may make sense to use your personal name rather than your business name as your domain.

Your Name or Your Business?

Depending on your business and your market, you may want to focus on building your personal name recognition rather than your business name. If your own name has not yet been registered as a domain by someone else, it is probably worth investing in registering it yourself on the chance that your clients and prospects know your name so well that they would expect your website address to be your name.

Marcy Phelps, of Phelps Research, for example, uses PhelpsResearch.com for her business website, but she uses MarcyPhelps.com for her blog. Her website is primarily a static marketing avenue so it makes sense for the name of her website to be her business name, whereas her blog is where she can be less formal and more personal in her writing, so she publishes her thoughts and ideas under her personal name.

That said, in my opinion, the only useful format for a personal name domain is YourFirstNameYourLastName.com, with no punctuation between your first and last name. If someone has already registered your name.com, don't register a similar version of your name, as most of your visitors will forget your URL and will go over to the owner of YourFirstNameYourLastName.com. For example, if your name is Clark Kent, and ClarkKent.com has already been registered to someone else, I wouldn't advise using a variation such as Clark-Kent.com, ClarkXKent.com, ClarkKent103.com, TheClarkKent.com, or ClarkKent.net. Most of your contacts will head over to

ClarkKent.com regardless of how many times you explain the correct spelling of your domain.

Other Domain Name Considerations

In addition to the simplicity/memorability factors, consider registering domains of likely misspellings of your own domain. While my business website is BatesInfo.com, I can also register domains such as bates-info.com, bates information.com, batesinfo.biz, and bates.info, and simply have them redirect the browser to my primary site. These may be ways that people try to find me on the web, so I try to anticipate where they might go.

Make sure your primary domain is a .com or .co.*xx* address. Besides the problem of people defaulting to .com when typing in a URL, having a .net or .biz domain emphasizes the fact that you are relatively new to this domain. The (often erroneous) assumption is that you and your business are new to the web, since "everyone" has his or her own .com address. If you are located outside the U.S., consider registering the .com version of your domain in addition to .co.*xx*. Likewise, if you have—or expect to have—much of a presence in another country, it's smart to reserve the domain with that country's top-level domain. (What's that? The top-level domain, or TLD, is the two-letter acronym indicating the country where the website is located.)

Remember to do a reality check before you settle on a domain name. Ask some of your friends how they would pronounce your domain name if they saw it spelled out. Then ask them to spell your domain name if they heard it spoken and ask them what it suggests. Does it turn out that your domain inadvertently spells something other than what you had in mind? Try to avoid the problem of the "Experts Exchange," a site where programmers can exchange ideas, whose unfortunate domain was expertsexchange. Are they in the business of exchanging expertise or trading info on sex changes?

This may seem too obvious to mention, but keep in mind that just because you can't find a website for a particular domain doesn't necessarily mean that the domain is available. Many people "park" domains—register the domain on the chance that they will want it (or be able to sell it) later, never bothering to set up a webpage for the domain. Before you settle on the perfect domain name, be sure to check a domain look-up service such as DomainTools (www.domaintools.com) or

Network Solutions (www.networksolutions.com) to see if the name you want is even available.

Be liberal in purchasing domain names and register them for as long as possible. It costs under $10 to register a domain for a year. Given the low per-year cost to protect your brand, it makes sense to register any obvious permutations of your chosen domain to ensure that you will be findable and to register at least your primary domain for as many years as possible to ensure that you don't inadvertently let your domain lapse.

Use a reputable domain hosting company. Sure, there are companies that offer to host your website for practically nothing, as long as you have ads on your site, which is a nonstarter if you want to look like a real enterprise. And some companies will host your domain at a low cost, but they won't offer you support when you need additional features or support. What you need is a company that is responsive to your needs and provides help when you want to add a shopping cart to your website, have to handle a spam attack, or simply can't figure out how to get something done. I have almost always used local companies to host my website; I appreciate the fact that they pay attention to a customer who isn't paying them thousands of dollars a month, and I find that they are much more responsive to my needs and concerns.

On the other hand, I run a slightly higher risk of the company going out of business and me having to scramble to restore my website. If I used a large domain hosting company, I get stability at the cost of not having the same personal service I get when I call Chuck at my local domain hosting company, Warp8.com. I manage that risk by going with local companies that have been in business for several years, that have been referred by colleagues I know and trust, and that answer their customer support phone with a real person (yes, that's the first thing I test when I am considering a hosting company).

Creating Your Website

You have probably seen some great company websites as well as some that should have been outlawed, and it always surprises me that some businesses don't think about how their website appears to others or what message it sends. The goal for your website is to ensure that it represents you in the most professional way possible.

For starters, this means that you don't put pictures of your children, dogs, or house on your website; this is solely for your business. (If you just can't resist, create a "friends and family" area and do not create a link from your main webpage to your personal pages. Or just break down and get another domain; remember, they're inexpensive and, if it is just for personal use, the domain name need not be catchy or memorable.)

Do It Yourself or Hire Out?

Unless you are truly a gifted designer, leave the actual construction of your website to an expert. You can find a good web designer through several channels:

- Find websites you like for other small businesses and ask them who designed their websites.

- Ask your colleagues who they recommend.

- Contact a local high school or college web design class and invite them to take your company website on as a project.

- Use a bidding site such as Elance.com or Guru.com, in which you describe what you want and freelancers bid on the job. While you are purchasing an unknown quantity rather than someone recommended by others, your risk is reduced by the fact that the cost to hire someone from these sites is usually modest.

(As a side note, the usefulness of freelance sites like Elance.com or Guru.com is that you can contract for skilled work at a low price. And that is exactly why we info-entrepreneurs should run the other direction—fast—from any offer for us to participate in this type of bidding forum. If we are bidding against others to be the cheapest researcher available, we attract clients who see our services as commodities and us as replaceable. These are not clients you can build a sustainable business around.)

There are a number of advantages of using a web designer rather than doing the work yourself. First, remember to make all your decisions with a five-year view. You want your website to look polished, easy to use, and appealing to your market. You want to take advantage of recent web design and functionality. You want the pages to load quickly and have a consistent look across browsers. Sure, you could probably figure all this out yourself, but is this really the best use of your time, energy, and focus, just as you are getting your business off the ground? A better approach, and one that you will carry with you as your business grows, is to value your time appropriately. If you do, you will probably decide that the time you spend learning how to do what a designer already knows how to do is a poor investment of your time. This is a skill that you can easily subcontract; you need a fresh set of eyes to ensure that your website is clear and easy to use, and you can spend the time marketing your business so that you can start bringing in revenue.

If, like me, you enjoy rolling up your sleeves and getting your hands greasy from coding HTML, just ask your web designer to keep the design simple enough for you to maintain and update yourself. Ask that your site be tested on multiple browsers and browser versions so that you don't inadvertently turn off an entire segment of your market because your website looks awful on their older browser.

Five Factors for Web Design

While I assume you will use a web pro to create your website, you are still responsible for ensuring that your website accomplishes your goals—to be found, to be seen as professional and trustworthy, and to stay in contact with your clients and prospects. Regardless of who designs your website, you will want to take these five factors into account.

The first is findability. As I have mentioned before, I do not expect to generate new clients from my website; a professional who has more money than time won't be spending her time surfing the web to find an independent info pro. Rather, I want to make sure that a prospect who has heard about me can easily find me on the web and read about my qualifications. There is an entire field of marketing called search engine optimization (SEO), designing websites with the specific goal of getting to the top of the search results for given queries. While info-entrepreneurs don't generally need SEO, make your site search-engine friendly. This includes considerations such as ensuring that every webpage has a unique title metatag, putting your name and your business name near the top of the page, creating a site map, putting all text in a nongraphic format, and including keywords that people who are looking for you will use in a search engine. If, for example, your clients are likely to be looking for a "business intelligence analyst" rather than an "independent information professional," include the former phrase on your webpages. There are many sites for SEO professionals; see, for example, Search Engine Guide (www.searchengineguide. com), which focuses on search engine marketing for small businesses, and Google's

Search Engine Optimization Starter Guide, available in the Webmaster Central section of Google's site (www.google.com/webmasters).

The second factor for web design is accessibility. Ensure that your site is viewable by your nontypical users: those with vision impairments or others who have tools that convert the text on a webpage to spoken word, those who have their screen on magnification to aid in viewing, those who are viewing your website on a mobile device, and so on. If you have a graphics-heavy site with many icons for navigation, your visitor will find your site very difficult to use. Likewise, if you use cutting-edge technology on your website, you run the risk of making it inaccessible to users with older browsers.

The third factor is navigability. Now that a prospective client has arrived at your webpage, how easy is it for him to find what he is looking for? Do you have clearly visible links or tabs that enable a visitor to go easily from one page to another? Do you have a site map to help visitors find what would otherwise be hidden pages? Include plenty of internal links from one page to another. Make sure that there is a way to get back to the homepage from any other page on the site. Your goal is to make visiting your site a pleasant experience.

The fourth factor in web design is usefulness. You could have the best site in the world on the mating habits of adolescent echidnas, but that's not of much value unless echidna researchers can find your site. Make sure that your site offers real value. Is it simply a placeholder with your contact information and a paragraph of text? If so, it also sends the message to your clients that you aren't interested in giving them any background about you. See the sidebar, "Must-Haves for Any Website," for more discussion of the minimum content to make your site useful.

The final factor in web design is value. Do you give visitors a reason to come back to your site later or to refer someone else to your site? Viral marketing can be very effective, but it means that you must provide fresh content on your site that would be of value to your clients. The next section "What About the Content?" looks at the specifics of what you can include; keep in mind that the more information you give away, the more valuable you become. So write a couple of white papers on an aspect of information that would be of interest to your clients. Publish a newsletter. Post your presentations on your site. Always think about what new content you could add to your site that would make it more valuable to your client base.

Must-Haves for Any Website

Your website may include hundreds of pages, or it may only have five or 10 pages. Regardless of the size and complexity of your site, you need to provide the following at the minimum:

- Your full name: Yes, you want to build your business name, but if you won't provide your name on your website, how can your clients feel comfortable working with you?

- Your snail mail address: Would you do business with a lawyer or accountant who wouldn't give you his or her mailing address? One of the key indicators of a bogus site is the lack of a street address. So show that you are a real business by providing your address. Use a post office box or virtual office service if you have privacy concerns.

- Your telephone number and VoIP address: Make it as easy as possible for your clients to reach you. As with addresses, I am reluctant to do business with companies that don't list their phone numbers on their websites; to me, this indicates a lack of commitment to their customers.

- Your email address: Yes, some spammers will snag your email address from your webpage, but that isn't a sufficient reason to hide your email address. And always use your business domain—me@mybusiness.com—not a personal or generic email address like me@my-local-ISP.com.

- A brief bio: Your clients don't expect a resume (in fact, a resume sends the message that you are looking for a permanent job and not committed to your business). However, they do want to know something about you. What's your background? Why are you qualified?

- Links to all your web presences: Include links to your blog, your profiles on social networking services, your microblogging account, your virtual world identities, and so on. Of course, this assumes that all your web activities reflect your professional image; if you are tempted to post pictures of you having a little too much fun at the open bar at the last conference you attended, either take a deep breath and let it go or post them under a pseudonym. Your clients want to see you online, but there's a point at which you might be giving out too much information.

- A clear, jargon-free description of why your clients use you: This is different from a description of what you do; you want to focus on what benefits you provide your clients, and the best way to do that is to shift the question from "What does your company do?" to "Here is how I make a difference to my clients." This is more difficult to do than you might think; be sure to test your answer on friends who aren't in your field, and see if, based on your description, they can describe what you do to someone else. If they can't, then you need to clarify your message.

- A page of benefits: Why should people hire you? What are you offering them that they can't live without and that no one else does as well? What pain points of your clients have you addressed? You could be the best researcher in the world, but your prospective client will want to know not only your background but specifically what you can do for him.

What About the Content?

You have lined up a web designer and have identified the essential pages and content from the "Must-Haves for Any Website" sidebar. Now how do you create the content? This is where even the most seasoned writer can get writer's block; web-page writing is different than any other type, particularly because you can't anticipate who your audience is.

What I found most helpful was to use a marketing professional to polish and refine my writing. So I composed the text for all the basic pages on my website, and then passed them to my consultant, who transformed what I had written into web copy. And, being a marketing pro, she also suggested I add a few pages—one for media inquiries, a page linking to my blog, and an FAQ on info-entrepreneurs, for example.

At the least, provide enough of a description of your business that someone visiting your site understands what you offer and why your prospective clients should care. While it is tempting to be as generic as possible, focus on writing for your core audience. Without lapsing into excessive acronym-ese, use the language of your clients. If they value creativity and out-of-the-box thinking, make your site fun and exciting. If your clients value stability and authority, write copy that is calm and professional.

Be sure to have a few friends or colleagues review your entire site before you take it live. Ask them what they think your key message is. Ask them how easy it was to find useful information on the site and see whether any language is unclear or ambiguous. Although your site may seem to you to be very clear and easy to navigate, you need a fresh set of eyes to catch the glitches.

Keeping Your Site Fresh

The purpose of building content is to give people a reason to come back to your site and to refer it to their colleagues. Your website can be more than just a billboard, and there are lots of ways to create value and encourage people to return to your site. It is critical to always keep in mind who you are writing for; your key audience includes your clients, prospective clients, and colleagues. Here are a few ideas; keep in mind that newer tools and resources will have come out after this book went to press.

- Monitor the news in your clients' industry(ies). Publish a weekly list of headlines and sources, and offer a subscription-based version that includes an abstract of each article (written by you).

- Write white papers on issues of interest to your clients. Christine Hamilton-Pennell, of Growing Local Economies, focuses on helping local governments and public libraries develop programs to support local entrepreneurs. In order to provide value to each of these audiences, she writes white papers on implementing "economic gardening" programs and on the best information resources to support local businesses that are of interest to economic development professionals and public librarians, respectively.

- If you give presentations (see why it's a good idea in Chapter 26, Marketing by Writing and Speaking), post PDFs of your slide shows on your website. People who share information are seen, often rightly, as people who *have* information, which is an impression you would like to give on your website.

- Produce podcasts of interest to your clients. Since podcasts are so simple to create, especially when compared to articles or newsletters, you can podcast frequently. Provide your review of a new information resource, report on what you found most forward-thinking at a conference, and interview people of interest to your clients.

- Build a customized search engine to help your clients conduct more efficient research on the web. Consider other ways that you can create a go-to website for helping your client base search more effectively on the web.

Before you get started writing your webpage copy, spend some time browsing other info-entrepreneurs' websites and taking notes. What do you like the most about the site? Is it clear what this business is all about? Is it easy to figure out who the principals of the company are? Do you understand who this company's major clients are? Imagine what questions prospective clients would have when they first get to your site, and make sure those questions are easily answered.

Other Web "Homes"

There are lots of other places you can call home on the web. The ones that require more participation and interactivity, such as blogs, microblogging, and a cultivated presence on a social networking site, are covered in Chapter 24, Marketing on the Web. This section looks at the initial steps you need to take to establish your identity on the more interactive web.

The social networking services are perhaps the best places to start your foray into creating your other websites. Facebook (facebook.com) and LinkedIn (linkedin. com) are two familiar names in the social networking arena. Both offer ways for you to establish connections with not only your friends but the friends of your friends. Perhaps more importantly, however, is that for many people, their profile on a social networking service is their primary web presence. In a sense, if you aren't on their network, you are virtually unfindable.

This is an area of the web that is growing particularly quickly so the functionality of these social sites is bound to increase incrementally. The following are a few examples of how and why info-entrepreneurs can make use of social networks.

Finding an Entry Point

A client of mine was attempting to assign a value to the photographic archive of a well-known artist prior to offering it for sale to a museum. He knew about a similar

Publishing Your Rate Sheet

What about listing your prices on your website? My advice is that you probably shouldn't for a number of reasons:

- You may want to quote a flat fee for each project. By definition, an estimate for a customized deliverable can't be done on a rate sheet.

- Prospective clients may seriously overestimate how long a project will take. If they see an hourly rate of, say, $175, they may jump to the conclusion that a project will be beyond their budget, on the assumption that you take as long to find information as they do.

- A rate sheet doesn't convey all the value-added services you provide—analysis and synthesis of results, customized presentations, and so on.

- When you estimate a project, you will probably factor in what the job is worth to the client. If it is vital to him, you will estimate high; if it's a nice-to-know question, you may offer a lower estimate. If you post a rate sheet, you lose some of this flexibility.

- Your hourly rate is only part of the total cost of a project. It's difficult to explain or anticipate direct expenses such as the cost of a search on a professional online service, subcontracted work, or copyright fees for academic papers, all of which you will bill back to the client.

I conducted an informal survey of a number of independent info pros' websites. Interestingly, the only ones who listed their rates were those who priced their services at the low end of the range for independent info pros. (See Chapter 15, Setting Rates and Fees, for more about pricing your services.) My theory is that people who post their rates on their websites are catering to clients who shop for price rather than value. Do you really want that kind of client?

sale in the past, and he wanted to know details about that collection—how many images, how much did it sell for, what restrictions were on the gift, and so on. I exhausted my online resources to no avail; the museum made virtually no announcement of the acquisition.

I then looked in LinkedIn for anyone in my extended network who worked at the museum in question. As luck would have it, the head archivist was in my network so I contacted him and asked for any help he could give. He responded within hours with a detailed email spelling out the content of the archive the museum had purchased, describing the restrictions placed on the collection and, alas, declining to disclose how much was paid for the collection. My client now believes that I have connections around the world, and I now have an archivist to whom I owe a debt of gratitude.

A Virtual Contact Manager

In the old days, when an employee left his job, he grabbed his Rolodex off his desk even before he packed up his kids' pictures. All his contacts were in that little rotary file, and they were irreplaceable. Now, that employee's contacts may be spread out in a number of places—in an internal employee directory, a file in a contact management system, email addresses stored on the organization's server, and perhaps even in a rotary file. It's quite possible for one of your clients to leave her last employer without bringing all her contacts with her.

Assuming your client had already created a profile in a social networking site, she will have all her vital contacts with her, regardless of where she is. By having an account on multiple social networking sites, you increase the likelihood that clients will be able to find you, even if they have lost your contact information. As long as your client has created a link to you from her account, she will always be able to get in touch with you.

A Personal Branded Website

Your business website is intended to talk about your corporate services. It is often difficult to surface your own personality and expertise. By maintaining and updating a presence on some of the social networking sites, you let people get to know you in different ways. They can see what groups you belong to, who you know, what you're currently doing, and so on. This offers your clients an opportunity to have a better understanding of what interests you, how connected you are to others in your field, and interesting projects (anonymized, of course) that you're working on. Since many of these sites allow your network to be notified when you update your profile, you have regular opportunities to ping your contacts with news.

Going Where Your Clients Live

A webpage is like a storefront—you set it up and hope to attract people to it. Why not also work on exploring beyond your own (virtual) store and see where the gang hangs out? Your clients and prospects may belong to a Facebook group, a customized social network on Ning or another build-your-own network site, an email discussion list, an industry discussion forum, or a virtual world. And how do you find these places? I usually identify them by monitoring all the possibly relevant discussion lists until I find a few that look most useful. (See Chapter 24, Marketing on the Web, for information on how to find discussion lists.) Then I keep my eyes open for mentions of other hangouts. I also go to the social network profiles of industry leaders and see what groups or networks they belong to; I assume that if they belong to one or several, I should, too.

On a more practical level, it is a lot easier to find colleagues and groups if you already have a network in place in several different services. Most networks provide deeper searching ability to those who have profiles on the network than to nonmembers. Since virtually none of these networks has a sign-up or subscription fee, it makes sense to establish a presence on as many as look promising from a marketing perspective.

What if you can't find a relevant group? Your first thought may be to create one yourself. Before leaping into this, give some thought to why no one has organized a group already. Are most of the potential members reluctant to have an online home? Is it an industry in which professionals change job responsibilities so quickly that they don't identify with a particular function (e.g., competitive intelligence, business analyst)? If it seems that there is an ongoing interest and need in forming a virtual community, this is a great opportunity to establish yourself with your clients. Form a group in one of the social networking services and generate conversation. Invite all your likely prospects to join. Start some interesting topics. Build a collection of useful links or resources. All this work will serve to demonstrate to your prospective clients that you understand this industry, are concerned with professional development and collegiality, and are viewed as a leader in your field, whether you feel like you are a leader or not.

Knowing the Local Customs

If you have been in online discussion forums for a long time, you've heard of the scorned Clueless Newbie—the person who joins an email discussion list and immediately starts asking questions that have been answered many times before, that are far too basic for the audience, or that are outside the scope of interest of the group.

Learning the etiquette and customs of a virtual community is similar to learning the ways of any unknown tribe. Sit off to the side for a few weeks and just observe. Is the general tone very professional or quite informal? Is it considered good form to ask for assistance? For that matter, do you want to be seen as someone who asks questions or as someone who is helpful, resourceful, and a valuable asset?

Look around. If you are on an email discussion list, look at the footer of every message; there are probably links to the archive of discussions, a library of resources, and other useful information. Check them all out; they are there specifically to help newcomers familiarize themselves with the community. If the group you are joining has a website, go through the entire website. Look for resources, links to industry blogs, white papers, and anything else that would help you familiarize yourself with the group.

In Chapter 24, Marketing on the Web, I look at how to most effectively participate in the interactive web. In the context of this chapter—establishing your web presence—your membership in these online communities lets you learn how your clients think and speak, what their concerns are, and how you can provide services that they will value.

And finally, I approach the interactive web as a professional development exercise. I'll try just about any new community or network, at least for a little while. Learning how a new discussion forum works or how to navigate through a virtual world keeps me more flexible and able to adapt to new services and tools.

Top Tips for Building the Brand "You.com"

- ✦ Your website is a semistatic brochure for your clients, prospects, and colleagues.
- ✦ Choose your domain name carefully and register similar domains.
- ✦ Use a web designer to create your site.
- ✦ Content is king; create content that has value and is worth returning to over time.
- ✦ Maintain a presence on social network and virtual community sites.

Chapter 11

Business Apps for Info-Entrepreneurs

I will start by confessing that I am not one of those early adopters who loads every new piece of software that comes down the pike. I use as few programs as necessary, on the assumption that no one pays me for my learning curve, so I might as well minimize the time I spend getting familiar with new software. I make sure that my software is compatible with what my clients and contacts use; in fact, my concern when I upgrade is often whether the new version will still generate output in an older version for my clients who don't upgrade frequently.

The applications that I cover in this chapter are what most independent info pros would consider the bare necessities, along with some tools that are helpful in specific situations. As of late 2009, the behemoth of operating systems is Microsoft, which means that I have to be able to create and use files and applications that run on Microsoft's operating system, regardless of what operating system I am using. If your clients primarily use another operating system, then you will need to generate reports in a format they can read.

The Basics

Let's start with the can't-live-without software, much of which probably came preinstalled on your computer. In most cases, I recommend that you stick with whatever is commonly used. It is easier to find colleagues or friends who can help you troubleshoot any problems you run into, and it is much more likely that your clients will be running the same program.

Word Processing

Microsoft Word—need I say more? But I will. When you start your business, make sure you have the latest version of Word, then plan on upgrading every couple of years. You probably won't need any of the bells, whistles, and bugs added with each new iteration, but your clients are likely to be using a current version, and you want to make sure that you can exchange documents with a minimum of trouble.

These are the Word functions I have found most useful in my business over the years:

- Create a table of contents
- Create a template for reports
- Add and edit headers and footers
- Build simple macros for repetitive tasks
- Build simple tables
- Insert images and embed files

Email

Most people use Microsoft's Outlook; since it syncs with your calendar, it can be the easiest way to keep track of follow-ups with clients, the progress on a project, or a call you promised to make. You are undoubtedly using some email software already; if you are using something other than the marketplace standard, just make sure you have the features and functions for a business email application:

- Create address lists and nicknames for frequently emailed addresses
- Filter your incoming email into folders (one folder for email discussion lists, one for "stuff to be read later," and so on)
- Run your outgoing email through a spell-checker and format your messages in plain text or HTML
- Create customized signature files and stationery formats

Accounting

Intuit's QuickBooks products are by far the most popular accounting packages for independent info pros, at least in North America. In addition to the fact that they are powerful and easy to use, you are much more likely to find an accountant who uses QuickBooks than one who uses Microsoft Accounting or other accounting program. Intuit sells several versions of QuickBooks; even the most basic versions have all the features you will probably need. Note that Intuit also offers a free version of QuickBooks called Simple Start, which will handle invoicing for up to 20 clients. By the time you get close to that number, you will certainly have enough money to buy the full version, and you will probably welcome the additional features that the full version offers.

Work with your accountant to set up QuickBooks initially. As streamlined as the software is, an information business is not a typical business, and you will probably need to modify some expense and income categories. It is a lot easier to pay an accountant to get you set up properly than it is to re-do a year's worth of transactions at tax time when you realize that the categories you have set up don't mesh with the categories needed for your tax return (and yes, I am speaking from first-hand experience).

You will need the following functions in your accounting software:

- Create invoices

- Write checks

- Receive and deposit payments

- Generate profit and loss reports and balance statements

- Generate past-due collections reports

- Balance your checkbook

Backups

I feel fortunate that I learned early in my career to back up my computer regularly. My first computer, which I bought in 1984, crashed fatally within two weeks of purchase—everything I had stored was gone forever. No great loss of data at the time, but I have been scrupulous about backing up all essential files ever since.

The method you use to back up your vital data is not as important as the regularity of your backups. Make sure that the process is automatic so that every evening your critical files are saved in a place where you can retrieve them easily. At the least, you need to back up all your client files, accounting and contact data, calendar, email, and any other information that you couldn't function without. Note that you don't usually have to back up application software, as long as you either save a copy of the installation file or the original installation disk.

Free or Fee? Own or Rent?

While it can be daunting to look at the expense of purchasing all these applications, we now have the choice of not spending hundreds of dollars for each one. Yes, you can buy a bundle of applications when you buy your computer, but there are also web-based applications that you can use without ever downloading software. One such example is Zoho (www.zoho.com), which offers free word-processing, spreadsheet, email, presentation, conferencing, scheduling, and wiki applications at no charge, and accounting, project management, and contact management software available for a fee.

The advantage of a site such as Zoho is that you have access to virtually all the basic business tools you need, at no charge. The output is in a format that can be read by the Microsoft equivalent (Zoho word-processing documents are compatible with Microsoft Word, presentation files are compatible with Microsoft PowerPoint, and so on). The software is designed to be simple to use, which means that its user interface is intuitive, and there are plenty of help files and discussion forums for support. New functionality can be rolled out quickly with web-based applications—just update the software on the server, and all the users instantly have access to updated features. You can store your documents on the website and, as long as you have a internet connection, you have all your applications and files with you wherever you go.

The disadvantages are, of course, that all your applications and files are on the web, which means that if you are offline, you're out of luck. And because the programs are designed to be simple and intuitive, you do not have all the high-end features of a stand-alone application. Some web-based applications may not keep up with the latest version of the Microsoft equivalent, meaning that you may receive a file from a client in a format too new for you to open with the web-based service.

My advice is to only use these web-based applications to try out a new type of program to see if it will be useful for you. For example, I used a free PDF file converter until I decided that this was something I would definitely have a use for in my business, at which time I paid for the full features of Adobe Acrobat.

The most important consideration is to ensure that you never look cheap or unprofessional in your dealings with clients. If they send you a file or ask for the deliverable in a Microsoft format (including the latest version), you should have the applications necessary to open and use the file. While I do not buy software on a whim (at least if it requires real money and real time to master), I willingly maintain the latest version of the most common software applications if I know my clients are likely to have the latest version as well.

Some people prefer to back up their information onto another household or office computer or to an external device. You can't beat the security since you know exactly where the back-up copy is. Of course, if you are protecting against the possibility of losing your data because of a fire or other catastrophe at home, your back-up copy may be no better off than your computer. Others use a web-based back-up service, which automatically establishes a secure connection between your computer and the host at a scheduled time, determines what files have been changed, and then backs up all the new or updated files and file groups that you specify. The advantages of remote archiving are that your files are accessible wherever you are, they are housed in a more secure facility than your home or office, and you never worry about the details of having enough file storage space or maintaining the physical security of the backup medium. The primary concern some people have with this arrangement is that their vital data is being transmitted to and stored in a remote location.

Remember that backing up isn't just to protect yourself in the event of a computer crash. At least in my case, I also go to my archived files when I have accidentally deleted a file I need or when a file becomes corrupted and I need an earlier version. Be sure that, whatever back-up method you use, it is simple, easy to use, and reliable.

The following are the basic functions your backup method should handle:

- Securely back up all essential files

- Schedule unattended backups

- Easily restore files from the backup as needed

Virus Protection

Like backup programs, antivirus software is something you only truly appreciate after you have been caught without it. There are a number of reliable virus protection programs available. Be sure that you select one that offers automatic web updates to keep your software alert to the latest viruses in the wild. Of course, you also have to practice safe computing; never open an unexpected email attachment without scanning it first, regardless of who it is from, and always virus-check any files you download from the web, even those you purchase from a reputable vendor.

Make sure you know how to do the following in your virus protection software:

- Schedule automatic scans of your hard disk

- Automatically scan all incoming email and downloaded files

- Protect against intrusion attacks on your computer

- Get automatic virus protection updates from the vendor's website

The Nice-to-Haves

This section covers software that you will probably want eventually but may not use every day. If you have the cash to spare and you like knowing that you have a fully equipped tool bench, add these to your shopping list. As I mentioned in the "Free or Fee? Own or Rent?" sidebar, consider first using free alternatives or trial versions of software to determine whether it is indeed something you would find useful. Once you have identified an application that you can justify purchasing, buy the fully featured version.

Adobe Acrobat

I'm not going to bother using a generic name to describe Acrobat—this is one software application that not only owns the market (at least as of 2009) but has, in fact, defined the market for PDF (Portable Document Format) files. Acrobat allows the user to create text and image files that can be read across platforms, regardless of whether the recipient has the software that created the original file. You can download the free version of Adobe Reader, which enables you to read PDF files, from www.adobe.com. But the full-featured Acrobat is nice to have, as it enables you to convert word-processing documents, PowerPoint presentations, and so on into PDFs as well as edit your PDFs, create PDF forms, and so on. I often find this the best way to supply information to a client; PDF is universally readable and ensures that the material remains intact since PDF files are "sealed" and cannot be modified by the reader. (See Chapter 37, Deliverables, for more discussion about sealing material for clients.)

PowerPoint

Like Acrobat in the electronic publishing arena, PowerPoint has become a generic name for presentation software. PowerPoint is easy to use, it's a great tool for public speaking when done well, and it comes in handy when providing an executive summary of a report to a client who routinely receives information in PowerPoint slides. In fact, as people become more accustomed to getting information in small bites and on mobile devices, they place more value in making information easy to take in and digest. A PowerPoint outline can make a more compelling "story" than simple text, particularly if you can incorporate graphics into the presentation.

Webpage Editor

With a few exceptions, a website is a business necessity and having a website means that you need to keep it updated and fresh. I talk about content for your website in Chapter 10, You.com; you need some way to get that great content onto your website. While you can pay a website manager to handle this routine maintenance, it may be more cost-effective and efficient to do your own simple updating. If so, you will need webpage editing software so that you can make changes to your pages, add pages, and refresh content. Since the underlying code of the site won't be seen by others, there is no need to use a name-brand editor; just find a program that works for you and that does all that you need your website to do.

If you are going to be editing your website, you will also need a way to get your new or edited pages onto the host site. FTP (file transfer protocol) software is readily available and often free, and most browsers include an FTP client. Whatever you use, you need to be able to:

- Establish a secure connection with your host
- Easily transfer files between the host and your computer
- Easily create directories and move files among directories
- Search for files on your host

Screen Capture Software

It is likely that there will be times when you need to print or capture and save an entire webpage—graphics, tables, and all—even if the page requires scrolling to see in its entirety. While every computer comes with a simple screen capture function, you may find that you want to capture more than just what you see on the screen, or you may want to do some simple editing of the screen shot but not want all the bells and whistles (and expense) of a full-featured photo-and-image editing package. The middle ground is software that will let you crop or erase parts of a screen shot, add notations, and use drawing tools for arrows, circles, or highlights. Among the most useful features to look for are:

- Ability to capture your entire screen, the active window, or just specific parts of a page

- Automatic scrolling of a page to capture more than just what is visible on your screen

- Easy-to-use image editing tools that offer the features you want without too many extraneous gadgets

- Tagging of your images for easy organization and retrieval

- Options for saving the image in a variety of formats and sizes

Other Cool Tools

There are tools and utilities for just about all those tasks you do frequently and wish you could streamline. Here are a few with a big following in the independent info pro community:

- Link-management programs that check whether links on a webpage are still valid. These are useful for ensuring that your website doesn't have any dead links; run a link checker once a month and update any nonworking links.

- Time-tracking software for recording the time you spend on a project, down to 10ths of an hour. This is particularly useful if you do work for law firms or other organizations that track time in small increments. Most accounting software, including QuickBooks, have a time-tracking function that integrates smoothly into the invoicing function; however, if you routinely need to track most of the hours of your day, you may want a stand-alone package that offers more features than an accounting package has.

- Bibliographic management software that helps you organize bibliographic citations. If your work involves managing or editing extensive references to articles and other published material, your regular word processor may not be up to the job. The library world has a number of high-powered tools for this kind of work, some of which are free or low-cost.

- Dictation software that transcribes your speech to text. Many people think faster than they can type, and others have difficulty using a keyboard. For those people and anyone else who would rather not type, there are dictation programs that learn your speech patterns and transcribe your speech into text. These transcripts aren't perfect, and these programs require you to speak clearly and distinctly, but they are a gift to anyone who isn't a fast typist. Currently, the most popular package among info pros is Dragon NaturallySpeaking from Nuance Communications.

- Desktop search software. There are many free tools that index all the content of the data files on your computer (word processing, email and attachments, PDFs, spreadsheets, HTML, and so on) and make them searchable. Some of these also archive prior versions of documents; this can be a lifesaver if you are trying to reconstruct changes to a file.

Software Lessons Learned

- ✦ You don't have an IT department on call to provide tech support. Keep your computer free of unnecessary tools and utilities; you are the one who has to maintain them.

- ✦ Learn how to get the most out of your commonly used applications.

- ✦ Be as frictionless as possible for your clients; find out what version of a particular application they use or what file format works best for them and use it.

- ✦ Back up everything you wouldn't want to lose. Keep the backup files outside your office.

Chapter 12

Work and the Rest of Your Life

So far, I have covered lots of practical issues—setting up your office, writing a business plan, and even "softer" factors like making sure you have the personality to enjoy and succeed at being an independent info pro. But I haven't talked much about integrating your work into the other hours of your day—the time that you spend outside the office, having a life. This chapter will look at some of the issues that frequently arise when you own a one- or two-person business, especially if you work from home.

Living Abundantly

There are different ways of living life richly. You can spend money as fast as you make it and live from paycheck to paycheck (or, as an independent info pro, from client payment to client payment). Or you can focus on finding richness and wealth in whatever situation you're in, in ways that don't involve cash. The first six months or year of a new business are going to be hard; you will be working like crazy to find new clients, and at first you may be spending more money than you take in. You can react to this by feeling desperate, making cold calls to random prospects, accepting work in which you don't have enough expertise, and generally losing your cool. Or you can focus on the ways in which you are wealthy, right now at the beginning of your life as an entrepreneur. Here are a few of the riches I reminded myself I had during my first, lean year:

- I can set my own schedule and take time to walk the dogs during the day.

- I can develop a network of fascinating fellow independent info pros through the Association of Independent Information Professionals.

- I can play music as loud as I want all day long.

- I can try out new ideas without running them by my boss for approval.

- I don't have to sit through committee meetings.

You can pull together your own list of things that gratify you as you work. The point is that, right now, you are rich in ways that you might not have appreciated. You are following your dream, you are creating a business from scratch, you are embarking on a new adventure, and you are challenging yourself in ways you might not have thought possible. Think about what you feel rich in right now, and focus on that when you start feeling discouraged. I found it helpful to read the daily essays in *Simple Abundance: A Daybook of Comfort and Joy*, by Sarah Ban Breathnach (Warner Books, 1995). This may be a bit New Age-y for your taste but find something that helps you focus on wealth beyond the bottom line.

Time Management, or "I Think I'll Take a Little Break Now"

Unstructured time is difficult for some people. You show up at your office in the morning and find none of the usual cues to buckle down and start working—no ringing phones, no voices from the next cubicle, no boss walking by asking about the report that is due at noon. Unless you have a client's project staring you in the face or some administrative tasks that absolutely have to be done, you will need to create your own structure for the day.

If you find that the days keep slipping away from you and you feel like you haven't accomplished anything by 5:30 PM, work on being mindful of how you spend your day. If you have to, keep a diary for a week and see how you spend every hour (most accounting software lets you track your activities during the day). At the end of the week, add up the time and see where it went. Some people find that working at home creates all kinds of little time sinks: "I'll just run out now and do the grocery shopping while the store isn't crowded." "I'll just take care of the dry cleaning and run a few loads of wash." "I'll just meet a friend for a quick cup of coffee." It's great to be able to get a load of wash done while you work, but if that turns into two hours of tidying up the house, then you are not working. Likewise, the flexibility to meet friends, go for a walk, and take care of personal errands during the week is a real benefit of being an independent info pro, but if you find that you are spending a quarter of your week this way, it is time to rethink your schedule.

"The Info Pro Is In" ... or Not

Even if you have great time management skills, it sometimes takes a while for your family, friends, and neighbors to realize that just because you are home all day doesn't mean you can drop everything and chat. When I started my business, I stopped answering my home telephone during the day. (Yes, you do need a separate phone for your business. See Chapter 9, Setting Up Your Business.) I found that I was getting too many calls from friends who thought that I had turned into a lady of leisure and had nothing to do all day long but chat on the phone. I cannot remember life before Caller ID; this has been one of the best ways of enabling me to focus on work during the day and pay attention to home during the evenings and weekends.

Info-entrepreneurs who work from home and have young children find that the issue of boundaries is particularly important. There are times when you have to put your head down and focus all your attention on getting a report written or a project started by the end of the day. And there are times when your child comes home from school and needs to tell you something (or just wants to re-connect). You will need to create some way to indicate to your family whether you can be interrupted, regardless of whether you look like you're working. Marjorie Desgrosseilliers, of SmartyPants Research, described the issue this way.

> I have had to train my husband and daughter that when the door is shut, I am At Work. The kind of work I do requires a lot of think time, which sometimes looks like sitting and staring off into space while I noodle through something. I had to teach them that this wasn't a sign that I'm not doing anything and am free to chat. Now they only come in my office if someone is bleeding or the house is on fire, or to bring me a cup of tea or something to eat. They're wonderful!

Set firm office hours. It seems that there are two kinds of independent info pros: some have difficulty sitting at their desk from 9 AM to 5 PM, working all alone; others have trouble leaving the office at the end of the day and tend to let their work take over all their available time. Figure out which type you are and develop a strategy for sticking to the office hours that you set for yourself.

If you can hear your office phone from the rest of the house, you might want to get in the habit of turning off the ringer when you leave for the day (but remember to turn it on again in the morning) so that you are not tempted to take after-hours calls. If your clients discover that you will pick up the phone at all hours of the day and night, they will call at all hours, and that way lies madness. Instead, really leave the office at the end of the day.

As a way to remind themselves of the fact that the office is closed, several home-based entrepreneurs I know toss a towel over their computer at the end of the day or the week. Other techniques that you may find helpful include:

- Committing to regular office hours with consistent starting and closing times

- Defining intense time blocks during which you don't check email, answer the phone, or allow yourself any distractions; a couple of those stretches each day help you stay fresh and focused

- Closing down your business at the end of the day; spend five or 10 minutes straightening up your desk, check voice mail one last time (not to return messages but to know what to address in the morning), line up your to-do list of specific actions you need to take for each of your current projects, and generally organize your office so that you can start working as soon as you return to the office

- Being mindful of how you describe what you do, using business language such as, "I run a business" rather than "I work from home," or "I have meetings most of the week, but I could stop work around 4 PM tomorrow," rather than "Sure, drop by any time. I don't have anything going on"

Creating a Good Office Environment

I talk about the nuts and bolts of creating your office environment in Chapter 9, Setting Up Your Business. Now let's think of the ambience of your office beyond the desk and computer. Look around the room and think about what you need to make it feel right. Pictures of your family? A beautiful bowl you picked up on vacation? A comfy chair to sit in while catching up on your professional reading? Some hardy houseplants? You are going to be spending at least a third of your life in the office so you might as well make it as inviting, pleasant, and soothing to you as possible.

My first office was in the basement of my house, with one small window that looked out onto a busy alley with trash trucks rumbling by all day. Because I didn't get much natural light, I installed full spectrum lightbulbs that replicated natural light. I hung a calendar with pictures of the Rocky Mountains, where I would go backpacking, to serve as a reminder that I do have a life. I brought in a funky old couch so that my dogs and I could curl up on it when I had reading to do. My office setting has changed a lot since then, but I always have a skylight, a comfy chair, and a place for the dogs to nap.

Another part of your work environment is your *mental* space. Just as I make sure my office space is conducive to creativity, I make sure my head is clear. I sometimes get caught in that hamster wheel that repeats all the unhelpful messages in my head, over and over again, and when I see that happening, I physically change my position or setting. This is when the dogs get an extra walk, or I focus on writing a few blog entries, or I do some office filing—something to get me back on track. Christine Hamilton-Pennell, of Growing Local Economies, told me about a couple of techniques she has found useful. "I remind myself that even though I may feel angry, scared, or frustrated, I can still be successful. The two aren't necessarily entwined. And when I have too many deadlines and am having trouble focusing, I remind myself that I can still do the next thing. That helps me look at actions I can take right now to move forward."

Going on Vacation

Yes, you will go on vacation—or you'll go crazy. Some independent info pros like to tack on a few vacation days at the end of a business trip or attendance at a professional conference. I find that difficult on several levels. On a practical level, it means I have to pack two wardrobes—one for business and one for play—which doubles the luggage. I also tend to go into marketing overdrive while I am at a conference, and it is hard for me to switch from business professional to tourist overnight. Finally, by the end of a business trip, I am ready to get back in the office and get caught up with email and backlogged work.

On the other hand, these mini-vacations can be a nice way to get a few days of relaxation without the hassle of planning a separate trip. You have already written off the travel costs as a business expense so your only nondeductible expenses are the extra days of hotel and food. And, let's face it, professional conferences are often held at nice destinations.

However you arrange your vacation, you will need to plan what to do with your office while you are away. During business trips, you might check voice mail and email throughout the day and subcontract out any work that comes in. However, trying to do this during a vacation is no way to experience a vacation—you never really let go of your business, which means you aren't getting much of the benefit of, you know, *time off.*

You have several options for taking care of clients while you are away. Whichever you choose, be sure that you manage your callers' expectations. One is simply to change your voice mail greeting to tell callers when you will be back in the office and when they can expect a return call. You don't want clients to hear the standard, "I couldn't get to your call, but leave a message," and then not get a call back for a week. If you are concerned about alerting burglars that your home is unoccupied, leave a message like "I'm attending a local conference this week but won't be able to handle any calls until Friday" or even "The office is closed this week" without any indication that you will be away from town.

"Call My Associate"

The option I usually choose when I am traveling and know I won't be able to keep up with work is to have a trusted colleague handle any calls that come in. We agree ahead of time on what hourly rate to charge, how to handle calls from new clients, any special needs that existing clients may have, and so on. I then leave a message on my voice mail saying, "My office is closed this week. If you have any urgent research needs, please call my associate ..." and I provide her name and number. The advantage of referring callers to someone else is that they can talk with a live person rather than just leaving a message and waiting a week for a reply. The disadvantage is that I am sending callers to someone else with the inevitable risk that they may decide that they would rather do business with my colleague than with me. That is a risk I am willing to take, especially since the independent info pros to whom I refer callers when I travel are scrupulous about sending subsequent calls from my clients back to me.

"Here's My Password"

Linda Cooper, an information consultant in Pennsylvania, takes a different approach. When she was running an independent info pro business and had to leave the office, she gave her voice mail and email passwords to a colleague who would check for messages several times a day and follow up with any important matters. If you are comfortable with this arrangement, it may be the best solution because it appears more seamless to your clients. Your callers don't have to make another phone call; someone returns their calls or emails and can handle their information needs, and you don't have a voice mail and email box overflowing with messages when you return.

There are also virtual assistant companies that offer this type of service. They have the advantage of a lower cost than paying a colleague for his or her time; virtual assistants often charge no more than $25 to $30 an hour. However, they will not be able to answer questions about your service or handle any rush requests from your clients. If all you need is someone to return email and voice mail messages in a professional manner and tell your clients when you will be back in the office, then a virtual assistant may be a good choice.

"Good Morning, Research"

If it is very important that your clients reach a live person when they call you, another option is to arrange to have your calls automatically forwarded to a colleague. There was a period of a few years when I had a lot of clients who needed work done within 24 hours, and they did not want to wait until I got back in the office, nor did they want to have to call someone else for the work. Several colleagues had similar fast-turnaround clients, and we set up an arrangement to handle each other's calls when one of us was out. We all got in the habit of answering our phones "Research" instead of with our name; this more generic greeting meant that when Karen's calls were forwarded to me, her caller wasn't disconcerted by having someone answer the phone with an unfamiliar name. Of course, once the clients started talking, I could figure out that this was one of Karen's clients, and I would handle the job as she had instructed me and would let Karen bill the client when she returned. This arrangement can work well if you have a colleague who is in the office most of the day and who can handle the type of research your clients usually ask for, and if you can arrange some way of answering the phones so that clients who have had their calls forwarded do not immediately assume they have the wrong number.

"I'm Outta Here"

Alex Kramer, of Kramer Research, is of the opinion that sometimes it is best to just shut down the office. When she is out of town, either on business or vacation, she usually leaves a voice mail message telling callers that the office is closed and the date that she will return. She found that her client base tended to assume that the person to whom she referred callers when she was away was, in fact, someone who worked for her. They would call the colleague directly the next time they needed research, and Alex would lose the client's business. Now she may have an intern answer phone calls or faxes that arrive while she is gone, and she provides guidelines on how to handle any assignments. Otherwise, her clients just wait until she returns.

Use whichever approach works best for your clients. If your clients typically contact you via email, you might want to set up an auto reply that tells them you are away. See the sidebar "Email Vacation Message" for some thoughts on this approach. If you are not sure how your clients will respond to your planned method for handling their business while you are out of town, ask two or three of your best clients for their reaction and suggestions.

Email Vacation Message

Email vacation messages, or auto responders, are settings on your email software or on your internet service provider's mail server that generate an automatic response to every incoming email message or just messages from addresses you specify. You can tell senders when you will be back and, if you want, whom to call in your absence.

Be aware, however, that deployed inappropriately, an auto responder can earn you infamy. Anyone who has been on an email discussion list has seen messages like this: "I'm out of the office until February 15. If you need immediate help, contact Susan Smith at x1254 or Jim Brown at x4327, or go to the intranet site at private.acme.com for more information." The message might as well say, "Hi, I'm clueless about the impact of my vacation email message on others."

If you subscribe to any email discussion lists, keep the instructions on how to suspend your subscription while you are gone and make sure you put your lists on hold before you set up an auto reply. Otherwise, every time anyone posts a message to a list you subscribe to, they may get a copy of your out-of-office reply—and that may result in your banishment from the list or at least a scolding from the administrator. Check the auto-respond instructions on your email software or ISP's site; some allow you to specify that your auto-respond message be sent just once to any given sender, or no more frequently than once a week. That way, you don't bombard a discussion list or colleague with "gone fishing" messages. I manage a couple of professional discussion lists, and during holiday seasons, I handle six or eight out-of-control auto responders a day. Trust me; the list administrators will appreciate your care in setting up your message.

Business Coaches: Help, I Need Somebody

If you have issues to work out in your personal life, you might see a therapist or counselor. If you need help working out business issues, a business coach could be a godsend. Jan Davis of JT Research has worked with a business coach and described her experience this way:

> Business coaches get into the psychology of running a business—the personal baggage we may bring to the business as well as the issues of running our business in synch with our personal goals and values. They hold us accountable for the priorities we set, such as taking time off, raising rates, and saying "no." I found the experience of having a weekly phone conversation with a business coach very worthwhile. Like therapy, there were things I learned about myself that I didn't necessarily like but that I needed to change in order to run a business harmoniously. Having a business coach really is like having a business therapist.

Note that business coaches aren't mentors in the sense of unpaid guides or advisors. Rather, they are professionals with expertise and skill in helping people identify and think through the things that are keeping them from achieving their full professional potential. Finding a business coach is often a matter of word of mouth, asking colleagues whom they would recommend. Note that I offer strategic business coaching services for both new and long-time info-entrepreneurs. You can find more information about my coaching services at batesinfo.com/coaching.

Life Lessons Learned

◆ Focus on the things that enrich your life. What are the less tangible benefits you receive every day from being an independent info pro?

◆ Bring to your office reminders of the rest of your life—things that relax and inspire you.

◆ Create enough structure in your schedule that you can leave the office behind at the end of the day knowing that you spent your time well.

◆ Teach your family and friends that, even though you're at home, you're also at work.

◆ Find the right setup that lets you truly leave the office behind when you go on vacation.

Running the Business

Chapter 13

Managing Your Clients

Clients are strange creatures whom you love but who sometimes drive you crazy. If you didn't have clients, you would be out of business, but how do you know what kinds of clients to cultivate, how to manage their expectations and keep them happy, and how to handle those occasional situations in which everything seems to blow up?

Monogamy Versus Playing the Field

No, I am not offering couples counseling or marriage advice about the relative merits of monogamy and spouse-swapping—just a recommendation that, when it comes to clients, the more the merrier. It is great to have some big clients who consistently call you for large projects, who refer others to you, and who pay you promptly. Would that we were all blessed with many such clients. But relying on one or two big clients for all or most of your revenue can be a risky business. Here's why:

- Without diversity in your client base, you are much more vulnerable to an economic downturn because a dip that hits one client will probably affect everyone in the same industry. Downturn or not, similar clients will have similar seasonal fluctuations in their business, which means that certain times of year will be particularly lean for you in terms of cash flow. If you have clients in a number of industries or at least a variety of types of clients (large corporations, small consulting firms, and so on), it is much more likely that at least some portion of your customer base will need your services all year-round.

- If most of your work is for a single client, you may even be discounting your hourly rates in exchange for the steady income. But your client isn't really doing you a favor by giving you all that work. It means that you are, in essence, providing the client with an employee who doesn't need benefits, paid vacations, a retirement fund, or a steady paycheck. And you are running the risk of being classified for tax purposes as a de facto employee. That's not a good thing—you will lose the ability to write off your office expenses, and your "employer" is hit with a tax bill for its portion of employee taxes. See Chapter 9, Setting Up Your Business, for more on this issue.

- If one or two big clients take up most of your time, you are less inclined to think about marketing and building up your base of other clients and prospects. "Who cares?" you ask, "I've got a steady gig." Unfortunately, all good gigs end eventually, and usually with little or no warning. Your contact person will change jobs or get laid off. The client will have a budget freeze and eliminate contractors, despite contractual obligations or assurances to the contrary. The department you work for will be reorganized out of existence or into another group that doesn't need your services. Stuff happens, and unless you have been busily building new client relationships during the good times, you will find yourself with no work and no prospects when times turn lean.

- Limiting yourself to one or two large clients means limiting your vision of what you are capable of doing. All you see are the skills and abilities that your one or two clients draw on. Most of the growth in my business, in terms of services I offer and types of work I do, has sprung from a client saying, "Hey, I don't know if you can do this, but I really need someone to do such and such." You are far less likely to hear that from a client who has you pigeonholed as "the person we pay to do 25 hours of X a week."

The bottom line is that, while monogamy may be the way to a happy marriage, don't plan to marry any one client. Instead, think of yourself as a charming, attractive singleton, interested in going out for dinner and a movie but not in a full-time commitment any time soon. Don't let one or two clients monopolize your time; there's too much at risk.

Is Any Client Too Small?

You have probably seen those ads for general contractors and repair people—"no project too large or too small." It's true that I have never had a job too big for one of them to handle, but I have a heck of a time finding someone to come and do all the little jobs around my house—repair a faucet, rewire a light fixture, or paint a closet. Whenever I hear a contractor complain about a slowdown in work, I wonder why he is not willing to pick up a day's revenue, at least, doing all the handyman jobs I have accumulated.

Independent info pros aren't looking to fix leaky toilets or patch the hole in the roof, but we do have to figure out whether small clients are worth the trouble. My policy is that small jobs are worth it if I think I can cultivate the client into becoming more valuable over time, or if I have the free time and this small job won't displace a larger project. (By "small," I mean a job that takes no more than an hour or two and that isn't likely to provide any follow-up work; examples include looking up which U.S. Congressional committees have oversight over the Federal Aviation Administration or a quick search to see what newspapers reviewed a particular book.) Perhaps they will be a source of repeat business or good referral sources; maybe I can turn the small job into a stepping stone for bigger projects. It sounds cold-hearted to assess potential clients this way, but you have to work one of these angles; it does not make much sense to attract clients who offer nothing but low-end one-off jobs. The cost of attracting a client is significant; if you cannot recoup that expense with repeat business or steady referrals, you are losing money.

How small is too small? In part, the answer comes down to the type of work you do. Manual research such as public records research or document delivery services are sometimes simpler to juggle so you can take on a lot of little jobs and turn them into a steady source of income. Online research and telephone projects, on the other hand, require a certain amount of overhead and uninterrupted time, and most require more than an hour or two to complete. Of course, if you charge a two-hour minimum for online or telephone research, then even those small jobs can add up.

Sometimes, doing work for a small client or one that you cannot charge your regular rate is better than doing nothing. Small jobs can give you valuable practice in estimating projects, negotiating with clients, and writing executive summaries of your research results. You can always ask smaller clients if they can recommend any colleagues for you to contact, and you can include their positive feedback (with permission, of course) on your website or in your marketing package. Alex Kramer, the owner of Kramer Research, puts it this way, "The bottom line is that the value in business is always more than just numbers. Looking at any one client solely on how much you can bill him often underestimates his value."

Working for the Cause

I know of a number of independent info pros who will work for nonprofit organizations they support, or for a local startup business, or who will work on a project that is interesting but doesn't pay well, with the understanding that, when the info pro's time gets tight, the small client will have to wait. One reason to take on this kind of work is to keep you from going crazy when the phone does not ring; another is that it is satisfying to be able to provide your services to a nonprofit cause that you care about. When you don't have a lot of spare cash to give, offering your research expertise is a great way to support an organization in a tangible way. And remember that even nonprofits often have board members and trustees who are executives in their "real" jobs, and you will get to know them and show them the services you provide.

Tire-Kickers, Lookie-Loos, and Low-Ballers

I think we all know who tire-kickers are: They are the people who wander through the used car lot, kicking tires, and tying up a salesperson's time without intending to actually buy a car. "Lookie-loo" is the name given by real estate agents to the folks who love to wander through open houses and look around, but who have no interest in purchasing real estate. And low-ballers are the clients who always work on getting a "better deal"—who try to negotiate down any project and get the most they can from you for less than you want to charge.

I can almost guarantee that, within a month after you have opened for business, you will get a phone call from one of these characters. They will talk and talk and talk, they will ask you all about your services and imply that they are just about to buy … but they have to shop around a bit first. Your challenge is figuring out how to get off the phone gracefully without offending the caller or wasting your time with someone who is not going to turn into a good client.

My solution is to watch the clock. I have gotten into the habit of always noting the time at the beginning of a phone call. If we haven't gotten down to talking about the specifics of the job and the budget within 10 or 15 minutes, I assume that I am dealing with a tire-kicker. At that point, I will tell her that it sounds like a fascinating project, but it would be best if she could outline her needs and email me a description of the job so that I can review it and submit a proposal. The message that comes across, without my having to put it in so many words, is that this is going to cost money and we need to get down to business. As often as not, I've found that the tire-kicker will simply go away rather than go to the effort of writing up a description for a project that may be no more than a gleam in her eye.

How do you deal with someone who is shopping around for the lowest bidder? Easy—bid high. Who needs a client who only hires you because you're cheap? This is a client who will be gone as soon as he finds someone cheaper, and clients like this can turn into clients who don't pay their bills. If the caller tells you, or implies, that he has contacted other info pros, you may wish to end the conversation right there. My usual response is, "Well, it sounds like you have already identified several excellent companies. Rather than tie up your time talking about this project, I'd recommend you just go with one of the people you have already called." If that doesn't work and he insists on getting an estimate from you, give him a budget that is as high as you can name with a straight face and tell him that you require prepayment of at least 50 percent of the not-to-exceed budget. If he really does want you and comes up with the deposit, then you have yourself a new client. If not, he will go away, and you won't be bothered by him again. Either way, you were polite, gracious, and professional.

Free Samples, Anyone?

Prospective clients sometimes ask independent info pros for samples of their work. Occasionally this makes sense; usually, though, you are better off responding to the request by addressing the underlying hesitancy that your prospect is probably feeling. Is she worried that you won't be able to meet her needs? Did she have a bad experience with another researcher? Does she think that all you will do is surf the web and send her some URLs? Since most info-entrepreneurs offer customized information services, a sample project will not reflect the added value we can provide to each client. Focus your conversation on the kinds of services you provide and on how you can tailor the deliverable to just what your prospect needs.

Amelia Kassel, owner of MarketingBase, commented, "The point of providing a sample of work is supposed to be to make a sale. But my experience has been that it never works in this profession. The client will make a purchasing decision based on other aspects of how you present yourself. These factors include personal chemistry (a very important aspect of business), your background, your reputation (including whether you've been referred by someone the client respects), and so on. In my experience, anyone requesting a sample is usually wasting your time and is probably not a serious or qualified buyer."

Providing a sample project does make sense in one particular situation—when you offer, as part of your product mix, standardized, relatively low-cost, high-volume information services. If you provide fixed-price company profiles, for example, or news updates on a specific industry, you might want to show clients what they would receive for their money. The danger, however, is that by showing prospective clients one cookie-cutter product or service, you limit their expectations of what you are capable of doing. If you do furnish a sample of such a work product, be sure to emphasize that you also provide higher-end, customized, value-added services.

Sample projects should carry no indication of the client for whom you did the work. Going still further, you might have to change the description of the project or other particulars to ensure that competitors cannot identify the client by the nature of the request itself. Pick a project that sounds intriguing but that could have been done for just about any client. Avoid technologies, marketing ideas, and issues that are closely identified with a particular client. Depending on the agreement you have with your client, you may have to get permission before sending out even a sanitized version of the work you did for them.

Let's *Not* Do Lunch

One of the advantages of marketing to clients outside your local area is that they seldom expect you to get together for meetings or for lunch. Even though face-to-face contact is nice, it is also a significant investment of your time, when you count the time it takes to get dressed in your meet-the-client clothes, travel to the meeting, travel home, and change back into your home-office clothes.

If a prospective client asks you to meet her in her office to talk about a possible project, think twice before accepting. For one thing, you almost certainly will not be able to charge for this time since you haven't started working for the prospect. And look at how much time you are investing in marketing to one person. Unless you are almost positive that you will walk out of the meeting with a signed contract, you are gambling with one important asset—your valuable time. Agreeing to what is, in essence, a sales call sends a message that you have time on your hands and that you can be summoned into the office as needed. Keep control of your time. You could respond with something like this: "Although I'd love the chance to meet face to face, I'm quite tied up with other projects at the moment. Is it possible that we could schedule a telephone interview at a time that works best for you?" And finally, the time you would invest in this single sales call could be spent doing other, more efficient marketing efforts that put you in front of a large number of people at once. See Section Three, Marketing, for more thoughts on cost-effective marketing techniques.

Of course, if the request for an in-person meeting comes from an existing client, your approach may change. Does the client expect to pay for your time, portal to portal (that is, from the moment you leave your office to the moment you return)? I try to pitch every face-to-face meeting with a client as consulting time and bill accordingly. If I cannot charge for the time, I make sure my client introduces me to as many other people within the office as possible. The more people who know me, who have my business card (and, more importantly, whose business cards I have), the more I can count on keeping this client, even if my original contact moves on to another job.

The bottom line is to think about whether the meeting will pay off, either immediately or soon. One-on-one meetings are not an efficient marketing tool, but they can be a good way to cement a relationship with an existing client.

Handling RFPs

It is great when a client calls and says, "I want you to do this project for me. Just tell me how much it'll cost." For most independent info pros, negotiating with a client regarding the scope or budget of a project does not involve bidding against other info pros—your clients call you because they are already sold on your ability to do the work.

However, there will come a time in your business when you encounter a Request for Proposal (RFP). Government agencies are often required to competitively bid all contracts with outside vendors. Some corporations also have formal bidding procedures in which at least three or four contractors must be solicited for any project over a certain size. Responding to RFPs, almost by definition, puts you in a situation where you are bidding against other providers; your odds of winning that contract are, all other things being equal, at best one in three. And you have no assurance that the organization issuing the RFP will award the contract to any of the bidders. If all the bids come in higher than expected, the organization may simply decide to cancel the project. Given the amount of work involved in responding to an RFP—they usually require extensive descriptions of what you intend to do, how, and when—you are investing a significant chunk of time without any assurance that it will result in a paying job. But, to be fair, let's walk through the advantages and disadvantages of responding to RFPs.

Advantages of RFPs

- Contracts that are awarded through RFPs are usually substantial.

- You have spelled out all the particulars of the project ahead of time so any add-ons can be billed separately, thus helping stop "mission creep."

- Even if the person you originally deal with leaves the organization, your contract remains intact.

- If you always have a number of RFPs in the pipeline, you have the chance of at least one contract coming through at any given time.

Disadvantages of RFPs

- RFPs often require extensive descriptions of your services that can take days to prepare.

- The odds of being awarded a contract through a competitive RFP are not high; you will lose more RFPs than you win.

- There is no guarantee that anyone will be awarded a contract through an RFP; the agency may decide that no proposals were acceptable.

- RFPs are sometimes poorly written, but bidders have very little leeway in modifying the proposal.

If you do decide to respond to RFPs and you live in the U.S., you may find it useful to consult the Small Business Administration's site (SBA; www.sba.gov). Its Government Contracting section (www.sba.gov/GC) includes a collection of resources to help companies contract with the federal government. In Canada, potential government suppliers have access to a wide range of services on the Canada Business's website (www.canadabusiness.ca), under "Selling to Governments." The U.K. website

Government Contracts the Easy Way

Bidding for government contracts can be a time-consuming process, but there are other ways to land contracts with the government—depending, of course, on which government it is. Instead of looking for solicitations for bids, try to focus on finding contacts within government agencies that need your services. In a sense, you can treat the government like any other prospective client. Identify an agency's information needs. Figure out how you can solve those needs. Write a one-page description of what you offer and what problems you can solve. Look through the agency's website to identify who is most likely to need your services, recognize your value, and authorize a contract. Get on the phone and confirm the name, title, and address of each of your prospects. Then send each a personalized letter spelling all this out.

After all this, you still may have to respond to RFPs, but if you stay in contact with your prospects and talk with them about what they need and how you can meet those needs, it is much more likely that the RFP will be written with your services as the standard against which other bids will be judged.

for everything you need to know about bidding for public sector contracts is Supply2.gov.uk (supply2.gov.uk).

And if you decide that you are not interested in responding to RFPs, consider using the response that Amelia Kassel, owner of MarketingBase, gives when asked to submit a bid: "MarketingBase does not bid but instead looks for a fit between ourselves and potential clients. We are not in the business of 'competing'; rather, we base our success on working with clients who understand our particular methodology and reputation, and who consider us an excellent choice for their situation." This is a very elegant way of declining to bid but still welcoming business.

The Art of Proposal Writing

Although responding to RFPs may not be an efficient use of your time, writing a proposal for a client is a different matter. In this case, you have already been talking about a project, you agree on the scope of what is involved, and you prepare a formal proposal explaining what you will do and what it will cost. Such proposals are generally completed in a noncompetitive environment—that is, you are not bidding against anyone else for this job. Instead, you are formalizing the relationship, defining all aspects of the job, and getting a written commitment from your client.

I am mindful, though, of the late Sue Rugge's advice. She cautioned independent info pros against calling the proposal a "contract" or writing it in legalese with lots of whereases and party-of-the-first-parts, since that might trigger an automatic review by the organization's lawyers … and we know how long that process can take. It might also scare the client, who suddenly thinks, "Gee, what am I getting into here? Perhaps I should just reconsider the whole thing." A signed proposal or letter of agreement, while it does not contain all the dotted I's and crossed T's of a formal contract, indicates the understanding between you and your client—you will do the work and your client will pay you for it. Call it a statement of work, or a project description … just don't call it a contract.

A proposal serves several purposes. It defines the scope of the project, which ensures not only that you and your client are in accord but also that you can charge separately for any work the client requests that falls outside the original scope. The proposal also serves as a marketing tool; if you write it well, your description of the project will help answer the question, "Why should I pay you that much for your work? What am I getting for it?" And it articulates your payment requirements, which is particularly important if you require prepayment or payments at certain stages of the work.

Proposal Must-Haves

You will need a template of some sort that you can use for all your formal proposals and that you can modify for each situation. It is a wise investment to have your attorney review it; just make sure it stays written in non-legalese to avoid intimidating the client and to enable you to tweak it as necessary. The proposal can be as short or as long as you want, but it should include the following:

- Outline of all aspects of the project: Spell out the questions you are addressing or the problems you are there to fix, described in as much detail as you and the client think necessary.

- Description of deliverables: Are you providing a written report, a spreadsheet, a PowerPoint presentation, a database, an in-person consultation, or something else?

- Time frame and due date: If this is contingent on receipt of prepayment, indicate the total length of the project instead of an actual deadline.

- Whether the work will be done at your client's site or at your office: You may not need to spell this out, unless you want to ensure access to the client's office.

- The resources you will need from the client: If your client expects you to use online information services for which he has an enterprisewide subscription, you need to spell out how you will get access to those services.

- Budget: You need to provide either a not-to-exceed figure or a description of what you estimate the project will cost and a timetable for reviewing the total cost.

- Terms of payment: Spell out how much you require before work can begin and how soon after completion of the project you require the final payment.

- Liability statement or disclaimer: Ask your lawyer to write this in clear terms that a non-lawyer can understand.

- Copyright limitations: If appropriate, spell out that you are providing information for one-time use by the client and that posting the material on an intranet or redistributing multiple copies must be negotiated separately.

- "Sell-by" date for the proposal: Specify how long the quote is valid, lest someone comes back in a year asking you to perform the work at this year's fee structure.

- A reason to use you: Include at least a couple of sentences explaining why the client can rest assured that hiring you would be a great idea. Even if you know there are no competing bids, you are still competing against "no thanks."

Going Through the Steps

The larger the project, the more important it is that you estimate the budget properly. A 10 percent miscalculation on a $500 job only costs you $50; the same miscalculation on a $10,000 would cost you $1,000 … and that hurts. Chapter 15, Setting Rates and Fees, goes into more detail about pricing; here I am addressing the particular challenge of pricing a large project.

The technique that has worked best for me is to work simultaneously on scoping out the project and pricing it. I open a fresh document and start brainstorming. First, I write down the deliverable—a report of such-and-such, including X profiles of individual what-have-you's. Then I start listing all the steps that will be required to get there. I often find that as I think of one step, I realize that this will require another prior step and so on. It's an iterative process.

Recently, I wrote a proposal to provide an analysis of the most effective way to market a new soft drink to teenagers. Starting with that as my deliverable, I eventually identified the following steps involved in getting to the final product.

- Quickly review ready-reference web resources to get me started
- Write up a search map with ideas on terms to use, sources to search, and key players
- Conduct more extensive web research
- Conduct research on appropriate fee-based online services
- Review retrieved material
- ID key trends, issues, focus, and outline the sections for the report
- Fill in as much as I can from results of search
- Identify holes, new areas that need exploration, and continue research
- Incorporate additional material into report
- Create tables, graphs, pull quotes to break up the text
- Write an executive summary
- Allow the result to sit for a few hours before final review

Of course, your list will be different for each project; the important thing is to get to the level of detail necessary for an accurate estimate. After I had this list compiled,

I estimated how much time each of the items would take, multiplied that by my hourly rate, added my estimate on the online expenses, and then added 15 percent to the total budget to cover the unexpected. Then I let that number simmer in the back of my head for a while (24 hours if possible, but at least an hour or two). When I review it, I consider what that total number looks like in the context of my client's total spending. I think about how much expertise I bring to this job. I consider the value of my deliverable to my client. At this point, I have usually talked myself into adding another 15 percent to the bottom line. I take a deep breath, compose a couple of paragraphs that specifically talk about the tangible value my deliverable will provide to my client. For example, it will guide an executive in a strategic decision. Or it will provide the direction for a major communications effort. Or it will determine whether a new product is viable. And if at this point in the process you don't know what your client will be using your research for, just ask. How can you fully address your client's information needs without understanding what is driving those needs?

Be sure you save the outline of your work plan and estimated hours. Once you begin the project, monitor your time so that you do not expend too much time doing the research, with no time left for all the added value.

A Sample Proposal

```
A World of Information Inc.
              123 Main St.
     Buena Vista, CO 81211
             719.123.4567
```

[date]

```
Pat Adams
The Denton Corp.
123 First St.
Portland, OR 97204
```

Dear Pat:

It was good talking with you today about your project for the strategic direction committee. My understanding is that you will be using this research to determine whether to expand in the widget market or shift the financial commitment to other areas of Denton's business. Following is a proposal for our research and analysis.

Scope of Work

A World of Information Inc. will provide the following research services to The Denton Corp.:

- Identify the five major companies that provide widgets in direct competition to Denton's Widgelator
- Provide company information, description of products, distribution channels, and samples of widgets, if possible, of Widgelator competitors
- Develop SWOT (Strengths/Weaknesses/Opportunities/ Threats) analysis of Denton and its competitors Determine trends and forecasts in the widget market

My understanding is that we will focus initially on the North American market and that you would like forecasts for five years out, if possible.

Research Methodology

We expect to conduct research using several professional online services, both the open and deep web, and social media to identify the key players, their market strategies, and trends in the industry. We will also contact the key companies directly, without disclosing information about the client for whom we are working and while abiding by the Code of Professional Business Practices of the Association of Independent Information Professionals (www.aiip.org).

The business analysts at A World of Information collectively have more than 30 years of research experience. We have worked extensively with clients in the manufacturing sector, providing services ranging from market feasibility studies to SWOT analyses of competitors and benchmarking for best practices. Our principals have given presentations on market research at conferences throughout North America. We are prepared to commit all the resources necessary to provide you with the knowledge you need to decide the direction of the Widgelator line.

Deliverables

An industry analysis, company profiles, a discussion of trends in the market, a SWOT analysis of Denton and its five major competitors, and an assessment of the viability of the widget market will be prepared in Microsoft Word, along with an executive summary in the form of presentation slides. In addition to our report, we will include the full text of all the materials consulted during this project. The report will be delivered electronically; the product samples will be sent via overnight courier as we obtain them.

Budget and Time Frame

The total budget for this project will not exceed $20,000. Prepayment of $8,000 is required; work will begin upon receipt of the payment and will be completed within four weeks. The remainder of the budget will be billed at the conclusion of the project. Payment terms are net 30 days. We accept corporate checks and all major credit cards.

Liability and Copyright Statement

A World of Information, Inc. shall make a good faith effort to provide services and work product that are of a high quality and that meet The Denton Corp.'s needs and expectations. Every attempt is made to ensure accuracy; however, A World of Information has no control over the quality of the information retrieved from the various sources used, so we cannot guarantee the accuracy or completeness of the material provided.

The report provided is a work for hire; you retain the copyright to the material and may use it for whatever purpose needed. The background material is protected by copyright. If you plan to distribute copies or make the background material provided on an intranet or website, you must negotiate payment with the copyright owners. We can facilitate the licensing fees; this work would be billed at our normal consulting rate of $185/hour.

```
    This quote is valid for 45 days.
    Pat, if you have any questions about this proposal,
please don't hesitate to call me at 719.123.4567. I will
check back with you at the end of the week to see if
you need any additional information.

Best regards,
Robin
```

Get It in Writing?

Some independent info pros write up a proposal or statement of work for each job they do. Others—and I am in this latter group—only use written proposals for first-time clients and for projects that exceed a certain threshold in terms of either budget or complexity. One consideration is whether the client needs something signed before the work begins in order to get your invoice processed. Another factor is your gut instinct; if your client sounds like he may not understand the scope and limitations of the project or if you have any concerns about whether the client will pay your invoice, a written contract is essential. And if you require prepayment of all or a portion of the not-to-exceed budget before you will begin work, you need a written proposal.

If the project isn't big enough to justify a formal proposal and you work with the client regularly, it is still a good idea to at least confirm the request via email or fax. Your confirmation might be no more than the following:

```
Susan:
It was nice talking with you today. Glad to hear that
the speech you gave was so well-received. This is to
confirm that you want me to see what I can find on the
current state of K-12 math and science education. I will
email this information to you by close of business on
Friday, and the total cost won't exceed $1,200.
    As always, thanks for calling me. It's always a pleas-
ure working with you.
Best regards,
Robin
```

It's not fancy, but it reiterates the key elements of the project—subject, budget, and deadline—to ensure that you and the client are in agreement. Some info pros ask their clients to either initial a copy and fax it back or reply to your email indicating that they agree with the description of and budget for the project. It depends on your comfort level and your clients' schedules. I find this additional step a burden, and I want to offer my clients as frictionless an interaction as possible. On the other hand, if you have no prior experience with a particular client, it makes sense to be a bit more formal. It sends the message that you take this business relationship seriously and expect your client to do the same, particularly when it comes to processing your invoice.

When to Say "No"

I know—it sounds wrong to turn down work. However, sometimes it just doesn't pay to accept a job, and it is better to recognize this ahead of time than to try to extricate yourself from a mess later. Here are some situations that have "Just Say No" written all over them. If you find yourself in one of these scenarios, read Chapter 16, Subcontracting, or I'll Scratch Your Back If You Scratch Mine, to find out how to pass the work along to someone better suited for the project:

- Subject specialization: No one can do all kinds of research well, and we all have limited expertise outside our primary subject area. If you are a legal researcher, for example, you probably are not proficient in chemical research as well. If your expertise is in radiology, you probably should not take on research that requires in-depth analysis of financial statements. The time it takes you to get up to speed in an entirely new area will far exceed the hours you can justifiably bill your client and, frankly, you just may not have the background knowledge to do a competent job in an entirely unfamiliar area.

- Time crunch: There are only 24 hours in a day, and you do not want to spend every one of them working. Sometimes a client will call with a project that you simply do not have time to do, unless you work around the clock. Take it from someone who has tried the work-all-night trick— you can't do a decent job at 2 AM, regardless of how many cups of coffee you drink. Suppose a client calls late on a Friday afternoon and asks if you can get the results to him by Monday morning. Sure, you could work all weekend, but the message you are sending to your client is, "I'm available whenever you need me. No need to plan ahead; I'm always ready to drop what I'm doing for you." That sounds very customer-friendly, but it also means that you are willing to give up any free time you have—and that is a first-class ticket to burnout. Instead, train your clients to plan ahead and not assume that you will routinely give up your weekend for their last-minute requests. Believe it or not, they will find a way to call you earlier in the process once they learn that that's what it takes.

- Client conflict of interest. This is a tough call: If you work for one company, can you also work for its competitor? It depends on what the project entails, how much access you have to proprietary information, and whether you have signed a contract with a client that forbids working for its competitors. Use the "headlines test": How would you feel if tomorrow's lead story in the *New York Times* was that you were providing research services to both Toyota and Volvo? If you are simply gathering public information, my gut tells me you do not have a conflict. On the other hand, if the work you are doing for Toyota involves an intimate knowledge of its proprietary designs for new vehicles, you shouldn't be doing similar work for Volvo. (See Chapter 17, Ethics and Legalities, for more discussion of conflicts of interest and client confidentiality.)

- Personal conflict: If you are a strict vegetarian and get a call from the Veal Processors Association, you might want to turn down the work. If you believe that abortion is wrong, you probably don't want to take on a project from Planned Parenthood. But handle your refusal professionally; there is no need to go into the details of why you want to have nothing to do with a prospective client. All you have to say is, "I'm sorry, but I have a conflict of interest and can't do work for your organization." Period. Let the prospective client think that the conflict is with an existing client rather than with your conscience. It is not worth getting into an argument about why you find their stand morally repugnant; remember, the person you are talking with may eventually change jobs and call you from an organization that you would be glad to work with.

Do You Like Me? Really?

We all like hearing compliments, and very few people actively solicit criticism. On the other hand, nothing is more frustrating to a business owner than a client who is unhappy with the work and simply takes his business elsewhere, instead of giving the business owner a chance to rectify the problem. We cannot resolve a problem unless we hear about it and, human nature being what it is, people are generally reluctant to complain about service. If you aren't pleased with your accountant, aren't you more inclined to simply move your business elsewhere than to call her up and tell her how annoyed you are when she doesn't return phone calls promptly or has a too-brusque manner? If you did speak up, you might find that she was in the middle of an office move or just had a baby—whatever the reason for your dissatisfaction, try giving your vendor a chance to make the situation better.

Our challenge as business owners is to encourage these complaints. Always follow your projects up with a phone call in a day or two to make sure the client received the material and to see if any questions have arisen or if she needs additional information. Some info-entrepreneurs also follow up a week or so after the end of the project with an electronic survey or a mailed copy with a self-addressed stamped envelope to see if the client is satisfied, needs anything else, wants any follow-up work done, and so on. The way you elicit comments and complaints isn't as important as the fact that you do it.

If you feel queasy at the thought of eliciting criticism, think about similar situations in your personal life. We have all had experiences where a product or service was quite unsatisfactory, but the company was so responsive in rectifying the problem that we were left with a positive impression at the end. Everyone understands that life happens and that sometimes we make mistakes. The critical point is the next step—identifying the problem and fixing it by bringing the end result up to the expected level of quality.

The Project From Hell

What happens when you *don't* say no when you should? You can wind up embroiled in the "project from Hell." Established info pros have all, at one point or another, accepted a job that their gut told them to turn down. The result? The client is angry because he didn't get what he expected, or he thinks the bill is excessive, or he wants you to do far more than what you thought you had agreed to do.

The one thing not to do in a situation like this is argue. Your client is already unhappy/anxious/impatient/frustrated/you-fill-in-the-blank. If you get an irate-sounding phone call or email, try to put yourself in the client's shoes before getting defensive. At the moment, it doesn't really matter what happened; what your client wants to hear is that you care and that you will make it better.

What *not* to say in this situation:

- "This has never happened before."

- "But this is what you told me you wanted! I did just what you asked for. What's your problem?"

- "Well, as soon as you pay my invoice, I'll see what else I can do for you."

What you can say to defuse the situation:

- "I feel terrible that this happened."

- "I am so sorry that this wasn't what you expected; let's talk about what I can do to fix it."

- "Thanks so much for explaining what you had expected. Let me get back to work and see what I can find."

Note that you do not necessarily have to admit fault—although, of course, if the problem was your fault or due to a misunderstanding or faulty assumption that might well have been yours, you should say so. The object is to demonstrate to your client that you "share her pain." Once you both calm down, you can figure out where and why the miscommunication happened. In the final analysis, a "project from Hell" is usually caused by a failure to communicate. You did not explain to the client that you might not find exactly what she wanted, or the two of you did not come to an understanding on the parameters of the project, or you did not alert her early in the process that her initial expectations were not reasonable, or you took on a project that you did not fully understand, or your client simply did not accept the limitations of time frame and budget, or you did not listen to your gut when it said, "Walk away from this one … it's a loser."

You might notice a pattern here; just about all the reasons that this project went bad include you as one of the factors. That does not mean that the customer is always right; in fact, the client may be clinically delusional. But it is your responsibility to recognize and watch for those pitfalls and address problems before they become unsolvable—by taking more time to discuss and manage the client's expectations, by articulating the limits on what you can and will do within the client's budget, and by walking away from a job that you don't think you could do splendidly. Of course, this assumes that you keep your part of the bargain—you do deliver what you promised, on time and within budget. And what if you can't? You pick up the phone as soon as you realize that there is going to be a problem, and you negotiate, with the understanding that this is *your* problem and the client is under no obligation to let you off the hook. Your job is to take responsibility—although not necessarily blame—for any project that goes bad.

What do you do if, despite your best efforts, your client is not happy with the results of your work? Up to a certain point, it makes sense to absorb the cost, at least for the portion of your invoice that covers your time as distinguished from your direct expenses. Call it a learning experience. Remember that a client whom you treat respectfully will probably call you again. See what additional work you can do to make the client happy and don't bill the additional time. Consider charging the client for your out-of-pocket expenses (such as online research) only or invoicing for expenses and just a portion of your time.

I have several long-time clients with whom I have occasionally experienced miscommunications. I have always apologized, expressed my mortification that this misunderstanding happened, and either not billed them for the job or charged them only for my out-of-pocket costs. They have always returned with more work; I have demonstrated that I want their business and am willing to give them the benefit of the doubt. Up to a certain point, it's a good investment to let one invoice go, if it is very likely that the client will call you again.

Of course, you must see how the client behaves in the future. If you sense as you start to negotiate the next project that you are going to have problems again, you might want to politely turn down the work and refer the client to someone else.

How to Fire a Client

Wait—you're supposed to *find* clients, not fire them, right? In general, that is true, but one of the perks of running your own business is that you can gracefully get rid of clients with whom you just don't want to work anymore. It is always a hard decision; you hate to lose the income from any client. On the other hand, being an independent info pro means having to manage yourself, your time, and your energy. If a client becomes a burden to you—financially, mentally, or emotionally—it could be time to let him go.

When should you think about firing a client, or, to put it more gently, helping a client find another independent info pro who can better handle his unique needs?

- If you feel angry or anxious whenever the client calls
- If working for the client is significantly more time-consuming and less profitable than doing similar jobs for other clients
- If the client is consistently verbally abusive, offensive, rude, or demanding
- If the client complains about your rates
- If the client habitually pays your invoices later than agreed
- If the client pressures you to do something that you believe is unethical or illegal

Even though it is tempting to simply call the client and yell, "I'm never going to work for you again! Ever!" this is probably not the wisest approach. Life is too short, and the market is too small for you to create a scene. The person you hang up on today may be working for your best client next month. And, in most situations, the softer path is just as effective and far easier. The secret is not to let the client know he's being fired or at least not why.

Think back to high school. When you were dating and wanted to break up, the standard line was, "It's not you, it's me. I'm just not right for you." Take that sentiment, tune it to the business world, and it really can work. When I started my business, one of my first clients had me coming on-site for 20 hours a week at a greatly reduced hourly rate. For the first six or nine months, that was great; it was welcome revenue at a point when I did not have much other work. But I finally realized that it was taking the time I needed to devote to growing the business, and the money did not justify it. After a year, I sat down with my client and said, "You know, I have really enjoyed working with you folks. Unfortunately, I'm going to have to raise my rates in three months to double what I've been charging you. I know that's probably more than you can pay, and I'll work with you to find someone else who can take my place." In three months, we parted ways amicably, my client never realizing that I'd fired him. And as scary as it was to give up a client who took up half my time, within a week I had found two new clients who paid my full hourly rate and who more than made up for the lost income.

Another approach, if you can't just double your rates on a client, is to tell the client that her projects are falling outside your area of expertise or that you are becoming so busy with other work that you can no longer fulfill her requests within her deadlines. And if the client doesn't believe you, turn down her next request, using whatever reason you gave her—you simply can't meet the deadline, or you just couldn't take on the request because it goes outside your realm of expertise. Yes, it takes nerves of steel to turn down work this way, but you can do it. If possible, refer the client to a colleague or to the membership directory of the Association of Independent Information Professionals. Just because the client did not work well with you does not mean that someone else cannot handle her. Dog trainers say that there are no bad dogs, only untrained ones. Similarly, perhaps there are no bad clients, just ones who haven't yet found the independent info pro with whom they can work happily and productively.

Top Tips for Managing Clients

✦ A variety of clients makes for a stronger business than a client base of one or two.

✦ Value your time; try to deflect requests for face-to-face meetings with prospects.

✦ Learn to gracefully extricate yourself from conversations with prospects who will not turn into clients.

✦ Be sure the value of your clients is worth the cost of attracting them.

✦ Think twice about responding to competitive bidding requests.

✦ Use proposals to sell yourself and manage your clients' expectations.

✦ Turn down projects and fire clients if the chemistry isn't there.

✦ Accept responsibility (if not blame) when a project goes bad.

✦ Demonstrate to your clients that you want and value their business.

✦ Don't let a client know he's being fired; let him down gently.

Chapter 14

Money, Money, Money

I suppose that all of us start our own businesses because we love the work, love the independence, and love the challenge, but we also do it for the money. This chapter looks at the financial issues that are central to starting and running an independent info pro business.

Financing Your Business

Section One of this book talks about the things you need to do and the equipment you need to buy before you launch your business. It might feel rather daunting, particularly after you have read through Chapter 9, Setting Up Your Business, and you total up all those startup expenses. For many people, this can amount to $5,000 or $6,000—probably more than you have sitting around in your checking account.

You have several options for funding your business. The simplest and most typical is to pay for it out of your savings. If you are thinking about starting a business, set up a separate savings account now and plan to put $500 in it every month. Yes, that may mean eliminating some discretionary spending, but it also means that you can start your business without the burden of debt.

Another option is to write a thorough business plan (see Chapter 8, Before You Launch) and present it to selected family members and friends. Ask them to lend you a portion of what you need at an interest rate equivalent to what they would earn from the bank on a certificate of deposit, and for a period of, say, five years. Of course, you will treat this loan as one that absolutely must be paid off as promised—the last thing you want to do is lose a friend over a business debt.

Local banks may also be willing to lend you money, provided you can demonstrate that you have a sound business proposal. Some independent info pros tap into the value of their house by taking out a home equity loan. Note that most lending organizations expect you to invest your savings or personal equity in the business as well. A lender generally won't finance more than 50 percent of your business, which means that you will have to invest your own money even if you take out a loan.

The last, and least attractive, option is to put your expenses on a credit card and pay off the debt as you can. Given that the interest rate on credit cards can be at least 18 percent, this can be a quick path to failure. The total cost of an item purchased on a credit card and paid off gradually can easily double, once you factor in what you are paying in interest. If the only way you can finance your business is through credit card debt, my suggestion would be to hold off on starting your business until you are in a stronger financial situation.

The U.S. Small Business Administration has a discussion on finding startup money on its website (www.sba.gov). The section on how to write a loan proposal is particularly useful. The Canadian government's Canada Business site (www.canada business.ca) also has a section specifically on financing your business, including both national and regional sources for short- and long-term financing. The U.K. business website, Business Link (www.businesslink.gov.uk), has a section specifically on financing and grants, determining what kind of financing is most appropriate for your situation, and managing your cash flow.

Keep in mind that writing a formal business plan in order to obtain a loan can be difficult. The info-entrepreneurship profession is relatively small, and each business is unique to its owner, so it is virtually impossible to get reliable numbers on the size of the market or a projection of your sales. You will have to base your estimates on interviews with potential clients as well as conversations with established info-entrepreneurs in order to make sure that your financial projections are reasonable. The Association of Independent Information Professionals (AIIP; www.aiip.org) publishes results of its member survey; while your business may not be typical, at least this provides you with some basis for your estimates.

Accounting 101

Fortunately, you do not need to know much about accounting to run your business, particularly if you work with an accountant to set up your books. Unless you have a background in finance or accounting, you are probably better off with simple money management software such as QuickBooks (quickbooks.intuit.com), rather than trying to maintain your accounts manually.

If you choose not to have an accountant set up the initial accounts for you and you live in the U.S., go through the most current IRS Form 1040 and Schedule C and note how the IRS categorizes expenses and income for sole proprietors. For incorporated business, consult Publication 535, "Business Expenses" for information on what you can deduct. All the forms and publications are at www.irs.gov.

Canadian companies will be filing a T2 tax return and Schedule 1, if you are incorporated, or Form T2124, Statement of Business Activities, or Form T2032, Statement of Professional Activities, if you are a sole proprietor. Note how the CRA (Canada Revenue Agency) categorizes income and expenses, and then set up your accounting software with those same categories. Be sure you understand how to collect the GST; more help for setting up a business in Canada is available at the CRA website (www.cra-arc.gov.ca).

If you are doing business in the U.K., consult Businesslink for detailed information about how and when to charge VAT, how to set up an accounting system, and what reports you need to file. There is even a page with help on selecting an accounting application which, while not naming specific products, does help you identify your specific accounting needs so that you can select the most appropriate package.

Accounting for Non-Accountants

For the record, I am neither a lawyer nor an accountant. Before you set up your business accounting system, be sure that you have consulted with a lawyer for the form of your business and an accountant for the details of tracking your business. What I describe here are ideas for keeping a handle on your cash flow; be sure that your accounting system is appropriate for your situation.

When you are setting up your income and expense categories, think through how you want to track your money. For example, I have separate income categories for regular research and for research that I provide at a discounted rate as a subcontractor, for online charges that I bill to clients, for speaking fees, for consulting services, and so on. To the IRS, it's all just gross receipts, but I can generate reports in QuickBooks that show me how much of my revenue comes from each type of work, how much of my research time I discount, and so on. For expenses, I track the IRS forms as closely as possible, with a few subcategories that help me monitor my cash flow. For example, I have categories for advertising, business travel, health insurance, and utilities, all of which are line items on Form 1040. But I also break out my office expenses into specific subcategories that I find useful for various purposes. The "online costs" category, for example, enables me to compare my online costs to the online charges I bill back to clients (they should be roughly equal).

You will need to set up a business checking account and savings account in addition to whatever personal bank accounts you already have. Taxing agencies look more favorably on sole proprietors who keep their personal and business money separate, and it's just simpler this way. Note that some banks require proof that you are already in business before they will open business accounts. Make sure you have your business license or whatever other forms your local jurisdiction requires before you head to the bank.

Why should you have a business savings account? You will need to put money aside regularly for tax payments (see the later section on paying the tax man) as well as for new equipment and unplanned expenditures. And as you learn about the inevitable ebb and flow of income, you need to have saved up enough money to cover your overhead expenses during those months when your income is exceeded by your outgo.

The accounting issue that puzzled me most when I started my business was how I actually paid myself and reimbursed myself for petty cash expenditures. I finally realized that, as long as everything is eventually processed through my business checking account, I could account for it all. For example, I save my receipts for business expenses that I paid for out of my own pocket, such as cab fare and postage, until it amounts to $100 or so. Then I write myself a check from my business account just as I would pay any other bill and categorize the expenses appropriately. Likewise, I pay myself a salary by writing myself a check and categorizing the expense as either draw (when I was a sole proprietor) or salary (now that I am incorporated). If this sounds complicated, pay an accountant to walk you through the steps the first time. It is fairly simple once you get used to thinking of your checking account as the hub for your financial information.

One aspect of running a business that none of us enjoy is bookkeeping. While it is tempting to simply whip out an invoice when a job is done, write checks as needed, and throw all the receipts in a shoebox for your accountant to sort out at the end of this year, resist the urge. For starters, unless you keep track of your income and expenses on an ongoing basis, you cannot get an accurate idea of where your business is, how financially strong it is, where there are problem areas, and so on. And, of course, the end of the tax year is probably not a time when you or your accountant can address this. If you just can't keep up on the day-to-day accounting, bring in a bookkeeper. If you are a sole proprietor, probably all you would need is a careful—and entirely trustworthy—person to input your invoices and bills. If you are incorporated, consider using a bookkeeper to manage your monthly reports and payments. Regardless of your corporate form, once your income approaches what you were making before you started your business, consider having an accountant prepare your taxes to ensure you are taking advantage of any tax benefits. An accountant with a strategic perspective can be a great advisor—my accountant advises me annually of what I should do this year to minimize my taxes.

Billing and Collections

Unlike employees who receive a steady paycheck, independent info pros only get paid after they have billed their clients and collected the money. In order to maintain at least some semblance of a steady cash flow, it is important to invoice quickly and follow up promptly on any invoices that are past due.

The Check's in the Mail

Some info pros require prepayment in full for every job. This works well if you price your projects on a flat fee basis rather than on time plus expenses. (See Chapter 15, Setting Rates and Fees, for a discussion of the pros and cons of each approach.) However, you often won't know the exact cost of the project ahead of time. It is still wise to require prepayment of at least a portion of the not-to-exceed budget, particularly if it is a large project. The advantages of requiring prepayment are:

- You ensure that the client is willing and able to pay you.

- You are protected from a total loss if the client contests the invoice.

- You help your cash flow by receiving money up front for expenses that will come due before your client pays your invoice.

The disadvantages of requiring prepayment include:

- Some organizations cannot generate a check quickly enough to let you get started in time to meet the deadline.

- Your client may be reluctant to pay you before seeing the results of the work.

An alternative to requiring a prepayment is to set up what is called a merchant account with a bank so that you can accept credit card payments. Then you have the

"Will That Be Visa or MasterCard?"

In the early 1990s when I started my business, it was very difficult to convince a bank to grant me merchant status so that I could accept credit cards. Fortunately, banks' attitudes toward small and home-based businesses have changed a lot over the years, and now the hardest part is figuring out which merchant account is the best deal for you.

The easiest approach is to go to the websites for Visa and MasterCard and look through their lists of "acquirers" or "merchant service providers"— banks and other financial institutions through whom you can process credit card charges. Shop around and compare costs before you sign up. As with any other financial service, charges vary considerably. Expect to pay either a one-time charge or a monthly service fee for a terminal or the software to process charges. The bank charges a certain percentage of each transaction (usually 2 to 4 percent, depending on how fast you want to get paid), and most also impose a monthly minimum fee of $20 or $30. While the monthly minimum may cause you alarm, think of it as payment insurance and just build the cost into your overhead.

American Express has a different setup than MasterCard and Visa; instead of going through a bank, you establish a merchant account directly with AmEx. Go to www.americanexpress.com and click the Merchants link to apply for a merchant account.

choice of either charging the client immediately for a portion of the project or holding his credit card number, so you can charge him at the end of the job. Of course, in the worst-case scenario, the client might dispute a charge, but I have found that any client who trusts me enough to give me her credit card number is going to be a good client. See the sidebar "Will That Be Visa or MasterCard?" for a discussion of how to accept credit cards.

My own guideline is to require either a credit card number or partial prepayment on the first job I do for any client and whenever a project's not-to-exceed budget exceeds $2,000 or so. Use your own judgment, balancing the need to manage your cash flow with the flexibility and trustworthiness of your clients.

And what happens if your client tells you that the check is in the mail? Should you start work immediately? Only if you have money to burn. If I have decided to require prepayment from a client, I always wait until I have the check in hand. Even then, I sometimes call the bank and ask for confirmation that the account has enough money in it to cover the check. Banks will not disclose an account balance, but they may tell you whether it contains sufficient funds to honor the check at the time you call. In these days of electronic funds transfer and overnight courier, if a client really wants you to get started immediately, she can figure out a way to get the prepayment to you quickly.

Be Explicit

When you are discussing a project with a client, take time to explicitly discuss payment terms, and listen to the client's response. If your client is a consultant and will be billing a third party for your work, you must spell out that you expect your invoice to be paid within the agreed-upon time. My usual speech goes something like this: "Although I know that you're working for your own client on this job, *you* are my client so I'll need to be paid within 30 days of the invoice, regardless of when or whether you're paid by your client. Will that be a problem?" If the client sounds hesitant or ambiguous, I ask for prepayment or a credit card number. It is always foolhardy to agree to wait for payment until your client gets paid; you have no idea when that happens and, in any event, his cash flow (or lack of it) is not your problem. You have to manage your cash flow, and your client must manage his.

Listen to your gut. There are times when, as soon as you bring up the matter of payment, you get a sense that this client just isn't going to pay the bill. If that happens, it is perfectly reasonable for you to require prepayment or to decline the work.

Presenting the Invoice

When you invoice a client, you are sending a message about the value you attach to your services. Whether you use preprinted invoices or simply your letterhead, you want an invoice that looks official and is clear and concise. Be sure that, whatever format you use, you include:

- The date

- The word "INVOICE" (some accounts payable departments will not pay from a "statement of accounts," for example)

- Your company name, address, and telephone number

- The name and address of your client

- The invoice number

- The payment terms (e.g., net 30 days)

- A description of the services provided and the cost for each item

- The total charges for the work

- Your Taxpayer Identification Number (U.S.), Business Number (Canada), VAT registration number (U.K.), and whatever other information is required by your tax agency

With a new client's first invoice, I include IRS Form W-9, which provides my Taxpayer ID number in a format that accounts payable departments expect. If you don't include it, your invoice may be delayed while the accounting folks mail you a copy of the W-9 to fill out and return. Save them the trouble and time by sending it with the invoice. You can download a PDF version of the W-9 from the IRS's website.

Make your description of the services you are charging for as professional sounding as you can. Rather than charge for "library research," note that you "provided analysis of the Chinese tungsten industry." Make sure that the invoice reflects value provided, not just work done. Some independent info pros like to list all aspects of the project individually, such as "Conducted six telephone interviews, obtained three market research reports, conducted extensive online research," and so on. Others prefer to simply describe the focus of the project without going into detail: "Development and presentation of strategic analysis of the dry dog food market." I think the latter looks more professional, but some clients like to have all the charges spelled out.

Some independent info pros send out all their invoices at the end of the month. There is a certain efficiency in this, but it also delays payment, in some cases by several weeks. Instead, consider sending out the invoice as soon as the project is completed and you have confirmed with the client that he is satisfied and no additional work is needed at this time. One exception is if you are doing several small jobs for a single client. As a courtesy, ask the client if she would prefer to receive one combined invoice at the end of the month or individual invoices as you go along. Some of my small-but-steady clients like separate invoices because they pass along the costs for each project to their clients; others prefer one invoice because it means less paperwork to process on their end. If a project extends over several months, establish at the beginning that you will invoice at the end of each month for the work conducted during that month.

Net 30 Means Net 30

Most companies send out bills with an indication of the date by which you are expected to pay. In the business world, this is often written as "net 30" or "net 15." Net 30 means that you expect to receive the net total (that is, the total after taking into account any credits or refunds) within 30 days of the date of the invoice. Net 30 is typical, but other payment terms exist. You can set any terms you like, but regardless of what you tell your clients, most of them will cut you a check 30 days after the date of the invoice. I always chuckle when I receive invoices marked "payment due upon receipt." Unless the vendor and I negotiated that beforehand, I pay the next time I'm writing checks; I'm not going to stop what I'm doing and pay it immediately or even the next day.

It is important to stay on top of your receivables. Your accounting software can generate past-due reports that show you which invoices have not been paid on time. I usually give my clients a few days after the due date because I have found that some companies have a policy of mailing the check the day it is due. But once an invoice is more than two or three days beyond the due date, call the client's accounts payable office to confirm that the invoice was received and to check whether any additional information is needed. (Did you include a W-9 with your invoice?)

If everything is in order and the accounting folks say the check is coming, give it a couple of weeks and then, if you still have not received payment, call the accounting department to check the status. (Leave your actual client out of it at this point. You want your client to have nothing but positive experiences with you, and a collections call isn't usually a positive experience.) Be courteous but firm. See Chapter 17, Ethics and Legalities, for a discussion of collections issues, and keep in mind that it is often better to walk away from a deadbeat client than to take him to court. If you have a client who is habitually slow to pay, you may want to require prepayment of some or all of the budget before you begin work on the next job. There is no reason for you to act as a short-term lender for clients who have trouble managing their cash flow.

If you are dealing with a small organization, there is probably one person handling all the company's bills. If so, get to know that person, who is going to be your new best friend. Ask him what he needs to process your invoice smoothly. Enclose a self-addressed stamped envelope. I am on a first-name basis with the accounting people of several of my clients, and my invoices always get paid promptly.

On the other hand, be mindful of the limitations of a large organization. You may be one of hundreds of vendors, and their accounts payable department's policy may be to cut checks 45 days after the date of the invoice. You can complain all you want, but they will not change their procedure for one relatively small vendor. If necessary, build an annoyance factor into your price and resign yourself to waiting 45 days for payment. While others may have a different policy, my feeling is that it is better to wait an additional 15 days than become a source of irritation to my client.

Deadbeats and Other "Learning Opportunities"

If you ensure that you have prepayment or a credit card from every new client, and if you maintain a good relationship with your clients, you should have no problem with nonpayment of your invoices. Unfortunately, in the real world, there are people who seem very nice but who choose not to pay for your services. First, remember that you should never take a risk with a new client; even if she was referred to you by your brother-in-law, get a credit card or prepayment. (My accountant has agreed to be the fall guy for this; if I get resistance to this request, I say, "Oh, my accountant is just a tyrant about this. He insists that I get a credit card or prepayment from every new client.") However, there may come a time when a repeat client refuses to pay an invoice, or you forget to request prepayment or a credit card number from a new client. And yes, this has happened to me three times over the course of two decades of business. In my experience, these situations are not matters in which a faceless accounts payable department is sitting on your invoice; these are almost always cases of an individual consultant or business owner refusing to pay. Hence, your collection efforts will probably be directed at your client, not an accounting department.

These are the steps I have taken, in escalating order.

Keep a paper trail of everything. If you have a phone conversation asking about the status of payment, follow up with an email—"as we discussed today …"—outlining what was said. You want to be able to say, "When I called you last week, you told me that you were writing a check that day. I haven't received it yet. Would it be easier for you to just give me your credit card number to take care of this?" If nothing else, you have a record of how many times and over what period of time you have tried to collect on the invoice.

If you can set this up with your domain host, send one more email, this time from accounting@your-company.com. Spell out the amount due, your efforts to collect, and a deadline for payment.

Have a colleague, friend, or relative call the client as your "Accounts Receivable associate" or "on behalf of" your business. This person can take a more stern approach, telling the client that payment needs to be received by a certain date. The important thing is to have someone speak with the client directly, rather than simply rely on your email from "Accounting."

Have your lawyer draft a letter requesting payment. Sometimes this is sufficient to get the attention of a deadbeat client. If the client is in your local area, you can consider taking him to court. However, the time involved in this may exceed the value of the money you are recouping.

If it is clear that you are not going to get paid, forgive the debt. My philosophy is that bad clients don't deserve any of my energy or focus. I wait until the debt is six or nine months old and then write off the amount owed. I send the client a letter to that effect; it usually includes wording such as this: "I am sorry that you are unable to pay my invoice for the work that I did for you in April. It is clear to me that you do not intend to honor this invoice, so I am forgiving the debt. I trust that, in your business dealings, your clients respect your time and expertise more than you have respected mine." This has the effect of removing the source of irritation from my life, and I release that energy-drain from my business. I know that when it comes right down to it, it will not be cost-effective, in terms of time, money, and energy, to pursue payment from a client. I would much rather move on and focus on my good clients.

And, believe it or not, two of my three deadbeats eventually paid me the full amount owed, albeit a year late.

My Loyalty Can Be Bought … or at Least Rented

Retainers or deposit accounts are nice ways to manage cash flow, offer priority service to specific clients, and provide you with a reliable income. They work similarly; the main difference is what obligation each party has.

In general, a retainer is an amount paid to you monthly (or quarterly or annually) for an agreed-upon amount of work. The ideal retainer situation for most info-entrepreneurs looks like this:

The client pays you $1,000/month. You guarantee that you will be available to provide up to seven hours of research a month for this client, and her requests will have top priority. If you provide more than seven hours of research in a month, you bill her at your regular rate of $200/hour. (Her retainer entitles her to a 30 percent discount off your regular rate.) In exchange, if she does not use you for at least seven hours, you keep the remainder as payment for your promised availability. The client gets a guarantee that you will work on her projects first, and she has a predictable cap to her research expenses, provided she doesn't use more than seven hours a month. Most retainer contracts last a year, with the option for either party to renew or renegotiate the contract after 12 months.

Deposit accounts are prepayments for your services, usually with no direct obligation in terms of hours worked or billed. Clients who have budget concerns may want to "spend" the available money now and use your services later. Some clients may find it more convenient to draw down an account than issue checks every month for your services. There is usually an expectation that you give a deposit-account client priority, and most info pros offer a discount of 10 or 15 percent off their hourly rate for deposit account clients.

If you set up a deposit account for a client, make sure that:

- The client understands that any money not used by the end of the year or by another agreed-upon deadline belongs to you (after all, your client is paying for you to be available for him with little or no notice).

- You provide a monthly statement of the account.

- You establish how low the account balance can go before it must be replenished.

Cash Flow

Do you remember the character named Wimpy in the old Popeye cartoons? He struggled with cash flow, and his refrain was, "I will gladly pay you Tuesday for a hamburger today."

During your first couple of years in business, you may feel a bit like Wimpy. The phone bill comes in and has to be paid, regardless of whether you have been paid by your last client. Get in the habit of banking every client payment. You don't know yet where your business's peaks and valleys are going to be, and you need enough money in the bank to pay the bills. This is particularly true if you do a lot of research using the professional online services; you will inevitably receive the invoice from your online vendor before you get payment from your client.

Watch your overhead expenses—the costs you incur independent of how much work you're doing and how much income you expect. (See the sidebar, "Overhead Versus Cost of Goods Sold" for a discussion of what overhead is.) It is nice to take potential clients out to lunch, and you are going through those expensive color inkjet cartridges awfully fast, and you really need that new electronic gadget, and, and … suddenly you wonder where all the money went. Particularly when you start your business, think long and hard about any potential expense that is not directly related to gaining new clients or providing billable information services to existing clients. After you have been in business a year or two, you can think about buying that high-end gadget; until then, keep your overhead to a minimum.

Some professional online services impose monthly service charges or minimum usage fees. If you are a member of AIIP, you can take advantage of discount programs that eliminate the monthly fees for a number of online information sources.

In general, avoid buying anything in bulk that you can pay for a la carte. For example, instead of signing up for unlimited online searching at $1,500 a month, stick with the pay-as-you-go option, even though you will be paying a nondiscount rate per search. Why risk not being able to bill out the entire $1,500 expense every month when you can buy (and charge the client for) only what you use?

Keep track of when bills are due and make sure that you pay your vendors on time. Your credit rating is a valuable asset and, once lost, is difficult to restore. If you think you are going to be late in making a payment, call the vendor immediately, explain the situation, and see if you can negotiate a better payment option. You do not want your phone line to go dead or your email address to disappear because you did not pay your bills promptly. Your clients will be inclined to shop elsewhere if they have trouble getting in touch with you.

There are lots of ways to get the most from your accounts payable and accounts receivable. These are a few techniques that can work well for info pros.

For money coming in:

- Offer a discount for full prepayment of your fee (10 percent is reasonable).

- Accept credit card payments. This can significantly speed payment.

- Always discuss payment at the beginning of the project; ensure that your client agrees to pay you within 30 days.

For money going out:

- When possible, pay on a credit card, but only if you will be able to pay it off in full when the bill arrives. This allows you to postpone payment until a client's check arrives.

- Eliminate finance charges and late fees. Pay off any interest-incurring debt as soon as possible.

- Whenever you can, ask, "Is that the best rate you can give me?" rather than, "What discounts do I qualify for?"

Even if a bookkeeper routinely manages your invoices and payments, you should monitor your cash flow weekly. Know how much money you have available, what bills are coming due, and when you can expect to receive payment from clients.

And finally, I will lapse into my coaching personality and encourage you to view your business with abundance. They call it cash "flow" because it flows in and out. Imagine what happens when you put a kink in a hose—the water stops flowing. Think of the money that comes into and out of your business as being part of a flow. If you feel constricted and afraid, you kink the hose. If you act from a perspective of expansion instead of constriction, the money often seems to flow more easily, too. I give money to several nonprofits whether I feel I have it to spare or not on the assumption that this keeps the flow going. And sure enough, it always seems to. When I can feel (responsibly) generous with my finances, I make decisions from a bigger, more expansive place, and I have yet to regret any of those decisions.

Overhead Versus Cost of Goods Sold

There are two broad types of expenses in business: overhead and the cost of goods (or services) sold. Overhead is what you spend to establish your company and stay in business, including items like your internet connection, business cards, health insurance, and office supplies. These are expenses you have to pay, whether you have any money coming in or not. You can't charge any of them directly back to a client, although your hourly fee is calculated to cover overhead costs. (See Chapter 15, Setting Rates and Fees, for more on setting your hourly fee.) It is critical to keep an eye on your overhead expenses because they can eat up a good deal of your profit.

The cost of services or goods sold is what you spend in the process of providing your information services. It includes expenses such as searching professional online services, royalty fees for a client's journal articles, books or reports you purchase on behalf of a client, and fees you pay subcontractors for research. These costs are directly tied to how much and what kind of work you do. Generally, you pass along all these charges to your clients. Make sure that your cost of services per project isn't too high so that there is nothing left in the budget to bill for your time; if you have a not-to-exceed budget of $1,000 and you spend $800 in direct costs to obtain the information, your profit on that project is awfully low.

Paying Yourself

Believe it or not, paying yourself is sometimes one of the hardest aspects of managing your money. How do you determine how much to take out of the business checking account as salary or draw? What if you need the money later to pay bills?

I have found it helpful to work backward. At the end of each month, look at how much money came in. Subtract any income you collected for expenses you must pay, such as online research; you will just be sending that money right back out when the vendor's bill arrives. Assume that 25 percent of what is left will be paid out in income taxes soon, either as an estimated tax payment or a deduction from your paycheck. Then take out whatever is required to pay your overhead bills, including regular payments to a retirement fund, and set aside an amount for the business savings account—for new equipment, for unexpected repairs, and to pay other bills when you don't have enough income to cover them. What is left after that is your salary.

Some info pros find it difficult to be this disciplined about money; they tend to spend it on whatever seems most pressing at the moment as soon as it comes in. If that sounds like you, just remember that you do not have a choice about paying bills or your taxes. If what is left over only pays for peanut butter sandwiches and spaghetti, well then, next month you will redouble your marketing efforts.

Paying the Tax Man

If you live in the U.S., about one-fourth of every check you receive will go right back out again to the IRS. You are no longer a payroll employee; no one is withholding the IRS's take on your behalf. Four times a year, even before they ask for it (yes, I know it's painful), you will pay the IRS a percentage of your estimated total income tax for the year. This process is commonly known as paying your estimated quarterlies. For other countries, consult your tax agency to learn what taxes you are liable for during the year and which ones you can pay at the end of the tax year.

And how do you know what your total income tax liability will be, when you are just starting your business? After you have been in business a year, it's pretty easy. The IRS lets you base your quarterly payments on the prior year's total tax liability. Note, however, that tax laws change all the time, and if you expect your revenue this year to be significantly larger than last year's, consult a tax advisor.

All well and good, but what about the first year you are in business? Ask colleagues who went through a similar start-up what you might expect to spend, talk with an accountant, and then make a reasonable guess. Revisit your business plan as the year progresses and make any necessary adjustments in your cash flow projections. But remember to make those quarterly payments. Go to the IRS website (www.irs.gov) to read about estimated tax payments and to download Form 1040-ES. Note that if your state has an income tax, you will have to send quarterly estimated tax payments to the state revenue office as well.

Be sure you keep track of receipts for and records of all your business expenses. And keep in mind that your definition of a "business expense" has to match that of your taxing authority. Sole proprietors and small businesses seem to be disproportionately targeted for audits, and you want to be sure that you have documentation for anything you claim as a business expense. Most countries' tax agencies offer fairly clear descriptions of what constitutes a business expense for a small business or self-employed individual. The common-sense answer to "What is a business expense?" is that it has to pass the straight-face test. You can often tack a vacation onto the end of a business trip, for example, but you cannot write off the entire expense of your housecleaning service if your office occupies only one-tenth of the total floor space of your house. And though your health club membership keeps you fit and alert, it is not a legitimate business write-off.

Living Large or Managing Your Money

- ✦ Be prepared to invest your own money in your business before you start looking for loans.
- ✦ Watch out for unnecessary overhead expenses and recurring costs.
- ✦ Keep your business finances separate from your personal accounts.
- ✦ Consider requiring prepayment from clients, particularly for large projects.
- ✦ Learn to be comfortable talking about payment terms with clients.
- ✦ Stay on top of your receivables.
- ✦ Monitor your cash flow.

Chapter 15

Setting Rates and Fees

As any marketing manager knows, setting prices is an art as well as a science. It's a combination of covering your costs, ensuring a fair profit, indicating your estimation of your value, and determining what the market will bear. For most retail products, a business owner can easily compare his prices against his competitors'—he can just walk down the street from his widget store and see what Sue is charging for *her* widgets. But info pros generally don't run storefront shops with prices in the window. And because the cost of our work varies with the requirements of each project, we don't usually have rate cards either.

Your fees will be based on a combination of factors, including the type of work you do, your client base, the going rate both for the industry you are marketing to and for the independent info profession itself, and the salary you want to pay yourself. This chapter will help you think about how you want to charge for your services, what your hourly rate should be, and how to talk to clients about your fees.

Setting an Hourly Rate

There are two ways to determine your hourly rate. The first is to just do a gut-check, decide that you're worth, oh, $175 an hour, and go with it. (And I hope that, if you do set your rate this way, you have a healthy amount of self-confidence. If your gut tells you that you are worth $25 an hour, keep reading.)

If, on the other hand, you prefer to take the analytical approach—or at least be able to justify your fee in your own mind—here is a formula to help you. It takes a little while to work through this process, but you will end up setting an hourly rate that will sustain you. The idea here is to figure out what you need to bring in to cover your costs and earn a satisfactory income:

- First, decide what annual salary you want to pay yourself. Be honest; don't estimate too low and don't expect to pay yourself $200,000 the first year. Self-employment has some intangible benefits, such as flexibility, independence, and the satisfaction of running your own business. However, you also have to factor in the downsides—erratic cash flow, no employer-sponsored retirement pension or paid vacations, the constant need to market. Be sure that the salary you set for yourself reflects the added stress of running your business. Remember that this won't be your take-home pay; you will still pay taxes on your income, just like a regular salary.

- Calculate what you will have to pay in taxes. Remember that, since you are now a business, even if just a sole proprietor, you will have to pay the taxes that your employer would normally pay.

- Now calculate how much money you need to set aside in a year for retirement, children's education, and other long-term financial goals.

- Next, figure out your nonreimbursable and overhead expenses for a full year. This includes everything except expenses you can bill back directly to clients, such as the cost of online searches or overnight delivery. It does not include your one-time office setup costs (described in Chapter 9, Setting Up Your Business), but it does include just about everything else you will be writing checks for, such as:

  - Office rent for 12 months

  - Utilities (electricity, telephone, internet service) for 12 months

  - Insurance payments (health, property, liability) for 12 months

  - Online information overhead or administrative fees for 12 months (subscription or minimum usage charges; not actual search costs, which you will directly bill back to the client)

  - Office supplies (paper, toner, business cards, stamps, and so on); the amount of office supplies you will consume in a year may surprise you, so estimate $2,000 or so annually

  - Annual membership dues for professional associations, both info pro-related and those of your client base

- Travel and registration costs for a minimum of two professional conferences a year (yes, you need to attend at least two—to market yourself,
  refresh your research skills, and stay on top of the issues in your clients'
  industry)

- Office equipment (assume that you will have to replace your computer
  every two to three years and that you will eventually need to purchase
  or upgrade other equipment, such as your phone, printer, and so on)

- Accountants' fees, magazine subscriptions, and other miscellaneous
  costs

Yes, it is hard to estimate all of this ahead of time. For most people, these overhead costs add up to between $20,000 and $40,000 a year.

Now let's figure out how many hours you can bill in a year. It is probably not as
many as you think. Start with 52 weeks. Subtract two weeks for vacation if you live in
the U.S. (one week of actual vacation and a week of random days when you need to
take a "mental health day"). If you live in a country where 10 vacation days a year
sounds uncivilized, subtract as many weeks as you expect to take off. Subtract
another week for doctors' appointments and sick days. Subtract another two to
three weeks for nonbillable holidays (all the holidays that regular employees get;
they won't be calling you on those days—and, let's face it, do you really want to be in
your office working on New Year's Day?). Subtract one to two weeks for attendance
at professional conferences (as I said, this is essential for your business). And finally,
subtract at least one week for unexpected IT or software problems. Remember, you
don't have an IT department, and you have to get your problem resolved without
relinquishing your computer while it is being repaired. That probably leaves you
with about 42 to 44 weeks. It's amazing how fast the time flies, isn't it?

How many hours will you bill each week? For most independent info pros, the
answer is no more than 20 or 25—and that assumes a 40- to 45-hour workweek. If
you are approaching this as a part-time job for now, remember that you still have the
same fixed overhead costs but now you have fewer hours in a year in which to
recoup those costs. Even though you are only working at this part time, you still have
the same telephone costs, ISP and web-hosting expenses, office equipment, and
professional dues and expenses as you would have when doing this full time.

Note that if you plan to do primarily manual research in libraries, courthouses,
and government agencies, your billable time may be closer to 30 to 35 hours. You will

be billing your clients for your travel time, and you can bill each client for a share of the travel time even when you combine several projects into a single trip. But for those of us who provide the more customary online and web research, analysis, and writing, 25 billable hours in a week is considered a good week.

You will spend the rest of your time marketing, answering email, marketing, preparing for presentations, marketing, sending out invoices, marketing, paying bills, marketing, and so on. Trust me on this, you will spend a lot of your time marketing. Even if one major client takes up most of your time, you still need to invest in marketing. As I explained in Chapter 13, Managing Your Clients, relying on one client for more than 25 or 30 percent of your revenue is dangerous; if you lose that client, your income will plummet. Bottom line is that you will be able to bill no more than roughly 1,000 or 1,100 hours a year, assuming you can generate that much work, week after week.

So what do we have? In simple math, it's comes out to the following:

Your annual salary plus taxes plus savings plus your overhead
<u>divided by</u>
The number of hours you expect to bill in a year

What's the result? Probably somewhere between $100 and $175 an hour (or $70 to $100 an hour for manual research, since you can bill more hours in a week than you can for online research). That is how much you have to bill per hour to pay your salary and cover your overhead expenses—again, in order to meet your salary needs, you have to be generating enough business to bill all your available hours.

For many beginning independent info pros, this rate may sound absurdly high; others may look at the number and imagine six-figure salaries their first month in business. Reality lies somewhere in between. Your clients probably won't focus on your hourly rate—particularly if, when you quote on a project, you present the total, not-to-exceed budget. Most clients—the kind you want to attract anyway—are accustomed to paying hefty rates for consultants. If your intended client base is likely to balk at your rate, think long and hard about whether you are willing to take a substantial pay cut to work for people who cannot afford your fees. If, on the other hand, you look at an hourly rate of $80 and imagine that you really will be able to bill 40 hours a week, 52 weeks a year, think again. Finding clients means marketing, and marketing takes time, particularly the first year.

Hourly Rate or Flat Fee?

There are two approaches to pricing a project: You can bill at an hourly rate plus expenses, with a not-to-exceed cap, or you can set an all-inclusive flat fee. Of course, both are based on your hourly rate; the difference lies in the amount of risk you want to build into the estimate.

If you are billing a project by the hour, you and your client have probably established a not-to-exceed budget—you agree that the *total* cost will not exceed a set amount. If you finish the work in less time than you expected, the final cost will be lower than the estimate. You have a strong incentive to watch your time and your expenses because you have agreed to a cap on the total amount. Once you begin work, if you realize that the project will take significantly more time or money to complete, you can go back to the client as early in the process as possible and try to negotiate a larger budget. Keep in mind, though, that you cannot make this a habit. If your clients see that your initial budget is usually inappropriately low, they will look for someone else who can estimate accurately.

If, on the other hand, you set a flat fee for a project, you are in a sense gambling that you know how much time the job will take. In reality, what you are doing is value pricing; you are setting a price that not only ensures your normal hourly rate but also reflects the value that your years of experience bring to the project. With flat-fee pricing, you must build in a cushion beyond your best estimate; remember, you are taking the risk that you will encounter unexpected problems or delays, and with flat-fee pricing, you cannot pass those unanticipated costs on to your client. Of course, if you come in significantly under budget, that additional profit is both a recognition that you were paid what you are worth, and insurance for those times when you fall flat on your flat fee and must absorb some of your time or expenses because you underestimated the scope of the project.

If you offer a prepackaged product or service, such as a standardized profile of a publicly held company or a two-hour workshop on web research, flat-fee pricing is the most appropriate option.

Estimating a Project

Suppose you get a call from a client who wants you to identify the latest trends in intermodal transport in Australia. You discuss the parameters of the project, figure out how much information your client is expecting, and agree on a deadline. Now she wants to know how much it will cost. Gulp. What do you say?

There is no easy answer for "How do I estimate the cost of a project?" After a while, it becomes second nature. "Hmm, this sounds like a five-hour project, plus about $300 in online costs," for example. But even if you've been doing research for years, it still takes a while to develop that gut feeling for how long a job will take. There is no firm guideline for estimating projects, but my first piece of advice is to resist the urge to blurt out a price. Say, instead, "Let me think about this for just a bit, and I'll call/email/fax you with an estimate."

What's Involved?

Now, take a deep breath and think through all the aspects of the project carefully. Do you understand the subject matter? Will you need to allow extra time to familiarize yourself with industry terms? How much information do you think is out there? You might want to run a very quick search in one of the professional online services to get a sense of the scope of the material available. Note that this is *not* the time to start spending money; instead, check a web search engine and see what comes up in five minutes of quick research, use Dialog's free Dialindex service or run a quick search through one of the value-added databases available through your local public library to business users, none of which will incur charges. See Chapter 34, Professional Online Services, for an overview of these value-added databases.

What about telephone research? Will you need to contact experts for information that doesn't exist in print or online sources? If so, will you be doing extensive interviews? Allow at least a couple of hours per interview. The interview itself won't take that long, but when you factor in the time to get the contact's name and phone number, exchange voicemail messages a few times to schedule the interview, conduct the interview, and write up your notes, it can easily take several hours. See Chapter 35, Telephone Research, for more details of what is involved in this specialized area of research.

Next, think about whether you need to factor in time for manual research in a library or government agency. Will you do this yourself or subcontract it out? If you are doing it yourself, be sure to include your transportation time. You are charging your clients for your dedicated time. When you are en route to and from a library, you are not available to take calls from other clients, to work on marketing, and so

What'll It Cost?

Even if you are an experienced researcher, it helps to map out how much time each part of a project will take. It is easy to minimize the labor involved in preparation and administrative tasks of the project, but if you don't factor it in, you will wind up seriously underestimating the total cost of the job.

Task:	Time (hours)	Cost
Reference interview	_____	
Research preparation	_____	_____
Online research	_____	_____
Telephone research	_____	
Manual/library research	_____	_____
Reports or documents purchased		_____
Subcontracting expense		_____
Editing and formatting online search results	_____	
Review of results	_____	
Analysis of results	_____	
Report preparation	_____	
Total time:	_____	
Time x hourly rate:	(a)_____	
Total costs:		(b)_____
Total expenses (a + b):		_____

on. If the project requires that you leave the office, the meter starts running as soon as you walk out the door.

If you are subcontracting this aspect of the project, be sure you know in advance how, and approximately how much, your subcontractor will charge you, so you can build it into your estimate. Alternatively, you can contact your subcontractor and ask her what she would be able to do for $X. See Chapter 16, Subcontracting, or I'll Scratch Your Back If You Scratch Mine, for more on this topic.

I find it helpful, both for myself and for my client, to write out a detailed "scope of work" proposal for each project. I begin with a paragraph describing what I understand the project to entail. Then, just for my own reference and not to show to my client, I spell out all the types of research I'll be doing—for example, a web search for company product specifications, online research for relevant patents, a search of trade and industry publications, interviews with government industry analysts, and so on. As I write a paragraph on each of these approaches, I often think of additional aspects of the project that my client may not have thought of herself. In fact, I often find that the intended scope of a project increases significantly once I have thoroughly thought through the specific approaches I might take.

Pricing Permutations

Once you have a feel for the extent of the research involved, use the worksheet in the sidebar "What'll It Cost?" to develop a rough estimate of the budget for the project. Notice the wide range of activities involved, from the initial conversation with your client through doing the actual research, cosmetically enhancing search results, and so on, down to the final analysis and report preparation. It is tempting to charge different rates for different kinds of labor; why should your client pay you $100 an hour while you are "just" setting up appointments for phone interviews? Remember, your client is paying for the exclusive use of your time. Your time is worth whatever rate you set (remember the math you did earlier in this chapter?) and discounting any of that time is cheating yourself. When you are cleaning up a downloaded file of articles or entering figures into a spreadsheet, you are not able to work for or market your services to other clients. This is sometimes referred to as the "opportunity cost," that is, what you give up by choosing to do something else. If you were not working on this job, you might be calling a potential client or working on a new proposal. Whatever you are doing for your client, you are spending time that you cannot devote to something else.

What if the client needs the project sooner than you would normally be able to deliver? What if it requires that you work evenings and weekends in order to meet the deadline? Most independent info pros charge a rush fee for anything that will require putting aside other work or working outside normal business hours. Think of it as overtime pay or as a means of ensuring that your clients really, truly need the information right away. If they aren't willing to pay a rush fee, it probably isn't an emergency after all. If you demonstrate that you are always willing to drop every-thing to work on a client's "rush" jobs, never charging a fee for the added service, you have in essence trained that client to wait until the last minute to call you.

How to charge a rush fee depends on the type of project. You can simply tack on a specific amount—say, $500—on top of the normal cost of the job. Or you can place a surcharge on your hourly rate, charging 50 percent more, for example. Obviously, the first alternative is more attractive for smaller jobs, and the second is better when the project involves more hours of labor.

Pretend I'm Not Here

I'll admit it … I am in my office way before 9AM, I don't leave at 5PM, and I usually put in some time over the weekend. In fact, I sometimes take on work knowing that the only way I can get it done is to work all weekend. But I never, ever admit that to a client. In fact, I have turned down clients who called on a Friday afternoon and asked if I could work on a project over the weekend and get it to them first thing Monday morning.

Am I crazy? No, I am just training my clients. If they know that they can get me to work on a weekend, they will start expecting it—or at least they will hope I will be willing to change my weekend plans. The more I meet their expectations, the less incentive they have to call me before the last minute. And the more I will feel that I have completely lost control over my free time.

However, what I will tell that Friday afternoon client is that I can get started on the project the very first thing Monday morning and get it to him by the end of the day. He doesn't have to know that I might in fact tackle it over the weekend—and yes, I make sure that I don't send it to him until at least midafternoon on Monday. It is important to manage your clients' expec-tations, and your actions—not your words—are what your clients notice.

Another add-on to the bottom line is the mark-up you may choose to add to out-of-pocket expenses. When you use a professional online service for research, you may incur significant charges that you will have to pay whether or not you have collected the money from your client yet. Likewise, you may have to purchase consulting reports, books, articles, or other material on behalf of a client. Those charges often go straight to your credit card, which means, again, that you have to pay them before your client has paid you. Because carrying expenses like this can have an impact on your cash flow, you may want to mark up out-of-pocket project costs by a small percentage. Note, though, that some professional online services forbid mark-ups. Be sure to read your service contract carefully.

What about fees for small jobs that you estimate will take less than an hour or two? I impose a two-hour minimum for projects; some independent info pros draw the line at one hour or at five hours. The rationale for a minimum fee is that every project, no matter how small, requires a certain amount of overhead time for routine tasks such as logging in the job, preparing and sending out an invoice, and so on, not to mention simply the time it takes you to shift gears and think about a new project. Half-hour jobs don't pay, and if you accept them, your clients will begin to think that you are the person to call just for those little jobs. Instead, if a client calls with a project that won't take more than 45 minutes, tell her that you have an *X*-hour minimum, then offer to provide additional research or analysis to bring the project up to your minimum. Your client benefits from the extra work; you benefit because you have demonstrated that you are capable of more than quickie research.

Quote High or Don't Play

It is tempting to quote a budget for a project at the lowest price you think you can manage in order to get the work. Resist that urge! For starters, you are probably not competing with anyone else. Most clients are not shopping around and comparing prices—they call someone they know will do the work well. If you are in a competitive bidding situation, think twice about bidding for the job. Why? Because you are dealing with someone who is basing his decision to work with you on cost more than anything else. Even if you get this job, you will have to win over your client for each new project, based on the fee you set. Yes, it's nice to get the work, but if you cut your fee in order to get the job, you have lowered that client's expectations of how much you are worth.

My experience has been that cost-sensitive clients tend to be the most labor-intensive. They are the ones who call during the project to add "just one more little question"—without an increase in budget, of course—and who call after the project is completed to ask for clarification of this item or that website you pointed them to. In a competitive bidding situation, bid what you normally would and stick to your price, and focus on finding clients who do not feel the need to get competitive bids for every project.

Be sure that your bid is high enough to reflect your value. This is hard to gauge; you often do not know what other independent info pros are charging, so it is difficult to know if you are high or low. My technique is to listen to clients' reactions to my estimate. If they accept without hesitation, I suspect that I am pricing myself too low. When I first started my business, I would work up an estimate and then gasp to myself: "Eight hundred dollars! Oh my gosh! That's a lot of money!" Well, it is a lot of money when you compare it to the cost of a meal out, but in the business world, $800 is chump change.

Price your services as high as the market will bear. That sounds awful, doesn't it? What's funny is that clients really do believe that the price you assign to your work reflects its true value. If you price yourself low, you are unintentionally telling your client that you don't think your work is worth much. Price high, and you project the image that you are expensive and worth every penny.

Judy Koren, of ResearchWise Associates, tells the story of a friend of hers, a now-retired medical cosmetician:

> She sold her own private-label face creams at her salon. When I visited, she showered me with little jars of her products. I said, "I can't possibly accept all this as a gift—look how much they cost!" She answered, "I won't tell you how much the contents actually cost *me* because it would embarrass me, but it's pennies. The only reason they cost so much is that that's the going rate. If I charge less, my clients are convinced my creams aren't as good as higher-priced brands they can get in the drugstore. I have the highest accreditation in my profession and I'm supposed to produce the best facial care products, not the cheapest. When I priced them lower, they didn't sell. But priced the way they are, they account for a sizeable percentage of my profits."

Presenting the Estimate

Once you have written up a description of the scope of the project, thought through all aspects of the research involved, estimated the total charges using the table in the sidebar, "What'll It Cost?", tacked on any additional rush fees, added an insurance factor of, say, 15 percent, and done a final reality check, it is time to discuss your proposal with the client.

I usually quote a total, not-to-exceed, budget rather than bringing up my hourly rate. Most clients have no idea how efficiently an info pro can work. Imagine the following conversation:

> *Info Pro:* Yes, I'd be happy to work on that project. I charge $150/hour, plus online costs, and this job might take me about …
>
> *Client:* [interrupting] Oh, no! Forget it. [thinking "I already spent eight hours on this and found nothing. I can't afford to spend another $1,500 or $2,000!"]

Now imagine this conversation:

> *Info Pro:* Yes, I'd be happy to work on that project. Based on my past experience, this type of research usually runs around $900. What if we set a not-to-exceed budget of $1,100, and I'll just charge you for my actual time plus expenses?
>
> *Client:* That sounds OK. You promise you won't bill me for more than $1,100?
>
> *Info Pro:* Absolutely. And if it looks like there just isn't anything out there, I'll stop before we spend very much time or money, and we can talk about other ways to approach the research.

For larger projects, it is even more important to couch the estimate in terms of a possible range of prices with a corresponding range of services. For $X amount, you will provide the in-depth research, analyze the information, and prepare an executive summary of the results. For 75%-of-$X, you will provide the research and write up a summary of what you have done and found. For 50%-of-$X, you will provide preliminary research and a set of recommendations about further research options you would suggest. Note that you offer the high end first, and then work down. This conveys the message that a complete research package includes all of these services, but your client can choose to receive a less complete package by selecting one of the less expensive options.

What happens if your client balks at the price you quote? What if she says that she thinks the job is worth only half of what you bid? That is when you offer a slimmed-down version of the project, priced accordingly. Instead of doing in-depth telephone interviews, you will limit the search to what you can find online. Instead of a high-level summary of the results, you may just clean up the results of your search, write an executive summary, and let her do the analysis herself. Be sure that you draw the line before you negotiate the project down to a budget that doesn't allow you to do a creditable job. Sometimes the answer simply has to be, "I'm sorry, but even the preliminary research will cost you $X. Perhaps your best option would be to go to your local library and see what information they can offer you at no charge."

What if your client says that other independent info pros would cost much less than you? My favorite response is one suggested by T.R. Halvorson of Synoptic Text Information Services, Inc.: "We set our prices according to the value we know we provide." If you have trouble saying that, practice it in front of a mirror until you can say it with confidence. And keep in mind that the client may be comparing you to someone who does not have access to the value-added online services and who cannot offer telephone research or public records searching—someone, in other words, who isn't in your league at all.

One of the most common mistakes made by new info-entrepreneurs is to take on a job with a budget far too small to be profitable with the justification that "I need the practice" or "Anything is better than nothing." Unfortunately, my experience is that neither of these reasons holds water. You do not need practice working for someone who cannot pay your normal rates. You are merely learning how to do low-budget, low-value work for clients who cannot afford your regular rates. Likewise, sometimes nothing—that is, turning down a low-paying job—is a better use of your time than doing a job that will yield you a low-rent client and that takes your time and energy away from marketing to a sustainable client base.

Can You Get the Money Up Front?

As independent info pros, cash flow is always in the back of our minds, and often in the front of our minds as well. On a big project, I may be incurring hundreds of dollars in out-of-pocket expenses doing online searching, purchasing hard-copy reports, and so on. Perhaps I am also subcontracting work to other info pros who will expect to be paid promptly. How do I manage all of these expenses before I get paid by my client? I generally require the client to prepay one-third of the not-to-exceed budget for any project over $1,000 or so. This ensures that I will have cash up front to cover online charges, subcontractors' bills, or other direct expenses. It also ensures that the client is serious about the job.

Requiring a prepayment does have downsides. Some companies seem to find it impossible to cut a check in less than 30 days and delaying work until you receive the money may be difficult if not impossible. Ask the client if his organization has provisions for expedited payment or electronic funds transfer to your business checking account. You might also consider establishing a merchant account so that you can accept major credit cards, assuming that your clients can pay that way. (See Chapter 14, Money, Money, Money, for information on accepting credit cards and on cash flow generally.) My experience has been that if the client really wants the work done, he will find a way to get payment to me within a few days.

Another option is to have your clients establish retainer or deposit accounts. In this arrangement, they prepay a set amount and then use your services until the account is depleted. In theory, this is a great deal for the independent info pro. You get the money up front and you are assured of a certain amount of work from the client. In fact, you may be able to offer priority attention to the client's requests in return for a use-it-or-lose-it monthly minimum. If they do not call on you during a particular month, you still deduct a predetermined amount from their account in exchange for your willingness to give precedence to their research needs. See Chapter 14, Money, Money, Money, for more discussion of deposit and retainer accounts.

In practice, very few independent info pros have clients on a retainer basis. The exceptions are document delivery businesses or other services that typically bill small amounts to clients with predictable research needs on an ongoing basis. Most clients are reluctant to obligate themselves to a set amount of research in a given period of time. Many clients simply don't know how much work they will be giving an independent info pro at all, so they are not inclined to send any money up front. Also, the accounting for retainer clients is less straightforward than for your pay-as-you-go clientele. The bottom line is that deposit accounts are great if you can get them but don't expect them to be the norm.

Recalibrating Rates

Picture yourself in three or four years. You are charging the same hourly rate that you started with. However, it's quite likely you are worth more now than when you started, even if you came from a library or research background and did similar work for years. You have become more efficient in your research, so you take less time to do the same amount of work. You have probably been subcontracting with other info pros, so you have a better sense than you did initially of what other people are charging, what their deliverables look like, what added value they provide, and so on. And the cost of living has certainly gone up since you started your business. It is time to think about raising your rates.

After I had been in business for a few years, I wanted to up my hourly rate, but I hesitated because I could not figure out how to tell my clients. Somehow, a postcard saying "Guess what? I cost more now!" just didn't seem appropriate. Then I realized that practically none of my clients knew what my hourly rate was. It does not appear on my invoices; I just list the total cost for my time. When I estimate the budget for a project, I give a round number without breaking it out into "This much for this many hours at $X an hour, plus this much for online, plus this much for document costs," and so on.

I realized that if I raised my hourly rate 15 percent, each project was simply going to start costing a little more. It would take the same amount of time, but that time would now cost $X plus 15 percent. As it turns out, I have raised my rates a number of times since then, and no client has commented or even, as far as I can tell, noticed the increase. I do have to renegotiate with my corporate clients with whom I have an annual contract that spells out the hourly rate but, as businesspeople, they also expect that rate to rise over time.

Of course, I am not suggesting that you initially set your rates low with the assumption that you can raise them to an acceptable level later. Start out with a rate you are happy with and that reflects your value and raise it when you feel that you can justify the increase. If you begin with a low hourly rate to attract clients, the only clients you will attract are those that want to pay a low hourly rate. By taking a strategic view of your business, you can set a rate that will sustain you not only during the first six months but through your first several years.

Top Tips for Rates and Fees

◆   Take the time to figure out an hourly rate you can live with … and live on.

◆   Be sure to include all overhead expenses when calculating your hourly rate.

◆   Get comfortable pricing jobs at what the market will bear.

◆   Prepare for clients' questions about the budget for a project.

◆   Clients assume that your rate reflects your value. A low rate signals low value.

Chapter 16

Subcontracting, or I'll Scratch Your Back If You Scratch Mine

One of the most important reasons to establish your own network of independent info pros is that you will eventually land a project that you cannot do yourself, and you will have to bring in someone else. You may get a question in an area that you know nothing about—for me, that would include medical, legal, and chemical searching—or a request for a type of research you do not offer—maybe patent searches or in-depth telephone interviews—or perhaps you are simply swamped with work and do not want to turn down a client but cannot accommodate the work because of other projects you are doing. In all these situations, as long as you have a network of other experienced info pros, you can keep a client happy even though you cannot do the work yourself.

How Does Subcontracting Work, and Why Should I Share?

Subcontracting turns you into a client: You have a project that needs doing, and you contract with another independent info pro who will do the work for you. As a matter of professional courtesy and because you are accepting the risk of not getting paid, the subcontractor usually agrees to work at a discounted hourly rate. You invoice your client at your regular rate, and the difference between what your subcontractor charges you and what you charge your client is profit. Alternatively, you can calculate how much you want to charge your client for the subcontractor's work and offer the job to your subcontractor at a flat fee that leaves you with a profit on the subcontracted portion of the work.

Depending on the situation, the subcontractor may not ever talk with your client directly; you act as the intermediary between the client and the subcontractor. This arrangement works best if you thoroughly understand the client's request and are able to accurately pass questions and answers back and forth between the subcontractor and the client. There are some situations in which you just don't want the subcontractor and client to talk. I have a couple of clients who are, well, challenging to work with, and my subcontractors are grateful that I buffer them from any direct interaction with my problem children. The situation in which this type of arrangement may not be ideal is when both your client and your subcontractor are much more familiar with the subject area than you are; in this case, it is probably better to let the two of them talk directly. About half of the jobs I subcontract involve putting my sub in contact with my client. When I work as the subcontractor for others, I occasionally am asked or encouraged to speak with the client directly, which I always welcome.

You may choose to introduce the subcontractor as your associate and indicate that, although the client may call the sub and interact with him directly, all the accounting, project management, and so on will come through you, and that all new projects should be directed to you, not to the sub. I have often been the subcontracted researcher, and I usually feel more confident that I have filled the client's information need if I am able to speak directly with the client. However, when I am working on just part of a larger project, it is usually simpler for me to talk only with the contractor who is managing the process and who knows what specific part of the puzzle I am responsible for doing. In any event, be sure that you discuss the issue of client contact with your subcontractor up front so that the sub understands with whom he will be dealing.

Calling in the Experts

Why would you send work to someone else instead of doing it yourself? The simplest answer is that you want your clients to come to you for all their research or information needs, regardless of the scope or topic; you want to be seen as their one-stop shop. But the challenge lies in providing high-quality research involving topics or methodologies that you are not familiar with; the last thing you want to do is take on a project in an area you know nothing about and wind up providing erroneous or incomplete information to your client. This is one major benefit of membership in the Association of Independent Information Professionals (AIIP; www.aiip.org). AIIP's annual conference and private email discussion list help you get acquainted with colleagues, observe how professionally they present themselves, and learn about their backgrounds and where their expertise lies. (That is also why you should maintain a professional demeanor whenever you participate in professional discussion lists. If you are argumentative, unprofessional, or rude, your colleagues will be disinclined to subcontract with you or refer others to you.) Working within your network, you can call on fellow info pros who have the skills you need for particular projects, thus enabling you to provide your clients with information from the best possible researchers.

On the Road Again

Bringing in subcontractors is also a way to provide services to clients while you are traveling or on vacation. When I am on the road, for example, I may ask a colleague to handle my clients for me. I leave a message on my voice mail explaining that I am out of town but that clients should call "my associate" so-and-so at such-and-such phone number for any rush research needs. My colleague then handles any calls that come in and bills me for her time (at a discounted rate) and expenses; I then bill my client for my colleague's time at my regular hourly rate, plus expenses. I make a little profit, my clients are happy, and I did not have to leave the office unattended while I was away. See Chapter 12, Work and the Rest of Your Life, for more discussion of how to keep your business going during a vacation.

Needing Low-End Labor

You may occasionally need to hire subcontractors to help with simple research that you do not have time for or that you do not want to bill out at your regular hourly rate. I ran into one of these situations when a client asked me to look at more than 800 websites. I knew that not only would I run out of time, but my client could not afford to pay my hourly rate for this kind of work. More importantly, my client did not need my expertise when reviewing each site as much as she needed my oversight and guidance of the project. For jobs like this, you might find graduate students who want to work a few hours a week or a mom with small kids at home who is not interested in full-time employment but wants to stay in the work force. You will have to supervise these subcontractors more closely than you would a colleague because you must train them from scratch, and they are bound to make some mistakes in judgment as they learn. On the other hand, you will probably be paying them a fraction of your hourly rate so you can build in some overhead time for training and oversight.

The Challenges of Subcontracting

Of course, some disadvantages come along with subcontracting out work. The issue foremost in most contractors' minds is that they must rely on someone else's work. It is usually not feasible (or even possible) to replicate the subcontractor's work or check it thoroughly before it goes to the client, so you have to accept on faith the subcontractor's assurance that she did a thorough and competent job. When you send a subcontractor's material to a client, *you* have to answer for its quality even though you did not do the research yourself. If the client is not happy with the results, you cannot simply throw up your hands and say, "Well, I didn't do the work … go talk to my subcontractor."

I routinely subcontract out a portion of my research work, and in one or two situations, I have been left high and dry by a new subcontractor. The person did a merely cursory job, or overlooked a crucial piece of information, or completely misunderstood the scope or focus of the project, or missed my deadline, or far exceeded the budget cap. The few projects that have gone bad have been learning experiences for me. I now know how to avoid most of the problems that can arise—by staying in touch with the subcontractor, by having her send the information to me during the course of the project rather than all at the end, and by making sure that she is not overworked or distracted.

Your subcontractor may legitimately need more hours than you expected the project to take. That, of course, eats into your profit, because you have probably agreed on a not-to-exceed budget with your client. The subcontractor may not use the same resources that you would have used or may not write up the results the way you would. Given that some of us independent info pros have a stubborn streak a mile wide ("It's my way or the highway"), dealing with subcontractors who have their own way of doing things can be an exercise in frustration.

In addition to the problems inherent in having someone else do the research for you, a remote possibility exists that your subcontractor will approach your client directly and solicit business. This is considered unethical and should never happen, but there are a few less-than-sterling people in any profession. Make it clear when negotiating with a new subcontractor that such conduct is unacceptable.

Points to Ponder

Imagine you have just landed a project that requires you bring in a subcontractor for a portion of the work. How do you formalize the relationship? The exact format does not matter as much as the fact that you clearly spell out your expectations for the subcontractor. AIIP offers a sample subcontractor agreement that its members can use. Whether you use the AIIP form, have a lawyer draw up a contract, or write your own, you will need to spell out the following:

- A detailed description of the nature of the research to be done, analysis to be provided, and other aspects of the project

- Whether the subcontractor may contact your client directly

- The format of your search results—full-text articles, an executive summary, printouts of webpages, and so on

- The not-to-exceed budget or the maximum number of hours the subcontractor is authorized to work and the hourly rate you will pay

- The deadline by which the information must be delivered to you

- Whose fee-based online accounts, if any, to use—the subcontractor's or yours

- The payment terms for the subcontractor (e.g., within 30 days of the invoice date)

- A nondisclosure agreement (NDA) in which your subcontractor promises to maintain client confidentiality and not disclose the name of the client or the nature of the research without prior approval; AIIP has a sample NDA available to members

It is important to spell out all the details of the subcontracting relationship, in writing, before you begin. It is tempting to just call a colleague, describe the project, and let it go at that, particularly if you are in a hurry. Resist the urge; in my experience, the most significant cause of subcontracting relationships going bad is treating a subcontracted job too casually. Even if I have discussed a project thoroughly with a subcontractor, I always follow up with an email that spells out the details of the project (at least, the details that I can disclose to the subcontractor without violating client confidentiality), an itemized list of what I expect the subcontractor to do, a description of the deliverable—that is, the form and format in which the results will be delivered, the final deadline for the project and any interim deadlines, and the maximum number of hours, the hourly rate, and the dollar amount of expenses authorized—or just the total not-to-exceed budget the subcontractor has to work within. See the sidebar "Points to Ponder" for the items to include in your subcontracting agreement.

Following the Golden Rule

If you are like most independent info pros, you will find yourself on both sides of the subcontractor relationship; you will be sending work to others, and others will be asking you to work on their behalf. The Golden Rule of doing unto others certainly applies in this setting; the person to whom you subcontract a job today may hire you as a subcontractor tomorrow.

If You Are the Contractor

Buddhism teaches the practice of "detachment"—the art of appreciating and enjoying life without focusing on possession or need. As a contractor, you must develop a form of detachment as well. Your subcontractor will work the way he thinks best, using the sources and techniques he believes will get the best result. You have to let go of the urge to second-guess and micromanage the process, provided you are confident in his ability to conduct the research. Take a deep breath. Detach. Understand that many paths lead to the same truth or at least to the information your client needs. No two researchers ever approach a project in quite the same way, and there is seldom only one right answer to a research question. As long as you have confidence in your subcontractor's abilities, let him follow his own path.

But how do you develop the confidence to let go? To switch metaphors from Buddhism to romance, consider going out for coffee before you start dating seriously. Try a new subcontractor on a small project with a long lead time. If it does not work out, you can still find someone else to finish the job. You might be less prone to micromanage on something that is not a major, rush-rush project. Starting off this way also lets you discover what communication style works best with that particular subcontractor. Does she need a lot of hand-holding? Does she like to check in every day to give you an update? Do you like it when she does? Does she ask questions if she isn't clear on the parameters of the project? Is she flexible about the format in which the results are to be delivered?

Speaking of deliverables, make sure to tell your subcontractor how you want the results delivered to you. Supply a copy of your Word template with whatever formatting you prefer and the headers and footers that you normally insert. (Headers and footers are a nice way to polish your report; the page numbers help the reader locate specific items from a table of contents, and a footer that contains your company name and contact information ensures that every reader down the line will know who is responsible for this fabulous report. See Chapter 37, Deliverables, for more discussion of packaging your research results.) Do you want the subcontractor to highlight key portions of the documents he has found? Do you want a table of contents at the beginning of the report? Do you want a list of all the resources used during the search? Be sure your subcontractor knows your requirements so that the material he sends you is ready, or nearly ready, to forward to your client or incorporate into your report. And when you first negotiate a project with a subcontractor, be sure to factor in enough time for you to tweak the deliverable to your own specifications. If your client needs the results by Friday, ask your subcontractor to send you the material by Wednesday evening at the latest. Once you have established a working relationship with a subcontractor and have confidence in his ability to deliver results that are up to your standards, you can reduce the amount of lead time you factor into the process.

Tell your subcontractor as much about the project as you can within the bounds of client confidentiality. The more he knows, the more focused and on-target the research results will be. Stay in touch during the course of the research. For complex projects, it is usually best to get interim results as the job goes along to make sure that the subcontractor is on schedule and generally in the right area. Even though that principle of detachment I mentioned applies throughout the project, you are ultimately responsible for the results of the research, and your client will expect you to stand behind what you deliver.

Remember that you are the subcontractor's client. That means that you must pay his invoice within the agreed-upon terms, whether or not you have been paid by your client. If you are working on a large project and you are concerned about cash flow, negotiate with your client for prepayment of a portion of the not-to-exceed budget. That way, you can afford to pay your subcontractor on time. And paying your sub on time is critical if you ever want to use him again. Mary Earley, of MME Research, said it best:

> It's critical to pay promptly and to communicate with your subcontractors. In addition to being the professional thing to do, you engender loyalty and your projects will get higher priority than those of companies whose payment is not reliable. Also, your subcontractors may be willing to be flexible about payment terms if you have been reliable in the past. In one case, I had a client who switched from a 30- to a 60-day payment frame, meaning that I was going to need to pay later on a specific project. Because I was candid with my subcontractors at the outset, they were able to accept those terms.

Much as you want to be able to handle anything a client asks you to do, in some situations it makes more sense to refer a project out entirely to a colleague—taking yourself completely out of the loop—rather than subcontracting and retaining ultimate control of the job. When I get requests for complex medical or legal research, for example, I know that I would not be able to do a competent job of translating the client's needs for a subcontractor. I would not know what questions to ask during the reference interview with the client. I would not know if the information delivered by a subcontractor was reliable or not. And sometimes I step out of the middle of a transaction for reasons of liability. I do not take on intellectual property research, for instance, because there is a risk—small but real—of being held liable for enormous damages if a relevant patent or trademark was missed during the search. Rather than subcontract the work to an expert intellectual property researcher—which would mean sharing any potential liability—I simply refer the client to someone who I think would do a thorough and professional job.

John Levis, retired owner of John E. Levis Associates, said it best: "It takes a healthy ego to be an information entrepreneur—you have to be confident that you've got what it takes to provide high quality information services. But successfully running an information business also takes a healthy *lack* of ego. You have to be able to recognize when you just don't have the knowledge or expertise to do the best possible job for a client. And believe me, if you take on a job that goes beyond your abilities, your client can tell, and he just won't call you again."

What About Referral Fees?

Independent info pros have various policies regarding the payment of referral fees when a colleague directs a client to them. I work on the assumption that, in the long run, referrals go both ways and it's more trouble than it's worth to pay referrals whenever a colleague sends someone to me and vice versa. Some info pros will pay to the referring person either a fixed amount or a fee equivalent to some percentage of the time that they billed to the client. If you expect a fee for referring a client to a colleague, be sure to discuss this with the colleague ahead of time. And remember that there is no assurance that the colleague will actually complete the sale; even if you do agree upon a fee, it is usually contingent on the info pro getting the job. Referral fees, unlike payments to subcontractors, are usually sent after the client has paid the invoice.

If You Are the Subcontractor

What I enjoy most about being a subcontractor is the variety of projects I get to work on. I can see how other independent info pros package projects for their clients. (See Chapter 37, Deliverables, for more on packaging research results.) I enjoy having colleagues as clients—someone who understands what information I need to do the research. And I enjoy being spared from having to interact directly with problematic clients. The downside is that I don't get to hear from the happy clients who were impressed with the research, and I generally cannot call the client directly to ask questions or clarify a point.

When a colleague asks me to subcontract, it is a sign of trust. It is my responsibility to decide whether I really can do the work. Do I have the time? Am I familiar enough with the subject to do an excellent job? Am I comfortable with the budget, deadline, and description of the work? I know that my contractor is depending on me; if I botch the job, I have caused her to look bad to her client.

A subcontractor's responsibilities are pretty straightforward:

- Do not take on a job you cannot do well.

- Never, ever exceed the agreed-upon budget without explicit authorization by the contractor.

- Do whatever it takes to get the job done by the agreed-upon deadline.

- If you run into problems as you are working on the project, contact the contractor immediately. No surprises!

- Make sure you understand how the contractor wants the results delivered.

- Be professional. The contractor is your client. Even if you are just getting started as an independent info pro and relying on subcontracted work for most of your income, you should cultivate a number of clients and not just one contractor.

- Above all, be mindful that your contractor is counting on you. He has made a commitment to his client and is relying on you to deliver the goods.

Being a subcontractor also means that the contractor trusts you to maintain client confidentiality. In some instances, a contractor asks me as the subcontractor to contact the client directly in order to clarify the research; I then introduce myself as my contractor's "associate." Once in a while, the client, assuming that the contractor and I are business partners, calls me later with a request for another project. It is critical for me to pass any such requests to the contractor; this was not my client to begin with, and I am ethically bound to decline any work from the client directly. When this situation comes up, I usually talk with the client just long enough to figure out that this is a new project, and then explain that my colleague so-and-so handles all new projects and that I will ask her to call the client back shortly to discuss the project.

Before you start a job for a contractor, find out how the end result should look. Does she want a Word file? If so, ask her to send you her template so you can use her standard formatting. (See the earlier section, "If You Are the Contractor" to see the same questions from the point of view of the contractor.) Does she want a cover memo? Even if she plans to incorporate your work into a larger deliverable, write up a thorough description for her, if not for the client—of what you did, what you found, what you didn't find, and what additional research you would recommend (remember—one can almost always do more work on a job).

Finally, you have to market yourself as a subcontractor just as much as for any other type of work. The subcontracting portion of your client base will consist of your fellow independent info pros, but you still need to remind them occasionally of the services you provide. You are more vulnerable to economic downturns as a sub-contractor; if the economy gets tight, independent info pros may have less business coming in, which means that they will have less work to subcontract to you. So this kind of work should not be your only marketing focus. If you have your own base of direct clients, you have a better chance of drumming up business than if you have to wait for your contractors to do so.

Running a Subcontractor-Based Business

Up to this point in our discussion of contractors and subcontractors, I have pretty much assumed that both parties do most of their own research, farming out work to colleagues occasionally. However, in another model for independent info pro businesses, the business owner focuses almost entirely on marketing and relies on a small cadre of subcontractors for all the research. Sue Rugge, one of the pioneers in our industry, built several successful businesses this way. Others have done so as well. This type of business works well even if you do not have a research background, as long as you enjoy—or at least don't mind—marketing.

The idea behind a subcontractor-based business is that you, the owner, focus on building the business and managing clients while subcontracting the work to expert researchers—all of whom are independent info pros running their own businesses; they are not your employees. You need to develop strong relationships with five or six subcontractors, all of whom are willing to give your jobs top priority. In exchange for a steady income stream, they agree to discount their hourly rate for you. Assuming that you can mark up your subcontractors' rates by a third or half, this can be a profitable business model.

You may have to hire someone to help you manage the flow of work through your office—taking the initial calls from clients, conducting the reference interview if you are not available to do so, tracking which subcontractor has which job, making sure the results of each job are returned to you and then sent on to the client in time, keeping track of expenses for each project, and so on. You do not have to be a researcher yourself to run a subcontractor-based business, but you do need an understanding of information resources and realities so you can discuss the project intelligently with the client. You can either estimate the budget yourself or discuss the details with the subcontractor who will be working on the job and get his or her estimate of the total hours and expenses involved.

If you are going to rely on subcontractors to do most or all of your research, you need to identify info pros who are very good, who have enough open time that they can set aside a certain amount of time for your work, and who are willing to discount their hourly rate in exchange for steady work. This may be harder than it sounds; most independent info pros who are worth their salt are busy with their own clients, and many are not willing to substantially reduce their fees. The effort to find the best info pros you can is worth it; they will enable you to offer top-quality research services to your clients, ensuring that they remain repeat clients.

For this kind of business to succeed, you have to be a good marketer because that is what you will spend much of your time doing. You have to be organized and willing to set up procedures for managing the flow of work through your office; when every project goes out to a subcontractor, it is a lot easier for an occasional job to slip through the cracks. You have to focus on the bottom line because overhead for your office administrator cannot be directly billed out to a client. And you have to be comfortable relying on others to do your research for you. Unlike the ad hoc subcontracting that the typical info pro occasionally engages in, running a subcontracted research company requires that you involve your subcontractors in your business. They will get to know your clients, they may use your account to search the professional online services, they will occasionally mess up, and you will have to cover for them with your clients.

In spite of such challenges, the subcontractor-based business model can be lucrative. You can grow your business as large as you want; your only limitation is how much marketing you want to do and how many subcontractors you want to manage.

Top Tips for Subcontracting

For subcontractors:

✦   Never exceed the agreed-upon budget.

✦   Always deliver your results on time or, better yet, early.

✦   Never take on a job you cannot do superbly.

For contractors:

✦   Treat your subcontractors as partners. Give them as much information as possible about each project.

✦   Detach. Find the best subcontractors you can and then let them approach projects however they want.

✦   Pay your subcontractors promptly, regardless of when your client pays you.

Chapter 17

Ethics and Legalities

I will begin this chapter by saying that I assume you will treat all your clients, colleagues, and vendors with courtesy and integrity. It's a small world, and your actions do have a way of coming back around to you. Your reputation is one of your most valuable assets, and it is far easier to maintain a good reputation than it is to repair a bad one.

The best way to maintain your sterling reputation and avoid the aggravation (not to mention expense) of lawsuits is to err on the side of caution and to run your business as if your spiritual advisor, your mother, the government, and an investigative reporter were watching your every move. It is great to be a risk-taker when it comes to trying new marketing strategies or expanding your business; risk-taking in legal or ethical matters is just foolish.

IANAL

IANAL is a web acronym for I Am Not A Lawyer and that describes me. This chapter provides commonsense guidance on how to conduct your business ethically and legally, but what I have to tell you, based on my own and my colleagues' experience, is no substitute for legal advice. You will undoubtedly need to consult a lawyer occasionally; I recommend that, as soon as you start your business, you find one you are comfortable with and who understands your concerns as an independent info pro.

Ethical Quandaries

All independent info pros place certain limits on what they consider to be ethical behavior. One info-entrepreneur, who will remain nameless, told me about a client she had when she first went into business. The client had a project funded with grant money and at the end of the info pro's work, there was still a bit of money left over. Apparently, it would have been unseemly not to have spent all the funds allocated, so he asked the info pro to just bill him for some extra time without actually doing any additional work. As she told me later, "I didn't have the moxie to say no, but I regret to this day that I did as he asked. When I later came to my senses, I gave an equal amount of money to a charity, and I severed my relationship with the client. No client is worth compromising my basic ethics." Although the client may have characterized his action as a bonus for work well done, the info pro felt that it was simply a form of theft.

Of course, it is also unethical—as well as unprofessional—to accept work that goes beyond your area of expertise, or that, because of time or budget constraints, you know you will not be able to do well. It is great to challenge yourself by taking on new types of work, but be confident, in your heart of hearts, that you can provide the client with high-quality, professional service. Likewise, there will be periods when you are fully booked with work, and a client calls offering you a project you really do not want to turn down. If accepting it means giving short shrift to one client or another, you must turn down the job or be willing to subcontract it to someone else. Taking on a project that you are not confident you can handle harms the entire profession; a client once burned is unlikely to use any independent info pro again.

This is where the network of colleagues that you have built up comes in handy. One of the reasons I belong to the Association of Independent Information Professionals (AIIP) is that I am able to meet experienced info pros in virtually every area of specialization—legal research, document delivery, medical information, even fields as specialized as architectural research or aerospace engineering. I have a small cadre of people to whom I routinely refer projects that I cannot handle or subcontract out myself. These are people I have gotten to know over time, virtually all of whom I have met in person at an AIIP annual meeting or at other info pro conferences. If I do not have an appropriate referral among the people I already know, I will browse the AIIP membership directory to remind myself who does what among the info pros I already know and might have dealt with already.

Handling Conflicts

Many independent info pros specialize in a particular industry—pharmaceuticals, advertising agencies, and so on. Sooner or later, they encounter the situation in which two of their clients are direct competitors. How would you handle this? If you are working closely with the marketing department of one company and you get a request from its competitor to dig up marketing strategy of your client, you should turn down the job. Even if you limit your research to publicly available sources, your original client might not want to find out that you are providing information to its competitor on a topic about which you have possibly had access to proprietary information. You may also have been required to sign a contract with your first client, promising not to do any work for any of its direct competitors. I use the "clear light of day" test: What would happen if both clients found out that you were doing work for the other? If you are simply providing research services to both using publicly available resources, my gut tells me that you do not have a conflict. If, however, you know that one client or the other would find this objectionable, or if you signed a contract not to work for a direct competitor, then you will have to turn down the work. (See the section, Reading the Fine Print, later in this chapter, which discusses how to handle contracts that unduly restrict your business activities.)

Client Confidentiality

It should go without saying that independent info pros must maintain strict confidentiality with regard to every project and every client. That means you never disclose the nature of a project to a third party. (You can usually describe projects in very general terms in your marketing material or when discussing the kind of work you do, such as "provided in-depth information on the ice cream market" or "developed a profile of the information technology needs of a government agency.") Likewise, you do not mention or list the names of your clients on your promotional material or website without specific, written permission from the client. Some info pros get around this by coyly describing a client as, say, "a major software company based in Redmond, Washington." Yes, they don't, strictly speaking, mention Microsoft by name, but most people will be able to figure it out. It is better to stick with a more vague and generic description ("a *Fortune* 100 information technology company") or get permission to list the company by name.

Similarly, do not use clients as references without asking. They may have a corporate policy prohibiting employees from endorsing a third party, they may not want outside entities—possibly their competitors—to know whom they use for information services, or they may simply not want to be bothered with calls from your prospective customers.

Reading the Fine Print

Reading the small print in contracts, licenses, and agreements gets harder every year, at least for those of us who have graduated to bifocals. But you ignore the fine print at your peril. Signing a contract without reading it or hoping that no one will actually enforce all of its provisions is asking for trouble. I will never forget the difficulties I went through the time that I unthinkingly signed a client's contract requiring that I carry $1 million (!) in automobile insurance; this was for a job that did not require me to leave my office chair. When I submitted my not-insignificant invoice, the client's billing department asked for proof of that million-dollar coverage before they would cut a check. Eventually I was able to get a short-term retroactive policy from my insurance carrier, but I learned then to always read the fine print and cross out any provision that I could not or would not fulfill.

As it turns out, it is sometimes easy to eliminate onerous and unreasonable requirements such as that $1 million in auto insurance coverage for an in-office project. Just cross out the offending paragraph, initial it, and note the change when you send the signed copy back to the client. Ask that they return a signed copy to you, and you are done. And what if the client refuses to modify the contract? Well, you can take a chance like I did back then, or you can walk away from the job as I would do now. My feeling is that the clients who are sticklers for your accepting their terms also tend to enforce those terms.

Some clients will ask that you sign a confidentiality or nondisclosure agreement (commonly known as an NDA) before you begin work. This is standard operating procedure for larger companies, and these agreements are usually not objectionable. However, look for a clause that also prohibits you from doing similar work for their competitors, often for a period of years. Unless you truly intend to comply with such a requirement—and how do you know ahead of time whom they might consider competitors?—be sure to negotiate. My experience has been that clauses like this one can sometimes be eliminated. Often it is just a matter of pointing out that

Playing by the Rules

Many independent info pros start their businesses while still working in a corporate environment. It is tempting to squeeze in some of your own work during the day—accepting clients' calls on your cell phone, using the information resources available to employees for your outside research projects, and so on. It is especially tempting to take advantage of your organization's flat-fee contracts with the professional online services such as Factiva or LexisNexis. "Hey, we're paying for all-we-can-use as it is; what's a little additional research?"

Resist that little voice in your head. It is wrong, it is unprofessional, and it is cheating. It is as tacky as stealing office supplies to furnish your home office. On top of all that, you will never learn how to determine the true cost of online research if you piggyback onto services that you do not have to pay for yourself; when you finally do quit your day job to run your independent business full time, you will have no idea how to accurately estimate costs. And finally, you will never forget or forgive yourself for these ethical lapses.

The same principle applies when using public library resources. It is tempting to call your local library and ask the reference librarian to conduct a search for you. "I mean, they'd do it if my client called directly, wouldn't they? I'm just the client's agent, right?" In this case, no. You are passing off the results of someone else's work as your own; you are using the scarce resources of a local library on behalf of someone who probably does not live in the community that the library is intended to support and that, in turn, supports the library through its taxes. Last but not least, you are using the necessarily limited resources of a public library when you should be providing your client with the full breadth and depth of resources available to you as an independent info pro.

(a) you are a small business serving their industry, and the restriction is unduly onerous, and (b) their basic concern is confidentiality, isn't it, and the rest of the contract—

which you have no trouble signing—assures that you will comply with that. Sometimes, however, they just will not budge, and you will have to consider declining the work, as I have done on occasion. You will also have to scrutinize the fine print in contracts you sign with online information providers. By now, most of them have learned what independent info pros are and what we do. One of their concerns was that we would act as "resellers"—that is, we would turn around and re-market access to their information to third parties at a lower price than they charge. Of course, that is not what independent info pros do; we just pass along selected information for one-time client use. However, some contracts do prohibit users from passing the information along to anyone else. AIIP members get the benefit of special contracts that the association has negotiated with a number of information vendors. These contracts specifically grant us the right to pass along the results of any search to a single client. If you are not an AIIP member, read carefully any information vendor's contract to ensure that it does not prohibit you from passing work along to your clients.

Contracts and Agreements

As I discuss in Chapter 13, Managing Your Clients, you need a standard form for contracts or letters of agreement, as well as a basic disclaimer statement that spells out what your client can and cannot expect from you. While it is not cost-effective to have a lawyer draft each contract or proposal for you, it is wise to have a generic one that you can modify as necessary. As long as you are at it, you can also ask your lawyer for a standard nondisclosure agreement that *you* can offer to clients—thus avoiding the problem I described earlier with noncompete clauses hiding in clients' NDAs—and for a subcontracting agreement for when (not "if") you subcontract work to another independent info pro. If you are a member of AIIP, you have access to sample nondisclosure and subcontracting agreements, which you can take to your lawyer and ask for any recommended modifications based on your specific situation and business model.

Remember that a contract by itself does not necessarily protect you from being sued by a client. Good communication and listening to your instinct are just as important. Make sure that you have managed your client's expectations. Is he asking for a promise up front that you will find specific information? Does he sound like he expects more than you think you will be able to deliver? Is this the kind of project that may require a lot of research with very little in the way of results? If so, make sure you have brought up, discussed, and dealt with any unfounded assumptions or unrealistic expectations. And by "dealt with," I do not mean just spelling out your caveats and cautions in a liability statement. Rather, you must say directly to the client, "I can't promise ahead of time what I'll find. In fact, I may find very little information on this subject. I will use the sources that I think are most likely to produce the information you want, but remember that you are paying me for my time and expertise, not for the information per se. Even if I don't find what you're looking for, you will pay for my work in finding what is available." If this sounds harsh, consider how much more harsh your collections call will sound three months from now when the client refuses to pay your invoice because you never dispelled his mistaken assumptions about the services he engaged you to provide.

Although it is tempting to turn every conversation about a potential project into a sales call with the objective being to close the sale, this is the time to be modest and actually *under* promise. If a client cannot deal with the possibility that you might not find what he wants, you do not want this client.

Dangerous Words

Every research project is restricted by budget and time constraints. Information resources are inevitably incomplete. All published sources contain inaccuracies. Given the limitations that we info pros have to live with, make sure that your marketing material, website, and client contracts do not include any of the following words. All of them promise what—by definition—you cannot deliver.

- Complete
- All-inclusive
- Exhaustive
- Comprehensive
- Thorough
- All sources
- Best

Keeping Your Word

"I meant what I said and I said what I meant. An elephant's faithful, 100 percent." Dr. Seuss's *Horton Hatches an Egg* featured an elephant who, having promised to tend to an egg newly laid by a bird who then disappears for months, maintains his post on the nest until the egg finally hatches.

Even though your jobs probably won't entail hatching bird eggs, Horton's promise to live up to his word is instructive. Clients do not like surprises, particularly when they involve invoices that are higher than estimated or results that are not as promised. It is often difficult to estimate at the outset how much time and money a project will involve. Rather than guaranteeing a complete job for a set fee, you are much better off phrasing your quote in terms of what it will take to "see what's out there" or setting a cap on how much you will spend on the "first phase" of the project. If, when you reach that point, you have not found what the client wants, your report should spell out the approaches you took, what you did find, and what further research you recommend. If the client wants additional work, fine; you can negotiate a fee for the next phase of the project. If not, at least you have kept within the originally approved budget. In either case, you never, ever exceed an agreed-upon budget cap without clearing it first with the client.

This concept is hard for some researchers to accept. "But there's so much more that I could find." "I'm not providing my client with truly professional service if I don't follow up on all the research leads I uncover." This train of thought can go on forever, though. You could almost always do more work on a project, but without your client's approval, you have no right to expect him to pay you for that extra work. And if you just don't bill for some of your hours and deliver a package that is disproportionately information-rich for what the client has agreed to pay you, you set up false expectations of what the client can expect in the future for a similar budget.

Copyright Perils

Copyright, in its most elemental form, is intended to protect the rights of authors, photographers, artists, musicians, and other creators of original works. The owner of the copyright has the exclusive right to reproduce the work, distribute copies, or make other use of the work, and to authorize others to do so. For example, I own the copyright on this book, but I have authorized the publisher to make and sell copies of it and to pay me a portion of the revenue from the sale of the books. If you want to make a copy of a chapter of this book for a friend, you will have to arrange for permission from the publisher and from me. Similarly, if you want to provide a copy of an article to a client, you need to arrange for permission from whoever owns the copyright—either the publisher or the author.

Copyright is a tricky issue and is still an unsettled question, at least in the U.S. It has become even more complicated since the web, where electronic copying is easy—and rampant. Although the "fair use" provision of the copyright law permits one-time photocopying under certain specific circumstances, copies made in a business or for-profit context may be subject to a copyright fee. As I noted at the beginning of this chapter, I Am Not A Lawyer, so I am not going to opine on what exactly the current copyright law does and does not cover. What I can recommend is that if you anticipate needing to make photocopies of articles or sections from books on a regular basis, you either establish an account with a copyright licensing organization such as the Copyright Clearance Center (www.copyright.com) or subcontract to a document delivery service that will handle payment of the appropriate copyright fees for you. You can find document delivery companies listed in the AIIP membership directory.

What about copyrighted websites and material downloaded from professional online services? The accepted truth among independent info pros is that we are merely acting as agents for our clients, and so as long as we comply with copyright restrictions on their behalf, we are in compliance with copyright law. That means, for example, that downloading or printing a page from a website is generally OK because we are only doing what our client would do for her own use. A royalty payment to the copyright holder is built into the fee we are automatically billed for material we download from professional online services; again, we are simply acting on behalf of our client, who is not obligated to pay any additional fees for her own use of the information.

However, our clients do not automatically have the right to redistribute material you provide to them, whether by posting it on a web or intranet site, making photocopies, or forwarding electronic copies to others. If your client wants to distribute copies of the information you send him, you can offer to help him negotiate with the appropriate website owners and online information providers. Dialog and DataStar offer a streamlined method for purchasing the rights to redistribute or archive individual articles through their Electronic Redistribution and Archiving program.

To ensure that your clients understand that they do not have unlimited use of the information you provide them, you may want to include a copyright notice along with your cover memo when you send your research results. An example of such a notice is:

> The attached has been compiled [or derived] from copyrighted sources and is provided for your individual use. If you plan to archive or distribute copies of this information, you must seek permission directly from the copyright holders. [Independent info pro's company name] is not responsible for copyright violations by you or your organization.

Recycling Results

I am often asked whether clients have requested the same search twice and whether I wind up using the information from one research project for another client—to recycle the results, as it were. In two decades of business, I have not once run into a situation in which two clients asked for the same information; every project has a different spin or emphasis. In the extremely unlikely event that two clients asked for exactly the same information at the same time, the answer would still be that I have to redo the work on behalf of the second client. A colleague of mine once received a project from a law firm client on an aspect of engineering technology. It was very broad, and the client insisted he wanted "everything" on the subject. Ultimately, my colleague complied and handed the client reams of search results, along with a very hefty bill. Just a few days later, she got a call from another client, an engineering company, asking for a search in a particular technical area, one that happened to be a subset of the information requested by the law firm client. As she did the search, using the same databases and pulling up much of the same information that she had for the first client, it struck her that the two requests must have been connected. Indeed, they were: The two clients were on opposing sides in a patent infringement suit. Effectively, she had done the same search for two clients. But the second client, who focused his request much more tightly, paid a small fraction of the cost for essentially the same quantity of useful information.

The rule for research using any commercial, fee-based online information service is "one search, one client." That means that the results of a given search can be provided to one client only. If a second client wants the same results, you have to pay for the material again. The same is true for photocopies of copyrighted material. Note that most professional online services do allow you to keep a backup copy of information you send to clients—and, yes, there have been times when I have had to send the results again because a client lost the file. The online vendor may stipulate how long you can keep the backup copy; some limit you to several months. I generally keep backup copies no longer than six months; if the client needs the information again, she will probably need an updated version of the research anyway.

Legal Collections

Very few independent info pros have been sued directly as a result of work they performed. What does sometimes happen, though, is that the results do not meet the client's expectations, the client decides not to pay the bill, the info pro threatens to take the client to small claims court, and then the client starts talking about the poor quality of the research. Suddenly the info pro is put on the defensive and things get ugly. (See Chapter 14, Money, Money, Money, for a general discussion of how to avoid getting stiffed by a client.)

So how do you deal with slow- or no-pay clients? To begin with, for any job that is large enough to really hurt if you do not get paid, obtain at least partial payment up front. Period. A client who does not have enough confidence in your work to put down a deposit may well also be difficult to collect from at the end of the job. And be willing to walk away if the client disputes your invoice at the completion of the project. Suing a client for nonpayment is often not worth the risk of being counter-sued for damages on the basis of having done an inadequate job. You may feel confident that you can defend the quality of your work, but do you really want to be put in the position of having to do so? And despite your best efforts, you may fail; any lawsuit is a gamble.

However, there are ways to encourage a client to pay that do not involve harassment, lawsuits, or undue anguish. First, always contact the client as soon as an invoice is past due. Ask if the client needs another copy of the invoice on the chance that the original was lost in the mail. If you forget to include your Taxpayer ID or Social Security number (or VAT, GST, or other business identification number) on your invoice, your client's accounting department may delay payment. Offer to fax or scan any necessary documentation such as the IRS's form that provides your Taxpayer ID number or Social Security number.

Keep in mind that your client may not be the person responsible for writing and mailing out checks. More likely, she signs off on the invoice, then sends it to the accounting department for processing. Many companies cut checks only once or twice a month, so if you just miss a payment cycle, you are out of luck and will simply have to wait. Once you have ascertained that your client has done her part, limit your calls to the accounts payable person responsible for your invoice, and escalate the discussion to that person's manager if necessary. Your contact with your client should be positive and focused on your services, not on getting your invoice paid. Of course, if you find that your client is sitting on the invoice, then you do need to impress upon her the necessity of doing whatever paperwork is necessary to get it off her desk and into the accounting system.

You might consider having someone else make collections calls for you—subcontract them to a colleague or hire a skilled temporary worker with a business background to make the calls. You might even ask a spouse or other household member who is willing and able to make the call or a business partner who is calm under pressure. It is easy to get angry or embarrassed when calling about an invoice that is seriously in arrears, and if you are not careful, you will wind up personalizing what is in fact just a business matter. Someone who is paid simply to make such calls in a professional manner may be better able to negotiate with the client. Be sure to give the person some negotiation points ahead of time; you might offer to accept payment in several monthly installments or to put the charge on a credit card, or, if circumstances warrant it, to forgive a portion of the total amount due. In any event, having a friendly but stern and emotionally uninvolved person make your collections calls may keep an unpleasant situation from turning into a hostile one.

As I mentioned earlier, be willing to walk away from an invoice if it becomes clear that your client simply will not pay you. Interestingly, I have only had to do this a few times. After it became obvious that the client was not going to pay me, I wrote him a letter forgiving the debt, expressing my regret that he was not able to live up to his promise to pay, and hoping that he treated his clients better than he had treated me. In two instances, I eventually *did* get paid by the client, albeit a year late. But the biggest benefit was that I did not let the debt weigh me down in the meantime. Running an independent info pro business requires an extraordinary amount of energy, and expending that energy on a deadbeat client is simply not useful.

Top Tips for Remaining Lawsuit-Free

✦ Be modest in what you promise your clients and manage their expectations.

✦ Establish a not-to-exceed budget for every project, and never, ever exceed it without prior approval.

✦ Be courteous, fair, and generous in dealing with clients.

✦ Subcontract or refer out any project that goes beyond your area of expertise.

✦ Keep clients in the loop when you are not finding what you expected.

✦ Listen to your gut and gracefully turn down work that does not feel right to you.

✦ Read the fine print in any contract you sign, and be prepared to negotiate.

Chapter 18

Professional Development

Back when I worked in corporate libraries, I always made sure to include money in my budget for professional conferences and subscriptions to library-related publications. Now that I not only set but approve and fund the budget for my one-person business, I still set aside a certain amount for professional development. Although it is hard to make time to read up on new developments in the field and tough to get away from the office to go to conferences, I know that my clients are paying me for my expertise. I have to continually refresh my skills, or I will become stale and lose my edge.

AIIP: Your Secret Weapon

I mention the Association of Independent Information Professionals (AIIP; www.aiip.org) in virtually every chapter of this book, and there is a reason for that. AIIP is an invaluable resource for anyone who is running an independent info pro business or considering becoming an information entrepreneur. I joined AIIP before I went independent, and I even took personal leave from my job to attend the association's annual conference. I am so glad I did; the opportunity to meet with experienced independent info pros, to just sit and listen to them talk about their current challenges and triumphs, was priceless. It gave me a real appreciation for what I was getting into. I will never forget one of the sessions I attended at that meeting—a panel discussion on "My Biggest Marketing Mistakes." It was so surprising to see such a collegial group, willing to share their own follies in the hope that others would not make the same mistakes. And my initial impression of AIIP has held up over the 20 years I have been a member.

AIIP was founded in 1987 by a couple of dozen independent info pros who barely knew each other but who shared a vision of forming an association of fellow info-entrepreneurs. Since then, it has grown to more than 600 members in more than 20 countries. AIIP offers several types of membership, including *full membership* for people who have already established an information business, *associate membership* for those who are considering becoming an independent info pro or who are otherwise interested in the profession, *student membership* for individuals enrolled in a degree-granting college or university, *supporting membership* for individuals or organizations wanting to provide additional financial support to AIIP, and two categories for retired members. Dues are relatively modest when you consider the benefits that come with AIIP membership.

Why do I renew my membership every year?

- I have access to the lively private email discussion list, AIIP-L, in which members discuss topics ranging from strategies for dealing with difficult clients to the newest electronic gadget to project-specific help such as tips for finding famous hot dog stands.

- My business is listed in the AIIP membership directory. My listing includes a description of my background, the type of work I specialize in and the services I provide, my website URL, and the specialized resources to which I have access. Other info pros who want to subcontract work can find me through the directory.

- I can attend the annual AIIP conference and learn firsthand how other information entrepreneurs deal with business issues similar to mine.

- I can develop business relationships with info pros from around the world.

- I am eligible for discounts on a variety of information-related services and products, many of which have been negotiated specifically for independent info pros.

- I can participate in the volunteer mentoring program, which matches experienced AIIP members with new info pros who need informal assistance in developing some aspect of their business. (I used to serve as a volunteer mentor and enjoyed it immensely, and now I offer a fee-based strategic coaching service for info-entrepreneurs.)

And finally, through AIIP I have built friendships with some of the best and the brightest people in the information industry. Working as an independent info pro can be an isolating experience; most of your friends probably have no firsthand knowledge of what you are talking about when you complain about cash flow, collections, or the challenge of closing a sale for something as ephemeral as "business intelligence." Imagine tapping into a network of hundreds of people who experience these same challenges every day. *That* is why I belong to AIIP, and that is why you should seriously consider joining as well, even before you launch your business.

Associations Galore

In addition to AIIP, you may find a number of information industry-related associations useful to join. Librarians and other info pros are often great sources of referrals—even librarians occasionally are stumped by their clients' questions, and they sometimes outsource such requests—and being active in a librarians' association is a great way to both learn from the pros and develop informal business relationships with them. See Section Three, Marketing, for more discussion of how to promote your business within associations.

The following associations would be of most interest to independent info pros:

- Special Libraries Association (SLA; www.sla.org): "Special" in this context means specialized; SLA is an association of librarians and other information professionals and knowledge workers who work in corporations, government agencies, business and industry organizations, universities, and other nontraditional settings. The membership also includes independent information consultants. SLA has about 11,000 members around the world, although the group as a whole has a North American focus.

- Public Record Retriever Network (PRRN; www.brbpub.com/prrn): Members conduct research in and obtain copies of public records from government sources. Note that this is not an association per se; it is hosted by BRB Publications, and principals of BRB serve as the directors of PRRN. It has more than 700 members, all in the U.S.

- The Chartered Institute of Library and Information Professionals (CILIP; www.cilip.org.uk): Based in the U.K., membership ranges from corporate information specialists to public librarians to knowledge managers. CILIP has about 21,000 members, most of whom are in the U.K.

Other country-specific librarian associations abound; some are more business-oriented than others. Associations also exist for librarians in specific industries and fields—the American Association of Law Libraries (www.aallnet.org), the Medical Library Association (www.mlahq.org), even the North American Sport Library Network (www.naslin.org). You may want to join a subject-specific library association, depending on the focus of your business and the type of information services you provide. The San Jose State University School of Library & Information Science maintains a reasonably thorough list of North American library associations (slisweb.sjsu.edu/resources/orgs.htm). SLA also maintains a calendar of industry events, which includes info pro-related conferences around the world. Skim SLA's list to find associations in your geographic region and subject interest.

In addition to formal associations, shared-interest groups and virtual groups are offering professional development opportunities in specific areas. One of the best-known groups within the information industry is the Patent Information Users Group, better known as PIUG (www.piug.org). I cannot imagine referring a client of mine to any patent researcher who is not a member of PIUG; I consider that to be a significant indicator of the commitment and professionalism of the researcher.

If your business focuses on a specific industry or subject, join your clients' major professional association. If your clients are primarily advertising and public relations professionals, for example, you can join the Public Relations Society of America (www.prsa.org) or the equivalent where you live.

Use your research skills to identify the leading association in your clients' industry or ask some of your clients which association they consider to be the most valuable. Keep in mind that you can often join as an associate member, which may not include all the privileges of full membership (e.g., voting or serving as an elected officer). This type of membership is available for those who are not necessarily practitioners. In addition to the benefits of networking with potential clients and getting your name out to members, joining an association usually entitles you to a journal or newsletter that will help you keep on top of issues that matter to your clients and help you anticipate their research needs.

Getting the Most Value From a Conference

In addition to the networking opportunities in attending a conference, here are some tips for keeping you focused on professional development while you are there:

- Look through the program before you arrive and decide which sessions will be most useful. Plan to spend at least three-quarters of the day in sessions—not playing hooky and visiting the local tourist attractions. (This is not to suggest that I have ever been guilty of that!)

- Allot time to visit the exhibit hall. Don't just walk down the aisles avoiding eye contact with the vendors; stop at each booth and ask the exhibitors to tell you (in 30 seconds or less) what sets them apart from their competition.

- Find the blog tag or keyword being used in the social web for the conference; often, the conference website will suggest what tag to use. Search your social network to see who else will be attending and consider meeting them during the conference. Also, identify the bloggers who will be covering the conference; I find that these folks often know who are the best speakers and which sessions are can't-miss, and they will cover sessions that I might not be able to attend.

- Talk to your clients ahead of time, if the conference is related to their business, and let them know you are attending. Offer to collect relevant exhibitor material or make contacts on their behalf and send the information to them when you return to the office.

- Look through your contacts and see if there is anyone in the conference city who you want to visit while you are there.

- If the conference is organizing groups for dinner at local restaurants, sign up. It is amazing what you can learn from colleagues during the course of a meal.

- Bring plenty of business cards and commit to not only handing them all out by the end of the conference but also collecting cards from as many prospects as you can reasonably market to.

Staying Sharp

It's hard for a one-person business to close up shop in order to attend a conference. You have the direct costs of travel, hotel, meals, and the conference registration itself, as well as the indirect costs attached to being away from the office and unavailable to clients who might have revenue-producing work for you. On the other hand, attending at least one info industry conference a year will keep you informed about new resources, research tools, vendors, and search techniques. Unlike the hours you might spend reading industry blogs, newsletters, or magazines, attending a professional conference is a full-immersion experience. You are (or should be) totally focused on your own professional development while you are there, and that is a useful annual exercise. Conferences also present a great opportunity to meet fellow independent info pros, build your subcontracting and referral network, and get inspired and re-energized.

When you figure out the overhead expenses for your business (I walk you through this exercise in Chapter 15, Setting Rates and Fees), include the cost of at least one information industry conference every year. Save up your frequent flier miles if you have to. I use a credit card that awards me a frequent flier mile for every dollar I charge—an easy way to accumulate those miles. Set aside $25 a week and within a year you'll save up enough to cover the entire cost of a conference. If your budget is tight and you don't mind giving up a little privacy, consider sharing a hotel room with a colleague.

In addition to attending conferences to keep up on new resources, technologies, and analytical tools, you need to stay updated on all the professional information services you use. (See Chapter 34, Professional Online Services, for more about background on fee-based resources.) Most of the vendors provide free user training and updates; take advantage of anything they offer that will help you search the system more effectively and make use of all the added-value features available. Dialog is well-known for its extensive free learning programs, including self-paced courses, live and recorded webinars, and numerous tutorials. Dialog also offers test databases and passwords so that you can practice what you learn at no cost. Factiva and LexisNexis also offer professional training webinars and tutorials. LexisNexis also provides information on marketing for libraries and information centers, some of which translates well to independent info pros.

I usually commit to spending three or four hours a week just for professional reading—this is in addition to my routine reading of email discussion groups and

RSS feeds. I might read a magazine on innovative business strategies or on new technologies or on marketing for entrepreneurs. All of these expand my mind and keep me thinking more creatively. Since we generally work from home or in other solo environments, we need to make an effort to expose ourselves to unexpected ideas and insights.

The Invisible Network

In addition to published news sources, make sure to discover the invisible network of experts available to you as an independent info pro—people who know something you don't know about the information industry or about research. I make a point of tapping into my network of colleagues whenever I can. I subscribe to a number of info pro-oriented email discussion groups. In addition, I make a point of staying in touch with independent info pros who I know and respect. I call all of them periodically, just to say hello and see what's new. I ask what amazing new web resource they've found lately, and I share with them an interesting source, product, tip, or technique that I've turned up.

When I talk to clients about their research projects, I often ask if they have done any initial research themselves or have any sources to recommend. Often, they will simply tell me to use my best judgment, but once in a while, I will learn about a great resource that I would never have found on my own. We independent info pros do not have a monopoly on research skills, and it is useful to remember that our clients may know about industry-specific sources that we can and should use.

I have been publishing a free monthly email newsletter of research tips (www.BatesInfo.com/tips) as a marketing tool for many years. (See Chapter 24, Marketing on the Web, for more discussion of this type of marketing.) An unexpected benefit has been the response I get every month from readers who point me to additional sources or other ways to find information. I think I gain more from my readers than I give them; my newsletter is one more way to tap into that invisible network of expertise that surrounds us as information professionals.

Top Tips for Maintaining Your Expertise

✦   Join and become active in AIIP.

✦   Find out what associations your clients are most likely to belong to and join those associations.

✦   Attend info pro conferences and focus on making the most of your time at each conference.

✦   Identify and participate in virtual discussions that address your area of expertise.

✦   Spend several hours a week on professional reading.

✦   Solicit recommendations of new information sources from clients and colleagues.

Chapter 19

Strategic Planning

"Strategic planning" sounds so formal—and formidable. *Fortune* 500 companies dedicate entire departments to this function. But independent info pros can, and should, do their own strategic planning as well. It need not involve a Harvard MBA; fortunately, all that is required is the ability to look at your business from an arm's-length perspective once a year and evaluate where you are and where you would like to be heading.

Getting a Yearly Check-Up

Think of this as your annual visit to the doctor, except without the embarrassing paper gown. Every year, schedule a day to sit down and evaluate where you are and, just as important, where you want to be a year from now. It is easy to coast along from year to year, particularly because we do not have annual reviews with a boss or annual meetings with a board of directors. But if we do not take time to reflect on our business and our competitive environment, we might find ourselves adrift or headed in an undesirable direction.

Go through your annual accounts (I hope you are using a financial management package such as QuickBooks; see Chapter 11, Business Apps for Info-Entrepreneurs) and print out a report of your sales for the year, sorted by client. Look at your records on every client for whom you did more than one or two projects. Where did the client come from? Was it a referral from an info pro colleague or another client, a conference you attended, an article you wrote, your blog, or a contact from your last job? Ask yourself if you can get more clients from the same source.

Saying "Thank You"

I do the annual review of my business in December, when the pace is a little slower. As I look at the work I have done for my steady clients, I want to express my gratitude for their business over the year. That brings up the question of whether or how to send holiday gifts to clients. Some independent info pros send boxes of candy, fruit, or snacks to their good clients. Others make a donation in their client's name to a noncontroversial charity. But some info pros worry either that clients will expect generous gifts every year or that corporate policy prohibits them from accepting gifts from vendors.

I do not have a set policy on gift giving; it depends on my relationship with the client. For a couple of clients I know well, I donate to a charity I know they support and send them a card telling them what I have done. For a client who is a speechwriter, I sometimes send a book I think he would enjoy. One of my favorite clients gets flowers every so often, just because I know she likes them, and I want to tell her that I am thinking of her.

Having been on the receiving end of vendors' holiday gifts, I know that the thought really does count. I do not keep track of who sent me something last year and who did not, but I do remember the occasional gift that shows that someone really thought of me. I forget within a month who sent me a tin of popcorn, but I remember for years a gift that has personal value. One year, a publisher I worked for sent me a beautiful print of a photo he had taken in the Sierra Nevada. I will always be grateful for that one gift, and I hope that some day I will be able to give a client something with equal impact.

What More Can I Do for My Clients?

Look at the kind of work each client has brought you. What else could you do for him? What is driving your client? Is his business growing or shrinking? What about the industry he is in—is it healthy or struggling? What could you provide to your client to help him grow his business? John Levis, a retired info-entrepreneur, once told me, "If you're going to grow your business, you need to be able to solve problems, not just find information. I wound up getting into the competitive intelligence field by listening to my clients and understanding their needs, sometimes even when they didn't know what they needed. Most clients are interested in getting answers to solve yesterday's problems; strategic planning focuses on solving tomorrow's problems. That's what keeps your clients—and you—in business."

Review your sales records to see if any one of your clients accounts for more than 20 or 25 percent of your revenue. If you find one that fits this criterion, ask yourself:

- What would happen if I lose this client? What impact would that have on my business?

- Why is this client giving me this much work? What can I do to generate similar amounts of revenue from other clients?

The practice of reviewing how much revenue each client brings in also helps you recognize how much business a "small" client may give you, cumulatively, over the course of a year. I remember my shock upon realizing the number of projects one consultant had sent me over the course of six months. It was all in one- or two-hour increments so I never thought of her as a particularly large client, but the business she sent my way certainly added up.

Spotting Troublesome Clients

During my annual review, I watch to see if anyone in particular has referred a disproportionate number of questionable, difficult, or potentially deadbeat clients. If so, I make a mental note to impose a more stringent rule regarding prepayment for clients referred from that person.

Reviewing your accounts will also help you determine whether you have clients whom you need to drop altogether. Do any of your clients call frequently for estimates without following through with the project? Do you spend an inordinate amount of time with them during or after each project, answering follow-up questions or justifying your bill? If so, it is probably time to fire the client because the time you spend with them could more profitably be spent doing billable work for other clients. And, yes, you *can* fire a client, provided you do it gently and professionally. See Chapter 13, Managing Your Clients, for more information on how to gracefully let go of a client.

Looking at the Revenue Mix

After I have reviewed the work I have done for my clients over the past year, I generate a report of income sources—how much I made from subcontracted research, how much for business intelligence, how much from consulting work, how much from speaking fees, and so on. I try to keep my income stream diversified; that way, even if one industry or group of clients is hit hard by an economic downturn, other clients may be unaffected, which means that my revenue is not hit as severely as it would be if all my work came from one small market niche. Having different types of clients and offering a variety of services also helps even out the workflow over the course of the year; a slow period for one group of clients may be a busy time for another.

Planning to Plan

Doing a yearly check-up is simple, provided you have set up your accounting system in a way that lets you easily extract useful information. With most financial management software, you can set up separate income subaccounts for the different types of work you do. For example, I maintain subaccounts for regular research, subcontracted research (work that I do as a subcontractor for other independent info pros), consulting, business coaching, speaking fees, and writing income. Using these separate categories takes no additional effort during the year—I just select the appropriate subaccount when I am writing each invoice—but doing so makes it easy for me to review my income at the end of the year. I can look at the totals and see exactly how much of my revenue comes from each type of work. In addition, I can categorize my clients by industry or market. For example, you may want to track how much of your revenue comes from law firms, consumer product companies, or whatever your major client groups might be. Think about how you want to monitor your business, and then build the tools that will enable you to do that. And remember, you can always set up new account types and update the account codes in existing invoices as your business grows and diversifies.

Not only do I review the diversity of my revenue sources, I also consider whether and how I might like to change that mix in the coming year. Do I want to travel more or less? Are my webinars profitable? If so, how can I increase the number that I do in a year? What impact will that have on my ability to maintain the other parts of my business?

I also think about maintaining a mix of clients and markets that respond quickly to marketing efforts—perhaps small clients with quick-turnaround projects who just forget to call—and big-ticket spenders who require longer-term marketing. With a blend of both types of clients, I can continually market to the latter group and can ratchet up my marketing efforts to the former group, if I find that I am not as busy as I would like to be.

Learning From Your First Year

I will talk more in Chapter 20, Your *Next* Five Years, about looking at the long-term direction of your business. Even if you have not been in business for five years, you want to learn from your experience as you go along—so that you will be here in five years. At the first anniversary of your business launch (and yes, celebrate it!), set aside time to review your year and decide how you will adjust for the next year. The following are some of the issues and questions I address each year:

- "What measurable goals did I set for this year? How many of these goals did I achieve?" For each of the goals that you did not meet, think about what happened. Did you misgauge the market for your services or products? Did the competitive landscape change? Did you run out of time? Did you just not want to do it? For the goals that you did meet, do a similar exercise. What was the hardest part of meeting the goal? What can you do next year to meet or exceed this year's goal, assuming that there will have to be some adjustment each year? What was particularly gratifying or rewarding? What did you enjoy doing the most and the least?

- "When I look back on this upcoming year, what do I want to have accomplished?" This is a variation on the usual question, "What do I want to aim for this year?" and I do that intentionally. I have learned that it is much more effective to imagine myself at the end point and then think back on what I will need to have done to get to that place. This way, you are able to plan out the steps you will have to take to achieve your goal, and you are much more likely to succeed.

- "What do I have to do differently this year?" In my head, I know that the competitive market changes constantly, the needs and priorities of my clients will change, and there will be new tools and resources on the web that I will need to use. But most people default to doing what they have been doing until there is a reason to change. So at least once a year make an opportunity to challenge yourself to move out of your comfort zone. You will find that your most creative ideas come when you are pushing yourself beyond where you would naturally go.

Taking Time to Think

Some businesses actually schedule formal retreats for top management to spend a weekend at some nice resort and think about the coming year and the company's strategic plans. That may be a bit much for a one-person business, but you will want to identify opportunities to sit back and reflect on where your business is going and your vision for the coming year. I travel frequently and have found that train trips and airline flights are great times for contemplation. I am away from the phone and email, and the distractions are limited (believe me, airline food is not a distraction). I usually bring some professional reading and either a handheld PC or a set of index cards for jotting down thoughts. I intentionally let my mind wander as I read, thinking about alternative ways to run my business, new services I could provide, or just new developments in the information world.

As Alex Kramer, owner of Kramer Research, reminded me once, this kind of thinking can be done during a vacation or while attending meetings as well. "I use the AIIP conference as a time to do strategic thinking about my business," she said. "It's time away from the day-to-day worries of my business, but it's still a business-oriented setting. Hearing myself talk with colleagues and hearing what others say during all the conference chit-chat helps me a lot. Even the session during the conference in which everyone has two minutes to introduce themselves helps me think about how I define myself."

Building a Brain Trust

While Franklin Roosevelt was governor of New York and during his first term as president, he had an informal group of advisors who he consulted regularly; he referred to that group as his Brain Trust. Consider taking a cue from FDR; a small cadre of advisors can be immensely helpful. As one- or two-person businesses, we sometimes lose that broader perspective; we can all benefit from ideas and feedback from people outside our business.

Some independent info pros create relatively formal advisory boards, comprising selected clients, colleagues, and others who understand the issues pertaining to small, service-oriented businesses. Other info pros simply pull together small groups of clients for dinner and brainstorming. What matters is that you identify people who understand your business, who are articulate, and whose instincts you trust.

Amelia Kassel, of MarketingBase, took this less formal approach and has been happy with the results. She invited four good clients who were within driving distance of her town, treated them to dinner at a local restaurant, and offered a certain number of free hours of research in compensation. She asked for their thoughts on her services in general as well as for recommendations on how to expand her business by finding other, similar clients. Because her clients represented ad agencies and public relations firms, they had all kinds of ideas about approaches she could take. In fact, they contributed so many thoughts that Amelia spent much of the next five years putting their suggestions in action.

It can be scary to solicit this kind of advice and feedback from customers. "What if they tell me they don't like my work?" you might be thinking. "What if they suggest things that I can't do?" For starters, if they did not like your work, they would not be your clients. And listening to ideas generated during a brainstorming session can be enormously useful. Some may be nonstarters, but you will probably want to try out one or two. The fact that your clients came up with the ideas is a good indicator that other clients will want similar products and services, too.

If you are not comfortable asking clients to offer their thoughts and you are based in the U.S., consider contacting SCORE (Service Corps of Retired Executives; www.score.org), sponsored by the U.S. Small Business Administration. A volunteer from SCORE can help you think through where your business is going and how you want to get there. SCORE offers both face-to-face and email counseling at no charge.

Some independent info pros prefer to work with a business consultant or coach; if your finances are tight, see if the consultant will agree to a barter arrangement in which you supply him or her with research services in exchange for help with strategic planning. I also provide strategic coaching services specifically for new and long-time independent info pros. One of my clients noted that it was important for her to feel that she had skin in the game—that is, that she was investing her company's money in building her marketing skills.

Expanding Your (and Your Clients') Vision

Once, in the middle of teaching a workshop, I had an epiphany: Clients won't ask you to do anything they don't think you can do. As simple as that sounds, it helped me recognize two things:

- Clients tend to pigeonhole you. "I call John when I need a profile on a competitor." They forget—or never realize in the first place—that you can provide other information services as well. Your job is to constantly remind your clients of all the ways in which you can make their lives easier or provide the information they need to do their jobs better. If they do not think you offer a particular service, they will never ask you to supply it.

- You may pigeonhole yourself. "I do secondary research for public relations and advertising firms." Suppose a client asks you to provide a market analysis or to develop a presentation for the client's boss, based on the information you have located? Your client may recognize a skill or ability you do not yet see in yourself; listen to the requests that push at the edges of what you think your capabilities are, and be open to saying, "Yes, I can do that." Of course, if you simply do not have the skills or background to do a competent job, either subcontract the work or refer it to a colleague. Many independent info pros have formed alliances to enable them to provide more complete information services to their clients. Sometimes these are formal partnerships; more often, they are casual arrangements to subcontract work to someone they know and can rely on. As you talk with clients, and as you do your own strategic planning, identify areas in which you can better solve clients' business problems by expanding the services you provide, either directly or via subcontracting. (See Chapter 16, Subcontracting, or I'll Scratch Your Back If You Scratch Mine, for a more thorough discussion of subcontracting.) Recognize the difference between being asked to tackle something you have not done before but are capable of doing and taking on a request in an area you know nothing about.

Finding a Sounding Board

I am immensely fortunate to live near a number of other longtime independent info pros, several of whom have become dear friends as well. We talk frequently, about everything from a challenging client to how to get motivated to get a presentation ready and how to evaluate the pros and cons of a new market.

You may not live close to anyone else who does what you do, and I suppose that advising you to move would be a bit drastic. However, you can still establish relationships with other info pros with whom you feel a bond. Reva Basch, editor of the first edition of this book, and I first got to know each other thanks to my rather presumptuous adoption of her as my informal mentor when I started my business. Although we lived on opposite coasts, we talked in email frequently. Living in the same city—or even the same time zone—is not a requirement. What is important is to find someone off whom you can bounce ideas and with whom you feel comfortable. You are not looking for a teacher or an expert to guide you through all the steps of your business (if you are, then consider paying a consultant). Rather, you are looking for an empathetic colleague whose instincts you trust and who can, by listening and occasionally offering the benefit of his or her own experience, help you think through thorny issues. The Association of Independent Information Professionals (AIIP; www.aiip.org) offers a volunteer mentoring program through which new members can be paired with more experienced info pros who have agreed to provide informal advice and support.

Top Strategic Planning Tips

✦   Schedule time once a year to evaluate and reflect on your business.

✦   Track your best clients and figure out how you can find and attract similar clients.

✦   Identify any problematic clients and evaluate whether to retain them as clients.

✦   Use clients or, if you prefer, a business coach or consultant for brainstorming and guidance about the direction of your business and new ideas you can implement.

✦   Find at least one colleague who can serve as your sounding board.

Chapter 20

Your *Next* Five Years

I am not convinced that info-entrepreneurs need to—or even could—write a strategic business plan extending five years out. In our industry, there are simply too many variables to predict what the information environment will look like or what we will be doing. It reminds me of driving up the northern California coast on a foggy night (is there any other kind?). I can see a little ways ahead, but then it all gets murky, and I have to keep moving in the direction that I know the road will be, even though I can't see it. Likewise, the best that we can do in terms of strategic planning is observe all the signs and indicators, and boldly drive forward in the direction that calls the loudest to us.

In that spirit, this chapter will look at how to know when to turn to a new direction, what questions to ask yourself, how to shift your perspective to a more expansive view of what you do for your clients, and what to do next. You will have to repeat this process yearly because I can predict with certainty that the weather will continue to be foggy.

Warning: Sharp Curves Ahead

I gave a presentation at the 2009 Association of Independent Information Professionals (AIIP) conference on recognizing and making strategic change. In preparation for the talk, I interviewed a number of longtime info-entrepreneurs about how they recognized the need to change and how they made a significant change in their business. Some expanded their business, a couple closed their businesses, and others moved into completely new directions. When I asked them what prompted each of their change of direction, I consistently heard the same factors. As you read the following list, consider if any of these issues apply to you and your business:

- "In my field, we constantly have to adapt. The industry changes rapidly, and if you don't keep up, you're left in the dust."

- "I wanted to expand my business, which meant that I had to bring in others to my business. Hiring an assistant gave me the energy and focus to go get new business."

- "I needed to diversify my revenue stream; I realized that I am too dependent on providing a single service to a niche market."

- "The market changed and I found myself competing with 'bottom-feeders'—companies or individuals who were charging a quarter of what I was—and my clients didn't value my analytical services."

- "I found myself in a rut. I was doing the same old same old, and I wasn't feeling challenged or energized. I was stagnating, so I needed to stir things up."

- "I was given the chance to work closely with one of my clients." (One of the people I interviewed used this as an opportunity to close her business and work full time for her client. The other person chose to expand her business with subcontractors so that she could provide more extensive services to her client.)

What I found particularly interesting about these reasons for making a big change was that most of the info-entrepreneurs felt that they simply had no choice—they had to adapt to a changing environment, or they would be out of business. While that sounds somewhat negative and reactive rather than proactive, in fact it demonstrates a functioning early warning system. Many small businesses are loathe to recognize that their markets have changed and that they must change as well. As I was writing this chapter, I read a *Wall Street Journal* article about the problems of near-empty shopping malls. The journalist interviewed a woman who operated a business out of a kiosk in the mall. She said, "I've made my business here. I don't want to move to another mall. I want [this] mall to be like it was eight years ago." While I can sympathize with her longing for the shopping mall to return to its former vitality, choosing not to move to a more economically viable location means that she will likely suffer the same fate as the rest of the mall.

Questions to Ponder

Although we may be reluctant to admit it, many of us only make changes when we have to because we are unsatisfied—for whatever reason—with the status quo. To speed up your planning process and to prompt new ideas, look for things that you are dissatisfied with or situations that you think you could improve. Here are some of the questions I ask myself every year to help me identify what needs to change:

- What business(es) am I really in? Is there an additional service I could provide that dovetails nicely with my existing services? What business have I wanted to get into this last year?

- Where is most of my revenue coming from? Is that where I want to be making most of my money? Is there something I could productize? Or would that just turn me into a commodity in the eyes of my clients?

- What am I really excited about? What do I look forward to working on? What kind of project is particularly satisfying for me? If what I really love to do won't support me directly, how can I take that passion and convert it into a revenue-producing effort?

- What are the primary industries that I am known in right now? How strong are those industries? Should I expand to a new market? Do I have the time and energy to face the learning curve of unfamiliar jargon, new issues, and all new players?

I find that the best indicator of an area that I need to focus on is the one that causes my stomach to clench up and try to hide behind my spine. In some years, that might be the question about what really gets me passionate. One year, during my annual strategizing, I recognized that I just wasn't as excited about my work as I used to be and—sure enough—my stomach started tying itself into knots. When I thought back on what had given me the most satisfaction over the past year, I realized that I really enjoyed mentoring other info-entrepreneurs and that I was skilled at it. That was when I developed my business coaching service, and it continues to be the most rewarding part of my business.

Just as I recognize an issue by my stomach, I also recognize an inspiration by how much lighter I immediately feel. When I had that moment of realization about offering coaching services, I felt like a huge weight had been lifted off my shoulders. When you think you can float on air, you have just found your new calling.

Moving to the Next Level

Once you have been in business for a few years, you will have a sense of what, for you, constitutes a "small" and a "large" project. While most people gauge the size of a project by its total budget, I focus more on projects in which I net the most profit. In some situations, that might mean serving more as a project manager and wrangler of researchers than a researcher and analyst. A smaller project that fills up much of my time during a slow period brings a welcome influx of cash when it is most needed, but it is more difficult to make a profit with smaller jobs.

There are a number of ways to cultivate these larger projects, both by expanding your existing clients' understanding of the range of your services and by reaching out to new client bases. Note that these are not mutually exclusive—you can move up the value chain with your existing clients at the same time you move into other markets or groups of clients.

Building on Your Existing Clients

One of the easiest ways to get larger projects from your clients is simply to ask. Clients may not know the extent of your services (especially once you add in the services you can subcontract to other info-entrepreneurs), so they would not necessarily think to ask you for in-depth analysis, or a summary presentation, or primary research. See Chapter 37, Deliverables, for more ideas on the added value you can build into your information services. I usually manage to work in a casual reference to a recent large job when I am chatting with a client; this way, they are reminded that, yes, I handle large projects.

Build relationships with your clients. They need to have confidence in you before they entrust you with a large project with high stakes. That may mean working with them on a volunteer project for a professional association or getting together with your client every few months—assuming you are in the same city. Remember to ask about the client's family or latest trip or anything else that expands your relationship beyond the immediate project.

With Clients, Is Bigger Always Better?

My general approach has been to look for the biggest clients I can find; they are less price-sensitive, they understand the added value I can provide, they are more likely to use me consistently, and there are usually multiple departments or functional areas I can serve.

You have to be careful, though, of becoming too dependent on any one client. Things happen in large organizations, often with little warning. Your main contact may leave the company, the organization may have a spending freeze or merge with another organization, or it may decide to hire someone directly to provide the services you now provide. If you count on any one client for more than 25 percent of your income, you are putting your business at significant risk when (and yes, it almost always does happen) you lose that client and have to immediately find new clients to replace that revenue.

On the other hand, having only small clients who use you once a year is a tough way to make a living. Some smaller clients—defined either in terms of revenue or size of projects—can be your best clients, as long as they use you consistently and are good referral sources. Some of my favorite clients are small in both senses of the word, and I value them highly because it is a more personal relationship.

I think of building my client base much the same as building a stone wall. The base has to be composed of large stable rocks, but I need the smaller rocks and mortar to support and hold together the larger boulders. As long as I have a healthy mix of clients, I know my business—or my wall—will last.

Move into more of a consultative role with your clients. Look through Chapter 29, The Reference Interview, to remind yourself how to explore more deeply as you conduct the initial assessment of what your client needs. Find out if you can provide added value that your client might not have thought of; approach this as a consultation rather than you taking a fast food order from your client ("Would you like a milkshake with that?").

Building a New Client Base

While it is usually easier to generate larger projects from existing clients than it is to find new clients, the latter is sometimes the best approach. If your current client base tends to be budget-conscious or if they tend to only want your services for lower-end projects, it may be time to move to a market that requires less active selling on your part.

Remember when you identified your client base when you started your business? See Chapter 5, Who You Are and What You Do, to remind you of how to focus on the best prospective clients and how to tailor your services to meet the critical needs of your market. Your criteria will probably have changed since your launch; you now know what kinds of services are the most rewarding and profitable for you and what kinds of clients you want to attract.

Just as it took time to build your initial group of clients, it takes time to build a new client base. Expect this to extend over the course of a year or more before you truly benefit from your efforts. Keep in mind that the investment of your time will pay off in more profitable clients down the road. Identify industry conferences that are nine months to a year out, and then decide whether it would be more beneficial for you to exhibit or speak at the conference and make the appropriate contacts. If you are not yet a member of the association your prospective clients belong to, join and start volunteering in a member-facing role. Employ all the other techniques you used when you built your initial client base, focusing now on your new market. Remember that it takes time to establish a reputation; start getting in front of your new prospects early and often, and treat this with as much energy and focus as you had when you began your business.

Rootbound Versus Bonsai

One of the problems you may experience once you have been in business for a while is consistently having more work coming in than you can comfortably fit into a day. When you are at that point, you may feel as constricted as did the root ball of my long-suffering Norfolk pine. It was moping in its corner of the living room, looking forlorn. A quick look at its base told me that it had outgrown its pot and needed more room to support its nine feet of trunk. In order to keep it healthy, I had to repot it so it can continue to grow.

On the other hand, a friend of mine cultivates bonsai plants. The patience and care she gives them is extraordinary, and she is repaid by having a perfectly formed miniature juniper, seemingly bent over from years in the wind. For her, growth for the sake of growth has no appeal; she is more interested in creating something on a scale that she enjoys and that requires as much focus as someone maintaining a tropical rain forest in her living room. Either approach can work well, and—unlike in horticulture—you have many options between a bonsai maple and a maple tree towering 50 feet overhead.

Where Am I Headed?

This may be an appropriate time for you to sit back and consider in which direction you want your business to go. What are your long-term goals and aspirations for your professional life? You may fall somewhere along this continuum:

- You want to build a business that you can eventually sell. In this case, your focus should be to create a strong company brand, form relationships with several good subcontractors who support the underlying services you provide, and ensure that your clients are loyal to your company, not just you personally. As your business can support it, hire full-time employees to do as much of the work as possible so that you can present a stand alone business to prospective buyers.

- You want to make a high salary so that you can support yourself until you retire. You will probably need a reliable group of subcontractors who can handle a percentage of your work. While you will always be running the business, you want to ensure you have enough back-up that you can increase your revenue as much as you want.

- You want to build a successful business, but your goal isn't to make a high salary—you have a bonsai business. You market aggressively when you need to, but you are more interested in cultivating the clients you have than in bringing in new clients. You may find that you are consciously or subconsciously making choices that limit your growth. As long as you recognize these choices and think through the consequences, opting to turn down large projects rather than subcontract them may be an appropriate way to keep your business at the size you want it.

If you are feeling rootbound by having more work than you have the time or resources to do, it may be time to consider enlarging your pot. You could do this by bringing in a business partner, hiring employees—either full- or part-time—or using steady subcontractors that you promise a certain amount of work to each month in order to have priority in their workflow. Each of these choices has its own challenges, but the subcontracting option is usually the least risky, and one that you can either expand or pull out of if necessary. See Chapter 16, Subcontracting, or I'll Scratch Your Back If You Scratch Mine, for more discussion of what is involved in working with subcontractors, and Chapter 7, Structuring Your Business, for things to think about before forming a partnership.

Making the Shift

OK, you know what you need to do in order to move your business in the direction you want. You know what steps you need to make. Now is the easy part of just doing it, right? If it were easy, you would have done it already. But there really isn't much more to it than that. I have talked with hundreds of independent info pros about their businesses, and one thing I hear consistently is "Well, failure just wasn't an option." Some people have children's college tuition to pay for, some are the primary earner in the household, and some could simply not imagine going back to a traditional job.

It also helps to remember that it was hard to start a business, too. You have done something this difficult before and obviously succeeded so you already have the skills you need to move your business up to the next level.

When I need to make a strategic shift in my business, one thing that keeps me focused and moving forward is thinking of how great it is going to be *after* I have accomplished my goal. I know that I will be re-energized with this challenge, and I keep reminding myself of that when I have trouble getting motivated.

Tips for Making a Strategic Change

✦ Consider all your options; don't make a decision based on fear, indecision, or a sense that you have no choice.

✦ You have to be willing to fail in order to take reasonable risks. If you never fail, you aren't trying hard enough.

✦ If an idea doesn't work out, remind yourself that you didn't fail—the idea just didn't work out.

✦ Make your own decisions; don't be overly influenced by what did or didn't work for others.

✦ Follow your passion. If you have an idea that gets you energized and makes you feel 10 years younger, go with it!

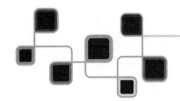

Marketing

Chapter 21

Marketing Dos and Don'ts

You have read Section One, Getting Started, so you have decided what products and services you will be offering, you have set up your office, and you are open for business. You have read Section Two, Running the Business, so you have your subcontractors lined up, you have your accounts lined up, and you have your strategic plan lined up. Now you are sitting there, waiting for the telephone to ring. I don't know about you, but during my early days, I would actually check the phone every few hours, just to make sure it was still working.

The rest of Section Three, Marketing, goes into detail about specific techniques and approaches for telling people about your business. This chapter will set the stage for those marketing efforts. Here, I will talk about some general marketing thoughts as well as some of the basic dos and don'ts that apply specifically to info-entrepreneurship.

You're Always "On"

In Chapter 5, Who You Are and What You Do, I look at the advantages of cultivating clients outside your local area. That said, never miss an opportunity to unobtrusively market yourself in person. Perfect your "elevator speech"—a quick two- or three-sentence description of what you do that you could deliver while riding the elevator with someone or in the grocery store, on a plane, or at a meeting. Here is how I might perform my "elevator speech" as I chat with someone sitting next to me on a flight or a neighbor down the street:

> *Prospect:* That's an interesting assortment of reading material. What do you do for a living?
>
> *Me (spoken with enthusiasm):* I have the greatest job in the world! I run my own research company, providing the intelligence behind my clients' strategic decisions. In other words, I make 'em look smart.
>
> *Prospect:* Really? I sometimes need information on competitors. Can you do that?
>
> *Me:* I just finished a project analyzing the competitors for a financial services company. You know, I send out a monthly enewsletter about doing research on the web. May I email you the latest issue?

Notice that I didn't just hand the prospect my business card; it is much more important for me to ask for hers. Who knows if she will remember to call me when she gets back to her office? More likely, she will leave my card behind in a taxi, forget about the conversation, and that is the last I hear of her. But she gave me her card. When I get back to my office, I can email her the latest issue of Bates InfoTips, along with a note mentioning how much I enjoyed chatting with her on the flight on Tuesday, so that she is reminded of who I am.

To follow up on my initial email, I look her up in the major social networking sites, and I check out her website and blog, if any. If she seems like a prospect, I would link to her in my social network, perhaps post a thoughtful comment on her blog, and subscribe to any relevant newsletters her organization puts out. These are ways to establish a professional connection and, provided you offer high-quality content on your website and blog, you can turn a one-time contact into a client.

"Can You Do This for Me?"

As I explain in the "Calling in the Experts" section of Chapter 16, Subcontracting, or I'll Scratch Your Back If You Scratch Mine, even though your prospective clients may think of you as "the expert on the aerospace industry" or "the business valuation researcher," they may ask you to do research in other areas as well. If it is a subject about which you know you can educate yourself quickly, or that is related to a topic you are familiar with, or that requires the same information resources you use all the time, it's a safe bet that you will do a fine job. However, if it goes way beyond the subject areas and research tools you know, consider outsourcing the extra-challenging jobs to colleagues who *do* specialize in those areas. Chapter 16 says more about how to subcontract out or refer work out and still make points with your clients.

Amelia Kassel, principal of MarketingBase, described one exception to the rule of always subcontracting or referring out what you do not know how to do. On two occasions, clients asked her to use specialized software or a professional online service that was new to her. She explained that she did not routinely use the product and that the client would have to pay for her learning curve. In both situations, the client knew her, valued her expertise, and was willing to be billed for the time required for her to get up to speed. This was a great solution for both parties—the clients could use an info pro in whom they already had confidence, and she was able to expand her knowledge of information systems into new areas while being paid to learn. It worked because Amelia explained in advance that she would need time to teach herself how the new information service worked; also, as an alternative, she offered to outsource the work. The clients appreciated her willingness to bring in an outside expert and, fortunately, could spare the time for Amelia to get proficient.

You must be confident that you can deliver what you promise. Clients—for that matter, people in general—are attracted to people who are positive, upbeat, and self-confident without being arrogant. Presumably, you are in this business either because you are an excellent researcher and analyst or because you can subcontract the billable work to people who are the best in their field. You have a right to be confident, but that right only lasts as long as you resist the urge to tackle jobs that are way over your head in terms of subject expertise, access to resources, or availability of time.

Ten Mistakes New Independent Info Pros Make

One reason why starting an information services business is so challenging is that it is unlike most other small businesses. The corner market can put big signs up in the window advertising this week's special on strawberries or dog food. The dry cleaner can place flyers on all the neighborhood cars. Website promoters can—and, alas, do—send out unsolicited email by the thousands, offering to increase traffic to your site for a "modest fee." These techniques may work for some entrepreneurs, but they are not particularly useful for marketing an information business. Think about how you would go about finding a lawyer, accountant, or real estate agent. You would ask your friends, neighbors, or colleagues; you would not wait for a cold call or a postcard in the mail nor are you likely to look in the Yellow Pages. Most people locate some-one who provides professional services via word of mouth. And that is how people will find you, too.

Of course, I read a paragraph similar to what you just read when I started my business: "Direct mail, cold calls, and Yellow Pages ads don't work." Sure, I thought, maybe they don't work for *you*, but I've got this great idea, you see … Suffice it to say, sometimes I need to learn things the hard way. In the interest of keeping you from wasting too much time and money on marketing efforts that don't pay off, here is my top-10 list of what not to do. And yes, I tried most of them myself during my first year.

1. *Using direct mail lists and sending unsolicited marketing material.* Regardless of where you found or purchased the list—a professional association, a local business directory, the phone book—a mass mailing is more than likely a waste of time and money. Unless the recipient already knows you and recognizes your name, it will be seen as junk mail and dropped in the nearest recycling bin.

2. *Focusing on marketing exclusively to your local area.* It is easy to assume that local businesses are more likely to use a local researcher. From that conclusion, you may decide that the best way to find those local customers is to attend Chamber of Commerce meetings or informal networking groups such as "leads clubs." The disadvantage is that you wind up spending your time marketing to a broad cross-section of people—most of whom are not your target market and would never become clients—rather than focusing on your target audience.

3. *Telling prospects that you can find any kind of information.* "Whatever you need, I'm an expert at finding it!" Sounds like a compelling marketing line, doesn't it? However, most prospects will figure that you are promising more than you can deliver or that you are not actually expert at finding anything at all. People will remember you if you tell them that you specialize in tracking down government files from a hundred years ago, or that you focus on research and grant writing services for the nonprofit sector, or that you help consumer food companies understand their competition. Concrete examples give people a way to describe you to others. While many people will not need your expertise themselves, they may know some-one who does. That means that every person you tell about your business becomes, in effect, part of your marketing staff. Make yourself easy to remember.

4. *Offering to discount your fee for new clients.* Customers assume that you set your rates based on your assessment of how valuable your services are. Offering a

lower price shows a devaluing of your time and, no matter how you present it, charging your regular rate after an initial discount will feel like a price increase to your client. In addition, you probably do not want to attract excessively budget-conscious clients. If a reduction of 10 percent makes the difference in getting this job, are you going to have to haggle over every future project?

5. *Making cold calls.* One side of your brain may be calmly saying, "Cold calling must work. Why else do stock brokers, insurance agents, and aluminum siding contractors insist on calling me, usually during dinner?" But if you are like me, the other half of your brain is screaming, "No! I'll do anything but make cold calls!" Fortunately, you can listen to that screaming half; in my experience and that of the vast majority of other independent info pros, cold calling simply doesn't work. There are several good reasons why cold calling is a bad idea. First, how many customers do you think would decide to spend hundreds or thousands of dollars, in preparation for making an important business decision, on someone they have never heard of who just happened to call them up? That's right … mighty few. Second, in these days of voice mail and effective administrative gatekeepers, you will spend an inordinate amount of time just trying to get your prospect on the phone. Third, you will have to get 15 or 20 people to answer the phone and engage in a conversation before you find one who is vaguely interested. That means that you will have spent several days with one prospect to show for your efforts and that person may never get around to using your services. At that rate, you will never land a real, live, paying client.

The only exception to the No Cold Calls rule is what some people call "warm calling." This presumes that you have already made contact with your prospects in some way so that they will recognize your name when you call. One way to do this is based on an approach described in the book *The Consultant's Calling: Bringing Who You Are to What You Do* by Geoffrey M. Bellman (Jossey-Bass, 2001). First, you need to identify a specific, high-level executive position within the industry, for which you believe you can provide unique, high-value services. Perhaps your target position is the head of international accounts in *Fortune* 500 food companies. Then, using the companies' websites or annual reports, identify the person in that position in eight or 10 corporations. Be sure to call the company to confirm that the information is still current. Then write a letter to each executive, introducing yourself and offering "name a topic and I'll send you an article a week for six weeks—no charge"—or a similar offer that highlights the custom research services you provide.

Be sure to include your email address and toll-free phone number, if you have one. Follow up a week or so later to ask what topic the executive would like monitored. If you cannot get through to your contact, try his or her assistant who may be able to help you identify a topic of interest. Then monitor the leading business and industry publications, major newspapers, and news headline services on the web, and send each executive one article a week with a brief cover memo. Remember to abide by copyright restrictions in choosing your articles; download them from an online service that permits redistribution of the material or avoid the copyright issue by sending your prospects the headline, a brief summary of the article, and perhaps a pointer to the URL where the rest of the story can be found. (See Chapter 17, Ethics and Legalities, for more information on copyright issues.) At the end of six weeks, you can place a warm call to these executives; if nothing else, they will probably remember who you are. But have you noticed how time-consuming this approach is? All that work just to make a sales pitch to a handful of people who might be prepared to accept your call. This illustrates why cold calling, without any preparatory work and demonstration of your value, is usually pointless.

6. *Marketing to the wrong people.* It is easier to market yourself to people you know and feel comfortable with than it is to market yourself to strangers. Unfortunately, unless all of your friends and family members just happen to be people who are eager to use—and pay for—your services, you will not generate much business talking only to the folks you know. Deciding on your client base requires a combination of following your heart and cold-eyed realism: Will these people be regular, repeat customers; good sources of referrals; and relatively price-insensitive? If you cannot stand working with your clients, you will not be in business for long. If you share a common bond with your customers, you will find communicating with them that much easier. But take a good hard look and make sure that you are not letting your comfort level override the basic business considerations of finding good, steady clients.

7. *Relying on a website or a listing in a business directory or the Yellow Pages to generate business.* "Build it and they will come" might have worked in the movie *Field of Dreams*, but it does not work for independent info pros. Although it is important to have a website and a listing in the business section (*not* in the residential listings) of your local telephone book, very few clients are going to find you through either of those means. I have had a website since 1996, and I can recall only a handful of clients over the years who located me through a web directory or a search engine,

and then actually picked up the phone and called me. Yes, I maintain my website and pay for listings in a few business directories that my clients use. But I do this as a way to confirm the stability of my business, not as a marketing technique. Prospects expect me to have a webpage, and they like being able to find out about my background and see how I present myself on the web. Likewise, if a prospect hears me speak at a conference, she can go back to her office, look me up in an association directory, and find that, sure enough, I am listed there; that suggests that I am familiar with the issues that she deals with every day. Websites and directory listings are great ways to reassure clients that you are in business, but you cannot count on them as primary marketing tools.

8. *Sending unsolicited email promoting your business.* As long as email exists, so will unsolicited commercial email, affectionately known as spam. Spam is also one of the most effective ways to repel potential clients. Not only that, it is forbidden by most internet service providers. Even if you have already had contact with a prospect, unsolicited email is just that—unasked for and usually unappreciated. Do you really want to be seen in the same light as those companies that offer to sell you a college diploma, an improved sex life, or a way to erase all your credit card debt immediately? Rather than sending email ads, write a short newsletter and offer a free opt-in subscription to your clients and prospects. See Chapter 24, Marketing on the Web, and Chapter 25, Print and Eprint Marketing, for more discussion of newsletters and other regular marketing contacts.

9. *Designing your marketing materials yourself.* Unless you are a professional website designer or have years of experience designing marketing material, resist the urge to develop your own logo or write your own website copy. I have seen far too many brochures, logos, and websites designed by independent info pros themselves, and the majority of them are, well, awful. Your marketing materials are an investment you have to make when you are just starting out. Graphic designers don't come cheap, but the money you invest at the beginning will be well spent; you will have a business image that looks established, professional, and polished. The same applies to your website. Some software packages provide you with fill-in-the-blanks templates for building your own homepage, but they often do not project a very professional image. See Chapter 23, Your Business Image, for more on your marketing materials.

10. *Scaling back your marketing if you have one big client.* Imagine the scenario: You just landed a big client, who is paying you for 30 hours of work a week. The client

promises that you will be kept busy for months—nay, years—at this rate. You sit back and think, "Now, this is how to run an info pro business." Unfortunately, you still have to market because all that work from that one great client will eventually dry up. It always does, regardless of the client's well-meaning assurances and best intentions. Sometimes your contact leaves the company or is transferred to another division. Sometimes the client's business slows down and the first budget item cut is outside contractors. Sometimes the client decides to take the work in-house. And even a contract promising you a certain amount of revenue every month is not really a guarantee, as it probably would not be worth the expense or ill will of litigating if the client chose to cancel it. So although a steady gig is nothing to complain about, it is important to realize that sooner or later it will end, and the end of a contract is not the time to start marketing efforts that often take months to produce results. Because you usually cannot anticipate when the work will end, you need to market constantly, even when you are fully booked with work.

Successful Marketing Techniques

✦   Market vertically rather than to a geographic region.

✦   Only accept projects you know you can do well.

✦   Use focused marketing techniques, not direct mail or cold calling.

✦   Think niche, not generalist. Focus on services that set you apart from your competitors.

✦   Show self-confidence and enthusiasm when you contact prospective clients. People are drawn to upbeat, positive people.

✦   Take the long view. Good, steady clients take time to cultivate.

Chapter 22

Your Marketing Plan

Your business plan is something you work on once, as you prepare to create your business. Your marketing plan, on the other hand, is a living document that will be driven by your vision of what you want your business to look like.

A marketing plan need not to be a formal document with headings, subheadings, footnotes, and appendixes. However, it does have to provide you with a framework within which to think about how you will find your clients. Many people find it difficult to sit down before they launch their business and think through their marketing strategy, but there is no better time to plan how you will get clients than before you have started your business.

Lots of books and websites focus on writing a business plan, but fewer relevant sources exist to help you develop a marketing plan that is appropriate for an independent info pro business. You probably will not be relying on your storefront displays, advertising, or a trained sales force to generate business, so most of the generic resources are not particularly helpful. Instead, design a marketing plan that feels right for you and consider it a work in progress. You will modify it as you learn what works and what doesn't work for your particular business and client base. In fact, I review my marketing plan once a month to see what activities I should schedule for the upcoming month and to decide whether I need to alter any of my marketing efforts for the rest of the year.

What Are Your Goals?

It is hard to know if you have arrived somewhere if you did not have a destination in mind. Likewise, you need business goals for the year that will guide your marketing activities and enable you to track the success of various marketing efforts. Your goals right now—before you have started your business—may turn out to be overly ambitious or far too conservative; you may want to talk with a few colleagues to see if your expectations match their experiences.

To achieve your strategic goals for the year, plan backward instead of forward. That sounds counterintuitive doesn't it? But often the most effective way to complete a project or to solve a problem is to identify what your goal is or what the resolution of an issue would look like, and then figure out how to get from here to there. You establish the end point and then look back to see what needs to be done to get to your end point. This strategy helps you identify the specific actions you need to take and that in turn enables you to set deadlines and quantifiable results. Each of your marketing activities is tied directly to one or more of your specific goals.

I encourage new info-entrepreneurs to set a variety of goals that reflect the different aspects of your business. These could include:

- My business will net (after expenses) $_____ this year.

- I will have ___ active clients within 12 months.

- I will develop at least __ prospects in this/these industry/ies_____.

- I will give at least __ presentation(s) to likely prospects.

- I will develop one new information product or service this year.

What Info Pro Marketing Entails

Many generic marketing plan templates assume that you will be operating a storefront operation and marketing to the local consumer. The techniques that work for that market do not work well for our type of business. We are selling our services and expertise—we are telling our clients that they can have confidence that we will provide them with the knowledge they need within their budget and time frame. Our biggest competitors are often simply our prospective clients' beliefs that they already have the right information, in the right format, at the right time, all the time.

The rest of Section Three covers specific activities that often work well for independent info pros. At this point, it may be helpful to group marketing activities into broad categories of approaches. The first category is starting and building your word-of-mouth marketing. Most of your clients will eventually come to you because they heard about you specifically. As the late Sue Rugge, an info-entrepreneur pioneer, said, all your business comes from word of mouth, and you have to be the first mouth. Activities to create word of mouth include public speaking, publishing an enewsletter, actively networking, and so on.

The next category is building your credibility and your personal brand. You will be establishing a name and a reputation as someone who is an acknowledged expert in her field. Yes, this can be difficult, at least for those of us who absorbed the childhood message of not bragging about oneself or, as the Australian expression goes, of cutting tall poppies down to size. Thankfully, there are plenty of marketing activities that can promote Brand You without making you feel self-aggrandizing. Having strong content on your blog and website, writing for publications your clients read, taking on a leadership role in a professional association, and offering webinars on research-related topics are all ways you can establish your credibility without feeling that you are overtly tooting your own horn.

The final category of marketing activities is creating publicity about yourself. This might include sending out strategic press releases, being featured in an article or interviewed on the radio or a webcast, or even being prominently linked to from an influential blog. (Note that this can include "manufactured publicity," such as having someone record an interview with you that you can post on your website, as long as you do not misrepresent the interview.)

Writing Your Marketing Plan

After you have read the rest of Section Three and have an idea of what types of marketing efforts would be best for your business and your goals, it is time to spell out the specific actions needed to achieve your goals. The key element is to let your goals drive your strategies and actions. Work from the end backward rather than simply thinking of activities you could try out. Unless you know the purpose of each marketing goal, you cannot develop a strategy to achieve that goal.

While the specific format does not matter, it is important that you design a marketing plan that enables you to see both your strategic goals for the year and your week-to-week activities. You will be consulting this plan at least once a month, and you may have to modify your plan as the year progresses, so it needs to be organized in a way that works for you. You will also always be working on several marketing efforts simultaneously. Some of your efforts may be done within a month or two, and some will be ongoing.

Neurologists have identified differences between the right and left hemispheres of our brains. The left hemisphere handles analytical, logical, and sequential functions; the right hemisphere is responsible for more intuitive, holistic jobs. In most people, one hemisphere or another is dominant, which means that different people tend to organize their thoughts in different ways. To accommodate these differences, I have proposed separate marketing plan templates for right- and left-brained people, only somewhat tongue-in-cheek. We left-brained folk do feel much more comfortable with the nice neat table in Figure 22.1, whereas the right-brained among us prefer a more visual map of what they are doing and why, like the one in Figure 22.2. And you may find that a hybrid of these two formats works best for your brain's wiring.

Activity	Purpose	Actions	Time frame*
Get active in my clients' professional associations	Get three CI clients in the consumer products industry by establishing reputation as expert	1. ID possible associations	1Q
		2. Research associations, ID volunteer opps	1Q
		3. Contact president of assn to volunteer	2Q
Work my network	Get three CI clients in the consumer products industry by building word of mouth	Notify all network contacts of my CI services	1Q
		Participate weekly on listservs my prospects read	all year
		Spend three hours/week building my LinkedIn network	all year

*I include the time frame so that I can space out my activities throughout the year.

Figure 22.1 Marketing plan template for left-brained people

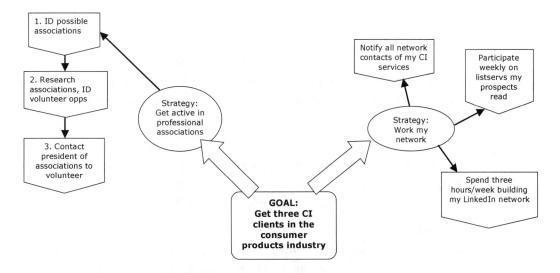

Figure 22.2   Marketing plan template for right-brained people

For either format, you will identify your business goals for the year and, for each goal, the strategies to meet that goal and the actions required for each strategy. In the examples here, I have as one of my goals to gain three competitive intelligence clients in the consumer products industry. Two of my strategies to meet this goal are mining my network for contacts in the industry and getting active in a relevant association. You will notice that one of these strategies requires three sequential actions, whereas the other strategy simply involves three simultaneous activities.

22 Ways to Kick-Start Your Marketing

Every business experiences lulls, times when it seems that you barely have the energy to drag yourself into your office, and you cannot stand the thought of having to go out and generate business. This happens to everyone, and it can be disconcerting when it does—you suddenly notice that business has dropped off, and you cannot seem to get back into the swing of marketing.

The following are some of the actions I add to my marketing plan when I need to rev my marketing efforts up a notch:

1. Ask directly for referrals from your existing clients. "Who do you know who needs to compete better in their marketplace, who I might contact?"

2. Get in touch with your clients, just to check in; I never cease to marvel at how effective this technique is. Our clients often have a need for our services but need our prompting to engage our services. Remember, our clients have already shown that they are sources of business.

3. Revisit your existing client list and evaluate who your best clients have been, in terms of project budgets, repeat business, and referrals. Think about what these clients have in common and how you found them. Where could you find other clients like these ones?

4. Look through your social networks. If you have not established connections with all of your clients, now is the time to do so. And see who their contacts are; if you see any that you think may use your services, ask your client for a connection or introduction.

5. If you identify a new issue or concern to your clients' businesses, design a specific research product or service that would address your clients' specific needs, and send a (hard copy) letter to your affected clients telling them about your new offering.

6. Write an article for a publication that your clients read. It need not be long, and it should be practical and nontechnical. Offer tips on staying updated on new web resources in their industry or review a new information source.

7. Write 10 blog posts and queue them up for posting over the next couple of months.

8. Prepare for and conduct three informational interviews with prospects in an industry that is new to you. (See Chapter 8, Before You Launch, for more discussion of informational interviews.) Learn what their specific pain points are and develop an approach to market to this industry.

9. Identify a current topic of interest to your client base—best practices for using social media for business intelligence, for example. Conduct your own survey of your network; this is a great time to ping your clients, colleagues, and prospects. Write up the results into a white paper, promote it on your website, and notify all your clients of the availability of your resource.

10. Look through all your projects from the last six months or year. Follow up on the issues that are regular concerns for your clients and send them a recent article on the topic with a note saying, "I saw this and thought you might find it useful with regard to [our recent project]."

11. Commit to three networking outings a week. This could be anyone from a colleague to a prospect to a client. Take a friend to lunch and focus on building your mutual networks. Ask him what kinds of leads he would like to hear about; depending on what he does, that might be sales referrals, job opportunities, leads for good employees, or client projects. Tell him what kinds of clients you are specifically looking for. These kinds of meetings are great ways to hone your 15-second "Here's how I will help you make strategic decisions" speech, and they keep that word-of-mouth network humming.

12. Use an obscure holiday as an excuse to send out greeting cards to your clients and vendors. I remember a family friend who sent out cards for Groundhog's Day every year; if your contacts are familiar with this North American holiday, this can be a fun way of staying in touch. The Spring or Fall Equinox, the Queen's Birthday, Mardi Gras, or even something as silly as International Respect for Chickens Day (May 4) can serve as a reason for sending a card. And yes, these are real cards that get stamped and put in the mailbox.

13. On a related note, check the social network profiles of your clients. If they list their birthdays, be sure to send a card. And yes, that's a printed birthday card, not an ecard.

14. Call a fellow info-entrepreneur. Ask her how her business is doing. Ask what was the most important change she has made to her business in the last year. Share an interesting resource with her.

15. Call someone who is reliably upbeat and positive. That kind of energy is contagious.

16. Commit to reading every issue of several business newspapers or magazines for a month. Cut out at least two articles from each issue that a client may find useful. Send a hard copy along with a couple of business cards and a note saying, "I saw this and thought of you."

17. Identify one new association that your prospective clients are likely to belong to, join it, and evaluate how you can volunteer strategically in a member-facing capacity.

18. Attend a local chapter meeting of an association you find interesting, even if you do not expect to find clients. Consider the visit to be professional development, not just marketing. I sometimes find my best clients when I am not looking for them.

19. Schedule a meeting of your advisory board. If you do not have one, this is a good reason to set one up. Identify four or five people who you respect, who understand the issues of running a professional services business, and who are willing to give you honest feedback. Ideally, these are people who live in your general area and can meet with you. If that is not reasonable, build a virtual advisory board that "meets" online.

20. Look at your upcoming trips and identify your clients and prospects in those cities. Send notes letting them know you will be in the neighborhood and see if you can set up a time to meet. (This is why I always arrive early on the day before a speaking engagement so that I have time to meet clients or prospects wherever I go.)

21. Review all your professional listings in the professional associations you belong to, on your social networks, and anywhere else you have your company listed. Upgrade and freshen up your listings, revising them to target your current market and to reflect your clients' current concerns.

22. Identify an issue of interest to your clients and create a white paper with some key resources. The topic could be "Most Significant Competitive Intelligence Blogs" or "Best Uses for Twitter"—whatever is relatively simple to research and of interest to your client base.

Marketing Plan Essentials

◆ View your marketing plan as a work in progress; review it monthly.

◆ To achieve your strategic goals for the year, plan backward from your end point.

◆ Set tangible, realistic, and measurable goals.

◆ Plan activities that create word of mouth, build your brand, and create publicity.

Chapter 23

Your Business Image

Everything you do is part of your image, right down to how you answer your phone and how you package your deliverables. Every time your client sees you, hears about you, or looks at your work product, you are sending a message. Fortunately, what that message says about you is, for the most part, under your control. This chapter looks at the ways you establish your business image even before you start talking with someone.

You in Print

As much as we have all gone "virtual," there is still a need for something as quaint as business cards—not to mention stationery, mailing labels, envelopes, and all the other accoutrements of the hard copy world. We do still meet people face to face, and—old-fashioned as I am—I believe that sending a thank-you note or follow-up letter on paper makes a positive impact. And while I sometimes see people exchange virtual business cards via wireless devices, the need to hand someone something tangible still remains.

Going Hard Copy

As you set up your business, it will be tempting to simply browse through a clip art collection to find a nice image, slap it at the top of a document, add your company name in some unusual font, and call that a letterhead. Resist the urge. Having a professional design your corporate image is an investment with both immediate and long-term payoffs. Trust me, people can tell the difference between a company logo designed on a word processor and one custom-designed for your business. Having a professionally designed logo and letterhead sends the message that you are an established and committed businessperson, not just a hobbyist. (And if you are entering the independent information profession as a hobby, I advise you to change your thinking immediately and turn it into a real business!) Do-it-yourself marketing materials, on the other hand, scream, "I'm new, I'm cheap, I may not be in business tomorrow!" Clients may wonder whether it's worth investing in you if you are not willing to invest in your own business.

Whenever I see stationery or a business card that was obviously created from generic clip art or otherwise designed by an amateur, I wince. It is a short-term savings that costs you in the long run. If you are planning to do much of your marketing on the web, a professional image there makes a huge difference, too. (See Chapter 10, You.com, for more discussion of your website.)

What your logo looks like will depend on who your clients are. You will want a design that speaks to your client base. If you are marketing to law firms, think Staid and Serious. If you're targeting high-tech advertising or public relations firms, you might try a flashier logo that resonates with those creative types. If you work with unions, it's probably wise to use a union printing firm so you can display the tiny symbol at the bottom (called the union bug) indicating that it was printed at a union shop. Know your audience and make sure your image is appealing to them.

How do you find a design professional to develop your logo and letterhead? Ask around. If you know any consultants or small businesses whose logos you find appealing, ask them who they used. There are also sites that allow freelancers to bid for your project. If you go this route—Elance (www.elance.com), Guru (www.guru.com), or craigslist (www.craigslist.org) are three options—be mindful that some of the people bidding on your project may not be familiar with your industry. Ask to see other work the freelancer has done. Does it look professional? Are his or her other clients happy with the work? Many office supply stores provide customized logo design as well as printing services, often for a reasonable cost, so having a custom logo is within the budget of anyone in business. Make sure that what you get has been designed exclusively for you, that you have the rights to any images used, and that your logo is not simply clip art with your name and contact information appended to it.

In fact, if you want to do without a logo and just use text in your letterhead and other marketing materials, most printers can design something for you in a pleasing font, layout, and, if you choose, color at a modest cost. Be sure to get a copy of your design in digital form so you can incorporate it into your website, handouts, and so on. This last bit of advice comes from having had my first business logo designed long before the web or electronic publishing and then spending a small fortune having it converted to a professional-looking electronic format.

Business Cards for Every Occasion

While I have my standard business cards for most situations, I also create specialized cards for every conference I speak at. I create a special page on my website specifically for that conference, and I print that URL on the back of a business card. I give those out at my presentations so that I can drive people to my site to download the handout and other material, and perhaps to subscribe to my newsletter or order some of the products in my online store.

Some info-entrepreneurs have an event-specific URL printed on the back of their usual business cards; this ensures that their branding is consistent. The quality of the printed cards will be high, but it can be expensive. An alternative is to have cards printed for each event, using one of the web-based stores that specialize in this. I have the same caveats here as I do with PaperDirect or other sources for preprinted cards: Be careful that the cards look professional, are on heavy stock, and are consistent with the rest of your marketing material.

Fortunately, many websites offer high-quality business cards that you can have printed in reasonably small quantities. The cost is relatively small— often $20 or so for 200 business cards. This is a smart investment for a single event, but it's not the best option for everyday use.

Preprinted Paper

If you cannot wait for the graphic designer to finish your logo, there is an alternative, though I think it is a second-best option. Paper Direct (www.paperdirect.com), for example, sells predesigned color letterhead paper and envelopes, business card stock, and brochures. You feed this preformatted stationery into your printer and add your company name and contact information to give it a customized feel. You can also purchase designer paper from many office supply chains.

The advantages of this approach are a low initial investment of no more than the cost of a box or two of predesigned paper stock, your order can be delivered within a day or two so you can start sending out marketing material with minimal delay, and the coordinated designs available give a consistent look to your stationery, business cards, envelopes, mailing labels, brochures, and postcards.

The disadvantages of using predesigned paper include possibly selecting the same design as someone else in your industry, thus diluting the distinctiveness and impact of your material, the relatively high cost compared to ordering your own stationery from a printer, and the chance that your supplier will decide to discontinue your design in the future. Although most of the paper is relatively heavyweight, most preprinted business card stock is light when compared to regular business cards, and the micro-perforations along the edges are a give-away—the sign of a do-it-yourself print job. When I see a letter on preprinted paper, my first impression is of someone who is not sufficiently committed to his business to invest in custom stationery; then I wonder how long he intends to stay in business. Preprinted papers can be useful for brochures and other specialized printings such as promotional mailings, but you run the risk of sending the wrong message if you use them as your regular letterhead.

Business Cards and Logos That Work

You will live with your logo for quite a while. You may eventually decide to update your corporate image if you change your company name or feel that your logo looks dated, but you want to start with a business identity that you are going to be happy with for a long time. What you select will depend on your client base (do they expect something flashy or conservative?), the type of work you do (do you want your logo to indicate that you specialize in the publishing industry?), and your personality and taste.

Your logo and business card tells others something about you so consider all of the following aspects as you choose your business card design:

- Paper stock: Make sure it is heavy card stock that can easily be written on.

- Font: Make sure it is easy to read and consistent with your business image. Try out a number of different fonts until you find one that reflects your business.

- Color: Use a white or light background and a black or very dark color ink for the lettering. If your card isn't easy for your contacts to read, what does that say about how you relate to your clients?

- Contact information: Include a mailing address as well as your phone number, email address, website URL, and any other necessary contact points; for some people, that might include a pager number or a toll-free number.

- Bilingual information: If your client base spans more than one language, consider having your contact information in a different language on each side of the card. For example, see the card in Figure 23.1 for Udo Hohlfeld, who does most of his business in Germany but used an English-language tag line to emphasize the international scope of his work and client base.

Figure 23.1 provides examples of a variety of business cards used by several established independent info pros. As you can see, they vary widely in design and feel, but they all look professional, and the company name is clear and easy to read. Although you can't tell from the images, all of these business cards are uncoated. I remember one experience when an info-entrepreneur proudly handed me her business card and asked me to get in touch with her about a project. Unfortunately, her card had a fancy coating on it that resisted all my efforts to write a note on the card so I nearly forgot why I had the card when I got back to my office. However you design your card, make sure that there is plenty of room to write notes on the back and that you can write those notes in pencil, ballpoint pen, and roller ball pen.

Debbie Wynot of Library Consultants LLC uses a virtual business card—people send a text message to an address and immediately receive her contact information on their phones:

Debbie Wynot
504-885-5926
Debbie@libraryconsultants.com
Business research
Law library management
Library consulting

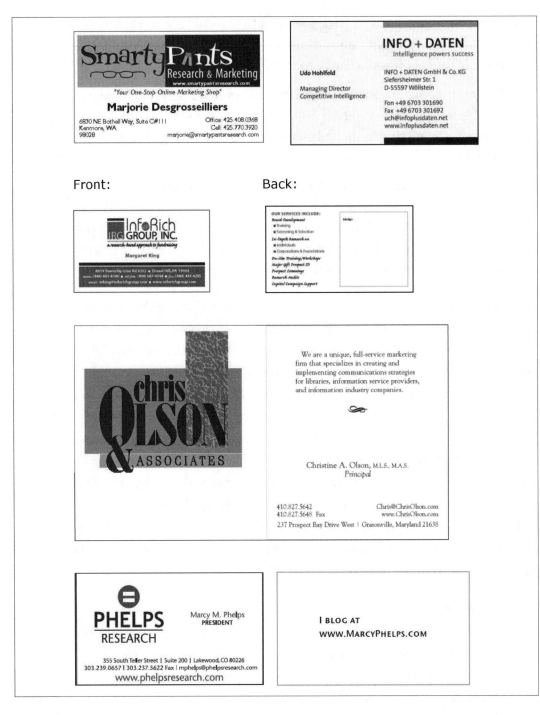

Figure 23.1   Business card examples

As she said, "I think the novelty of it has a bit of a wow factor. I haven't had anyone ask me for more than what's in the ecard, probably because the information is already electronic and they can add it to their contacts with any notes they want."

Your Web Image

Chapter 10, You.com, and Chapter 24, Marketing on the Web, go into more detail about how to manage your web presence. In the context of your business image, remember that your web profile says something about you and your business. Be sure to keep your messages consistent across media as well as relevant to each audience.

I hesitate to mention any social media site, as I am sure that the hip, happening place to be seen in will have changed by the time you read this. Wherever you set up a persona—Twitter, LinkedIn, Facebook, or wherever you are—there are some items you always need to include:

- An appropriate photograph: It's tempting to post a fun photo of you on the beach sipping a drink with little umbrella in it, but you want to maintain a professional image throughout the web. See the sidebar, "Get Shot Professionally," for thoughts on using a professional photographer for your headshot.

- URLs to your website, blog, and other online presences: Include pointers to all the places on the web where you maintain a profile.

- A brief description of your business: Keep in mind that this is your one chance to market yourself, so have a pithy phrase you can use as your description. Make it compelling enough that people will want to click through from a search results page to view more information about you. Use phrases such as "Helping clients make strategic decisions" or "Creating a competitive advantage" that emphasize your value to clients.

- Your credentials and experience: In addition to college degrees, list professional groups and associations you are active in, significant awards you have received, and any activities that highlight your expertise. Do not include a resume or CV; remember, you are a business, not someone looking for a job.

- All your contact options: Include your mailing address, phone number(s), and email address, along with links to any other relevant ways to contact you, including your Skype address, Twitter name, and so on.

Get Shot Professionally

People like seeing who they are dealing with, whether it is having you provide research services, a webinar, or consulting services. You can make yourself seem more approachable and businesslike if you have a professional headshot that you can post on your website, in your marketing material, and on your social networking site profiles. It is tempting to just stand up against a wall and have your spouse catch you while you are smiling. Unfortunately, these photos usually look unprofessional and probably are not the most flattering you could use. Instead, invest in a few hours with a professional photographer and, if you are a woman, have a professional do your make-up, too.

A good photographer will offer you a number of different poses and images, from very professional to more friendly and personable, and he or she will do minor touch-ups to make you look your best. Ask for digital copies of your best color and black-and-white shots; your best color shot may not be the best one in black and white. After my last photo session, I came away with two different shots in a business suit and one more casual shot that still looks professional but a bit more friendly. (Yes, that's the one I use on my coaching webpage, and I use the more formal shots in the rest of the website.)

Keep your profiles current. This means posting regular updates on what you are doing, listing upcoming presentations you are giving, and participating in discussions. Remember to keep all your profiles consistent; although networking sites may have different expectations in terms of formality and presentation, you want to maintain a professional image throughout the web. Make your presence known and become seen as a thought leader. Post links to thought-provoking articles or blog posting, offer your perspective on industry news, or share what you learned at a conference.

There are lots of social aggregator sites that specialize in crawling the web looking for all the places where people congregate and converse. That means that your prospective clients are probably able to see what kinds of pictures you share on a photo site, what you say you're doing on Twitter, what music you like, and how you act in Second Life.

Answering Your Phone

It seems unnecessary to advise you to answer your phone when you are available and to return calls promptly, but you would be surprised. Paul and Sarah Edwards, home-office gurus, once told of calling five independent info pros, leaving five messages, and having not a single call returned. Nada. Zip.

Being in your office to answer your phone can be a competitive advantage, particularly now that so many businesses seem to rely heavily on automated responses and voice mail menus. It demonstrates to clients that you are available when they need to reach you. If you are going to be out of your office for more than an hour or two, change your voice mail message to let callers know that you will not be able to call them back immediately. I cannot count the number of times I have left messages after hearing, "I'm in the office but can't take your call right now" or "I'm either away from my desk or on another call but I'll get back to you as soon as I can," and then found out a week later that the person was actually on vacation but never bothered to change the outgoing message. By managing your callers' expectations, you can leave the office and still assure your callers that you really are glad they called. If you anticipate being out of your office frequently to do on-site research or consulting, do not advertise or guarantee 24-hour turnaround.

What about giving clients your cell phone number and listing it on your business cards? Maybe it's just me, but I'm put off when someone gives me a laundry list of numbers to call if I want to reach them. Why should I have to call your voice line, your pager, your cell phone, and your home phone, and leave messages at each number? If you plan to be away and want to take calls on your cell phone, set up call forwarding on your business line, and then forward your office phone to your cell when you leave the office.

But think about whether you really want to take calls wherever you are. Suppose you are in the car or out with your family; you won't be able to concentrate on your client's needs when you are negotiating traffic or watching your daughter score a goal. As Alex Kramer, of Kramer Research, commented, "Your callers can hear what's going on around you, and if you're not doing something business-related at the time the call comes in, you may not be in the right frame of mind to take the call. That's why my voice mail refers people to my pager number and not my cell phone. I'll answer a page if I'm someplace quiet and I can focus on the call; otherwise, I wait until I'm back in the office."

Wherever you are when the phone rings, you need to sound polished, professional, and focused when you answer. Many independent info pros answer their phones with their name—"Robin Smith" or "Hello, this is Robin." I prefer this approach because it reminds my clients that they are dealing with me, not with a faceless company. Other info pros prefer to answer the phone with their business names. That's OK, if the name is easy to say out loud, since it reinforces the brand of the company. And some info pros simply answer the phone by saying, "Research" or "May I help you?" While it may seem off-putting to some callers, this rather generic greeting is a good choice if you are subcontracting and talking with your contractor's clients or acting as someone's "associate" while he is on vacation. However you choose to answer the phone, watch your tone of voice. You want to sound upbeat, crisp, and professional. One of the tricks recommended by a telephone researcher (and who would know more about cultivating an effective phone manner?) is to stand up when you talk on the phone. This helps you feel more focused and energetic.

Checklist for Polishing Your Business Image

✦   Have your logo and letterhead done by a graphic designer.

✦   Have your business cards and stationery professionally printed on high-quality stock.

✦   Keep all your online personas consistent and professional.

Chapter 24

Marketing on the Web

There are hundreds of good books that focus on how to use the web for marketing your business and uncounted businesses that owe their existence to the web. However, marketing an information business requires more than a robust web presence; it means bringing people to your website, establishing your credibility, and giving them a good reason to initiate contact with you. This chapter looks at the approaches that work well for info-entrepreneurs. Keep in mind that this is one aspect of your marketing plan that you can expect to modify every year. Resources come and go, people's use of the web changes, and the use and functionality of a particular site may change dramatically.

Where Can You Live Online?

In Chapter 23, Your Business Image, I talk about how to present yourself to the public in your print and online identities, and Chapter 10, You.com, addresses what you want in a website. But having an online presence alone is not an effective marketing approach. It requires a strategic approach that examines all the possible places where you can establish your presence and evaluate which ones offer the biggest bang for the time you invest in the virtual world.

What places you are seen in can tell a potential client a lot about you. Are your blog postings well-written and useful? Has your blog been updated within the last week or two? Is your profile in LinkedIn or Facebook written to appeal to your potential clients, or are you sending the wrong signal by failing to observe the local culture? This means always taking a while to learn your way around a new community before you start contributing. See how formal or casual the conversations are. Does everyone post a photo with his or her profile? Are the conversations rough and tumble or measured and deliberate?

I generally advise new info-entrepreneurs to set up profiles in whatever social sites their clients are likely to be on. Your goal is to be as frictionless as possible when it comes to clients getting in touch with you. Are they likely to want to connect to you in LinkedIn? Make sure you are there. Do they all hang out on Twitter? Learn how to tweet effectively. In addition to simply making yourself easier to find, there tends to be a land rush every time another social network gets popular, and the "good" user names get snapped up quickly. In order to protect your own brand, it's a good idea to use a consistent name across the social web—either your name or your company name—and to register that name on new networking sites before someone else does.

Think strategically as you set up your profile in any of your online homes. What do you want to say about yourself? Use words in your description that clients might use to find you. For example, instead of describing yourself as "experienced online researcher," try something like "strategic business intelligence" on the assumption that your clients are more likely to look for what they need rather than who you are. List any professional honors or awards you have received, professional associations you are active in, and books or articles you have written.

Include information about volunteer, advisory, and board positions you have held, unless the organization is involved in a controversial issue that your clients might find objectionable. I would certainly list a position on the local Humane Society board, but I probably would not mention a leadership position in NORML (National Organization for the Reform of Marijuana Laws) or the Wiccan church. Even if I believe both are laudable organizations, I would run the risk of offending clients by highlighting my association with what could be seen as a controversial organization.

Building Brand You

Kim Dority, of Dority & Associates, introduced me to the idea that we each have a personal brand, in addition to our company brand. As she described it,

> Contrary to what many of us associate with the concept of branding—
> that it's inauthentic, artificial, self-promoting, etc.—intelligent personal
> branding is all about showcasing your *authentic* self in a way that lets

others understand your value. Think of branding as simply taking the initiative to shape others' perceptions of your skills and abilities before they form opinions based on faulty assumptions—assumptions that may very well limit your ability to contribute. It's a way to showcase your strengths in the areas that matter to you.

Since I do a lot of speaking and writing for the information industry, before Kim got me thinking about personal branding I had not considered the need to introduce myself on the networking sites where my clients hang out. They already know my name, right? Kim reminded me that it was still up to me to manage my reputation and to profile the aspects of my business and my expertise that are most relevant to my clients. That old saying "There's no such thing as bad publicity, as long as they get your name right" does not apply to info-entrepreneurs. We rely on word of mouth, and it is our responsibility to frame that word of mouth. The social network sites are all avenues for you to position how people see you and how they describe you to others.

Finding and Building Groups

Social networking sites such as Facebook or LinkedIn are for more than just establishing your profile and linking to your friends and colleagues. Look for groups within the social networking sites that your prospective clients frequent. Right now, for example, I am actively participating in various groups of fellow info-entrepreneurs, business intelligence researchers, bloggers, professional speakers, and even one group of more than 5,000 people who all worked for MCI Telecommunications Co. back in the 1980s.

These groups can be great ways for you to market yourself gently to clients. Focus on answering rather than asking questions. Provide thoughtful comments and insights. Always, always be courteous and respectful of others; when people only see you through your words, you are judged on those words. If you are sarcastic, critical, or rude to others—regardless of the situation or provocation—others will assume that you may treat them uncivilly as well. And remember that your words live on, long past the momentary aggravation or criticism. Three years from now, someone could easily pull up that intemperate remark out of context and conclude that you are not someone to do business with.

If there does not appear to be an online group for your marketing focus, create one yourself! It takes time and effort to build an online community, and you will be responsible for creating most of the content until you get a critical mass of members. On the other hand, it can be a tremendous way to establish yourself in a niche; if you are marketing to economic development agencies, you can build your reputation as a leader by creating a virtual home for others in this field. Most of the major social networking sites support private groups formed by their members, and services such as Ning exist simply to host social networks built by members.

Marketing With Your Website

A business website is one of those business marketing tools that are necessary but far from sufficient. I always look at the website of any potential client or subcontractor; if I do not see a website, I wonder whether the person intends to be in business for the long haul.

Chapter 10, You.com, covers what is required for you to set up your business website. This section looks at how to get the most out of your site. Note that I am assuming that you are not operating a business that is focused on selling products or offering low-end research for people who fill in an order form. These types of commodity businesses require a far more intense focus on maximizing your website for ecommerce than most info-entrepreneurs require.

Getting Found in Search Engines

An entire industry has developed around what is called search engine optimization (SEO). The idea behind SEO is employing particular techniques to make your website appear near the top of a search engine's results list for specific search words. Keep in mind, though, that most of your business will not come from people cruising the web looking for high-value researchers. You want your site to be found if someone is looking for your specialized type of information services, but it is not necessary to try to get your website at the top of a search for, say, "competitive intelligence." There will always be ecommerce businesses that are willing to pay SEO professionals thousands of dollars to ensure that their websites show up at the top of any search for common descriptions of our type of work. Phrases like "web research," "business research," and "patent search" are too high-value for a one-person business to optimize its way to the first 10 search results.

Instead, create a website that is inviting to visitors and friendly to search engines, with useful content that others are likely to link to. Use words that people would use to find you, rather than simply words that describe your business. If, like my colleague Christine Hamilton-Pennell, you provide consulting services for communities implementing an entrepreneurship support program, you want to include the phrase "economic gardening" in both the text of your website and the meta-description field. Use your key phrases in subheadings. Include a clear site map with links to all the areas of your website.

As long as your site observes the basic principles of good web design, such as using descriptive page titles with words that search engines will pick up and that people are likely to use when they search, you probably have no need for a concentrated SEO effort.

Getting People to Visit Your Site

Although listing your site in directories and search engines is useful, it is even better to create content that makes people want to bookmark your site and visit it frequently. Make your site worth coming to and worth going back to again. Think about why you visit the sites that you have bookmarked yourself: They contain valuable information, are updated frequently, and are presented in a format that is easy to use. You can create a destination that your clients will find just as useful with a bit of creativity and time. Write a client newsletter and publish it on your site (see Chapter 25, Print and Eprint Marketing, for more about newsletters). Build an annotated guide to the best web resources for your client base and be sure to update it often. Post your press releases (see Chapter 28, Public Relations) and announcements of upcoming speeches. And be sure to check all your web links regularly to make sure they are still live. You can use a shareware or inexpensive software package to check all your links automatically. One that I like is Xenu's Link Sleuth (home.snafu. de/tilman/xenulink.html).

If you give a presentation, put your URL at the bottom of every PowerPoint slide. Post a copy of the talk or the slides at your site and tell the audience how they can download a copy. If you post anything in an email discussion group or web forum, always include your URL at the bottom of your posting. (See the section "Participating in Electronic Discussions" for more thoughts on low-key marketing through discussion groups and forums.)

One colleague of mine used her website to get some great coverage for her company. She conducted a review of consumer-oriented health websites, evaluating how current and accurate the information was and describing how much misinformation she found. She then published her report on her website and sent out a press release announcing her findings. She got great coverage of both her report and her company, and she was even invited to testify before a White House commission.

Blogging Your Business

As with any other type of web content, it is quality that counts, not just quantity. Write about things that matter to your clients. Remember, people are investing their time and attention on you when they read your blog; make it worthwhile.

You will not get much marketing value from your blog if you don't know what the point is. Why are you writing a blog? (And if the answer is "because Mary Ellen Bates said to," you need to come up with a better answer.) You may want to be seen as the go-to researcher who shares search tips with the public. Perhaps your goal is to be seen as a thought leader in your clients' industry or to be the place people go to find free resources that help them find and use information more efficiently.

Keep your blog articles relatively brief and interesting; make your point within the first two or three sentences, expand on your idea for a couple of paragraphs at most, and then stop. If you have more to say, put it in a newsletter or white paper, where it will stand alone as your thoughts on a topic. Your goal is to make your blog articles easy to read and point others to the post. Most people are disinclined to read blog postings that require more than a screen or two of text. Add images or graphics when appropriate. People are drawn to pictures, and your blog is more appealing visually if it is lightened up with screen shots, logos, embedded videos, or other images.

Use enticing titles for your blog posts to encourage readers to click through an RSS feed or a search engine search results page. "Five Ways to Find People on the Web," or "Top Tools for Business Intelligence Research," or "Field Report From the Annual Widget Conference" all suggest that the reader will benefit from reading your blog.

Get a custom domain for your blog so that your blog address is not tied to a specific blog host. For example, I point people to my blog at www.Librarianof Fortune.com, rather than the "real" URL of maryellenbates.typepad.com. I can always move my blog to another host or host it on my own site without my readers needing to know.

As with your website, list your blog URL wherever you can—list it in your email signature file, mention it in your presentations, and point to it in your enewsletter.

Use your blog to promote your upcoming talks, the availability of your latest white paper, and any awards you have won or volunteer positions you are elected or appointed to.

Even more so than for traditional webpages, linking is a critical part of the blogosphere. If your purpose is to get people to read your posts, then you need to get others to mention your blog. The best way to get links to and comments on your blog is, of course, to link to and comment on other blog postings. You won't see immediate results; building your reputation and standing in the blog world takes time. It is usually worth the time and effort, however, as you build a network of people who are interested in what you have to say and who are likely to refer you to others.

Minding Your Signature

All email software allows you to include a "signature" at the end of every email message you send out. Most people simply put in their names, email addresses, and website URLs, but you are wasting valuable real estate by merely listing your contact info. Think of your signature file as a way to say more to your clients and contacts than what is in the text of the email message. You can point readers to your blog, to a white paper you recently wrote, or to the subscription for your enewsletter. In order to entice your readers into clicking through—and interrupt their email reading to do so—the text in your signature needs to be compelling.

Instead of simply listing your URL, tell people why they should go there. Adding a note that says, "Read my latest enewsletter on five innovative competitive intelligence tools" is a lot more compelling than "Click here for my enewsletter."

Keep your signature to no more than six lines. Any more than that will look as though the message continues after your signature, and whatever message you are trying to send gets lost in the verbiage. You don't need to list your pager, your cell phone, your fax line, and your Skype ID; just include enough to enable readers to contact you.

Participating in Electronic Discussions

An effective way of establishing your expertise is to participate in the email discussion lists and web-based forums where your clients and colleagues congregate. AIIP-L, the private email list for members of AIIP, is a tremendously useful way to network with fellow info pros, brainstorm about difficult situations and projects (while maintaining client confidentiality, of course), and get to know fellow AIIP members with whom you might be able to set up subcontracting relationships.

In addition to AIIP-L, do some research to find electronic discussion groups that your prospective clients are likely to read or that other researchers in your field participate in already. Obviously, this approach is not as useful if your clients are not accustomed to carrying on conversations with colleagues via email. Ask those in your industry whether they are aware of any discussion lists or would recommend one in particular. If they give you a blank look, assume that this may not be the best use of your marketing time and effort. If they rattle off the names of several groups they find stimulating or useful, take note.

You may also want to identify the trade and professional associations your clients belong to; like AIIP, these associations may host useful email discussion lists that make the membership dues a worthwhile investment. For more discussion of leveraging your association memberships as a marketing device, see Chapter 27, Starting the Word of Mouth.

Once you have identified a few electronic discussion groups that look promising, subscribe to them and just sit back and listen—well, read—for a week or two. Get a feel for the audience and the "culture" of each group. You don't have to scan more than a handful at first; in fact, you probably should not start with more than you can keep up with. It makes more sense to subscribe to three or four at a time that you will be able to participate in rather than spend all your spare time trying to keep up with 10 or 20 different lists. One of the unexpected benefits of reading these lists is that you may learn about additional, perhaps even more productive, lists. The private discussion list for AIIP members often includes references to other lists of interest to many independent info pros—the BUSLIB-L list for business librarians, or a group in Facebook for competitive intelligence researchers, for example.

When someone posts a question or raises an issue on a list that you can address, do so. Remember that this is a long-term marketing approach; you need to establish your expertise with the list participants over the course of months before you can expect people to contact you for work. Any posting on professional lists that smacks of blatant advertising is verboten; it can get you thrown off the list and will hurt your reputation. Be subtle. Saying "I know the answer and I'd be happy to do the research for you for a fee" will not win you clients. Rather, provide helpful pointers and advice when you can and be sure to include your name, company name, email address, and website URL at the bottom of every posting.

When networking, whether in person at a conference, electronically in an email discussion group or web-based forum, or in private email with a colleague, people notice the small things. If you are rude or snippy with someone, others may decide that they do not want to refer clients your way. If you are argumentative in a discussion forum, your colleagues may well conclude that they have no interest in engaging you one-on-one in the context of a subcontracting relationship either. Think of every professional encounter as a marketing opportunity. Just as you would never get into an argument with a prospective client during a sales call, you should also avoid needless or pointless arguments in an electronic discussion group.

Other Options to Consider

Depending on your business, client base, and your interest, there are other ways to market your business on the web. As I write this, Twitter is a popular way for people to microblog. While Twitter has taken some lumps for being nothing more than a list of what people had for breakfast, it can be a strategic tool for establishing yourself as a resource for information your clients want. As with blogging, the critical factor is in providing content your readers want. No one wants to know that you are stuck in the Denver airport because of a snowstorm; your words are far more likely to be redistributed across social networks if they are pithy, clearly written, and useful.

Podcasts, webinars, and other live (or recorded live) presentations can be valuable marketing tools as you establish your reputation within your client base. These require both more of a learning curve and an investment in high-quality equipment in order to ensure that the presentation reflects well on your professionalism. Make sure your finished product is easy to follow, requires no technical expertise to run, is immediately useful or relevant, and is of interest to your clients. You may wish to eventually turn these products into revenue streams; the production quality must be high but having a source of passive income is always nice for entrepreneurs. See

Chapter 38, Other Services You Can Offer, for more discussion of developing products to sell.

There are lots of so-called experts sites or Q&A (question and answer) sites, where people can tap into the knowledge of self-identified researchers or experts. These sites can exist independently, or they can be one feature of a social networking service such as LinkedIn. Some info-entrepreneurs are active participants in these expert sites, answering questions and providing quick research to find web resources. It does not take more than a few months to be seen as a helpful expert, but it is not likely that prospective clients with real budgets would be asking their question in an expert or Q&A site. If they have so little at stake that they are willing to rely on the advice of a virtual stranger, they are probably not likely to pay your hourly rates for more in-depth research. If, on the other hand, you are offering a service or product that is targeted to the general public, these sites may be helpful ways of building your reputation … and your client base.

Virtual worlds such as Second Life have not caught on as quickly as their early proponents predicted, but they may eventually become another place where you want to maintain a presence. As with a website or a social media site like Facebook, you have to design a virtual "place" that attracts people to you. This may mean "staffing" your online storefront during regular hours, giving free presentations, and providing useful content to visitors.

Regardless of what the virtual community looks like, remember that there are people behind each user ID. They can serve as your word-of-mouth marketing brigade if you treat the community with respect. You must earn the attention and respect of the group before you can expect to gain any business from your participation.

Top Tips for Marketing on the Web

✦ Clients are more likely to look for what they need rather than who you are; make sure your online presence includes words that describe your benefits, not just your features.

✦ Personal branding is about showcasing your authentic self in a way that lets others understand your value.

✦ A business website is necessary but far from sufficient.

✦ Make your web content worth reading and worth coming back to again.

✦ Your words live on in the web. Be professional and courteous in all your web presences.

Chapter 25

Print and Eprint Marketing

In the first edition of this book, I focused on print material such as brochures, Rolodex cards, marketing kits, and the like. We still are far from the paperless office envisioned by early computer proponents, and there is still a place for hard copy marketing and electronic versions of print material.

Even though much of your marketing will consist of activities that generate word-of-mouth buzz, there are some traditional print marketing techniques that work well for independent info pros. Chapter 23, Your Business Image, covers standard business identity such as business cards, stationery, and brochures. But keep in mind that there is far more to marketing than handing someone your business card.

Starting Your Mailing List

One marketing guideline states that a business has to "touch" or contact a prospect at least five times before the prospect remembers the business and responds to the marketing pitch. That sounds like a lot of touching, doesn't it? Fortunately, it does not mean that you have to pick up the phone and make five sales calls; you can send out a periodic newsletter or postcard to remind your prospects of your services.

How do you develop a mailing list of prospective clients? If you are reading this book before you have started your business, begin collecting business cards from everyone you meet. Once you launch your business, you will have an initial prospect list to work from. I encourage you to send material to everyone you have encountered in a business-related setting, announcing your new business, and including three or four reasons why the recipient should call you. ("We help you make better strategic decisions." "We free up your time from searching so you can focus on what you do best." You get the idea.) When I started my company and was flipping through my collection of business cards, I almost didn't send a brochure and marketing letter to a speechwriter I had worked with briefly a couple of years before, thinking that it was not even worth the cost of the stamp. I am glad I did though; he turned into a wonderful client and a great source of referrals. You just never know.

As you build your own mailing list, retain every name unless the mailing is returned as "addressee unknown." In saying that, I am assuming that you have at least minimally prequalified all prospects before adding them to the list; you have ensured that everyone to whom you send mail has met you, heard you speak, or otherwise had some direct contact with you. You never know who among your prospect list does not use you directly but is passing along your mailings and your name to colleagues. I learned this lesson when I met a prospect who had been receiving my newsletters and postcards for four or five years, with no noticeable results. As we got to talking, she commented that she was so glad that she was still on my mailing list, that she forwarded my newsletter to five other people, and that she routinely gave out my name as the person to call for research.

One advantage of public speaking is that you can use these events to gather subscriptions. See Chapter 26, Marketing by Writing and Speaking, for more discussion of how to offer incentives to get the right people to give you their contact information.

Direct Mail: Directly to the Wastebasket?

Your own mailing list will probably grow rather slowly and that is not necessarily a bad thing. Information services are not a commodity that can be mass-marketed, and a list of 200 qualified prospects who have heard of you is worth much more than a list of 20,000 people who have no idea who you are. It is frustrating to have to build a prospect list from scratch, and I estimate that 75 percent of all independent info pros try a direct mail campaign at some point. Maybe you are tempted to harvest names of executives from a directory. Perhaps you are thinking about building a mailing list from a professional association's membership roster. Or maybe you are looking into purchasing a mailing list from a list broker.

I won't get into a lengthy discussion of the copyright issues involved in taking names from a directory or membership list. Generally, that information is considered proprietary and is covered by copyright. Most publishers specifically state that you cannot compile your own mailing list from their directories without written permission and payment for the use of the information. But this approach is seldom cost-effective anyway.

Traditionally, a direct mail campaign is considered successful if 2 to 4 percent of the recipients *respond* to the mailing. That does not necessarily mean that any of that small percentage of respondents ever become paying clients. Those are not very good odds, particularly for a small business selling an intangible and relatively high-priced service. My hunch, based on conversations with many info-entrepreneurs over the years, is that the response rate to direct marketing for info pro services is much lower than 4 percent. Would you choose a lawyer, doctor, accountant, or therapist based on a mass mailing? I did't think so; I wouldn't either. Likewise, the odds of a likely prospect deciding to use your services because of a mailing—no matter how polished—are very low.

That said, there are circumstances in which some form of direct marketing can be effective. If you have an identifiable, tangible product—short company profiles, a weekly news update with summaries of key articles in a narrowly defined industry, a specialized piece of software for analyzing information—you may be able to develop a direct mail piece that works. To be effective, though, you need to describe what you are offering in clear terms, demonstrate the value to the prospective client, and compel the prospect to follow up with an order. The product must be something that many people in your client base would find cost-effective and valuable, something that they cannot do themselves and that is not available through other common sources. Expect to send out hundreds, if not thousands, of marketing pieces on a regular basis; remember that it takes five exposures for the prospect to remember who you are and to decide to make a purchase. Even with an excellent direct marketing pitch, do not expect more than the usual 2 to 4 percent response rate.

The more qualified your mailing list, the better. Rather than purchasing a generic list from a list broker, consider buying the membership directory mailing list from an association that your prospects are likely to belong to—and do some judicious pruning of that list before sending your mailing out. What is important is to purchase a list of people who, because of their membership in an organization, participation in an event, or subscription to a key industry publication, have already indicated that they are interested in a specific professional area—film production, patent research, electrical engineering, or whatever your area of specialization is.

Targeted Mailings

Although mass mailings are often ineffective, very focused mailings can be successful in some markets. The secret is to invest time up front in finding the organizations and individuals to target. First, identify 25 or 30 companies, government agencies, or other organizations that you know would use your services. Use your research skills to identify the name of a likely prospect in each organization and that person's direct mailing address. Do not rely on printed directories, which are often out of date before they are even published. Either confirm the contact information on the organization's website or pick up the telephone and call the organization directly.

Once you have your contact's name, write a one-page letter describing the information need that you are addressing and how you can meet that need. Tell the prospect that you will be following up with a telephone call to answer any questions.

Pace yourself so that you can indeed follow up each one with a phone call. By sending, say, five letters at a time, you can track the response you are getting and, if necessary, modify your approach for the next five letters. And even if a prospect does not immediately turn into a sale, at least ask if you can put him on your mailing list for your free enewsletter. He may just need to hear from you a few times before he decides to give you a try. Evaluate your success rate after you have tried this technique for several months. If it does not seem to be paying off in terms of actual paid projects, consider switching to another marketing strategy.

Client Newsletters and Postcards

Client mailings can be an effective tool for showcasing your expertise and reminding your clients of your capabilities. Unlike advertising, a mailing to someone you have had at least some contact with usually gets noticed. The key is to make sure that your clients and prospects hear from you regularly, preferably every month or two.

Newsletters and Enewsletters

One of the most significant impacts of the web is that it enables anyone to become a publisher. First, we published webpages. Then came blogs, which enabled us to create constantly updated journals, one blog post at a time. And now we have podcasts, videocasts, and who knows what else? We may start seeing intracranial implants for delivery of the news directly into our brain soon, although I intend to resist that as long as possible.

Interestingly, one communication tool that has not changed much over time is the newsletter. It is still an effective way to stay in contact with clients, colleagues, and—depending on your focus—the world at large. Many newsletters have dropped (or never had) a dead-tree version and are published directly to the web and sent to subscribers' email inboxes. These publications are known by various names: electronic newsletter, enewsletter, email newsletter, epublication, emedia, or even ezine. Whatever you call them, these publications can be fun to write and are cost-effective tools for keeping your name in front of your clients.

Writing a client newsletter is not as daunting as it might sound. For starters, it does not have to be a 10-page affair; you can begin with a one-page newsletter and expand it gradually as you become more adept at newsletter writing. The main concerns are that it be readable and frequent. As for what to write about, think about interesting websites you have encountered, a particularly intriguing research project you tackled (maintaining client confidentiality, of course), or a description of new products or services you saw at a recent trade show.

While you should post your newsletter on your webpage and create an RSS feed for those who want to read your newsletter through their RSS readers, do not count on your clients going to your site to read it. "Push" technology—sending information directly to the reader—has more impact than "pull" technology—placing it on a site that readers have to remember to visit.

One decision you will make before you write your first newsletter article is what the format and length of the articles will be. The most important factor is how long your typical clients are willing to read something. For some professions, anything more than two paragraphs looks like too much content. For others, clients assign more credibility to writing that has a scholarly or academic feel. Know your audience and write in a way that is likely to be familiar to your readers.

There are a number of ways to design your newsletter. The simplest is a plain text email or sheet of your stationery, with a short article or two, along with your contact information. Simple and easy to do, but it may not look very professional. While some people still prefer plain text, most prefer something more polished and, well, interesting; remember, you are competing for the attention of your readers, and you do not want to look boring. Consider creating an HTML template you can use for your newsletter so that it includes some graphic elements, a variety of font sizes, and live hyperlinks.

Some newsletter formats include just a teaser paragraph with a link to a webpage for the rest of the article. The advantages include the ability to publish longer articles without having the newsletter appear text-heavy, and the ability to track readership by seeing how many people click through, which can help you target your articles to what people are most interested in. If your newsletter comprises several articles, begin your newsletter with a table of contents or list of headlines and an excerpt from each article with a link to the full article (either later in the newsletter or on a webpage). This enables readers to skim the issue and jump directly to the articles of interest. It also lets you publish more in-depth articles if you want to without forcing readers to slog through two articles of minimal interest to get to the one that grabs their attention.

Since you are creating your newsletter from scratch, you have a lot of leeway in deciding what it looks like. Keep in mind that you want to make it appealing, easy to read, and entertaining as well as informative. Leave plenty of white space. If their first impression is one of dense text, people are less likely to read it. Use a font size large enough to be read by less-than-youthful eyes. As for content, write about topics that your clients care about or that they will find useful. Following are a few examples of what a client newsletter can cover:

- Trends in your clients' industry
- Reviews of professional resources (websites, value-added online resources, books, podcasts, and so on)
- Upcoming industry conferences
- Interviews with experts
- A fun or odd feature—a link to How Stuff Works (www.howstuffworks.com) or an interesting fact culled from Did You Know (www.didyouknow.org), such as the collective names for various groups of animals (a drift of hogs, a gang of elks, or a float of crocodiles)

Managing Mailing Lists

Rule No. 1 of managing an email subscription list is to make it 100 percent opt-in. That means adding no one to the distribution list unless they specifically request it.

The second rule is to include instructions on subscribing and unsubscribing with every mailing. In my monthly newsletter, I remind readers: "You are receiving this because you have subscribed to this free newsletter as {theirname@their domain.whatever}. If you would like to unsubscribe or change your email subscription, just go to www.BatesInfo.com/subscribe." Alternatively, people can just email me, and I remove their email addresses myself. The point is to make it as easy as possible for people to unsubscribe, if they want to.

When I first started sending out an email newsletter, I maintained the subscription list using my email software, manually updating it whenever someone wanted to be added or removed, or when an email address bounced. That worked fine when I had a couple hundred subscribers. But once my mailing list grew to 500 or 600, it became too time-consuming. At that point, I shopped around for a service that could host my email list for a modest fee. (I did not want to use a free service such as Yahoo! Groups, because free services usually insert ads at the bottom of each mailing, and because the return address indicated that the mailing was from a Yahoo! Group rather than my own email address. I felt that both of these "features" detracted from the professional image I wanted to maintain.)

Commercial email list hosts handle most of the administrative details of a one-way (also known as broadcast or announcement) email list. They handle any rejected email addresses, they deal with subscription/removal requests, they will send out a message from you when someone subscribes or unsubscribes, and they provide the HTML code for you to add a subscription box on your webpage. The cost for any of these services is usually determined by the size of your mailing list and the frequency and file size of your mailings.

Promotional Postcards

You may not have the time or inspiration to create a newsletter every month. Postcards are useful tools for getting your name out to your clients even when you do not have much to say. Be sure to include your company name, something to pique the client's curiosity, such as a list of interesting recent projects or a new product you offer, and a call-to-action suggesting that the client call or email you today. Make sure your contact information appears in a large, bold font. See Figures 25.1 and 25.2 for two marketing postcard samples. Keep in mind that the postcard has to stand on its own; that is, do not simply point people to your website or ask them to

HELP!

Can't keep up with news in the automotive
industry?

We can help! Auto-Info-Direct offers a free
weekly enewsletter with the key news in the
automotive industry.

10% discount to new subscribers

Call us today at **303.555.1212** or go to
auto-info-direct.com for a sample issue.

Figure 25.1 Sample postcard for newsletter

call to find out what services you provide. An effective marketing postcard has to be
so compelling that your client is motivated to pick up the phone.

You can also use postcards as follow-up contacts after a presentation. How does
this work? Collect business cards during your talk with the offer of a door prize drawing. While you are speaking, notice which points generate the most interest. When
you get back in the office, create a postcard that—briefly—reminds people of your
talk, highlights several key points, and invites them to call you the next time they are
making a strategic decision.

Figure 25.2 Sample postcard for research services

You can buy colorful preprinted postcard stock from Paper Direct (www.paper direct.com) or any major office supply chain. Normally, these come two- or four-to-a-page with microperforations, so you can run them through a printer or photocopier. My experience has been that the larger postcards, 5-1/2″ by 8-1/2″, are more effective. You have more space for text, and they do not look as much like junk mail.

Directories

Most of your business will come from recommendations, from people who have heard you speak or read what you have written, gotten to know you from your participation in the social web, or from existing clients. But you want to make it as easy as possible for prospective clients to find you. A website is a necessity, and you will probably want to have a presence in some of the social networking sites. See Chapter 24, Marketing on the Web, for more discussion of these options. You can also pay for listings in print directories.

Yellow Pages Are More Than Just Doorstops

I used to recommend that info-entrepreneurs use a landline (that is, a phone that actually plugs into a telephone jack) for their business phone. It was important to have reliable phone service; you never want to be saying, "Can you hear me now?" when you are on a cell phone call with a client. The quality of VoIP service is now comparable to a landline connection, and cell phone sound quality is getting better.

With a landline phone, your business name will appear in the local print and web-based telephone directories. This makes it easier for someone to find you if they know your business name but not your website, and this is my last-ditch resort when someone inexplicably does not list their phone number on their website. As long as you make sure that a phone number is listed in all your web profiles, you are probably sufficiently findable for prospective clients who want to talk with you live.

If you have a landline phone, you will usually also have a standard listing in the local telephone company's Yellow Pages directory. Before you specify the category you would like to be listed under, browse through the other listings in that category and see if they are similar to your business. Bates Information Services was initially listed under "Information Bureaus," which seemed at first glance like the appropriate place. Had I looked at the other listings, I would have realized that my company would appear between the American Kurdish Information Network and the Chittenden Press Service. Needless to say, the few calls that I got from that listing were from people looking for news agencies, not research services. (The local Yellow Pages still doesn't have a category for Business Research, so now I appear under Market Research & Analysis—not ideal, but at least callers know that I'm a fee-based business rather than a wire service or a source for free information.)

Regardless of the category in which you list your business, do not count on getting much actual work from a Yellow Pages listing. You can expect many more calls from tire-kickers and people who are not prepared to pay for your services than from bona fide prospective clients. That is why I am not persuaded that display ads in Yellow Page directories are worth the expense. The money you spend for a larger ad in the local phone book would probably be better spent on listings in more targeted directories (see the following section). Remember, the vast majority of people who pick up the Yellow Pages are not going to be your clients. You will get better results with a listing in a directory that goes directly into the hands of people who are likely to be interested in the services you provide.

Specialized Directories

Clients are more likely to look up an independent info pro in a directory that is specific to their industry or market, rather than in the local phone book. That is why many info pros join associations that their clients belong to—to ensure that they are listed in the association's membership directory. Some associations have a less-expensive category for vendors or associates, as distinct from regular members. This usually entitles you to a directory listing, even though you may not want to take advantage of all the other benefits of membership.

Of course, merely having a listing in an association's membership directory won't bring you business. You need to make sure that people are going to that directory, looking for you, not just browsing the listings for one that sounds good. In order to get the value from your membership, you need to raise your visibility so that people know your name. See Chapter 27, Starting the Word of Mouth, for more discussion of how to get the most marketing benefit from your association memberships.

Print Advertising

You may have noticed that in this chapter devoted to print marketing, I have not mentioned plain old advertising—taking out ads in newspapers, magazines, or other publications that your clients read. That is because print advertising is an expensive proposition, and you often do not see results for months. For advertising to be successful, you need to have a well-designed ad—which means paying a marketing pro to help you with the layout and wording—that appears in at least six consecutive issues of the magazine or newspaper. Remember the guideline about having to "touch" prospects at least five times before they will call you? Unfortunately, when you run an ad, you have no assurance that your prospects will even notice the ads in any given issue; that is why consistent placement is crucial. More importantly, though, efforts you put into advertising do not generate any word of mouth. You never hear someone say, "Oh, I saw a great ad in the newspaper for a plastic surgeon. You ought to try him out!"

If you are considering running an ad, talk to a few of your existing clients and find out what kind of ad would make them pick up the phone and call you. What publications do they consider most reliable? Which ones do they read thoroughly? Look through a few recent issues and see what other types of companies advertise there.

Most importantly, before you embark on an advertising campaign, decide how you will measure its success. Do you see new business that you can attribute to the ad? Do any inquiries mention the ad? If you can see tangible results, then you have found a good advertising strategy. If you cannot attribute any business to the ad within, say, six or eight issues, you should reconsider your marketing mix.

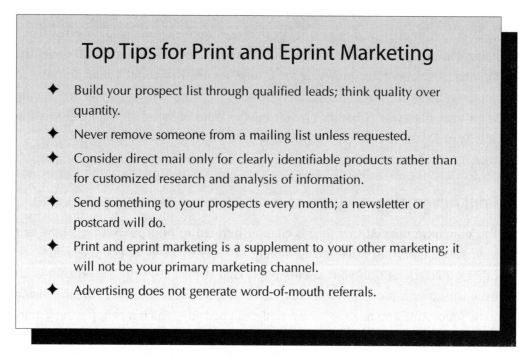

Top Tips for Print and Eprint Marketing

✦ Build your prospect list through qualified leads; think quality over quantity.

✦ Never remove someone from a mailing list unless requested.

✦ Consider direct mail only for clearly identifiable products rather than for customized research and analysis of information.

✦ Send something to your prospects every month; a newsletter or postcard will do.

✦ Print and eprint marketing is a supplement to your other marketing; it will not be your primary marketing channel.

✦ Advertising does not generate word-of-mouth referrals.

Chapter 26

Marketing by Writing and Speaking

Most new independent info pros do not have the advantage of being already well-known in their industry. One of the most effective ways of gaining credibility is to be seen as an authority; that can come from writing articles or books your clients read or by speaking at conferences they attend. An added benefit is that you can use these opportunities to remind people of what you know and what you do. Of course, you cannot turn an article or a talk into a blatant sales pitch; however, you can mention your website and your enewsletter (if you have one) in every speech and every piece of writing you undertake. Make it easy for your audience to find that website, read that blog, or subscribe to that newsletter by providing your email address and URL.

Marketing through speaking and writing can be tremendously effective, but it is a long-term process. It takes time to land a speaking gig or get an article written and published. Speaking and writing skills may not come naturally to you. Writing my first article was very difficult, and I was a nervous wreck during my first few speaking engagements, but I soldiered on under the assumption that (1) it would get easier in time and (2) I simply had to do this. It did get easier over time, and both writing and speaking have become both good marketing tools and sources of new insights for me. So even if the thought of public speaking makes you cringe, read on.

Author, Author!

You can get a lot of mileage out of writing an article. If you write for an industry publication that your prospective clients read, you are immediately seen as an expert. You can use that article as validation when you are trying to line up speaking engagements (more about this later in the chapter). If you either negotiate this ahead of time or purchase electronic reprint rights of your articles after publication, you can put them up on your website. Voilà: instant credibility.

Try writing for your local business weekly; the audience is more limited and not as focused as for industry publications, but it is great practice and a good way for a wide variety of people to see your name. As with industry publications, you can negotiate or purchase reprint rights of the article for your website. And you can write for publications that your referral sources read, which includes *AIIP Connections*, the quarterly newsletter of the Association of Independent Information Professionals (AIIP; www.aiip.org).

In fact, if you are really ambitious, you might consider offering to write a regular column for a publication whose readers you value. Of course, this presumes that you enjoy writing and that you will come up with something to say in every issue. Before you pitch the idea to an editor, outline five or six columns and see whether you have enough ideas to sustain it.

What's the Payoff?

The question that is undoubtedly at the front of your mind right now is, "How much will I get paid to speak or write?" The minimum for professional writers is currently around $1 a word, but mention this to an independent info pro who writes regularly and she will probably collapse in helpless laughter. If you contribute an article to a local business weekly, do not expect to be paid at all. That goes for *AIIP Connections*, too. If you write for an industry publication, the going rate is generally somewhere between $200 and $500 for an article of several thousand words. You probably won't be paid until the article is actually published. No, you are not going to get rich from your writing, at least not directly—but as a loyal member of the National Writers Union (www.nwu.org), I always encourage writers to negotiate the best rate they can for their work. The real payoff comes in the reputation you build and in the other ways you leverage your writing. Be sure to tell your clients about any articles you have written. Mention it in your newsletter and, where appropriate, in the email groups and discussion lists you participate in.

Querying Editors

How do you figure out what publication to write for? To identify the important publications in your clients' industry, go to your local library and look through the

Encyclopedia of Business Information Sources (Gale Group, published annually), either online in the Gale Directory Library or in print. In fact, consider purchasing this invaluable research tool. It is a great resource for identifying the key associations, directories, periodicals, websites, and databases for industries from Abrasives to Zinc. Then check out WritersMarket.com (www.writersmarket.com). This web-based directory lists contact information for thousands of publications, tells you what they pay, and whether they publish articles by freelancers as well as by their own staff writers. There are various subscription plans to WritersMarket.com, all averaging around $5/month—a modest price for the value.

Look up each publication you have identified through the *Encyclopedia of Business Information Sources* in WritersMarket.com, make sure they publish articles by freelancers, and note any particular submission guidelines. You should also check the publication's own website for a link to "author's guidelines" or "submission guidelines." These tell you what type of material the publisher is looking for, the format in which to submit articles, the style and tone expected, and so on. Look through recent articles on the publication site, if they are posted there, or the indexes of recent issues to see what types of stories the publication generally carries.

Now it is time to think about what to write. I cannot give you ideas; you know what you know, and you know (or can figure out) what your clients would find interesting to read. Focus on topics that are timely, that are useful, and that tie together your expertise and the concerns of your client base. Once you have an idea of what you would like to write about, send a query letter to the submissions editor to find out if he or she is interested in your article. You don't have to write the article in advance, but you should be able to describe your idea in a paragraph or two. Explain why you think this article would be appropriate for the publication, why it is timely and interesting, and why you are the person to write it. If you have written other articles, you can include two or three of them with your letter. These previously published articles are called "clips"; they are often used to demonstrate to an editor that an unknown writer is, in fact, competent and has indeed been published before.

Send your query letter in hard copy, not through email. Many editors (wisely) will not open unsolicited email attachments, and your query will have more impact on real paper. Enclose a self-addressed, stamped envelope for the editor's response; editors receive query letters all the time, so you want to make it easy to reply. It is acceptable to send query letters to several publications about the same general topic. If you are fortunate enough to have your proposal accepted by two editors, make sure that you can write two distinct articles, taking a different perspective or emphasis in each one. It is verboten to submit the *same* article to two publishers.

Always get a publication agreement in writing. Spell out the topic of the article, the length, the deadline for delivery, who owns copyright of the article, and the details of payment. Some publishers will insist on seeing the article before agreeing on a price, particularly if you are a new writer. Ask for the right to publish the article on your own website after a suitable embargo period, such as three months.

Writing Well

What about actually putting words to paper ... er, to computer screen? First, look through some back issues of the publication you are writing for to get a sense of the style and tone of published articles. Ask the editor for a style sheet or author's guidelines. Some editors like lots of sidebars and checklists, others want a list of referenced URLs, some have specific rules for subheadings, and so on. Make your article inviting by starting out with an attention-getting or intriguing first paragraph that catches the readers' attention and makes them want to read more. Pack your article full of useful information, so that people will want to keep it around for future reference. Remember, every time they look at it, your expertise is reinforced.

I remember a discussion among AIIP members in which one person maintained that it wasn't smart to give away your "trade secrets" in an article. On the contrary, I have always operated from the belief that whatever I put down on paper just serves to highlight my background and years of experience. Our trade secrets consist of our skills, experience, intuition, and contacts, and you cannot give those away.

As for the more mundane aspects of writing a professional article, consider the following:

- Write in simple, straightforward language, not "academese." Forget the extensive footnotes and pedantic prose.

- Keep your article focused and on point. Most readers don't have a long attention span or a lot of spare time to read articles, so don't inflate the length of your article beyond what you think the subject requires.

- Use descriptive subheadings to break up the text.

- Include a mention of your client newsletter, website, or other marketing tools in your author biography at the end of the article, along with your contact information.

- Stay within the word count agreed upon with the editor.

- Ask a couple of colleagues to give you their honest assessment of the article before you submit it and make any necessary changes to ensure that it is as polished as possible.

- Meet the agreed-upon deadline. Remember, the editor may be holding space in an issue for your article. If you cannot deliver the article on time, you have just made an editor's life a whole lot harder. Missing a deadline is one of the most unprofessional things you can do—when writing an article as well as in your own info pro business.

Once the article has been accepted, find out whether the article will appear on the publication's website and link to it from your own site. If it is not destined for publication online, ask how long the content will be embargoed before you can post it on your own website. And get more mileage out of the article by mentioning it in your blog and your client newsletter, as well as in any talks that you give on the same or a related topic.

Speaking Your Piece

Writing is one way to establish your credibility within your client market. Another technique that works for many independent info pros is public speaking. A room full of people staring at you may not be your idea of a fun time, but it does get easier with practice. Every time you give a talk, you have the undivided attention of everyone within earshot.

Starting Local

Unless you are already well-known in your field, you probably won't get invitations to speak, with all expenses paid, at conferences around the world. That's OK; you can start local and work out from there. To begin with, identify the events and association meetings that your prospective clients are likely to attend. If they are marketing executives, look at the local chapter of the Business Marketing Association or similar organization. If you provide in-depth biomedical research, the local chapter of the Medical Library Association could be a great source of both direct business and referrals.

Find the appropriate organization's website and identify the person responsible for planning the local meetings. Write, email, or call the meeting planner and offer to speak (for no charge, of course) on a topic that you think would interest the group and that highlights your expertise. Offer to send the planner copies of any articles you have written. You will probably find that you are welcomed with open arms. It is difficult to pull together local events, and an offer to speak (for free) is usually the best thing a meeting planner can hear.

Prepare, Prepare, Prepare

Once you have landed a speaking gig, do your homework. Make sure you develop a talk that addresses the interests and concerns of the audience. The traditional formula for speakers—tell them what you're going to tell them, then tell them, and finally tell them what you've told them—still works. Build your talk with an introduction in which you get their interest, set the stage, and tell the audience what they will be learning; follow this by the body of the talk, in which you cover each of the topics you promised at the beginning; and conclude with a wrap-up that summarizes what you talked about and, if appropriate, end on a thought-provoking or inspirational note.

One of the hardest aspects of speaking is to not cover too much. We info pros are a collegial and sharing lot, and we want to tell others about all the things we have found and techniques we know. Unfortunately, that is not possible. I often need to remind myself that the goal of a good presentation is to include less than all I know but as much as the audience needs to know. There is always more than I will have time to say; my mission is to select what part of what I know will fit into the time allotted.

Some speakers feel most confident if they write their speech ahead of time. If you take this approach, assume that between 10 and 15 pages of single-spaced text translates into a one-hour talk. Others work best with just an outline or PowerPoint presentation to guide them. If you are the latter type of speaker, figure on roughly three minutes of speaking for each PowerPoint slide. If you move through slides any more quickly than that, your audience will be more interested in watching the quickly changing screen than paying attention to you.

You will give a better presentation if you practice your talk ahead of time. Stand in front of a mirror, set a timer to the number of minutes you have been allotted, and start talking. Allow 10 or 15 minutes for questions and make sure that your talk fills but does not exceed the agreed-on time. Whether it is a half-hour talk or an all-day workshop, it is disrespectful to have too much or too little content for the time allotted. If you try to cover more material than you have time for, your audience will leave feeling confused, frustrated, and unsatisfied. If you have too little material to fill the time, you will give the impression that you do not have much to say. Either way, you won't look good, but going over your allotted time is the worse of the two offenses.

Be brutally honest with yourself as you practice your presentation. If you find yourself trying to cram too much information into the time you have, cut back. Yes, there is always more to say on a topic as fascinating as the one you have chosen to cover but rushing through your slides because you have run out of time looks unprofessional and does not add to your or your audience's comfort. And do not be tempted to exceed your allotted time. You will accomplish nothing except alienating your audience and ensuring that the organization will not invite you again.

Finding a Test Audience

Joe Flower, an experienced writer, speaker, and consultant (www.ImagineWhatIf.com), has some great advice for anyone considering public speaking. Because so much of successful speaking is practice, he recommends finding volunteer speaking opportunities where you can improve your skills before making your big presentation at that major conference. As he said to me once: "Where do you find volunteer audiences? Local organizations such as women's clubs or the Rotary, the human resources or education specialists of companies in industries that might be affected by your talk. Offer them a free lunchtime talk that is relevant to their people. I once called up every stock brokerage in town, and gave a bunch of lunchtime talks about dealing with an aging population, for example. You need real audiences; there is no substitute."

Going Global

Once you have become somewhat comfortable in front of a room, it is time to expand your horizons. Instead of just speaking to local chapters of national associations, get in touch with the annual conference planner or program committee and propose a talk that you think would be of interest to the membership as a whole. It might be an expanded version of your presentation to the local group or something else that a broader audience would find appealing. Keep in mind that conference planners often work six to 18 months out, so you may be making a pitch for a talk quite a ways in the future. But the opportunity is worth waiting for; your credibility among your clients will grow significantly once you are known as a speaker at the national or international meeting of their professional or trade association.

When you reach this point, you may be in a position to ask for money. Depending on the organization, they may pay an honorarium to speakers. Even if they do not pay speakers directly, it is reasonable to ask for reimbursement of your travel expenses and to expect them to waive any conference registration fees. After all, you are providing the content that their attendees are paying for, right? If you want to expand your speaking into a more regular part of your business, see Chapter 38, Other Services You Can Offer.

There are more ways to be compensated than just by an honorarium. Approach your discussion with the organizer with the attitude that everything is negotiable. The following are all ways that you can get more from your presentation and that generally do not involve any direct costs to the organizer:

- Placement of your ad in the conference program and/or the organization's newsletter

- Distribution of your marketing material to all attendees

- A booth at the trade show (be careful what you ask for, though—a booth has to be staffed in order to be effective)

- An interview while you are at the event with the organization's newsletter editor for a profile article about your business

Going Virtual

At some point, you will likely ask yourself why you are going to all the trouble of taking time away from the office and traveling to an event, enduring hotel food, and sleeping in a strange room, when you could just deliver the presentation via webinar or podcast. Unfortunately, even in the best of situations, a remote speaker is not as engaging as one who is at the event in the flesh. The primary purpose of public speaking is to generate new clients, and you simply cannot make the kinds of personal connections via a pre-recorded presentation that you can when you are there in person.

That said, there is a place for webinars and podcasts in your marketing mix. (If you are thinking about selling these as stand-alone products, see Chapter 38, Other Services You Can Offer.)

Pros of webinars as a marketing tool include the following:

- They are good for viral marketing. Multimedia files are easy to link to and share, and news about a well-done podcast can spread quickly.

- Building an archive of podcasts can help you develop a revenue stream in the future when you start selling your podcasts.

- If you simply cannot travel to where your prospective clients will be meeting and they still want you, a recorded webinar is an alternative, albeit not an ideal one.

- Producing well-done webinars positions you as an expert.

- Conference planners can listen to your podcast or webinar and preview your speaking and presentation style.

- Webinars can lead to paid speaking engagements; a conference organizer will hear your webinar and decide that you simply must be in his or her next event.

Cons of webinars as a marketing tool include the following:

- It takes time to learn how to deliver a good webinar. Your speaking style is different, and you have to be able to speak energetically and enthusiastically when talking to a computer screen instead of a room full of people.

- Your initial learning curve may be steep as you develop the expertise to produce professional-level webinars or podcasts. That means judicious editing, polished packaging, and making them available in as streamlined a process as possible.

- Using podcasts or webinars as a free marketing tool may cut into your opportunities for in-person speaking invitations, if not positioned strategically. Your goal is to clearly differentiate the surface-level learning from a webinar and the in-depth coverage of a topic that you offer in your live presentations.

Learning to Speak

What if you are just not comfortable as a public speaker? Look for nonthreatening opportunities to speak in front of a group of people, even if they are not prospective clients. (But don't get comfortable in that environment; your goal is to "graduate" to groups of prospective clients.) That might be a talk at the AIIP annual conference or at the local Chamber of Commerce. Think about taking on a role that requires occasional public presentations at your place of worship or with an organization where you volunteer. Toastmasters International (www.toastmasters.org) is perhaps the best-known organization for honing your public-speaking skills. More than anything else, learning to speak publicly just takes a decision on your part to put yourself out there. The first few times you speak in public will be difficult, but it really does get easier the more you do it. You may even end up enjoying the limelight … who knows?

Public Speaking Pep Talk

The first time I stood in front of a roomful of people and started talking, I was a nervous wreck. I had trouble maintaining my train of thought, I worried about keeping the audience's attention, I even worried that I couldn't see over the podium! But I survived, and I have found that with practice, public speaking has become something I look forward to doing. Over the years, I have developed a few mantras that help me calm down when my stomach starts to clench up:

- The audience wants you to do well; they're silently cheering you on. As long as you make it through your talk and don't run screaming off the stage, you'll do fine.

- Most people can't imagine getting up in front of a room and speaking. They respect you for having the guts to do this. Your audience knows how brave you are because they know how scared they would be in the same position.

- What is the worst thing that could happen? Your clothes aren't going to fall off your body, so at least you know you won't wind up stark naked in front of a roomful of people. If you lose your place in your talk, you can stop, take a deep breath, smile, and start over at whatever point you find yourself. At worst, people may think you made a rather abrupt transition from one thought to the next.

- Perception is reality. Fake it 'til you make it. If you project an air of self-assurance and sound like you're having fun, your audience will pay attention to what you are saying and will enjoy your talk. They don't need to know that your stomach is in knots.

- Never tell the audience that you're nervous or that you don't have much to say. They don't need to know the former, and the latter isn't true, or else you wouldn't be standing at the podium.

- Find a few friendly faces in the crowd and speak to those people directly. Make eye contact, smile, and imagine that you're just practicing your speech in front of a few friends.

- Welcome the adrenaline. Studies have shown—and my own experience amply confirms—that adrenaline helps your brain process thoughts more quickly. You will think faster on your feet, and you will find insights that you didn't have when you were preparing the talk. In fact, adrenaline makes you a better, sharper speaker.

Maintaining the Buzz

Since you are speaking in order to market your business, always view your audience as a source of leads. For some events, the organizer will supply you with a list of attendees. Otherwise, offer a door prize as a way to collect business cards. Buy a copy of a recent book by a respected author that relates to the subject of your talk and bring it to the meeting along with a bookstand and an attractive basket. Display the book prominently and announce that you will have a drawing for it at the end of your talk. (Note that you can sometimes obtain free copies from the publisher if you offer to promote the book during your talk.) Hand the basket to the closest audience member and have the audience pass it around the room while you speak; have the audience members put in their business cards. When you are finished speaking, draw a name, award the book to the winner, and—more importantly—save all those business cards. When you get back to the office, go through the cards, weed out those from organizations that you don't think are likely prospects, and send notes to the others, thanking them for attending and inviting them to subscribe to your enewsletter.

I have found success in printing up business cards for specific talks and putting something on the back that summarizes your key points. For a talk on painless negotiation, for example, I had cards with my contact information on the front and my "Eight Keys to Strategic Negotiation" on the back. My 500 cards disappeared by the end of the day, and I know that this is one business card that people will keep at their desk, just where I want it. See Chapter 23, Your Business Image, for a discussion of business cards for every occasion.

Another way of keeping in touch with your audience is to offer a private URL on your website that has a free white paper, a webliography of the resources mentioned in your talk, links to material you have written on a topic, or anything else you can think would be of enough value to entice audience members to visit your website later. Of course, you can also mention those resources when you send your follow-up note to all the people who entered the door prize drawing.

Another technique that works on several levels is to get audience input during your talk, write any comments on a flip chart, then offer a summary of all the suggestions from the audience for anyone who gives you his or her email address. This not only provides you with a value-added follow-up offer but also helps you record ideas that you can take, expand upon, and work into your blog, enewsletter, future talks and articles, and so on. Additionally, this engages the audience and enables everyone to share their expertise.

Lessons Learned as a Writer and Speaker

- ✦ You gain instant credibility once you are a published author.
- ✦ Write for publications your clients are likely to read.
- ✦ Write clearly in straightforward language. Short articles are more likely to be read than longer ones.
- ✦ Get used to public speaking; practice, practice, practice.
- ✦ Plan on lining up speaking engagements for annual conferences at least six to 12 months in advance.
- ✦ Offer a follow-up of some kind—a private webpage, a summary of audience comments, a copy of your slides, and so on.

Chapter 27

Starting the Word of Mouth

As I say repeatedly in this book, you will get most of your clients from referrals. A client will mention your name to a colleague; a librarian will refer clients when he gets requests he cannot handle; a fellow independent info pro will send a client to you if the research goes beyond your colleague's expertise. As Sue Rugge, a pioneer in the info pro business, so memorably said, "It's all word of mouth, but you have to be the first mouth." This chapter looks at ways to get that word of mouth going.

Many new entrepreneurs find it difficult to market themselves. We were taught as children not to brag or be overly boastful. But when you are running your own company, you are the product. If you find it difficult to promote you, you, you, then focus on your company name. You're marketing John Smith Infotronics, not just John Smith.

In any event, keep in mind that everything you do has an impact on the reputation of your company and you as a professional. In a sense, you're always "on"—at least whenever you are in a business or professional setting. When you contribute to an electronic discussion group, watch your language and tone of voice. When you are at a professional meeting, dress appropriately; I usually try to dress a bit more conservatively than the average, just to ensure that I am taken seriously.

"What Does Your Company Do?"

When someone asks you what you do, what will you say? You need to have a concise, memorable response prepared and ready to go. This is sometimes called your "elevator speech"; imagine stepping into an elevator with your biggest prospect. She turns to you and asks, "So, what exactly do you do?" You have 15 seconds (the time it takes for the elevator to let her off at the 25th floor) to describe yourself in such a way that she immediately understands when she would call you.

Give your elevator speech some careful thought, keeping in mind that everyone you talk to is a potential client or referral source. Paul and Sarah Edwards, the authors of a number of books about home-based businesses, describe a useful formula for developing your 15-second introduction. The template they use is: "You know how [describe typical clients' information problem]? Well, I [solve problem] by [doing this]."

For example, "You know how frustrating it is when you have to make a strategic decision without all the information you need? Well, my company helps you make better decisions by providing you a complete industry scan, so you can understand the competitive landscape." Or, "You know how hard it is to find 'soft' information about your industry or your competitors? Well, as a telephone researcher, I can gather the insights of the industry leaders for my clients, and since my clients' names are never associated with the research, I can put my finger on information they couldn't have obtained themselves."

I like this formula because it forces me to focus on the benefits I provide to my clients, rather than simply describing what I do, and it keeps the entire description to 10 or 15 seconds. As you work on your personalized version of the answer to the "So, what do you do?" question, focus on the following:

- Avoid industry jargon or buzzwords such as "solutions." Word of mouth travels a lot farther if people outside your field understand and can describe to others what you do.

- Keep it short. They are asking you for a reason to use your services, not your life story.

- Make yourself recession-proof. What are your clients' critical information needs—things they view as essential, not just nice to have?

- Focus on benefits that provide clear added value. Offer services that your clients cannot or will not do for themselves and that enhance their bottom line.

- Make sure you can deliver your introduction with enthusiasm. If you are excited about your business, others will be as well.

Be sure your elevator speech includes phrases that the other party can easily remember. Rather than saying, "I provide innovative business intelligence solutions to support customer-focused initiatives and reallocation of resources to key value drivers," try saying, "I help executives make smart decisions when they are restructuring a business." Which of those descriptions would you find more memorable and easier to mention to someone else?

The Art of Schmoozing

Whether you are promoting your services at an exhibit booth, attending a local professional association meeting, or just chatting with someone at a conference, learn about the other person before you start describing your own business. Ask problem-seeking questions: "What do you use the social web for at your job?" or "What is the most challenging aspect of your work?" or "What do you do when you can't find the information you need?" Show a genuine interest in the other person's work and profession. Undoubtedly, you will learn something interesting about her line of work. You will also find out how you can help her and can fine-tune your introduction to address her particular information problems.

Many people are shy by nature and find it hard to make conversation with strangers. I had one of those "ah-ha" moments when I realized that most other people are equally concerned and delighted when they find someone willing to listen to what they have to say. I repeat the following reminders to myself before I walk into a room full of strangers:

- Pay attention. Focus on the person you're talking with and listen to what he or she is saying. Ask open-ended questions and find out about what the other person's key concerns are. Only then can you talk meaningfully about how your services can be beneficial.

- Be courteous. Obviously, you don't arrive late, leave in the middle of a presentation, or engage in antagonistic conversations.

- Be enthusiastic. Use your face and body to show emotion and to indicate that you are interested in the conversation. Show that you are passionate about what you do and that you love working for your clients. (And if that isn't the case, think about refocusing your business on a client base and type of work that you do love.)

My Launch Letter

When I launched my business, I sent out a (yes, hard-copy) letter to every-one for whom I had a business card or a snail-mail address, enclosing two business cards (one to keep and one to pass along to a colleague). It took time to personalize them to each contact, but I figured that this was my one chance to present my new business to my contacts. Here is what a launch letter might look like.

Dear { so-and-so},

I'm delighted to announce my new company, Smith Energy Information Services, which I launched in April of this year. I focus [note present tense, not "I hope to focus"] on providing business intelligence to the renewable energy industry, based on my 15 years of experience as corporate intelligence manager in the energy and engineering fields.

Examples of projects I work on include:

- analysis of recent legislation on tax breaks for residential wind power

- a competitive assessment of the smart grid technology industry

- state and local initiatives to bring clean tech to their region

I am really excited about this business, and I look forward to supporting your strategic decisions. FYI, you can see more information, and a copy of my free client enewsletter, at www.SmithEnergyInfoSvcs.com.

As you can imagine, information consulting businesses live by referrals. Please let me know who you think I could contact to tell them about Smith Energy Information Services.

Best regards,
Mary Ellen Bates

While your tone may be different, there are some features that should always appear in an introductory letter.

- Sound upbeat and positive.

- Describe your business as an ongoing concern, not something that "I am thinking about trying to start." For Star Wars fans, remember Yoda's words: "Try not. Do, or do not. There is no try."

- Always ask for referrals. People need to be reminded to pass your name along to colleagues.

- Give people concrete examples of the types of research you provide, making the value you provide clear, in memorable sound bites they can use when they talk to others.

- Offer a free enewsletter so that you can stay in touch with your contacts.

- Make yourself memorable. Know how to tell a story about your business in a way that makes it easy for the listener to describe your business to others. Think of three words or phrases that connote value and that you want the other person to remember in association with you. I sometimes use "librarian of fortune," or "the answer person," or "strategic decisions"—something that will stick in the other person's mind and make it easier for them to refer me to someone else.

- Perception is reality. Act self-confident, even if you don't feel self-confident, and eventually you will start feeling as confident as you act. Have a firm handshake and make eye contact with the people you meet.

An Introvert's Approach

Ruth Shipley, of SMR Information Solutions, described an experience she had at a local networking event. As a fellow introvert, I really appreciate her technique. Here's her story:

The first time I attended my Chamber of Commerce's "Business After Hours" event, I arrived right when it started; to my dismay, there were already a lot of people there. The room was packed with small groups, all facing inward like football huddles. And the buzz from all those conversations was close to deafening.

I remember standing up on the landing looking down at that mass of humanity and wondering, "How will I ever penetrate that? And I'll have to shout just to be heard!" But I went down and tried anyway. One by one, I stood fairly close to a few groups. But they never noticed me or opened up to admit me into the group. This was definitely not for the faint of heart or hard-core introverts.

Then I realized that most of the people in the room were not really interested in meeting new people but in talking to people they already knew and in catching up with friends. So I looked for people who were alone, and sure enough, I found one. She turned out to be very interesting and we talked for some time. I'm glad I got past that initial moment of dismay when I saw the groups and not the solos.

"How Did You Hear About Me?"

Whenever a potential client contacts you to ask for an estimate or to learn more about your business, ask how she heard about you. That is invaluable market research; it tells you how your word-of-mouth marketing is going and who is talking. I keep track in my client database of how each client found out about me, and once a year, I look through it to see where most of my new clients have come from. Was it from my website? Are several of my existing clients frequent sources of referrals? Did people hear me speak at a conference? Did they read a book or an article I wrote, which prompted them to call me? Use this information to maximize your marketing efforts by focusing on the word-of-mouth tools that work best for you. (See Chapter 19, Strategic Planning, for more about conducting an annual review of where you are and where you're going.)

Susan Detwiler, a retired independent info pro, took a systematic approach to this word-of-mouth analysis. As she described it, "I did a genealogy of my business—that is, I looked at each job I had done that year and thought through how I had gotten that particular client. Client A was a colleague of Client B, whom I had met at a Medical Surgical Market Research Group meeting. Client C was a member of the MSMRG. Client D was a referral from someone in the Association of Independent

Information Professionals. Client E was a referral from someone who exhibited at AIIP [Association of Independent Information Professionals]. And so on. I realized that most of my well-paying work came from my active participation in two organizations—MSMRG and AIIP." She learned that it took more than just being a member of an association or advertising in their newsletters; she was active, visible, and known for a specific type of research service. She did not do much work directly for AIIP members as a subcontractor, but she found that AIIP members were a good source of referrals.

Working the Associations

Detwiler also discovered that being active in selected associations can connect you to crucial sources of client referrals. The key is to look at an association's membership list before joining and determine whether its members represent businesses or other organizations that are likely to use your services. If access to the membership directory is restricted to existing members, use your research skills to get a sense of who the members are. Look through the association's website and note the affiliations of elected officers and committee chairs. Review its annual conference program and see what kinds of speakers are invited. Look in the social network sites and see who lists that association on their pages.

Once you have identified one or two professional associations that seem to be likely sources of leads, join and become an active volunteer. Membership itself is worth very little beyond a listing in the association's membership directory. Your prospective clients will get to know you by seeing you in action. Identify a volunteer opportunity that involves contact with members—writing for the newsletter or organizing local programs, for example. At one point, I volunteered to handle the logistics for local meetings of my local Special Libraries Association chapter. RSVPs came to me, which meant that every time members mailed in their checks and registration forms, they were reminded of Bates Information Services. And I was the one at the door handing out name badges and collecting tickets. It wasn't a sexy job, but it gave me the opportunity to meet most of the members of the local chapter, and they all knew my name and the name of my company. It was definitely a good investment in name recognition and brand awareness when I was just starting my business.

Moving Beyond the Chamber of Commerce

From my observation, most new info-entrepreneurs join their local chambers of commerce or similar group and expect to generate business from their memberships. I have also observed that most people drop their chamber memberships after two or three years. Most people find that chamber membership is useful in very limited ways and for limited periods of time. Look through this list of pros and cons and decide whether you believe membership is worth the cost and time.

Pros:

- Since membership is so diverse, you have lots of practice explaining what you do in ways people can understand.

- You can learn how to network in a low-risk environment because it is not a likely source of customers.

- You can find local experts you can rely on for IT support, accounting, web and graphic design, and other business support services.

- You get your word-of-mouth network started. In fact, there is something to be said for getting a referral as "his rates are too high for my business to afford, but he's really good."

Cons:

- Membership isn't cheap; chambers of commerce in large metropolitan areas charge members anywhere from $200 to $600 and more.

- Many of the members are owners of small or retail businesses—staffing services, real estate agencies, financial advisors, supermarkets, and so on. None of these types of businesses is likely to value your services, especially at your professional rates.

- In order to get value from your chamber membership, you have to invest time and energy into volunteer work. Your time may be better invested in other organizations with more (and probably better-paying) prospective clients.

In addition to, or instead of, chambers of commerce, identify all the local groups where your clients are likely to be. And keep in mind that your market ought to be at least nationwide, rather than only in your metropolitan area. Do not define your market by the kind of business you can find locally; rather, work from the reverse and identify your client groups and then decide how to find them.

There are lots of other local groups where you can both get new ideas and build your network. One U.S. website that local planners often use to promote and administer events is Meetup (www.meetup.com), which lets you search for any event within X miles of a particular ZIP code. So, for example, I see that right now there are 16 groups focused on various aspects of renewable energy, all within a half-hour drive of my house. If that were one of my market niches, I would check out the most likely groups and pick a couple to focus on.

The main thing is to show up consistently at meetings, participate, and commit to spending a full year putting energy into each of the groups. Showing up once in a while doesn't do it; you need to become a regular who people recognize and value. Give more than you get from others; remember, you are the new kid in school, and the other kids are waiting to find out if you play nicely with others. Your job is to demonstrate over time that you are smart, creative, strategic, and exactly the person they need to bring in for their important business decisions.

Leads and Networking Clubs

While asking for informal referrals from clients is a great way to generate that word of mouth, you might also consider joining a formal organization designed to fast-forward the referral process. These groups, called leads clubs or networking groups, offer members a structured way to exchange qualified business leads. Local groups often attract people from a wide variety of businesses—stock brokers, printers, interior decorators, cleaning services, and even independent info pros. Groups usually meet once a week, and each member has an opportunity to describe his or her business and exchange leads with other members. Expect to pay a yearly membership fee as well as local group dues.

Some independent info pros find these groups good referral sources; others value them for moral support and as resources for local business services such as accounting or graphic design. As with your local chamber of commerce, networking groups also provide a comfortable setting for you to practice your 15-second introduction. Since the other members of the group are trying to provide you with qualified prospects, they need to grasp what you do. At each meeting, you can hone the description of your business so that it is memorable and understandable.

In my experience, leads groups can be useful when you are starting your business as a way to learn how to network, describe your business, and share leads with others. In the long term, however, I do not believe they are worth the weekly commitment of time. In order to succeed as an info-entrepreneur, you need to find clients who have more money than time and who will recognize and pay for the added value you provide. The level of person you need to cultivate is usually not someone who has time to spend in leads groups; you want clients who are already so busy that they have to bring in outside expertise for their research and strategic analysis.

Asking for Referrals

It may seem odd, but we often forget to ask our clients and contacts to recommend others who might use our services. People appreciate the chance to spread the word about someone they enjoy working with, but they often need a reminder. I include a nudge in my enewsletter and marketing postcards: "Spread the word! Do you know anyone who might want to hear about Bates Information Services? Send me their email or postal address, and I'll send them a one-time mailing to let them know about my strategic research services." Note that I assure my clients that I am not going to put their colleague or friend on a junk-mail list, and I certainly won't call them with a sales pitch. When I do send out that mailing, I include the name of the client who referred me, which gives me instant credibility by saying, in essence, "This isn't a random sales pitch … Your colleague Steve recommended that I contact you."

Some independent info pros offer an incentive for a client referral—a discount on the next job for the referring client, for example, or a token gift. I am not convinced that such gestures are necessary or that they even make a difference. Use your judgment, based on your familiarity with your client base.

Another source of referrals may be the reference staff at your local public library. Although I usually recommend marketing outside your local area (see Chapter 13, Managing Your Clients), public librarians can be great word-of-mouth marketers. First, get to know the reference staff, and particularly the business reference librarians if your local library has a separate desk for business reference. You may not be a business researcher per se; you are simply targeting the librarians who deal with patrons whose information needs are more likely to be commercial in nature and who are therefore more likely than the average library user to be willing and able to pay you for in-depth research services.

Find out if the librarians outsource or refer out questions that go beyond the level of service they normally provide. Some libraries have policies that prohibit the staff from recommending any outside information professionals; other libraries maintain lists of local independent info pros that they hand out to patrons on request. Consider offering to give a free workshop on your specialized area of research to the reference staff; it is a nice way to give something back to a valuable local resource, and it doesn't hurt to be seen as a supporter of the library. I have occasionally worked with public libraries to present a half-day workshop on business research that they open to the public. I make sure to highlight all the services and resources available at the library; of course, I also mention my free enewsletter at the end of the workshop. Everybody wins; the library is able to offer a valuable service to its patrons, the patrons are exposed to some of the more advanced services the library provides, and I can market myself to a group of information-hungry prospects.

Top Tips for Starting Positive Word of Mouth

- ✦ Develop a memorable and descriptive 10- or 15-second introduction.
- ✦ Focus on benefits, not features; answer the question, "What's in it for me?"
- ✦ Keep track of how new clients hear about you.
- ✦ Become active in any professional associations you join; membership alone is not enough.
- ✦ Remind your clients to refer colleagues to you.
- ✦ Find local groups where your clients may be and that interest you.

Chapter 28

Public Relations

Public relations, also called media relations, involves efforts to get third-party news coverage of you and your business. You are not talking directly to prospective clients, as you are with most of your marketing efforts. Rather, you are addressing people who will deliver your message to their audiences. Public relations can be an effective component of your total marketing strategy, but it will not, by itself, bring you many clients. What a successful public relations campaign can do is greatly increase your credibility; nothing enhances your authority like being quoted in a publication your clients read or, better yet, having an article written about you.

Of course, generating publicity about your business means doing something newsworthy. It also means being comfortable talking with reporters, writers, bloggers, podcasters, and TV and radio interviewers. As with everything else, public relations takes practice. I remember an early interview I did with a reporter from a local business journal. I spoke too casually, and one quote that made it in the article was my comment that "my clients are clueless about finding information, and they're delighted that I can help them get what they need to make important decisions." I was mortified that I had called my clients "clueless," but I had only myself to blame. Reporters are entitled to use anything you say; you cannot go off the record after the fact and try to take back something you said. This was a great learning experience for me, and since then, I have trained myself to pause before answering any question and think about what I want my on-the-record response to be.

Doing Something Newsworthy

Some reporters and broadcast producers may find you through articles you have written, referrals from the Association of Independent Information Professionals (AIIP; www.aiip.org), or even by doing a web search. But they are more likely to call if you take the initiative and contact the media first with a story idea or newsworthy item. How do you find a newsworthy angle if you have just started your business? Think about what a reporter might find interesting:

- Send out a brief survey to your clients or prospects, asking them to estimate how much time they spend on the web looking for information and their favorite search starting points. Guesstimate the average salary of your contacts, multiply that by the amount of time it would take them to find the information, subtract what it would cost if they paid you to find it, and the result of this admittedly unscientific survey is how much money they would have saved by calling an independent info pro. You might also mention the fact that a professional researcher can find richer, deeper information in X percent less time than the average non-info pro. Summarize the results, along with a list of the respondents' favorite search sites.

- Identify the 20 or 30 publications most frequently read by your client base—advertising executives, chemists, healthcare administrators, or whoever your target market happens to be. Do some research to identify how many of those publications are available in full text, with both current and archived material, for free on the web. Odds are that less than 50 percent of the publications you have selected will meet these criteria. Pointing out two or three of the most outstanding gaps as examples, write this up in terms of "it ain't all on the web for free, at least if you're looking for professional-quality information."

- If you provide telephone research, develop a list of, say, the five best ways to get past executives' gatekeepers and the five conversation-stoppers that you should never use during a telephone interview. Package this list and present it as a tool to find the hidden information that never makes it into print—anywhere.

- If you are speaking at a professional conference, ask the conference organizer for help in contacting the local press and reporters in the industry.

They may share their media contact list, for example, or set up a "meet the speakers" reception for the press.

Amelia Kassel, owner of MarketingBase, developed a specialized information product and sent a press release to about a hundred regional business journals, from the Albany (NY) *Business Review* to the *Honolulu Pacific Business News*. Several publications picked up the story, and she was able to track some new clients back to that publicity. As she commented later, though, "Keeping something like this going on a consistent basis is tough to do as a one-person business. I tried another press release about some new services, sending it out just to business journals in my state, and I got no bites." The lesson she learned is that what works best is sending out a press release as widely as possible and featuring a tangible and easy-to-describe product.

Writing a Press Release

Once you have something newsworthy to publicize, the next step is preparing a press release to send out to the relevant reporters and broadcast producers (see the section "Getting Noticed" for more about selecting the appropriate media). Most press releases use a standard format; this is not the time to show your creativity by doing something completely innovative and off the charts. Make it easy for the recipient to skim the release and figure out what you are up to and what is interesting about it.

Press releases usually follow the following conventions:

- Use your company letterhead, or type your company name, address, phone number, email address, and website URL at the top.

- In all caps, center the phrase *Press Release*.

- Indicate that the information can be reported immediately (*For Immediate Release*).

- List your contact information—your name, phone number, and email address.

- Write a headline that emphasizes what is newsworthy; make sure your company name is part of the headline.

- Indicate your city and state, and the date of the press release.

- In the first paragraph, tell who, what, when, where, and why. Summarize the important points. Readers should be able to tell immediately why they should care about your story.

- In the next paragraph(s), provide additional information. Include a quote from you as the principal or president of the company; this adds interest and makes the reporter's work easier.

- In the last paragraph, summarize what your company does, give a brief company history if you have been in business for a while, and list your contact information.

- Double-space the body of the text with at least one-inch margins. This makes it easier for the reporter to skim the release and make notes in the margins.

- Indicate the end of the press release with "# # #" or the word END, centered on the page.

Sample Press Release

BATES INFORMATION SERVICES INC

PRESS RELEASE
FOR IMMEDIATE RELEASE
Contact: Mary Ellen Bates, 303.772.7095
mbates@BatesInfo.com

BATES INFORMATION SERVICES RELEASES
NEW WHITE PAPER ON PAINLESS NEGOTIATION

Boulder, CO (March 5, 2010)—Mary Ellen Bates, owner of Bates Information Services, today announced the availability of her latest white paper, Painless (no, really!) Negotiation. This free, five-page paper covers the Seven Deadly Sins of Negotiation, formulas for re-framing any situation into a negotiable interaction, and how to negotiate toward shared goals rather than opposing sides.

   Mary Ellen Bates, principal of Bates Information Services and LibrarianofFortune.com blogger, has more than 30 years' experience as an info pro, 20 of them as an info-entrepreneur. She managed to evolve from someone who couldn't negotiate if her life depended on it to someone who now enjoys the creativity involved in a successful negotiation. "If I can do this," says Bates, "anyone can."

The white paper includes the highlights of her insights in negotiation, along with some of the most effective words and phrases for moving a negotiation to the best outcome for both parties.

Mary Ellen Bates is the author of six books about the information industry, including two editions of *Building and Running a Successful Research Business: A Guide for the Independent Information Professional* (Information Today, Inc., 2003, 2010). Bates Information Services, established in 1991, provides business insight to business professionals and consulting services to the information industry. She also offers strategic business coaching for both new and long-time independent info pros. For more information about Bates Information Services, visit the website at www.BatesInfo.com or phone +1 303.772.7095 or Skype to mary.ellen.bates.

If possible, keep your press release to a single page and never exceed two pages. Write clearly and in plain language, avoiding buzzwords, industry jargon, and acronyms. Although you know what you mean by "reinventing interactive paradigms," a reporter may not. Avoid adjectives and hyperbole; you are delivering news, not a sales pitch. Use the active rather than passive voice ("The company provides business research" rather than "Business research is provided by the company").

Think of your press release as a piece of direct mail … because that is how it will be received. It is an unsolicited piece of mail that asks the recipient to do something for the sender—in this case, to cover your company's news item. Make it as interesting as possible so that it is not treated as another piece of junk mail. Your headline needs to stand out and promise something interesting. You have mere seconds to attract an editor's attention. Avoid hype or hyperbole; remember, this is a description of your news, not an advertisement.

Proofread—not just spell-check—your release before you send it out, and double-check that you have included today's date. See the sidebar "Sample Press Release" for an example of what a short press release looks like. The "Press" or "Newsroom" section of most corporate websites will show you many more examples.

Getting Noticed

You can address your press release to "Editor" in care of a particular publication, but that will not get you very far. Editors receive unsolicited press releases by the ream, every day. Take time to identify individuals to contact directly. Look through the print or online issues of publications that you would like to cover your news. Identify the columnists or staff writers who cover your area. Enclose a personal note with the press release, mentioning something they have written that you read recently, and explain what your company is doing that you think the writer would find interesting. Showing that you have actually read the writer's work makes a big difference in whether your press release gets used or tossed.

Use some creativity in developing a media list of editors, reporters, columnists, and bloggers with whom you want to stay in touch. You may want to send a release to the weekly business journals in major cities; if so, see BizJournals.com for links to about 40 business weeklies. Your local public library may have print or electronic media source directories you can consult for leads to publications in your industry. These directories include:

- Bacon's Media Database (www.cision.com)

- Gale Directory of Publications and Broadcast Media (www.gale.cengage.com)

- All-in-One Media Directory (www.gebbieinc.com)

- Media Contacts (www.burrellesluce.com.com)

You will certainly want to find out what publications your clients read (Hint: Ask them!) and to include in your contact list any publications produced by your industry's trade or professional association. Think about online publications as well as print; what ejournals or web-based periodicals, if any, cover your market?

There are also companies that specialize in distributing your press release to thousands of outlets for a fee. You are not guaranteed that the *Financial Times* or the *New York Times* will pick up your story, but your press release will be archived in a

"According to Client X"

It is always nice to mention success stories or interesting projects you have worked on. Reporters like examples, and telling a story is a great way to show your range of services. However, always ask permission from your clients before the interview if you can describe a project of theirs or mention their name. Some clients are delighted to be quoted, while other organizations prohibit their employees from endorsing outside vendors. If your client is agreeable, be sure to give the reporter their contact information. I have a client who is a communications consultant and a speech writer. She was happy to talk to a reporter about how she uses my services, and she got some free publicity from the article as well. In fact, she called to tell me that she had put her name into a search engine and found that, despite not having a website of her own, she does have a presence on the web—in the online version of the article in which she was quoted.

Also, encourage your clients to tell journalists about your services. Ask your clients (yes, ask 'em) whether they know anyone who writes for publications that they and their colleagues read. I am always amazed and gratified at my clients' responses when I try this. Because so many of them are consultants and also independent professionals, they understand the need to publicize one another. I refer reporters to my clients for quotes whenever I can, and they return the favor. Cultivating your good-karma network can be a splendid public relations technique.

searchable database, ensuring that journalists looking for a source could find you. You can filter the distribution to specific audiences—those in a specific geographic region, a particular industry, or a demographic group. While this moves your out-of-pocket expenses from zero to several hundred dollars, it ensures that your press release is included in the online sources journalists consult.

What about marketing to TV and radio and other nonprint media? My experience has been that this kind of exposure does not translate into business, perhaps because people are accustomed to having the TV and radio on almost as back-ground noise. I have been interviewed half a dozen times on TV and by at least 30 radio stations over the course of my business, and I cannot point to a single serious prospect I have gotten from any of those exposures. On the other hand, mentions in print media and blogs as well as articles and books that I have written have brought me a number of clients and prospects. I suspect that when people sit down to read, they are paying more attention, and they can save the article for later reference.

It is great to imagine yourself on the cover of *The Economist* or *Time*, but save that fantasy for when you are already famous. For now, it is more realistic—and you have a much higher chance of success—if you focus on publications and writers that speak directly to your audience. If you provide information services to design pro-fessionals in the automotive industry, instead of pitching your story to the editor of the *Wall Street Journal*, contact the journalist who covers the automotive industry for the *Journal*. Also, identify the leading publications that your clients read and get in touch with the journalists who cover automotive design.

It will be tempting to send press releases by email rather than in hard copy but resist. Journalists and editors get even more press releases in email than they do in print, and they tend to treat it the same way—straight into the trash. You are even easier to ignore in email than you are on paper. An email press release looks indis-tinctive if you include it in the body of a message, and a press release sent as an attachment is, almost without exception, deleted unread. Even discounting the annoyance factor of unsolicited email, your hard-copy stationery has more impact; you can include clippings of other press coverage you have received, and a copy of your brochure and business card, and—unlike unsolicited email—it does not look or feel like spam.

Becoming a Certified Expert

In addition to sending out press releases and staying in touch with the editors, writ-ers, and producers you are cultivating, you can take steps to become recognized as an expert in your field. For starters, you can get a listing in the *Yearbook of Experts* (www.expertclick.com). This directory is targeted to the media and is used by televi-sion, radio, and print journalists when they need to interview an expert on a partic-ular topic. Yes, as crass as it sounds, you can buy your way into expert-hood—assuming you do have expertise in a given subject area and can learn how to give good sound bites. It is not cheap, but if you compose a compelling listing, you will probably get calls from journalists and radio and TV producers looking for a pithy quote. Of course, it is your responsibility to turn what can be a very general quote or a brief mention into something your clients will hear about. Reference your interview in your client newsletter, on your website, and on the email discussion lists you participate in. Be sure to add each reporter or producer who calls to your media contact list for future press releases.

If you feel comfortable calling a reporter and touting your expertise on a specific topic, you can consult Help A Reporter Out (HARO; www.helpareporter.com). This unique—and as of 2009, still free—email list is maintained by Peter Shankman (www.shankman.com), a public relations entrepreneur who connects reporters with public relations folks and others who have an expertise to share. His thrice-daily HARO enewsletter distributes thousands of queries every week to sources who want to be quoted. If you see a query that you could contribute something interesting to, contact the reporter directly. Note that most of these queries are time-sensitive; if you cannot respond before reporters' deadlines, do not bother contacting them.

Building a Press Kit

A press release, accompanied by a personal letter, is a good way to let an editor, reporter, or TV or radio producer know about a specific news item. But you will also need a (hard copy) press kit that you can send to media contacts when you want to give them additional information about you and your business. A press kit should include:

- Your business card.

- A professionally done black-and-white photograph. Don't rely on family or friends to take a nice picture of you in your backyard. Pay a professional photographer. (See Chapter 23, Your Business Image, for more about professional headshots.)

- A biographical profile, no more than one page, highlighting your professional accomplishments, your educational background, and any awards you have won or professional recognition you have received. This is not a resume, and it should not look like one; rather, it is a single page with the highlights of your professional career.

- A one-page description of your business and the services or products you provide, focusing on the reasons why someone would use your services.

- Copies of articles you have written, articles written about or featuring you, and speeches you have given.

- Recent press releases.

- A page of pithy quotes and testimonials from clients willing to provide them; even an "anonymized" quote is worth using: "Around The World Information Services helped me win a million dollar account. Their market research and analysis were tremendous; I don't know what I would do without them." —Marketing Director, Fortune 500 pharmaceutical company.

Be sure to include a pitch letter—a one-page letter that introduces you and invites the editor to review the contents. The letter should concisely and clearly explain why the editor's audience—magazine readers, television audience, radio listeners, and so on—would be interested in your story. The pitch must be customized for each contact. Suggest a few different angles for coverage or for an interview, such as, "Did you know that 90 percent of the information on the web can never be found in a search engine? Let me explain why" or "Some of the most useful information on your company's competitors is right out there for anyone to find … but no one thinks to look at these sources." After you have sent your media kit to your contacts, complete with personalized pitch letters, follow up with phone calls to make sure they have received the material and to see if they have any questions. When you call, be cognizant that media people are often on deadline and be considerate of their time. Be prepared to give your pitch in less than two minutes or ask to call back at a more convenient time. Stay in regular touch with your contacts. Send them press releases, any new articles you have written, copies of your enewsletter, and so on. Even if they cannot use your story now, they may keep you in mind for later projects.

Giving Good Sound Bites

If your marketing efforts pay off, you will eventually be asked to appear as a guest on a radio or television program. This can be a fun experience and an excellent opportunity to establish your credibility. Although some people worry that they will be asked a challenging question or will be made to look bad, that almost never happens. The host wants the audience to learn something and to be entertained; unless you go in looking for an argument, you will find that the interviewer just wants to give you an opportunity to tell people about what you do and know.

The key to a successful interview is to prepare ahead of time and to relax. The following tips will help you stay calm and self-confident while you're on the air:

- Know the program. Is it informal and chatty, or businesslike and to the point? Will the audience be familiar with the type of services you offer, or do you need to explain them in layperson's terms? Is it a call-in show, a lengthy interview or conversation with the host, or a three-minute slot in a news program?

- Provide the interviewer or the show's producer with a list of questions ahead of time. Make them interesting and thought-provoking and, of course, be prepared with concise, focused answers. The interviewer may not use any of them, but it doesn't hurt to offer some pertinent questions that may help focus the interview.

- Provide the producer with a brief written background on you and your company.

- Even if the show is being taped for later broadcast, it may not be edited, so do not assume you will have a chance to redo an answer. Speak thoughtfully; it is all right to pause for a second to collect your thoughts before you answer a question.

- Speak clearly and at a normal pace. Do not use industry jargon or acronyms without first explaining what they mean. Keep such usage to a minimum.

- Answer each question as concisely as you can, without giving monosyllabic answers. Think and speak in sentences, not paragraphs, to hold the audience's interest. Two or three sentences (or about 20 seconds) is enough for most questions. Focus on the most important points rather than on details.

- Relax. You've been invited because you and your work will appeal to the program's audience. Tell the audience what they would find most interesting. Use concrete language and anecdotes where appropriate to illustrate your point.

- Don't argue with the interviewer or with a listener, if it is a call-in show. If you do get a sticky question or one that you would rather not answer, emphasize what is important and positive. Stay "on message"—don't get bogged down or sidetracked.

- Remember that anything you mention to the interviewer or production staff before you go on the air is fair game. Do not say anything off-air that you would not want repeated to the audience.

- After the interview, send a thank-you note to the interviewer and the program producer. Offer yourself as a source for information in the future, and suggest any additional program ideas you have.

Note that many of these suggestions apply to telephone interviews with print reporters as well as to radio and TV appearances. Reporters are looking for a few good quotes, so keep your answers short and focused. Pause at the end of every couple of sentences, in case the reporter needs a moment to catch up with her notes. Save the detailed explanations for follow-up questions, if there are any. And, as I mentioned at the beginning of this chapter, be very, very careful about what you say because the default assumption is that every utterance is fair game.

Public Relations Checklist

✦ Create something newsworthy—a survey, a report, a list of tips, or a unique information product or service—and write a short press release featuring your news.

✦ Develop a media contact list—editors, writers, bloggers, and producers whom you want to cover your news.

✦ Send press releases and newsletters to your contact list regularly.

✦ Ask your clients for press referrals and for permission to quote them.

✦ Prepare a media kit to introduce you to editors and producers.

✦ Plan ahead for interviews, and follow up afterward.

Researching

Chapter 29

The Reference Interview

Librarians call it a "reference interview." Consultants call it a "client information needs assessment." Researchers call it a "client interview." They are all referring to the conversation you have with a client in which he tells you what he needs, you negotiate the scope, deadline, format, and budget for the project, you thank him for his business, and you get to work. It seems like such a simple process, but if a project goes bad, you can usually trace it back to a reference interview that was poorly done.

The reference interview is the one time when you are guaranteed to have your client's full attention. He is calling you, he needs information and he knows it, and he wants you to do the work. This is the best chance you will have to negotiate with your client, and it is probably the only point at which he is willing to take the time to explain the details of the work he wants you to do. If you do not nail down all the particulars now, you will find it a lot harder to call back and explain that, well, you didn't really understand what he was talking about, and can you just have another little conversation to straighten out a few things?

This is also your best opportunity to make a subtle sales pitch. You can send out all the marketing material you want, but the stage at which the client will really listen to you is when he is calling you to perform a miracle ... er, provide high-value information services to him. This is when you can point out the added-value services you provide, in-depth research that he did not know you could do, or an approach to the project that he had not thought of yet.

Steps in a Reference Interview

You would not think that a simple conversation would require a series of steps, would you? Believe it or not, I teach a half-day workshop for info pros on the art of the reference interview. It is amazing how much is involved when you look at the dynamics of the negotiation that takes place.

Step One: First Contact

Your client contacts you and tells you what she wants done. If this initial contact is via email, try to set up a time to have a live conversation. While an emailed request may look straightforward, you would be surprised how often the request morphs into something else by the time the conversation is over. In my experience, most emailed requests wind up developing into entirely different projects. Even (and especially) if an emailed request sounds simple, do what you can to talk to your client directly before you begin. If that is not feasible, prepare yourself for a series of email messages to clarify and define the request.

Step Two: Explore the Question

Assume that what you are hearing from your client is probably not what you are going to wind up researching. No, your client isn't a fool; it's just that most likely she does not know what sources you will be using, or how much information is available, or what kinds of research you are actually able to do, or how much in-depth analysis you provide. Here is the key: Your client is asking a question that she thinks you can answer. She is not necessarily articulating her underlying information need. Your job at this point is to ask open-ended questions to help your client explore the topic and explain what exactly she is looking for. See the sidebar "Getting at the Underlying Question" for some sample questions.

This is the point at which you listen and let the client talk. Take in what she is saying and try not to jump to conclusions about the approaches you will take to the research, the sources you will use, or the information you will find. Make sure that you are not distracted by other projects, another phone call (that is why voice mail was invented), or whatever is on your computer screen right now. Be here now; turn all your attention to your conversation with the client. Whatever else you are working on can wait; this is not the time for multitasking.

Getting at the Underlying Question

How do you get a client to explain what she really wants without sounding like you are prying or interrogating her? Try some of these open-ended questions—and remember, this is the time to let your client do all the talking.

- What do you mean by _____?

- What do you already know about _____?

- What do you expect me to find?

- Are there any sources you have already checked or that you would recommend?

- Are there any other terms used to describe _____?

- I'm not familiar with _____. Can you explain it to me?

- If I can't find exactly _____, what would be second best?

What if you have no idea what your client is talking about? Yes, it does happen, and it is difficult to conduct an effective reference interview if you do not know the first thing about the subject. You have a few options at this point. If you have absolutely no knowledge of the subject matter (I know nothing about medical research, for example), you might want to halt the conversation and refer the client to a colleague who specializes in that type of research. Alternatively, if the subject falls outside your area of expertise but you want to retain "ownership" of the project, you may choose to subcontract all or part of the work. If that is the case, the reference interview process will be somewhat different because you may want to let your client know that you are bringing in "an associate" (or however you want to characterize your subcontractor). You may want to arrange a conference call in which your subcontractor and your client can discuss the project. Then the subcontractor can get back to you with an estimate, and you can work up your own estimate to give to the client. (See Chapter 16, Subcontracting, or I'll Scratch Your Back If You Scratch Mine, for more about contracting relationships.) On the other hand, perhaps the project just involves a topic you do not know much—or anything—about, but you are fairly confident that you can come up to speed quickly and do your usual superb job. In that case, you can tell your client that you need to do some preliminary research in order to develop an estimate. Spend a little time, no more than 15 or 20 minutes, getting familiar with the subject area. This assumes that your general research skills are fairly well developed; you do not want to flail about helplessly wondering where to begin. (If you do find yourself flailing, it is an indication to do what I suggested earlier in this paragraph: Subcontract the project or refer it out to a more experienced colleague.) Remember, you can build some learning time into the project budget; this initial research is simply to get familiar with the terminology and to ascertain whether it is an area that you can get up to speed on later. Then you call the client back and resume the reference interview.

Step Three: Negotiate Everything

Now that you and your client have explored what she is really looking for, it is time to negotiate. Does this project call for specialized research techniques such as telephone interviews or public records research? Does your client want an executive summary along with the research? Would she like relevant information extracted into a spreadsheet or a PowerPoint presentation? Would she like you to present the results in person or on a conference call with her colleagues? What about the deadline? Does she really need it in two days? Would she be willing to wait a week in order to get more in-depth research and analysis?

This is also the point at which you manage your client's expectations. You explain that, although you will use what you believe are the most appropriate resources available to you, you cannot promise ahead of time what you will find. The client is paying for your time and expertise, not for information per se. This means that even if you do not find exactly what she is looking for, she will still pay you for your research and expertise. Listen closely to your client at this juncture. Is she balking at "paying for nothing?" If so, she may not understand that finding nothing is sometimes very informative. Your deliverable will include a description of what you did find, what resources you used, what approach you suggest for further exploration, and so on. You will provide intelligence, even if it is not quite what the client wanted or anticipated.

At this point, is your client asking you for a guarantee of what you will find? Is she telling you that she just *knows* that you will find lots of information? If so, this is when you will have to spell out the rules of engagement: You cannot make any assurances of what you will find; you are not like a trial lawyer who only charges if he wins the case for you.

If your gut tells you that your client has unreasonable expectations, and if you do not seem able to modify those expectations with a reasonable explanation of what you can and cannot do, it is time to walk away from the job; it has "disaster" written all over it. This is not a failure on your part or your client's. It is usually a matter of different personalities or communication styles that just do not mesh. Presumably, someone else will be able to approach this client in a way that she hears and can acknowledge the inherent uncertainty of research. My usual tack in such cases is to say, "You know, I just don't think I'd be the right person for this job. Let me recommend a couple of colleagues who have more expertise in this area," or "Let me give you the URL to AIIP's membership directory, where you can get names of other info pros who might be able to help you."

Step Four: Stop and Estimate

Note that we still have not talked about budget. The first three steps in our reference interview have established what research the client needs, what additional work with that information she wants, and when she needs the final product. Now you have to figure out what it will cost. Even if you have been estimating projects for years, do not try to come up with an estimate while you are conducting the reference interview. Nine times out of 10, you will significantly underestimate the time involved. Instead, review what you understand the project to entail and tell the client that you will work up an estimate and email it back to her shortly. Be sure to describe the work in your own words; if the client originally asked for "background information on the shipping industry," you might reword and refine her request, as a result of the clarifying questions you've asked her, as "a review of the overnight package delivery industry, such as Federal Express and UPS." Rephrasing the request ensures that you catch any hidden assumptions—yours or the client's—about what is involved in the project.

So you hang up the phone. You sit back and start noting down everything you think the job will require. For example, if you are estimating the overnight package industry project, your list might include:

- Review and compare the major players' websites to see how they describe their services.

- Download and extract information from companies' U.S. Securities and Exchange Commission filings. Develop a chart that highlights the key differences among the players.

- Obtain industry surveys from government agencies and trade associations.

- Search one of the professional online services for articles from industry publications.

- Obtain market research reports on the industry.

- Conduct telephone interviews with major retail shipping customers such as L.L. Bean, Amazon.com, and Dell Computers to find out what concerns they have.

Would you have thought of all these possible research aspects while you were on the phone with the client?

Next, spell out what value-added services you will provide, such as an analysis of the results of your research or an executive summary of trends in the industry. See Chapter 15, Setting Rates and Fees, for more discussion of how to price a project, and a worksheet for estimating costs. Now write a summary of what you will do, what you expect your deliverables to be, when you will finish the project, and your not-to-exceed budget. Include some verbiage to the effect that you cannot promise that you will find the exact information that the client is hoping to find, but you will make your best effort, and you will consult with the client during the course of the project if you encounter unanticipated roadblocks or find that very little information is available. You also need to include a disclaimer; see Chapter 17, Ethics and Legalities, for a discussion of disclaimers.

Step Five: Get Buy-In

Finally, you are at the step where you send the proposal and budget to your client. Follow up with a phone call to discuss any questions and to nail down the project officially. Listen for any hesitancy about the budget. Does your client accept your proposal? Do you get the sense that she really expects you to deliver something more or that she hopes it will *really* cost much less than your not-to-exceed budget? If you do, speak up now because this is the last time you can easily clarify these expectations. Also listen for any clue that your client had expected a much higher budget. If so, that is an indication that either you are pricing your services too low or you miscalculated the extent of the work involved. You cannot correct your pricing if it is too

Am I Giving Away My Secrets?

Some clients require more hand-holding than others when it comes to a reference interview and an estimate. If they need a detailed description of the kind of research you plan to do, just build the extra time required to prepare that description into the budget for the project. They may become more confident after you have done a few projects for them, or they may just be the type of people who need to feel in control. In any event, their need for hand-holding is not a reflection on your abilities, so look at it as a good exercise in thinking through a project and chalk up the experience to the wonderful diversity of humanity that you get to work with as an independent info pro.

Some independent info pros are reluctant to spell out the particulars of how they plan to approach a research project, fearing that they will be disclosing their trade secrets or giving the client a roadmap with which he can do the project himself. This is a misplaced fear. What we offer our clients is not a secret stash of resources; rather, we offer the ability to search for information efficiently, follow clues to find information in unexpected places, and present the information in a way that makes it easy for the client to use. Telling our clients what resources we will begin with hardly gives them the tools and expertise to do the work themselves, just as a doctor explaining what technique she is going to use on me certainly does not give me the ability to do it myself, thank goodness.

low, but you must make sure that you have not seriously underestimated the amount of effort required. Talk through the work you plan on doing, and the format and scope of the deliverable, and make sure that you and your client are in agreement before you proceed.

Reassure your client that you will call or email if you have any questions as you go along or if you are not finding as much information as you had anticipated. Ask if her accounting department will require any special information in order to pay the invoice, such as a purchase order or authorization number. The time to deal with this is before you begin working; if there is going to be a delay because of paperwork that must be completed, you have a much better chance of getting your client to expedite the process now when she is eager for the work to be done, rather than after she has the results in hand and you are waiting for your invoice to be paid.

Even if you have an established track record with the client, you should get something in writing confirming the description of the project and the agreed-upon budget. Some independent info pros send a formal contract; others simply ask that the client OK the email message describing the job; their response is confirmation. The larger the project, the more formal the proposal. Ask your lawyer to draft a sample contract that you can use for projects that require a formal agreement. I tend to avoid anything that looks like a contract for smaller projects; I have found that they just scare clients, and they often delay the project while the client gets his legal department to go over them. On the other hand, if I am going to be working on a 40- or 50-hour project, I definitely want the client to take it seriously. In fact, I will probably require prepayment of a portion of the not-to-exceed budget, so a formal contract is called for.

Sources of Ambiguity

If all goes well, you will walk through the five steps of the reference interview, nail down the job, and be on your way. If, however, there seems to be some miscommunication, you may have stumbled into one of the following pitfalls. You cannot necessarily avoid these sources of ambiguity but being aware of them will help you recognize and address any misunderstandings during the initial interview, instead of at the end of the project:

- The client's familiarity with the subject: If the client does not know much about the topic, he may provide what he thinks are helpful tips or buzz-words, which turn out to be dead ends. One way to catch this is to ask your client if he would like you to find some basic background information on the subject.

- The client's assumptions about what information is available: It is human nature; we tend to ask the questions that we think people can answer. Your client may be asking for only the information he thinks you will be able to locate, instead of describing the deeper question he really needs answered.

- The client's personality: No, you cannot do anything about that, but you can recognize when your personalities clash, or your communication styles do not mesh. If that happens, see if you can bring in a subcontractor or just refer the job to a colleague.

- Misspellings or faulty memory: Librarians joke about the client who comes in asking for "that article from the *Times* a couple of weeks ago about fly fishing." Any experienced librarian will tell you that at least one and quite possibly two of those aspects is wrong—the article was from six months ago, it was in the *Journal*, or even *Angler*, or it was about deep sea fishing. Treat any statement along the lines of "I read about it last week" with similar skepticism. Likewise, double-check the spelling of any company or personal names your client provides.

- Dealing with intermediaries: One of the most difficult situations is when a client's administrative assistant calls you to relay a request for research. You cannot negotiate directly with the client, you cannot clarify or expand on the request, you cannot offer additional services, and you cannot meaningfully negotiate the budget. If you have worked with the assistant before, you may be able to simply ask to speak to the client directly. If not, see if you can email a list of questions that the assistant can pass along to your client. If you hit resistance, the only alternative—short of declining the job altogether—is to document what you understand the project to be, spell out in detail the kind of information you will be providing, and make sure that the client signs off on the budget directly. Be careful; this is the kind of situation in which misunderstandings are much more likely to happen, and they are usually not detected until after the project is completed. Again, listen to your gut. If you just do not feel comfortable doing a project that you cannot negotiate directly, offer to refer the client to a colleague. Turning down a project is always a better alternative than ignoring your instinct and winding up with a disappointed client who won't pay your invoice.

Top Tips for Negotiation

✦ Pay attention; do not try to multitask during a reference interview.

✦ Assume that there is a deeper question behind the initial question.

✦ Ask questions that elicit useful answers; ask open-ended questions.

✦ Avoid premature diagnosis; do not jump to conclusions regarding what the project entails.

✦ Paraphrase and reword the project to your client.

✦ Examine and be willing to negotiate all aspects of the request: information needed, scope and depth of the project, deadline, budget, and delivery method.

✦ Look for ways to upsell—tell your client about additional analysis or more in-depth research you can do on top of what he specifically asked for.

✦ Watch for possible areas of miscommunication and resolve them at the outset.

Chapter 30

Thinking Like a Researcher

I suspect that every researcher has a unique mental map he consults when preparing to tackle a research project. Your mental map will be built from your experiences in finding information over time—whether you learned to use the library as a child, how well the readily available web sources cover your area of expertise, your familiarity with relatively obscure information sources such as government documents, your comfort level when calling and interviewing industry experts, and so on. (For thoughtful discussions of researchers' mental maps, see Marylaine Block's articles "My Rules of Information," *Searcher*, January 2002, available at www.infotoday. com/searcher/jan02/block.htm and "Mapping the Information Landscape," *Searcher*, April 2002, available at www.infotoday.com/searcher/apr02/block.htm.) I cannot construct your research map for you, but I can show you some of the ways that info pros approach the research process.

Ready, Fire, Aim

The sequence for target practice or for research, of course, should be prepare, aim, and fire. However, researchers are often guilty of getting the order wrong and launching into a search before they have figured out what they should be looking for—the ready, fire, aim approach.

Assuming that you have already completed your initial interview with the client (see Chapter 29, The Reference Interview), the first thing you should do is just sit back and think. It is tempting to hop on the web, throw in some key terms, and see what pops up, but your initial research will be more productive if you have done some preparation first. Remember, you may not incur any out-of-pocket expenses in searching the web, but your client is paying for your time, and you have to manage it wisely.

What Form of Information Are You Looking For?

What do you really need to find? Does your client want information that you would find in white papers, policy statements, or position papers? Articles from magazines or trade journals? Conference papers? Chapters from authoritative books on the subject? Statistical material? Multimedia such as an audio clip, animation, video file, or image? Information from blogs, social network sites, online discussion forums or newsgroup postings? Does your client want plain textual material, an Excel spreadsheet, webpages, or some other format? Is the information you are looking for too current for a standard web search engine to retrieve? Or is it too old to appear online at all?

Looking at the question of form from a slightly different angle, does your client need:

- The full text of articles or summaries?

- Very current material or information from 10 years ago?

- Introductory material or more advanced treatments that assume the reader's familiarity with the subject?

- A good overview or an exhaustive search of everything written on the subject?

After you have answered these questions, jot down a checklist of what you are really looking for, and keep it close at hand as you begin your research. I am always surprised when I realize how easy it is to get distracted as I become engrossed in my research. It is tempting to follow tangential leads. Peripheral vision is a useful skill and will often enable you to discover new and valuable sources, but you can wind up far afield if you lose focus and try to follow every possible lead.

Will You Know It When You See It?

Do you have a clear understanding of what your client needs? For example, I worked on a project to identify the impact of imported Chinese tungsten products on the U.S. market, specifically the use of Chinese tungsten in strengthening sharp edges in products such as snowplow and saw blades. Before I began, I had to decide whether I wanted anything that mentioned Chinese tungsten or only material that looked at U.S. manufacturers as well. I knew I would have to look at import and export statistics to see the trends in the Chinese tungsten trade, and I had to determine the current strength of the market for U.S. tungsten. I had to identify experts to interview, which meant figuring out who would know about this specific issue; I could not just talk with someone on the mining and processing of tungsten in general.

If you have done a thorough reference interview with your client, you will have reworded the goals of the project in your own words to ensure that you understand exactly what the client expects. Justice Potter Stewart of the U.S. Supreme Court famously said that he could not describe obscenity but "I know it when I see it." That might work for Supreme Court justices, but it is not a good approach for independent info pros. If you do not know ahead of time what would answer the question and you are just hoping that you will know it when you see it, you might easily miss a spot-on reference.

How Much Do You Know About the Subject?

Is this topic one you are already familiar with, or do you need to do preliminary research in order to educate yourself? Be sure to factor into the total cost of the project the time required to bring yourself up to speed. Yes, it is all right to bill the client for that groundwork. My rule, though, is to not spend more than 30 minutes to an hour on self-education. If it takes me longer than that to get familiar with the topic, it is possible that this is far enough outside my area of expertise that I should subcontract or refer the project to someone else. For instance, the entire area of chemistry happens to be foreign territory to me. I do not know what any of the terminology and symbols signify. I do not understand what happens when you combine certain elements. I have no sense of which components might be significant in a search and which are common building blocks that I could safely ignore. I would be totally at sea if I accepted a search in this area. However, a topic such as the Chinese tungsten market felt "safe" to me, even though I had never researched anything quite like it before. I knew I could grasp what tungsten was and was it was used for; I knew from experience that certain questions and issues are common to searches of this general type. And I had done similar research on other types of saw blades, so I had a list of resources that could get me started.

What's at Stake?

How you approach a research project will be determined in part by what the information will be used for. Does the client just want to get up to speed on a new technology or product? Does she simply want an overview of an industry's trends? Does a client need to know what the market is like because he's considering going into a new line of business? Is the client making a strategic business decision and counting on the results of your research to help her reach a conclusion?

While clients may be reluctant to disclose the exact nature of the project they are working on, a skillful reference interview should give you at least a general sense of whether they expect you to deliver essentially a get-smart package or the informational equivalent of everything but the kitchen sink.

Seeing Horizons and Setting Limits

We info pros are a strange breed. We think about information in ways unlike most people. We know how much information is available beyond the web—in fee-based online services, government documents hidden in the recesses of a courthouse, print material in libraries, even telephone interviews with experts who could never put all their knowledge into print. We see how far the information horizon stretches, and part of our role when we discuss projects with clients is to expand their understanding of the wide range of resources available.

I find that one of my greatest challenges in providing research services is figuring out how to narrow my approach to the best, most relevant, and most cost-effective sources for any given job. Do I start with one of the professional-grade online services? Should I look for a trade association's website? Would it be best to search market research companies' catalogs for an appropriate consulting report? Should I pick up the phone and call an expert? The approach you take first will be determined at least in part by the deliverable your client wants. If she is expecting an analysis of articles from the trade press, you will focus on a fee-based online service. If she wants projections, you might identify market research reports or conduct interviews with the leading players in the field.

In fact, one of the biggest challenges for a longtime researcher is to get out of your rut and try new approaches. It is easy to get accustomed to using the same databases, websites, or printed reference works over and over again for a particular type of research. But your clients hire you because you are an expert in finding the best information sources today. Just as your computer automatically clears its memory cache on a regular basis, consider purging your "assumptions cache" every six months or so. Seek out new information sources instead of (or in addition to) your usual sources. It is a useful exercise, and it helps keep you refreshed and current on the newest and latest resources. See Chapter 18, Professional Development, for more thoughts on staying on top of information resources and trends.

Whatever research strategy you use, assume that you will be able to find something, even if the research topic is as narrow as the market for replacement shower heads, as one of my projects was. If you come up with nothing on your first attempt, try broadening your search by adding synonyms and alternative terms, eliminating date or language restrictions, and so on. For my research on shower heads, for example, I expanded the research to residential bathroom plumbing fixtures generally and then looked for statistics on trends in bathroom repair. We independent info pros sometimes forget that our clients need answers, not just data, and the information that fills their needs may not look at first glance like an exact match. We often have very high standards for what we deem to be relevant: "If this article isn't specifically about the market for replacement shower heads, forget it." Actually, the client is often just as happy with related information that points to the answer. Statistics on home renovation and repair as well as articles discussing general trends in consumer purchases of plumbing fixtures were sufficient for my client, who understood that it wasn't likely that anyone had studied the replacement shower head market specifically.

The flip side of expanding our vision of the information horizon is needing to know when to call it quits. I have always believed that what makes a good researcher is the presence of the "finder gene"—that urge to dig deeper, to try one more approach, to look through one more source to find the very best information. It is a useful trait but, like many skills, it can be taken to an extreme. Once we are off on the chase, it is hard to stop.

You know it is time to say "when" if:

- You run out of time; you have to have the answer by noon and it is now 11:59 AM.

- You start seeing references to the same sources over and over again; you feel like you are walking in circles. (Do you remember the story of Winnie the Pooh and Piglet tracking a Woozle around the tree and eventually realizing that they were only tracking their own footprints?)

- You have found enough information to satisfy the client and doing an exhaustive search is not appropriate for the project or the budget.

- You ask colleagues for suggestions, and all they mention are resources that you have already tried.

- You are doing research in a field or geographic region that simply does not offer many information sources, and you have tapped those out.

- You sense that the 80:20 rule has kicked in: You are pretty sure that you have found 80 percent of the information available, but the time, effort, and expense required to find the other 20 percent would match or exceed what you have already spent.

Sometimes you just have to sit back and decide whether you have found an answer that works, even if it is not an exact match with what the client asked for. Fortunately, charging for your time makes this task a bit easier. If the client is only willing to pay for a few hours of your time, then you know that he is not looking for a comprehensive analysis on the subject. We can see how far the information horizon extends, but often our client does not want us to go all the way to the horizon.

Mapping Out a Large Project

Some research jobs are so straightforward that your search strategy is determined for you: "I need a bibliography of what so-and-so wrote about organic farming in the 1970s" or "I need an Excel spreadsheet with five years of financial statements for these 10 companies" or "Tell me the latest trends in retinal scanning for security systems." Other projects are more involved and require research in a number of different types of information sources. For those more complex jobs, expect to spend time outlining your research strategy, thinking about all that is involved, and deciding what kinds of resources you will use. If you can, negotiate some interim deliverables; it is useful to get feedback from the client during the project, to make sure that your expectations match hers. It is a lot easier to adjust your approach midway through the process than after you have invested 20 or 30 hours of work in it.

Working for Free

Imagine that you are in the middle of an interesting research project. You are enjoying the process of learning everything you can about the ice-cream parlor industry, and you are finding leads for all kinds of great sources. During searches like this, it is hard to rein yourself in when you hit the end of your budget. "But there's so much more useful information out there!" you tell yourself. "My client is paying me to find the best information available, so I have to keep going. I just won't charge for these extra two hours."

BZZZT! Wrong answer. Giving free time to clients devalues your expertise and sets up the expectation that they will always get loads of research and analysis at a low cost. We have to stop when the client has decided it is time to stop; when you negotiated the not-to-exceed budget, your client was indicating how much value he assigned to this job. If he is only willing to pay for an overview of a topic, that is what he gets. Any additional time that you put into this project comes straight out of your bottom line.

Of course, there are times when you might be justified in throwing in a free hour of work, particularly if you feel that you were not working up to capacity. Were you distracted and not focused on the client's job? Were you off on a tangent that you should have recognized as irrelevant? If so (and this shouldn't happen often), then absorb the time and resolve to avoid the problem in the future.

When I map out a complex project, my timeline includes the following steps:

- Outlining all aspects of the research, listing what I need to find, what format it should be in, and what sources I think might be most appropriate

- Determining how much time to allot for analysis, synthesis, and review of the material after I have done all the research I can

- Evaluating my own schedule and skill sets to determine whether I should bring in subcontractors; if so, identifying the appropriate subs and bringing them up to speed on their portion of the project

- Educating myself on the subject; checking for industry buzzwords and acronyms

- Running a preliminary search using whatever research tool is most appropriate (professional online service, web, phone, or library research)

- Collecting all research so far from subcontractors

- Reviewing what I have so far, identifying problematic areas, and deciding which aspects I have covered sufficiently

- Continuing research for the aspects of the project that I have not nailed down

- Evaluating my progress

- Continuing research and evaluation until I (with help from subcontractors) have all angles covered or have exhausted the time I budgeted for research

- Reviewing my results, outlining my findings, writing my report and overview, and adding the analysis my client has requested

- Setting it aside overnight, reviewing it one last time before sending to the client, and making any final changes or corrections

Note that one of the first things I do is calculate how many hours I can spend doing the actual research. If my client has agreed to a budget that includes 25 hours of my time, that doesn't mean that I will be spending 25 hours doing research. I will probably spend an hour or two preparing for the research, bringing myself up to speed on terminology, organizing my thoughts, reviewing the power tools available in the professional online services, and so on. I will also set aside four or five hours at the end of the project to pull all the material together, put it into a format that is easy for my client to use, think through what all I learned in this project, write an analysis and executive summary of my results, and outline any additional work that could be done if the client needs more information.

Tutorials on Research Techniques

There are a number of web-based tutorials on how to embark on a research project. Most of them cover web research as well as the use of some other, more traditional tools such as library resources and the fee-based online services. Many of these tutorials were prepared by university librarians, either in conjunction with a basic course in library reference or in an effort to teach students that there is more useful information out there than can be found through web search engines or through their social network. As a result, the focus of such tutorials is fairly basic; a longtime independent info pro probably will not learn anything new. If, on the other hand, you are coming to this profession without years of experience as a researcher and you want an overview of what is involved, you will find these tutorials valuable.

Stanford University has developed an online tutorial, Stanford's Key to Information Literacy (skil.stanford.edu), that walks you through the process of defining all aspects of a project, searching library catalogs, databases and the web, and evaluating the reliability of the information you retrieve.

Another source of quick learning is the 21st Century Information Fluency project (www.21cif.com). This project began as a U.S. Department of Education-funded effort to look into the field of online information literacy, and it became an independent company in 2009. This site offers a wide array of tutorials, tools, wizards, podcasts, and other resources to help you from the start of your research to evaluation of what you have found.

Your local public or university library may also offer useful information on research basics—online tutorials, hands-on workshops, and other training material.

A Researcher's Checklist

✦ Do I have a clear understanding of what I am looking for?

✦ Do I know what type and form of information my client wants and why she wants it?

✦ Am I looking beyond my "usual suspects" to see what other information sources might be appropriate?

✦ Have I mapped my research strategy in advance and allowed for time to evaluate, organize, and synthesize the information into something more useful for my client?

✦ Do I know when to stop and am I willing to quit even though I know I could do more research?

Chapter 31

Online Research Basics

This chapter will give you an overview of what online research entails; the following chapters cover in more detail the various types of online information resources. For the purposes of this chapter, I have divided the online world into four broad categories:

- The open web: That portion of the web that you can access with standard search engines

- The invisible or hidden web: Sites that are accessible but have content hidden from or that cannot be "read" by most search engines

- The gated web: Content on websites that require registration and/or payment such as Britannica.com or eLibrary.com

- The social web: The content within social networks such as Facebook and LinkedIn, material in blogs and microblogs such as Twitter, and other collaborative tools such as wikis and mash-ups

- The professional online services: The high-end aggregators of information from many sources, such as Dialog or Factiva

I cover the various aspects of finding information on the web in Chapter 32, Web Research 101. I discuss the professional online services in Chapter 34, Professional Online Services.

It's All on the Web for Free, Right?

You already know that not all the useful information in the world is available via the web, just a mouse-click away—but sometimes it feels like the rest of the world is still laboring under that illusion. Every time another content-rich website starts charging for its services, I am tempted to smile. I know that it will remind at least one more web surfer, somewhere in the universe, that, no, it's not all on the web for free.

Let's look at some of the places where information exists but that a web search engine will not find. Search engines miss a lot of the information that is on the web. They may not know about a newly added or recently changed website. They may not dig deep enough into a site to find every page. They may not be able to read the textual or numeric data on a site if the information is not in a format they can process; graphics, databases, and multimedia files generally fall into this category. They have trouble keeping up with frequently updated blogs, and they usually cannot get into the social networking sites. In fact, some experts estimate that as much as 90 percent of the content of the web is invisible to search engines.

Another challenge with web research is that, while many publications make the current and recently published issues of their periodicals available on their website, a deep archive usually is not available and neither are the search power tools you need to find the key insights your clients need. There is the related problem of having to go from one publisher's website to another in order to search a wide variety of professional publications. There are some services, such as MagPortal.com, that offer free access to full-text articles, but these services include a very small subset of the material available through the professional online services, and they cannot be relied upon for professional research. And while Google offers an archive of news articles, its coverage is far from complete, and most of the articles from the professional and trade literature must be purchased; they are available through news aggregators but for a fee.

Other limitations of conducting research on the web include the impermanence of material—you have no assurance that what you find today will be there tomorrow. Then there's the lack of sophisticated search and retrieval tools. Even the advanced search features of search engines resemble blunt tools more than surgical instruments.

What's Missing?

As much as we would like to think that an electronic archive exists somewhere of everything that has been published, it isn't so. Publishers are not putting their content on the web in any complete or consistent manner. Unfortunately, we cannot count on the professional online services described in Chapter 34 to maintain a comprehensive archive of articles either. Even those databases that claim to provide complete, full-text coverage of a publication have gaps. Some very short articles are often omitted. Errors happen when articles are loaded into a database, and records get dropped. Syndicated features are routinely eliminated from the publications in which they appear. Advertising supplements, even if they include articles, are not preserved. Letters are transposed during data entry, so, for example, an article by Walter Mossberg will not be found if his name was input as Walter Mosbserg.

And then there are the Tasini gaps. *Tasini v. New York Times* was a case before the U.S. Supreme Court in which the justices ruled that database producers had to negotiate specifically for the rights to include articles written by freelancers. The fact that the articles had already appeared in print did not automatically give the publishers the right to license those articles for resale by a third party—in this case, the electronic database producer or aggregator. The result of this decision was that some online information providers deleted all existing content by freelance writers rather than attempt to secure the rights from the individual authors. So databases that at one point did attempt to include every article from a publication may now have gaps.

To further confuse the matter, many fee-based news aggregators explicitly choose not to include every article from a publication. If the focus of a particular database is the insurance industry, for example, the producer may add selected articles from a wide variety of sources, while omitting any material that is not focused on the insurance industry. And the articles themselves may not be complete. The records in most databases are plain text, which means that graphics, photos, charts, and graphs are often not included, even on the web. (One exception to this is the TableBase file, available on Dialog and DataStar, which extracts tabular material from business-related articles.)

Other factors that affect whether you will find a specific article include embargos and lag time in updating online files, policies of the aggregators regarding which edition of a wire service or newspaper to include, and the policy of the database or website regarding the retention of older records.

Free Versus Fee

Given the wide range of information sources on the web and in the fee-based online services, and given the fact that there is not a tremendous amount of overlap between what is available on the web and in the fee-based services, how do you decide where to start an online search? Longtime online searchers tend to default to the professional online services, valuing the power search tools, depth and breadth of information, search efficiency, and consistency among databases that they find there. Researchers who learned how to search the web before they had heard about Dialog or Factiva usually start with a web search engine, knowing that they can skim a wide range of information sources and that the only cost will be their time. Understanding the pros and cons of both approaches, I have developed a mental checklist to help me decide where to go first for any given research project, in which I ask myself:

- Who cares about this information? Would anyone be likely to collect it and give it away for free? If so, I will start with the open web.

- Do I need high-value search tools such as consistently applied subject indexing or the ability to construct a complex search statement? If so, I will start with the professional online services.

- Am I looking for information in a form other than plain text, such as an audio or video clip, a spreadsheet, or a photo? If so, I will start with specialized finding tools that mine the invisible web.

- Do I need all the output in a single consistent format? If so, I will start with the professional online services.

- Do I need very current material? If so, I will start with news sources on the open web.

- Do I need material from more than a year or two ago or material that I can be sure of retrieving again later? If so, I will start with the professional online services.

- Do I need articles from professional or trade publications? If so, I will start with the professional online services.

- Is this a quick search just to see what information is available on a subject? If so, I will start with a good web-based news aggregator.

- Is this project in support of a high-stakes decision? Is it crucial that I find a wide range of material? If so, I will start with the open web, then go to the professional online services, and then look information in the more opaque portions of the web, including the social or collaborative web.

Boolean Basics

If you have ever used one of the professional online services or clicked the Advanced Search link on a web search engine, you have probably been exposed to Boolean logic, which uses AND, OR, and NOT to define the relationship among your search terms. And if you made it past elementary school, you were probably exposed to Venn diagrams, which are a simple way to represent Boolean logic.

To refresh your memory, look at Figure 31.1 and imagine that the left circle (circle A) represents articles about long-distance running and the right circle (circle B) represents articles about Seattle:

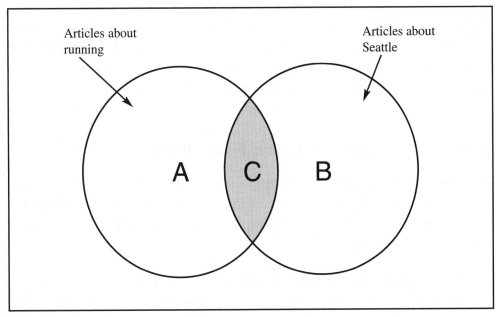

Figure 31.1   Venn Diagram

- Articles that mention both running and Seattle (expressed logically as A AND B) are represented by the center area of the figure, labeled C, where the two circles intersect.

- Articles that talk about running or about Seattle or about both topics (expressed as A OR B) are represented by all the areas of the figure—that is, the two circles as well as their intersection: areas A, B, and C.

- Articles that talk about running but that do not mention Seattle (expressed as A NOT B) are represented by the white part of circle A (which looks like a circle with a bite out of it).

The professional online services all use the syntax AND, OR, and NOT. Web search engines often support Boolean logic as part of their "advanced search" options. However, there is very little consistency in how search engines handle multiple words in a default or basic search. If you typed *running Seattle* into a search engine, it might be interpreted as *running AND Seattle*; it might be read as *running OR Seattle*; it might even be processed as the exact phrase *"running Seattle."* To complicate matters, some search engines let you indicate words or phrases that must appear in every retrieved webpage, either by putting a "+" at the beginning of each required word or by using a pull-down menu that indicates, "This word must appear." In this case, the search *+running +Seattle* would be interpreted as *running AND Seattle*, and the search *running Seattle* would be interpreted as *running OR Seattle*. If you are not sure how a search engine or online service is going to interpret your search, read the help files or search tips page before you get started.

Adjacency, Truncation, and Other Power Tools

The basic Boolean operators are pretty straightforward, as long as you keep those overlapping circles in Figure 31.1 in mind. But most online services and web search engines offer additional search tools to help you refine your query. Some of the more common power tools include:

- Phrase searching, interpreted as "look for these words in this exact order, with no intervening words." Most web search engines require that you enclose a phrase in quotation marks. Example: "tour de france"

- Proximity searching, interpreted as "look for these words within *N* words of each other, and in this order." This feature is most commonly available in the professional online services. Example: asteroid near10 dinosaurs

- Some search tools also let you indicate that you want the two words within the same sentence or paragraph. Example: asteroid same dinosaurs

- Truncation, interpreted as "look for any word that begins with these letters." This is used to search for variations of a word. Example: vaccin* (to search for vaccine, vaccines, vaccination, and so on)

- Field searching, interpreted as "look for this word only in this part of the document." This is an effective way to narrow a search by looking for the key concepts in the title or first paragraph of an article, for instance. Search example: title(autism)

- Date searching, interpreted as "look for any records before/on/after this date." This is useful for finding articles published within a certain time frame; however, limiting by date is not reliable when searching the web. Search example: date from 12/01/08 to 3/01/10

- Nested logic, interpreted as "look for this word AND any of these words." This is useful when you want to use synonyms or other alternative terms in a complex Boolean search. Search example: electric near2 (car or vehicle or automobile)

In addition to Boolean logic, most search engines, specialized finding tools, and professional online services offer a "softer" version of expressing your search concepts. This is the familiar default with most search engines—a simple box in which you type your key words. The search engine first displays webpages with all the search words next to each other, then those in which the words all show up near each other, then those in which all the words appeared anywhere on the page. This basic search option is fine for a quick search but keep in mind that you are undoubtedly missing some relevant material. You are letting the search engine evaluate the relevance of the retrieved material based on its proprietary algorithm; sometimes the calculation is pretty good, and sometimes it completely misses the concept you were looking for.

Get in the habit of trying your searches in both the basic and advanced versions, and you will begin to notice which searches work well in which search tools.

Little-Known Tips for Online Research

✦ Use Boolean logic when appropriate. It gives you more control over how the search engine processes your request, and the more control the better.

✦ RTFM. Yes, that's geek-speak for Read The Fabulous Manual. Click on the Help or Search Tips links, use the Advanced Search options, and read the documentation that comes with your subscription to an online service. Every online service has its own quirks and power tools; you are wasting your time and money if you don't take advantage of all the resources available.

✦ Practice "pearl culturing." Just as a pearl begins with a small grain of sand, start with a narrow search to identify a few key articles on a topic. See what keywords are assigned to those articles, which acronyms are mentioned frequently, and what synonyms exist for the term or concept you are researching. Then expand your search based on the new terminology you have picked up.

✦ Use tools for limiting your search. Restrict your search by publication year, if you are looking for current material only; by source, if you want material from a specific publication or type of publication; by article length, if you only want in-depth coverage of a topic.

✦ Use search terms to define the type of material as well as the subject, particularly when searching the web. If you are looking for statistical material, for example, include words like *table, chart,* or *graph* in your search.

✦ Use synonyms and alternative phrasings. A search for road rage might also need synonyms such as "aggressive driving," "traffic calming," and even "intermittent explosive disorder."

✦ Remember to account for variant versions of English. As George Bernard Shaw once said, "England and America are two countries separated by the same language." *Retirement* in the U.S. is *superannuation* in Australia. *Aluminum* in the U.S. is *aluminium* in the U.K. *Globalization* in the U.S. is *globalisation* in most of the rest of the English-speaking world.

✦ Watch for gaps in coverage. Not everything that you want to find is online—either because the source is incomplete or because the information simply is not available in an online format.

Chapter 32

Web Research 101

Almost all independent info pros use the web as a research source, even if the primary focus of their business is something other than online research. Telephone researchers use the web to look up contact names in companies, associations, and government agencies. Document delivery companies use it to confirm the title of a conference proceeding or an obscure periodical. Library researchers consult web-based virtual card catalogs before they head out the door to make sure that the books they need are actually at the library.

Aspiring independent info pros often ask me whether it is possible to successfully run a business based exclusively on searching for information on the web. Unfortunately, in my experience, I have found that is not a viable business model. As much as we would like to think that everything we need to know is on the web, much of the most useful information is hidden within proprietary databases such as those offered by Dialog, Dow Jones Factiva, and LexisNexis. (See Chapter 34, Professional Online Services, for more information on these resources.) Limiting your research to what you can find on the web does your clients a disservice; you are ignoring most of the high-value information sources and search tools that help you work most efficiently.

Whether it is true or not, most people assume that they are expert web searchers. Outsell, Inc., a consulting firm for the information industry, regularly surveys self-described experienced online searchers. According to its reports, more than a third of knowledge workers say that they did not find what they needed when they searched the web—despite the fact that most people judge their own web research skills to be advanced. Another study from LexisNexis found that most legal professionals believe they waste time looking for information and sorting through irrelevant material.

The challenge here is convincing clients who already use the web that you can find and organize information more efficiently than they do. Yes, you probably are a better searcher, you have identified some great resources, and you have the persistence of a bulldog. It is still a hard sell when the dominant perception is that anyone should be able to find what they need on the web.

That said, clients do value our ability to find information more efficiently than they can, to evaluate web information sources, and to select the most authoritative sources, if we package our expertise properly. We understand the limitations of the various web search engines, and we know how to find sources that lie hidden in areas of the web that search engines cannot get at. We also know how much information *cannot* be found on the web, and where else to look. As you read this chapter, think not so much about how you might build a business on web-based research alone, as about how you can integrate the web into the full range of information services you provide to your clients.

Note that this chapter is not intended to serve as a complete description of how to conduct research on the web. There are many books that focus on web research—I have written several of them myself. Here, I will touch on the various types of resources on the web that are of most value to info-entrepreneurs.

How Search Engines Work

Most people begin their research on the web by typing a few words into a search engine such as Google. It is a simple way to find hundreds—or hundreds of thousands—of webpages, at least some of which might be useful. You will get better search results if you understand how search engines are built and what their strengths and weaknesses are. Note that this is a simplified description of how search engines work. For a more detailed explanation, consult a resource that specializes in monitoring search engines, such as Search Engine Watch (www.search enginewatch.com) or a university library tutorial, such as the University of California at Berkeley library's "Finding Information on the Internet" tutorial. (Start at www.lib.berkeley.edu and search for the tutorial's title.)

Contrary to appearances, search engines do not conduct a live, real-time search of the web when you type your keywords in the search box. Instead, they search already compiled indexes of the websites they have reviewed in the past. And where do those indexes come from? Starting with a core database of websites, a search engine reviews each webpage it already knows of to see if it can "read" it (that is, that the content is in plain text or in a format that it can understand). It indexes all the useful words on the page, sometimes omitting common and relatively meaningless words such as *and*, *to*, and *the*, and then looks for any outgoing links to other websites. It goes to each of those linked-to sites, repeats the process of indexing all the useful words on those sites, looks for outgoing links, and so on. You can picture the automated program crawling through a site, and from site to site, and in fact, these search engine indexing programs are called crawlers or spiders. Needless to say, crawling the web is a time- and resource-intensive process; there is an inevitable delay between when a page is added or changed and when a search engine gets around to looking at it. There are also many pages that search engines cannot or won't read at all. See the later section, "The Invisible Web," for more about what search engines *cannot* find. One of the exciting aspects of web research is the development of new information sources and new types of information resources. As I write this book, I cannot anticipate the next "wow" web technology, but odds are good that it will take search engines a while to figure out how to index the content. As a result, there is an almost inevitable lag between the emergence of a new facet of the web and when search engines have begun to spider the content.

When you type your search terms into a search engine, the retrieval software analyzes your input and figures out, based on its own internal algorithms plus any special instructions you might have supplied, how to process your search. The software determines whether all the words you have specified—or most of the words, or any one of the words—must appear on a webpage in order for that page to be retrieved. It figures out which combinations of words, if any, it should interpret as phrases. It evaluates the words to determine which ones are uncommon and, therefore, probably more important to your search. The retrieval program then checks the search engine's index and finds the entries for websites that match your search criteria.

The final step is a relevance-ranking process in which the search engine sorts the sites—often tens or hundreds of thousands—so that the ones it calculates to be most likely to be useful appear at the top of its list of results. How the search engine does this calculation is a deep, dark secret; search engines live and die by their ability to present users with the most relevant material at the top, and none will disclose exactly how their relevance algorithms work. In general, the calculation is based on some combination of factors, including the number of occurrences of your search words on the site, where and how prominently the words appear on the site, how close to each other they appear, the relative rarity of the words in normal usage, the "popularity" of the site as calculated by the number of times users have clicked on it or other sites have linked to it, and numerous other considerations.

Because of all these variables—the frequency with which search engines "crawl" sites to build and update their indexes, the method they use to interpret and process your search, and their proprietary relevance-ranking algorithm—no two search engines have quite the same view of the web. Try it for yourself. Type the same search into three search engines and see how much (or how little) overlap you find among the top 20 or 30 sites in each search engine's search results page.

Getting the Most From Search Engines

Studies of search engine usage report that the average search only includes two or three words. That means that most people do not use synonyms or alternate phrasing or concepts, or take advantage of any of the search engine's advanced search techniques—limiting a search by type of site, language, format, or date; searching for two words near each other; looking only for a word in the title of the page; and so on. The best way to keep up-to-date on these features is to get in the habit of periodically clicking the "advanced search" link or the "help" link in any search engines you use regularly.

Many search engines provide power-search features such as:

- Phrase or proximity searching (coal near environment, or the phrase "strip mining")

- Truncation (any word starting with the letters econom)

- Field searching (the word plagiarism in the title)

- Date search (find sites updated within the last two months)

- Language (limit this search to sites in French)

- Adult filter (eliminate any porn sites from the search results; depending on the search engine, this may filter out useful medical sites as well)

Web Directories and Guides

Search engines are built to find and index as many websites as possible. Sometimes, though, you do not want *every* site that mentions a particular word, but just the best, most authoritative sites. That is where human-built directories and web guides come into play. Web directories are distinguished from search engines by the following characteristics:

- Websites are selected for inclusion by humans.

- Sites are organized by category and subcategory (e.g., Science-> Environment-> Hazardous Wastes), so they can be browsed by topic.

- Emphasis is on selecting the best sites rather than the most sites.

The granddaddy of web directories is the Yahoo! Directory (dir.yahoo.com), which was the basis for the Yahoo! search service way back in the early 1990s. Other well-organized, authoritative web directories include IPL2 (www.ipl.org)—the merger of the Internet Public Library and the Librarians' Internet Index—and the WWW Virtual Library (vlib.org). These are maintained by professional librarians and information professionals, and they are often a good starting place for research in an area you are not familiar with. One of a web directory's strengths, however, is also its weakness: The only resources included in a directory are those specifically selected, reviewed, and evaluated by an editor. That means that there is an inevitable delay in the introduction of a new information resources and its inclusion in a web directory.

Web guides or portals are similar to directories; they consist of sites selected by experts and are intentionally not comprehensive. However, web guides usually focus on a particular topic or type of information and are often more useful if you want to dig deeper into the web than you can with a general-purpose web directory.

You can find web guides on virtually any topic—government information, the plastics industry, professional and trade associations, online newspapers, or everything you wanted to know about Yorkshire terriers. A web guide is usually built by someone with a passion or a professional interest in a specific subject or by a librarian with an interest in building the best finding tool for a specific type of information. These guides are often excellent sources for independent info pros, as they provide a shortcut to the most useful and reliable resources on a topic.

Some web directories combine selected websites with databases of published articles, enabling you to conduct a hybrid search for, presumably, the best of both worlds. Scirus (www.scirus.com) is one such service, enabling searchers to conduct focused queries on science-related topics ranging from agricultural science to astronomy, medicine, materials science, and engineering. You can search and review article summaries for free, and pay for any full-text articles you want.

One particularly noteworthy web guide for business research is BizToolkit (www.biztoolkit.org), a free service of the James J. Hill Reference Library, a remarkable private business library that offers a wide range of services to the public at no charge. The library is supported by an endowment and other private sources, and offers a fee-based program that provides access to a number of professional online services. (Note that use of these services is only for personal use, so independent info pros cannot make use of this for their clients.) The BizToolkit is a well-designed directory of databases and other research resources, organized by broad category, such as Business Lists, Industry Research, and Market Research. The focus of the Toolkit is helping businesses grow, so many of the resources may be of interest to you as an entrepreneur as well.

Unfortunately, a single comprehensive directory of web guides does not exist, so how do you find these resources? You can start with a general web directory, click down to the topic you are researching, and then search within that category for the word "directory" or "guide." As you read articles on your subject, watch for mentions of online portals, metasites, and guides.

The Invisible Web

Earlier in this chapter, I described in general terms how search engines look for new websites by looking for outgoing links. However, much of the most valuable information on the web is never indexed by search engines, so it is "invisible" to anyone who is using only a search engine for research. There are a number of reasons for why search engines overlook or choose not to include information from particular webpages:

- The text on the page is not readable by the search engine spider (some search engines can "read" word-processed files, spreadsheets, or PDF files, but no search engine can read text that is embedded or expressed in a graphical or multimedia format).

- No other page has linked to the page, so the search engine has not learned about it.

- The webpage requires users to register before they can view its content.

- The information is contained in a database and can only be extracted via a separate search query at the website itself.

- The webpage has changed since the search engine last visited it.

- The information resides on a web bulletin board, discussion forum, or social network site that search engines cannot enter because they cannot "register" themselves.

- The website was down when the search engine attempted to index it.

- The page is many layers deep within a website, and the search engine does not look below a certain number of subdirectories.

- The webpage includes a metatag indicating that search engines are not to index that page.

Obviously, many barriers exist to finding information on the invisible web when all you use is a simple search engine query. So how do you get to this often-useful information? First, look for resources listed in web directories and guides like the ones I described earlier in this chapter. Note, especially, pointers to databases and other file formats that are not usually readable by search engines.

Also remember that even if some content is hidden from search engines, related pages may be visible. Say, for example, I want to find an interview I heard on National Public Radio concerning bioengineered foods. The webpage containing that interview will not be accessible via a search engine because search engines cannot interpret audio files. But if I enter the words *bioengineered*, *NPR*, and *listen*—assuming that somewhere on the webpage I am looking for there is a phrase such as "click here to listen to this interview"—I get the page that describes the program and, indeed, it has a link to the audio file. If you are looking for a page that you do not think a search engine will pick up, think of search words that imply invisible content. *Listen* or *hear* suggests a link to an audio file; *search* suggests access to a database with a "click here to search" link; *video, watch,* or *view* suggests a video clip you can watch.

And, finally, remember that much of the invisible web that is of particular interest to independent info pros consists of published material—articles on publications' websites, databases of market research reports, and so on. Develop your own collection of key web resources for the type of research you do, focusing on the sources that search engines will not pick up. And check out Chapter 18, Professional Development, for ways to stay up-to-date on new web research tools and techniques.

Searching the Social Web

The collaborative, or social, web is potentially one of the best sources for obscure or specialized information. You have millions of people self-organizing into groups with common interests; they build in-depth collections of information, and you can always find someone who has an insight into whatever you are working on.

Finding the information or individual you need within the social web can be challenging, however. Each social network is an entity unto itself; in this sense, social networks on the web function similarly to networks in the real world. You would not elbow your way into a group of people deep in conversation and expect them to stop what they are discussing and focus on your concern. Likewise, mining for the electronic equivalent of gold can require some sleuthing.

First, remember that the information in the social web is primarily user-created. There is usually no one vetting the quality of the information, and many online communities and networks do not require users to disclose their real names, which makes it difficult for info pros to evaluate the reliability of an online source.

The value of the collaborative web is in the networks established. Individuals who contribute more to the web are more highly regarded, and they in turn usually manage to stay on top of emerging trends in their area of expertise. Look for people who are often referenced in the context of a specific issue or topic. See whose blog is frequently linked-to by other bloggers and look through that blog for new resources or ideas on where to look for information.

Wikis and other collaborative tools represent communities that are focused on a shared project or goal. They can be tremendous resources for finding obscure bits of information, experts to interview, and links to authoritative sources. As with other nontraditional web content, wikis are not well-indexed by search engine spiders.

Look for mentions of wikis in web directories and finding guides, as well as for links from other wikis such as Wikipedia (en.wikipedia.org).

Info-entrepreneurs have two very different perspectives on how to make use of the social web. As I discuss in Chapter 24, Marketing on the Web, you can use social networking sites such as LinkedIn or Facebook as ways to effectively communicate with your clients and prospects. In order to market effectively on the social web, you need to be familiar with how to find people and information using Web 2.0 tools. As you make use of these resources, think of how you can tweak your own profiles to make yourself more easily found by prospective clients.

Discussion Forums and Lists

Although most research projects involve looking for written material or interviewing experts, sometimes we need to tap into the pulse of a particular group of people— electrical engineers, digital photography buffs, or international researchers, per- haps. The first stop may be email discussion lists, social networking groups, and web-based discussion groups. Locating these sources can be difficult; as a rule, they are part of the invisible web described earlier in this chapter. Fortunately, some directories exist that can help, and creative thinking will also guide you to the resources you're looking for.

In my experience, the most targeted discussions and best collections of experts can be found in email lists, also known as listservs (note that LISTSERV is a trade- marked name for the first email list management software). Although there is no comprehensive catalog of email discussion lists, websites that host public email lists usually provide searchable directories. Two of the most popular sites include:

- Yahoo! (groups.yahoo.com): One of the most popular free group hosting services

- CataList (www.lsoft.com): A directory of lists running on LISTSERV software

Many email discussion lists maintain web-based archives, often going back many years. Most restrict access to list subscribers, which is one reason why these archives are often not indexed by search engines. You may find yourself temporarily sub- scribing to a number of discussion lists simply so that you can tap into their archives. Be mindful of the fact that you are a merely a passer-by to the members of this group. Posting a request on the list before consulting the archive and doing as much legwork as you can ahead of time is considered rude and will generate nothing but ill-will. Instead, do as much background research as you can and, if you feel confident that you are not asking a question too basic or tangential for the list, then post your query and offer to summarize the results.

Online forums hosted by particular websites are also good sources for identifying experts. Unfortunately, as with other nontraditional areas of the web, such discussions are difficult to identify and search engines often don't pick them up. Two specialized tools that index discussion boards are BoardTracker (www.boardtracker. com) and BoardReader (www.boardreader.com). Both allow you to search words in individual board postings, for discussion threads on a topic, or for metatags assigned to a topic. You may also want to identify a web directory or guide that covers the industry or topic you want to research and then look at likely sources to see if they host a forum.

And if you want to consult with a large group of librarians and info pros before you visit your subject-specific list, try the resources at FreePint (www.freepint.com). This company offers a number of services and tools for information professionals, virtually all of which are free:

- FreePint Newsletter, a lengthy fortnightly enewsletter

- FUMSI, monthly articles and special reports on the various aspects of Finding, Using, Managing, and Sharing Information

- VIP Magazine, a monthly magazine that covers business research (subscription-based)

- ResourceShelf (www.resourceshelf.com), a prolific blog of web-based resources of particular interest to librarians and researchers

- DocuTicker, a daily update of free, full-text reports from government agencies, nongovernmental agencies (NGOs), and similar organizations (while it offers worldwide coverage, the emphasis is on U.S. content)

- FreePint Bar, a very active discussion forum where librarians and info pros can pose difficult research problems for thousands of FreePinters to help with (full disclosure: Willco, the sister company to Free Pint Ltd., has hosted my enewsletter subscriptions for years)

Top Tips for Internet Research

✦ Use "type of document" searches to narrow your search: Include the word *listen* to identify audio files, *forecast* to find industry projections, and *search* to identify databases.

✦ Always use several search engines when conducting a comprehensive search. There is surprisingly little overlap among search engine coverage.

✦ Get to know the power search features of the search engines you use frequently. Know how to use field searching, truncation, phrase searching, and so on.

✦ Remember that much of the valuable information on the web is not included in search engines. Tap into your invisible web resources as well.

✦ Watch for mentions of new resources, white papers, and other hard-to-find material in the articles and discussion groups you read.

Chapter 33

Specialized Web Databases

Chapter 32 looks at conducting research in what could be considered the traditional web—information that exists on the web and that can and sometimes must be searched for. Coming at research from the professional angle, Chapter 34 looks at the high-end professional online services that are specifically designed for researchers. There is, however, a middle ground—databases on the web that contain in-depth information in structured formats that make the information much more accessible but that do not require a large up-front payment or a subscription fee. This chapter looks at some of these databases, which are often excellent sources of authoritative information and not usually found through search engines.

Pay-As-You-Go Options

A number of online services, including several of the professional online services described in more detail in Chapter 34, offer access to their content to nonsubscribers. Users can provide a credit card and either pay per search or per downloaded article. The cost is higher than it would be for a subscriber, but these are ways to access sources that you do not use frequently and do not feel proficient in searching.

These services often include the same sources you can find in the professional online services. So why use the higher-priced professional services? For starters, your search options are usually quite limited in these alternative online services; typically, they are designed for the web surfer who is willing to pay a few dollars for a quick search to turn up an article or two, rather than for the professional online researcher who needs to do an exhaustive search on a subject. Your output options are also generally more restricted on these low-cost services. And the charge will go on your credit card right away as opposed to a monthly invoice, which means that you will almost certainly pay the bill for the search long before your client pays you.

Since most of these low-end services do not charge for searching (you incur a fee only when you request the full text of an article), they are often useful for scoping out the range of a topic. Sometimes I will try searching with a few key terms and see how much material I retrieve. I will scan the article titles and summaries if available to get a sense of how I might need to broaden or narrow my search. Then I will run the search on one of the professional online services, where I can take advantage of its power search tools to focus on the most relevant material.

I also use the low-end services when I just need a single article and know exactly what I want. This kind of simple document delivery search does not require any finesse; all I want is the full text, and any online service that includes that publication will do.

Dialog (www.dialogweb.com) and Factiva (global.factiva.com), two of the major professional online services, offer low-cost access to their content. Dialog, notorious for its obscure search language, offers a search-engine-like search box that you can fill out with your search parameters. You can display a brief listing of search results at no cost; you pay per item if you want the full text. Factiva's credit card subscription involves a modest annual fee, plus a per-article fee. In both cases, you search for free and know exactly what the total cost will be before you incur any charges.

Google Scholar (scholar.google.com) is another option for searching academic and scholarly articles. Through various licensing arrangements, Google offers the ability to search the full text of hundreds of academic journals, theses, preprints, and professional society publications. Google Scholar also includes links to books in its Google Books index, and it identifies multiple available versions of articles, often including prepublication copies and author's copies as well as the official, published version.

Google Scholar is a good choice if you want to get a sense of who the experts are in an academic field, get a rough idea of how much has been written about an issue, or purchase a copy of an academic or scholarly article. Many articles are relatively expensive, but price points are determined by the publisher, and scholarly publications are known for their high copyright fees. I would not rely solely on the results of a search in Google Scholar for a couple of reasons. First, even the Advanced

Search tools are relatively rudimentary so I am never sure that I have retrieved every relevant article. It is also problematic that Google does not provide a comprehensive list of the sources in Google Scholar so I cannot gauge how comprehensive my search was.

I am not covering the free article sites such as MagPortal.com or FindArticles.com. While they do offer free access to full-text articles, they are virtually never worth an info pro's time to use. They offer very little in the way of search tools, and they include only a small subset of information from the large aggregators. Your time is far better spent using other resources, even if they aren't free.

Public Libraries

One reason I love public libraries is that, contrary to their stereotype, they have often been on the cutting edge of information technology and access. Most public libraries have access to many fee-based information services, and any resident with a library card can search these databases from the convenience of his or her living room. Generally, the resources include a large aggregator such as Gale's General OneFile or EBSCOhost's Academic Search Premier or Business Source Premier, as well as specialized databases such as the Encyclopedia of Associations, Morningstar (stock and mutual fund research), Reference USA (business and residential directories), and even the Opposing Viewpoints Resource Center (collections of source materials offering arguments for and against issues such as assisted suicide, homosexuality, nuclear weapons, and abortion).

While you can often search the same content through your public library as you would be paying for on a professional online service, you often will not have the same power search tools that enable you to get all the relevant material efficiently. Most libraries have contractual restrictions on which databases can be accessed remotely and which ones must be used on-site in the library, which means that in order to use the high-end information sources, you will have to go to the library, conduct your searches, save the results to a portable medium, and then go back to your (home) office. If, once you are reviewing your results and writing up your report, you find that you forgot a critical aspect of the search, it's back to the library. As with the pay-as-you-go tools, I use the databases available to local businesses through my public library as a way to run a quick search to get the informational lay of the land and for one-off article retrieval, but I don't rely on them for the vast majority of my online research.

If your local public library does not have the funding for these online services, you may be able to buy your way into a better-funded library, many of which offer a non-resident library card for a fee. Before you sign up, however, make sure that they offer access to the high-end databases you want; as noted earlier, some libraries cannot offer remote access to some of their premium online resources.

Libraries' Licensing Limitations

Many new info-entrepreneurs with a student ID and university library card or a public library card figure they can save their clients money by using their free access to fee-based online services with their library card. In addition to the issue of this simply being an inefficient way to conduct research, as it often requires a visit to the library, there are legal issues to consider.

Many aggregators and online publishers place restrictions on how and which library patrons can use the material that is available through the library's subscription to an online database. Some public libraries have negotiated contracts that allow virtually unlimited use by anyone with a library card. If that is the case with your local public library, you are free to download articles and pass them along to your client without worrying about violating any licensing restrictions. However, the contracts that many public libraries and virtually all university libraries have with their online vendors prohibit commercial use of their databases. In fact, one library prominently displays the warning that "remote access to EBSCO's databases from non-subscribing institutions is not allowed if the purpose of the use is for commercial gain through cost reduction or avoidance for a nonsubscribing institution." That means that we independent info pros cannot legally use these resources for our business, as tempting as it may be. See Chapter 17, Ethics and Legalities, for more discussion of running an ethical business, and conduct your business as if any of your actions could be written up on the front page of the *Wall Street Journal* or whatever paper your clients read.

Open Access Publications

Academic and scholarly periodicals often have hefty subscription prices; the average annual subscription price of academic chemistry publications is well over $3,500. One result has been that fewer libraries can afford to maintain their subscriptions of the key sources of new developments in scientific fields. As subscriber levels drop, publishers increase their subscription prices to maintain their profitability. This vicious circle served as the impetus to the Open Access (OA) journals initiative.

The idea behind OA journals is that peer-reviewed publications need not be solely in the for-profit publishing model; the same editorial rigor could apply for publications that have no subscription fees. Just as with traditional scholarly journals, the OA journal publishers maintain their scholarly reputation, articles are peer-reviewed, and all articles are indexed and permanently archived. The difference with the OA model is that the publisher—often a university, professional society, or government agency—brings in revenue through channels other than subscription fees. The most well-known revenue model is to charge authors a fee, ranging from several hundred dollars to several thousand. Often, the author would simply build the cost of the submission fee into the grant or other funding proposal; if an author is unable to pay the submission fee, most OA publishers will waive the fee. Many OA publishers use other methods to generate revenue, including subsidies from government agencies, universities, libraries, foundations, and similar institutions. Some fund their operations with membership fees, advertising, a premium print edition, or other commercial products.

However they get funded, they pose a serious threat to the traditional subscription-based publishing model. As the influence and impact of open access journals increase, it will be even more important for info-entrepreneurs to include these sources in our online research. The Public Library of Science (www.plos.org) was one of the first organizations to seriously challenge the scientific and medical publishing community with its launch of *PLoS Biology* in 2003 and *PLoS Medicine* in 2004.

One of the challenges of searching OA journals is that they are not yet as well-indexed in the professional online services and, as of late 2009, there was no aggregator site that allowed searching many publishers' OA content simultaneously. PubMed Central (www.pubmedcentral.nih.gov), an arm of the U.S. National

Institutes of Health, maintains an archive of a number of OA publications and allows searching multiple OA journals simultaneously.

The Directory of Open Access Journals (www.doaj.org) is one effort to identify and index as many high-quality OA journals as possible. It includes brief descriptions of thousands of OA journals, as well as article-level indexing for some journals. This means that, at the least, you can use DOAJ to identify OA journals on a topic, and you can search the full text of a subset of the DOAJ journals.

Another tool for identifying OA resources is the Open Access Directory wiki (oad.simmons.edu). This publicly maintained wiki includes information on repositories of OA documents organized by discipline, databases of OA data, and a wealth of information for and by the OA community.

Government Databases

National, regional, and local government agencies are making their information available on the web. Much of this information is in structured databases, meaning that the information probably will not show up in a search engine's results. Because of the complexity of the available information and the wide range of formats and uses of the data, there is nothing even approaching a unified search tool for government information. The U.S. federal government is making efforts to aggregate access to all of its content through a few portals. Your best option is often to determine which agency is involved in regulating, measuring, or studying your topic, and then drill down into that agency's website for more information. Government agencies are sometimes a good starting point for research in an unfamiliar area because they generally include introductory or background information for the general public in addition to material for their specific audience. The following are examples of a few government databases of use to many info-entrepreneurs.

EDGAR

Edgar? Who's Edgar? The U.S. Securities and Exchange Commission (SEC) requires that all publicly traded companies file their financial and stock-related reports electronically through EDGAR, the Electronic Data Gathering, Analysis, and Retrieval system. You can search and retrieve EDGAR files at no charge through the SEC's website (edgar.sec.gov). As the SEC is moving toward requiring more detailed information in a format that allows for downloading and further analysis, researchers have access to some powerful tools for mining the financial reports that companies provide to the SEC. Several commercial sites sell access to the same EDGAR files, but with sophisticated search, monitoring and display options not available at the free SEC site.

STAT-USA

The U.S. Department of Commerce is charged with encouraging trade, both within the U.S. and internationally. To that end, it has created a rich collection of international trade information, called STAT-USA (www.stat-usa.gov). Most of the research-related material is in STAT-USA's National Trade Data Bank, which includes Market Research Reports, Best Market Reports, and similar material. These reports can be 20 or 30 pages long and are written by trade experts within the country in question. The reports tend to be quite specific—the telecommunications industry in Chile, the civil aviation industry in Austria, or the best markets for pollution control equipment worldwide. Unlike most government information sources, the National Trade Data Bank is not free; there is a fee to download reports, but it is a relatively modest $200 a year. You can also purchase a one-day pass to STAT-USA for $25.

Europa

The European Union publishes a wide range of reports, official documents, newsletters, procurement databases, and statistics through its portal, Europa (www.europa. eu). Not only is most of the material available online—either at no charge or for sale through its store—but much of the content is available in multiple languages. Given the range of information formats and languages, finding what you need within the Europa site can be challenging. On the other hand, this is one place to find data about and from all the countries within the European Union. Fortunately, Europa maintains the Europe Direct Contact Centre, staffed with multilingual staff whose job it is to help the public navigate the sometimes complex workings of the EU.

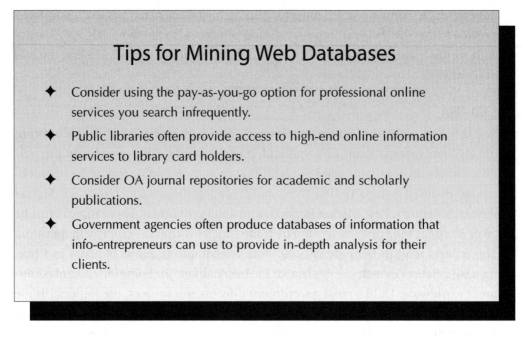

Tips for Mining Web Databases

✦ Consider using the pay-as-you-go option for professional online services you search infrequently.

✦ Public libraries often provide access to high-end online information services to library card holders.

✦ Consider OA journal repositories for academic and scholarly publications.

✦ Government agencies often produce databases of information that info-entrepreneurs can use to provide in-depth analysis for their clients.

Chapter 34

Professional Online Services

Long before the web, other vast electronic warehouses of valuable information were available to anyone with a subscription and the patience to learn the arcane command language involved. I remember taking a class in online research when I was working on my master's degree in library science in 1980. We learned how to log on to Dialog (see later in this chapter for a description of each of the major online services); once we had logged on, the system responded with simply a question mark: "?". Not very user-friendly, I would say. And it only got worse; a search request would look something like this: *s pfizer/ti and (eu or european()union)*.

A lot has changed since those heady days when we librarians-in-training were delighted with the novelty of electronic access to material that previously could only be found in printed indexes. But some things have not changed. The value-added online services still charge for access, and they still require somewhat arcane search syntax, at least compared to the simplicity of a web search engine. They also still offer an array of information you cannot find anywhere else—not on the web and often not even in printed sources.

This chapter is by no means a substitute for the training offered by the professional online services themselves and for the real-world experience of using them on a regular basis. Use this chapter as a tool to help determine which online services you should focus on. Then expect to spend at least six months learning how to make the best use of them and honing your search skills. Plan to spend several hundred dollars each month in the process of becoming proficient; this is probably not an expense you can bill back to clients, at least not in its entirety. Remember when you were learning how to drive a car? You might have learned by taking a driver's education class, or your parents took you out to a vacant parking lot and showed you how to safely handle two tons of machinery. However you learned, it took a while before you could be trusted to drive your grandmother to the store or your date to a movie. Of course, the consequences of flubbing an online search are inconsequential when compared to what an inexperienced driver can do to a car, but both require a commitment of time and money (insurance and gas on the one hand, per-search and per-document charges on the other).

"This Costs How Much?!?"

Let's talk about the cost first because that is what first-time users of any professional online service notice right away. Obviously, the price of online searches will vary, depending on the source you are using and whether you are downloading a single article or 50 market research reports. To give you a rough idea of the charges you will incur, expect to pay $10 or $20 for a few articles on a topic, $350 or $400 for the information required to compile a company profile, and $20 or $30 per page for market research or investment analysts' reports.

Each vendor has its own set of pricing plans, some of which are more attractive than others to the independent info pro. In general, we info pros look for subscriptions that do not impose a monthly minimum fee but charge only for actual use. Most online services offer so-called transaction pricing, based on some combination of the amount of time you are online, the number of records you view on the screen or download, the number of searches you run, and the complexity of those searches. Needless to say, most independent info pros gravitate to the plans that are the most straightforward and predictable. Factiva, for example, does not charge for the time you spend online or the number of searches you run; you just pay for each article you download, period. You cannot get much simpler than that.

Cheaper by the Dozen?

When I signed up at a local health club, I was given two options: I could pay $7 for each visit, or I could pay $50 a month for unlimited use. I knew I would be going at least two or three times a week (or at least that was my intention) so I figured that I would be better off with the flat monthly fee. However, the economics of saving money by buying unlimited access to a service don't apply to online services, at least for the average independent info pro. As I mentioned earlier, most of the professional online services offer some form of transaction-based pricing—at full retail price, of course—as well as a discounted rate if you commit to spending a certain amount every month. Most of these flat-fee arrangements allow you to search and download as much content as you want, with the proviso that if your usage winds up being much higher than expected, the fee will be adjusted higher. It sounds tempting; you can do $2,000 worth of searches, bill your clients the full retail price, and only pay your flat $1,000 for the month. That's a cool $1,000 profit, isn't it? Well, it is for that month, but what about the months when you can only bill out $500 to your clients and you are still stuck with that $1,000 invoice? Ouch!

My general rule is that anything that requires a minimum payment of $100 or more a month is a gamble, at least until I have used the online service for a year on a transaction-priced basis, and my experience shows that I will consistently incur at least that much billable usage every month. Otherwise, I opt for the undiscounted rate on a pay-as-you-go contract. Sure, I miss out on the windfall those months when I use the service more than usual, but I also avoid having to pay a high fixed cost that I cannot bill out during months when my workload is lighter.

That said, sometimes a flat-fee contract makes sense. Alex Kramer, owner of Kramer Research, was offered unlimited access to one of the major online services for $400 a month. She took that offer in a heartbeat, knowing that (1) her usage was at least half that amount already, (2) she could promote her online research business more aggressively to build up usage, and (3) the monthly fee was low enough for her to absorb as overhead during those months when she did not do many online searches. Alex has been in business for many years and can anticipate her usage and her cash flow needs pretty well, so this was a smart decision. But if you are just starting out, I would caution you against signing a flat fee contract until you have a better handle on your average usage. A new independent info pro simply does not need another fixed expense that must be paid every month, regardless of your usage.

The Big Three (Plus a Few)

There are three major online services in the U.S. market: Dialog, Factiva, and LexisNexis. All three are available in most of the world, either directly or through third-party marketers, and additional professional online services exist that are particularly competitive in specific regions of the world. This section will give you a brief introduction to the big three, along with some of the other major players in the value-added online arena. Members of the Association of Independent Information Professionals (AIIP; www.aiip.org) are eligible for discounts and the waiving of monthly fees or minimums on many of these online services.

Dialog

www.dialog.com

Description: Dialog has rightly been called the supermarket of online services; the combined breadth, depth, and scope of its databases are arguably the best in the business, particularly for independent info pros. Now part of ProQuest, Dialog gives users access in one online service to the full text of articles from a wide range of sources, including newspapers, business, and marketing literature; patent and trademark data; industry and company directories from around the world; chemical structure databases; summaries of articles from obscure medical, science, and technology publications; and even a database of tables and charts extracted from articles. Just about the only type of information Dialog lacks is legal material such as case law and statutes.

Pricing: In addition to its usual flat-fee subscription pricing, Dialog offers two transaction pricing options: One is based on how long you spend connected to the system plus per-record charges for every item you display, download, or print; the other is based on the amount of system resources required to process each command you enter, plus per-record charges. Both plans also involve a $200/year Dialog Services fee and a $16/hour "communications charge"; the annual fee is waived for AIIP members.

Dialog also offers stripped-down access to some of its databases with a strictly output-based pricing plan; there is no fee to search or review titles of retrieved records, and each record costs more to download than in DialogWeb.

Ease of use: Dialog offers a choice of user interfaces and pricing plans for various customer groups. The primary way to search Dialog is through DialogWeb (www.dialogweb.com), which lets you directly search any combination of Dialog's 600-plus files. Users have a choice of "Guided Search" or "Command Search"; the former provides search forms to fill out and that execute a search without the need to learn Dialog's search syntax. However, users lose much of the power of Dialog with Guided Search, as you cannot construct detailed searches, combine sets of results together, or perform any of the data-mining that you can do with Command Search.

Unlike most of its competitors, Dialog also offers specialized software to get more out of your searching. You can download the software, DialogLink, from the Dialog website (support.dialog.com/dialoglink). This software automatically saves the entire transcript of a search, lets you compose search queries offline to save money in connect-time charges, and makes navigation through Dialog somewhat easier. Report templates can let users take the results of a search, import the data into a spreadsheet, and generate charts or graphs to make the result more compelling.

Another way to search Dialog is through Dialog1 (www.dialog1.com). This requires a regular subscription to Dialog, but enables you to search files that you are not familiar with by using search forms that allow you to run reasonably sophisticated searches without having to learn the search syntax or even know which files to search. The pricing on Dialog1 is different than the traditional transaction pricing; unlike the rest of the Dialog offerings, Dialog1 does not charge for searching. Instead, users pay a higher per-article rate than with the regular Dialog service. Keep in mind that searching with Dialog1 is not equivalent to the DialogWeb alternative. Users are searching a predetermined set of files and cannot tweak the underlying search strategy embedded in the search forms. Use Dialog1 for tangential searches, but not for key aspects of your research. (If your project requires searching in files that you are not proficient in, consider subcontracting the work to a more experienced Dialog searcher.)

In order to get the most from your Dialog subscription, you need to develop a familiarity with the Dialog search syntax, which has not changed much in the last 30 years and is more arcane than most. Users have an astounding array of power search tools and information sources at their disposal, but this is a system that cannot be mastered quickly. You can download an extensive user manual, Successful Searching on Dialog Command Language (support.dialog.com/searchaids/success).

Training and support: Dialog offers a number of self-paced tutorials, web-based and classroom training, and an extensive collection of training workbooks, along with training passwords that let you try out your new search tools in a test database without incurring any charges. See support.dialog.com/training for more information on the various Dialog training options. Dialog maintains an information and professional development program for professional researchers, called Quantum[2], which you can tap into at quantum.dialog.com.

Factiva

www.factiva.com

Description: Factiva is owned by Dow Jones, one of the leading business information providers. As you would expect from its parentage, Factiva is strongest in business-related information sources. It offers an impressive array of publications, and it is particularly good for non-U.S. business-related sources. Factiva also offers what it calls Intelligent Indexing across all its content. That means that, regardless of the origin of the information, you can look for articles on a specific topic or about a particular company, using standardized terms. Factiva is weak in coverage beyond the business press and news sources; you won't find specialized directories, hierarchical indexing of medical subject terms, or intellectual property resources here.

Pricing: Factiva has by far the simplest transaction-based pricing plan. Users pay $69 a year for the annual service fee (waived for AIIP members) and $2.95 for each article they download.

Ease of use: This is a relatively easy-to-use online service. It doesn't have some of the specialized search tools that are available on Dialog (see the discussion later on Power Tools), but the search syntax is fairly intuitive. The fact that you incur no charges for searching means that you have more freedom to noodle around, try different search strategies, and fine-tune your search until you are happy with the results, all free of charge.

Training: Factiva offers scheduled online training sessions, web-based tutorials, quick-reference cards for specific types of searches and in-depth user guides. Its InfoPro Alliance program (www.factiva.com/infopro) includes webinars, quick search tips, case studies, white papers, and presentations of interest to info pros.

LexisNexis

www.lexisnexis.com

Description: Along with Dialog, LexisNexis is one of the oldest of the professional online services. It began as a resource for lawyers, offering full-text court decisions, and branched out to include the full text of laws and regulations, public records, and related material. What began as Lexis eventually came to include Nexis—an extensive collection of full-text and summarized articles from a wide range of sources. Because its original user base consisted of people who were not trained info pros, its search syntax and tools are more intuitive than those of some other online systems. You can subscribe to Lexis.com, Nexis.com, or both.

Pricing: Of the big three, LexisNexis has the murkiest pricing plans. Users can choose among several options including a per-search charge or a connect-time charge, plus output costs. It's difficult to ascertain the cost of a search ahead of time because detailed pricing is not readily available. If you expect to be using LexisNexis frequently, this is one online service that should be set up as a flat-fee account. In this instance, the predictability of the price is probably worth more than having to pay a monthly fee that you may not recoup.

Ease of use: LexisNexis manages to combine power search features with a very intuitive interface. Info pros who are not familiar with the service can use the Quick Search option, and experienced info pros can tap into the more advanced alternatives. The fill-in-the-forms interface helps users build searches in areas that they are not familiar with.

Training: LexisNexis enjoys a reputation for having the most in-depth customer support service among the professional online services. Having trouble constructing a search that gets you what you want? Call the customer support desk and a search professional will test different search strategies with you and send you the most effective search construction. LexisNexis' portal for info pros, LexisNexis InfoPro, is accessible at law.lexisnexis.com/infopro and offers training materials, case studies, professional development resources, and other support material.

The Best of the Rest

DataStar (www.datastarweb.com) is owned by ProQuest, the same company that owns Dialog. DataStar's strengths are in its coverage of European sources—published articles, company directories, and financial information—and the biomedical and pharmaceutical industries. Its web interface is simple to use, and an advanced user option is also available. Costs include a monthly Dialog Services Fee of $18 (waived for AIIP members). Search charges are based on how long you are connected to each database, plus a fee for each item displayed, downloaded, or printed.

Questel (www.questel.orbit.com) focuses on intellectual property (patents and trademarks) information from around the world. It is not a simple system to learn and, given that much of its content is in complex, highly structured databases, it is not for the faint of heart. If you intend to specialize in intellectual property research, this is a must-have online service; otherwise, you can access most of the databases you will need through other, simpler online systems. Prices include an annual service fee of several hundred dollars and transaction charges based on connect time plus output fees.

Westlaw (www.westlaw.com) is LexisNexis' main competitor in the legal research arena. In addition to offering full-text case law and legislative and administrative material, Westlaw also provides business information, although this is not its focus. Its user interface is reasonably easy to use, and most of its power search tools are accessible with pull-down menus. Pricing is negotiated separately for each subscriber with flat-fee subscriptions the norm.

Power Tools

Not only do the value-added online services provide access to material that you cannot find elsewhere, they also offer tools for fine tuning your search and analyzing search results. Each professional online service has a different suite of power tools; the following is a list of features to look for when you are evaluating which services to subscribe to:

- Truncation: Search for all words that begin with a specified word stem. You should be able to indicate single-character truncation (*calendar** will retrieve pages with the word calendar or calendars), multiple-character truncation (*humid**** will retrieve pages with the word humid or the word humidity), and internal truncation (*wom#n*).

- Nested logic: Construct a complex search with a combination of Boolean ANDs and ORs (*[alumina or [[aluminium or aluminum] adj oxide] and tape*).

- Atleast*N*: Require that a search term appear at least N times within the document (*atleast5 nicotine*).

- Field searches: Limit the search to specific portions of the document, such as title, author, lead paragraph, or source (*headline[color or colour]*).

- Boolean and natural language searches: Select either Boolean logic (AND, OR, NOT) or a "fuzzy" search algorithm that looks for close as well as exact matches (*global warming polar Europe* would retrieve articles that contain most or all of these words).

- Date and relevance ranking: Sort the results of a search either by date with the most current items first or by relevance with the items calculated to be the best matches first.

Dialog also has a number of unique specialized tools including RANK, which analyzes the number of times an author's name, patent assignee, journal title, or subject term appears in the search results, and MAP, which takes the results of one search, extracts key terms, and then runs a new search using those extracted key terms.

Make a habit of reading the help files and advanced search screen tips when you search a professional online service. Remember, you are paying good money to use the system, and you might as well get maximum search power out of it.

Controlling Searches With Controlled Vocabulary

Many database records in the professional online services consist of more than the summary or full-text articles; they also include subject words and metatags that have been added to improve the relevance and completeness of search results. For example, an article on the health benefits of walking as a form of exercise may have appended the indexing phrase "walking—health aspects." Other articles on this same topic will also be indexed "walking—health aspects." Database producers, and in some cases the online services themselves, have built detailed controlled vocabularies—that is, indexes of words and phrases used consistently to describe particular topics and concepts. These indexing terms can make your search much more focused and efficient. They allow you to fine tune what might otherwise be an overly broad query by searching for the controlled vocabulary terms in addition to whatever other words you think might appear in the article itself. So, for example, a search using the subject phrase "walking—health aspects" may give you more focused results than a search for the words "walking" and "health" anywhere in the text of articles. Many specialized databases also use controlled vocabularies; patent databases index each patent record by a complex classification scheme, company financial records are indexed by industry code, and so on. Check the database and system documentation for controlled vocabulary or thesaurus terms that may help you improve your search results.

Depending on the type of material it contains, a database may offer several types of indexing. Many assign subject words that describe the central focus of the article

(Agricultural Machinery or Intranet Portals). Some include additional subject terms that describe the type or format of the article or the way the subject is treated (Interview or Industry Survey). Some use codes to identify companies discussed in the article; these are particularly useful for company names that are frequently misspelled (Siemens), that involve odd punctuation (E*Trade), or that are inconsistently identified (W.R. Grace/WR Grace/Grace).

There are also hierarchical classification systems that, while somewhat complex, can be tremendous tools for expanding or refining a search. Examples of hierarchical systems, in which there are broader and narrower concepts, include:

> NAICS and SIC codes, used to describe types of businesses
>> 62: Health Care & Social Assistance
>>> 621: Ambulatory Health Care
>>>> 6214: Outpatient Care Centers

> MeSH medical subject headings
>> A07: Cardiovascular System
>>> A07.231: Blood Vessels
>>>> A07.231.611: Retinal Vessels

These are often called "cascading" codes; you can select articles that have a very narrow focus (MeSH code A07.231.611.647 for Retinal Arteries), or you can select all articles that discuss the cardiovascular system (MeSH code A07), which will include all articles indexed with any MeSH code that starts with A07. If you frequently use a database that includes complex codes, buy the print thesaurus or set a bookmark on your browser to the online version.

Tracking Your Costs

All three of the major online services let you assign a client name or number to each search session; this information will appear in the invoice, so you can track expenses for the online research component of any given project. Usually, this feature is called the "Subaccount" or "Client Billing" code. This is a useful tool because independent info pros generally bill out all of their research-related expenses.

Although you can wait to bill your clients until you receive your invoice and see how much you have spent online for each project, this often is not a practical option. Many clients want to be billed as soon as the project is completed, and you probably also prefer to bill them sooner rather than later. Dialog displays the total cost of a search when you log off, and both Factiva and LexisNexis let you check your invoice online.

When in Doubt, Subcontract Out

As I noted at the beginning of this chapter, the professional online services are expensive and more complex than, say, a web search engine. On the other hand, they offer powerful search features and deep resources of information not available on the web. If you are already a skilled searcher on one or more of these online services, these tremendously powerful tools will greatly expand the scope of your research offerings. If, on the other hand, you are not an experienced searcher or you get a project that requires the use of a professional online service on which you are not proficient, consider subcontracting that aspect of the research to a fellow independent info pro who is an expert. See Chapter 16, Subcontracting, or I'll Scratch Your Back If You Scratch Mine, for all you need to know about farming out research to a colleague. Given the high cost of a poorly done online search—in terms of both direct costs and information not found—subcontracting is often the best option for both you and your client.

Tips for Using the Professional Online Services

- ◆ Learn the power search tools of the online services and use the Advanced or Command Search option.
- ◆ Avoid flat-fee contracts where practical; transaction-based contracts help control cash flow.
- ◆ Stay up-to-date on pricing plans and changes in vendor rates.
- ◆ Use controlled vocabulary searches when appropriate.
- ◆ Subcontract online research if you are not an expert on a topic.

Chapter 35

Telephone Research

Info pros tend to think of all the information resources available online—on the web, in the professional online services, and in the specialized, niche databases—but we sometimes forget that the best information may not exist in any permanent medium at all. If you need information on what motivates people to purchase hole saws, the names of the most influential chiropractors in St. Louis, or a list of the minority-owned businesses that bid on a specific project, you are not going to have much luck online. These were all real-life research projects, and the answers were all found by interviewing real, live experts.

Telephone research is not for everyone. It takes persistence, creativity, patience, and great interviewing skills—a set of talents that many independent info pros do not possess. When I talk about phone research, I am not thinking about simple market surveys in which the interviewer is given a list of phone numbers to call and a script of questions to ask. That type of research doesn't offer any added value, and companies generally pay low wages to the people who conduct such interviews. Rather, telephone research as I discuss it in this chapter involves getting up to speed on an issue, identifying the key players, conducting in-depth interviews, analyzing the results, and writing up your results and conclusions.

If, after reading this chapter, you think that you would like to specialize in telephone research or add it to the mix of services you offer, I recommend *Super Searchers Go to the Source* by Risa Sacks (Information Today, Inc., 2002). This is a great collection of interviews with 12 experts in primary research, including a number of phone researchers, in which you can learn about the challenges and joys of this kind of information business. Although somewhat dated, most of the challenges and techniques they discuss still hold true. Even if you do not focus on telephone research exclusively, it is a useful skill to add to your information arsenal. Phone research can often help you provide a more complete information package, filling in the missing pieces you cannot get online.

What's Involved in Phone Research?

The principle behind phone research is that you often have to gather more than just the facts. After you have read the articles, reviewed the market research reports, and gone through the annual reports, you need to dig deeper and figure out causes, motivations, and underlying factors. Why is this industry in such turmoil? What is the executive of this company most likely to do in the face of this new situation? How did this company get where it is today? What was its strategy? In addition to digging up soft information like this, phone research is great for updating published statistics and covering just-breaking developments.

There are several types of telephone research. One project I was involved in had to do with how a typical toddler spends his day. How much time does he spend watching TV, eating, playing by himself, playing with others, napping, and so on? In addition to a good deal of online research, we had to identify parents who could describe how their toddlers spent their day. This kind of specific, anecdotal information-gathering lends itself well to telephone research. Another type of phone research involves digging up information so specialized that very little has been written about it—for example, the market opportunities for a specific type of carbide-tipped blade. And sometimes telephone interviews are used to follow up on a quote you have found in an article to discover what else the quoted expert has to say on the topic.

Offering telephone research services usually involves working as a subcontractor a fair amount of the time. A significant portion of your work may come from other independent info pros and from librarians, because not many people can do phone research well and most are happy to subcontract to an expert. You will need to cultivate clients who understand and value telephone researchers; these include market research companies, competitive intelligence departments within organizations, and public relations firms.

Characteristics of a Good Phone Researcher

Every independent info pro has a telephone, but not every info pro can be a successful telephone researcher. Here is a list of the characteristics shared by the best telephone researchers:

- Take a real interest in people. You have to be compulsive about asking "why," and you have to really want to learn the answer.

- Have the tenacity of a bulldog. It is often a challenge to get past the gatekeepers and voice mail and actually talk to the person you are trying to reach. You have to persevere and think creatively about how to get through the obstacles. That might mean calling early in the morning or during lunchtime.

- Don't get discouraged. You have to be able to hear "no" and keep on going, always assuming that you will eventually find someone who will tell you what you need to know. All telephone researchers have days when they just don't want to talk to anyone, or they feel they did a horrible job on their last interview. Some phone calls are hard to make, and some interviews go badly for whatever reason. You just have to pick yourself up and move on.

- Keep your schedule flexible. You have to call people when it is convenient for them to talk. If your target is five time zones away, you may have to set your alarm for 5 AM or be willing to call at 10 PM.

- Be insatiably curious. To do phone research well, you must be able to get completely immersed in an obscure topic. You have to enjoy the process itself, the thrill of the hunt, and the search for the one person in the world who perhaps knows everything you need to learn about this topic.

- Be polite and courteous. You are asking a favor when you call to interview someone, and they do not have to talk to you. Treat everyone you speak to with respect, whether it is the CEO, the receptionist, or the temp who is taking calls while someone is out sick. Try to make a personal connection with everyone you talk to. The person who answers the phone can either hang up or put you in touch with the ideal contact; a lot depends on how you treat that person.

- Listen carefully. Part of successful telephone interviewing lies in the ability to wait for people to say something interesting or useful. If you are patient, you will often get referrals to other sources that are vital to your research but hard to find—obscure websites, discussion lists, books, reports, other people you should talk to, and so on.

- Develop your online research skills as well as expertise in phone research. Almost every phone project involves a good deal of preliminary research—identifying candidates to interview, getting up to speed on an unfamiliar industry or topic, drilling down through company websites to see who is responsible for the product you are interested in, and finding out what a prospective interviewee has written already. You will either have to do this research yourself or subcontract it to an expert online searcher before you can begin the telephone phase of the project.

- Hone your writing ability. Not only must you be a good listener, you also have to write well. The report that you provide to your client will be more than just a transcript of your interviews; it should include a summary of what you learned, an analysis of the key points and issues revealed in the interviews, leads on other areas of research, and so on.

For more in-depth discussion of each of these characteristics—straight from some of the best telephone researchers in the industry—see *Super Searchers Go to the Source*, which I described earlier in this chapter.

Challenges of Telephone Research

Assuming you have the personality and skill set necessary, phone work is one of the easier segments of the independent info profession to break into. You don't need training and years of experience searching the professional online services. You don't need a private investigator's license or nearby access to a world-class library. And because it is a type of research that many people find difficult or less attractive because it is not online, you may find less competition than in some other fields of research. Of course, the usefulness of telephone research is less well recognized than that of online and web research so your marketing efforts may take longer to pay off. Clients often think about bringing in an expert online searcher, but few people realize how much information never gets published at all.

Telephone research poses some unique challenges. For starters, you only have one chance with any individual contact; if you fumble an interview, you cannot go back and try it again later. That means that you need to be prepared and energized for every phone call. Having an "off" day is not an option. In addition, telephone research usually can only be conducted during the normal business hours of the person you are calling. As a result, you are limited in the amount of projects you can take on at one time. Unlike online researchers, who can always squeeze in one more project over the weekend if need be, telephone researchers must work when their subjects work. And telephone work during holiday seasons and peak summer vacation periods is challenging. Your contacts are less likely to be in the office and less likely to be focused on work. (On the other hand, you may be able to get past gatekeepers more easily during these times because they also go on vacation.)

Telephone research is by its nature time-consuming. Even a couple of 10-minute interviews can easily take two or three hours, once you factor in time to prepare for the interviews, identify the people to interview, schedule the interviews, and write up your results. You have to reconcile yourself to losing some jobs when clients need phone work done but have limited budgets and do not realize how much is involved in doing this kind of research.

Successful Telephone Interviews

Telephone research differs from other types of research in that so much depends on human interactions. If you are having a bad day or you catch your interview subject on a bad day, that's it. Online services do not care one way or the other how you are feeling. The computer responds just the same whether you are polite or rude. Since phone research is such a high-touch business, your success depends on your skill in getting each interview right the first time. Here are some suggestions from expert telephone researchers, many of whom were interviewed in *Super Searchers Go to the Source*, on how to succeed in this line of work:

- Know how to estimate. Figure that the total project will take four to five times longer than you expect to spend on the actual interviews. So a one-hour interview could take five hours altogether, including the time to identify the right person to talk to, make several calls before you get that person on the phone, conduct the interview, and write up the results. Allow extra time for developing your discussion guide or list of questions and for a summary and final analysis of the results. Often, the write-up and analysis will take up 50 percent of the total time in a project. And remember, when planning your workflow and negotiating a deadline with your client, this process will stretch out over several days. Even if you are only doing five interviews, it is very unlikely that you will reach all five people on the same day—and you may have to make 20 or 30 calls to identify the right five people.

- Do your homework. Before you make any calls, educate yourself about the subject matter. Learn the buzzwords and acronyms used by people in the industry. You do not want to spend an expert's valuable time asking questions that you could easily find answers to yourself; you want to use the interview to gather information that cannot be found elsewhere. If you are planning to call a published expert, learn beforehand what that person has said or written on the topic.

- Think sideways. Rather than focusing specifically on where to find the information, think about who could answer your question. Who cares about this topic and might be willing to talk to you? Good sources for experts, or referrals to experts, include trade or professional associations, government agencies, directories, industry publications, educational institutions, nonprofit organizations, and even the exhibitor and speaker rosters for trade shows and conferences. And think about people you know in your nonwork life who might be helpful. I have called family members for projects, as well as people I have known for years through online discussion forums (but have never met face-to-face), and even someone with whom I had trained for a marathon.

- Have something to trade. See what you can offer your interviewees in exchange for their thoughts and comments. Will your client allow you to send an anonymized version of the summary report to a helpful contact? Can you offer a summary (over the phone) of what you have learned from other interviews?

- Start with your least important or low-stakes interviewee, and work your way up. If you are going to ask a dumb question or flail around, you want to do that during a less-crucial interview. For that matter, it is often helpful to identify someone with a general knowledge of the topic to talk to first. Try to save your most important interview for later in the process, when you are knowledgeable about the subject, you know what issues are particularly difficult or important, and you are comfortable in your approach.

- Always ask for referrals. An experienced telephone researcher once said, "Never, ever leave somebody without asking for a referral. And when you call the next person, say that you were recommended by the previous person. People respond so well to recommended calls." Always ask questions: "Who else could help me with this? Whom would you suggest I talk with? Do you know anyone else who is an expert on this topic? Where else would you suggest I look?"

- Prompt for more. It is useful to ask at the end of the interview: "Is there anything important that I didn't ask?" or "Is there anything else that you'd like to tell me?"

- Try to verify independently whatever someone tells you. Watch for bias in your interviews, particularly if you hear something from one interviewee that contradicts what all your other interviewees have said. Unlike published information, which an editor ensures that the writing passes a professional standard, what you learn in a phone interview has not been vetted by a neutral party. If you hear something that just doesn't sound right, be sure to question it or at least flag it in your report to the client.

- Ask one question at a time. Multiple or complex questions confuse and frustrate interviewees and make it harder to concentrate on the key information you are trying to find. Make sure that your questions are not "leading" so that you don't bias the responses you get.

- Stay focused. Before you make any phone calls, write up a paragraph spelling out what you are looking for and keep that in front of you during your interviews. On the other hand, be willing to go where the interview leads, within reason. Sometimes the best information is what you did not think to ask or expect to find. That is the serendipity factor of telephone research.

- Enlist the help of whoever answers the phone. Despite your best efforts to find an appropriate contact beforehand, sometimes you have to call an organization and blindly ask for suggestions as to who to talk to. Ask questions like, "Who in your organization lives and breathes this topic?" Sometimes it helps to throw yourself at the mercy of the receptionist or secretary with a question such as, "I need your help; can you tell me who I can talk to about this?"

- Know when to stop. Telephone research often involves soft questions that don't have definite answers so it is hard to know when to quit. When most of your questions have been answered or you keep hearing the same information over again, that should serve as an indication that you are ready to wrap it up. If you keep hitting dead ends, or people tell you over and over that no one knows the answer to your question, rethink your strategy. Be willing to try an entirely different approach or to scale back your expectations of what you will be able to find. Keep a careful eye on your time and budget throughout the project. You have to be skilled at estimating costs and keeping track of your time as you proceed. Be sure to communicate with your client on an ongoing basis if what you are finding takes you in new directions or if something comes up that affects the time frame or budget. In one project I worked on, for example, we discovered midway through that many of the experts were at an industry conference in Beijing for the next 10 days. In any event, never exceed your time or budget without the express agreement of your client.

Telephone Research Ethics

If you provide telephone research, you will eventually get a call from a potential client who, when told that the information he wants is most likely too confidential to be disclosed, will respond, "Well, just lie and tell them you're a student writing a paper." You will have to figure out a tactful way to tell the prospect that you simply cannot do that.

The Association of Independent Information Professionals (AIIP; www.aiip.org) addresses this issue with its Code of Ethical Business Practice, which requires that members "uphold the profession's reputation for honesty, competence, and confidentiality." Of course, this does not mean that you are required to disclose the identity of your client; in fact, clients often use independent info pros because we provide anonymity. When you call a contact, you will introduce yourself and tell them the name of your company and that you are conducting research. If they ask for the name of your client, you can respond that your client has not authorized you to disclose that information. Surprisingly, many people are satisfied with this answer and, even though they don't know whom the information will go to, will agree to talk to you. Some clients, though, have no objection to your disclosing their names. Be sure to clarify the level of required confidentiality at the start of each project. If there is any doubt, err on the side of maintaining confidentiality.

The bottom line is to listen to your gut. Do not accept projects that you are not comfortable with or that you consider unethical. If you are not happy doing the work, you probably will not be able to provide professional-quality research anyway. If necessary, see if you can negotiate with your client to refocus the project on information that is available through legitimate sources. As Andrew Pollard said in *Super Searchers Go to the Source*, "Most information that's of value can be gathered from ordinary open sources and by open means."

Checklist for Telephone Researchers

✦ Be prepared. Conduct background research so you know the basics about the topic before you call.

✦ Put yourself in the right frame of mind. If you are truly interested in the people you interview, you will be able to learn much more from them.

✦ Stay focused and determined. Just because the last person refused to talk to you doesn't mean that you are stuck. Pick up the phone and make the next call.

✦ Remain unfailingly polite. As a telephone researcher, you are relying on people's generosity; no one owes you an interview.

✦ Keep within the bounds of the law and your personal ethics. Do not accept a job that you do not feel comfortable doing.

Chapter 36

Public Records Research

Public records research is a specialized field best suited for independent info pros who are detail-oriented, enjoy doing on-site research at courthouses and government agencies, and have good people skills. Unlike online research, there is no massive aggregated collection of sources or databases you can consult; public records work involves going directly to where the records are kept and just digging around. Public records research is more art than science so you need to learn how to be a good searcher through experience. No one has written a definitive how-to manual on public records research because the techniques used for one source are entirely different from those used for another. One courthouse may have its own internally built database to index court cases; another may have a purely manual filing and indexing system. One government agency might feed all its records into a fee-based online service, and another might require that all requests go through a clerk.

Before I go into more detail about public records research, I will note that I am not a lawyer, and I cannot tell you about the regulations that apply to public records research in your state or country. As an example of why this matters, in some states in the U.S., you are not permitted to disclose information about criminal cases if the person was not eventually convicted, whereas in other states this information is considered public. Be sure to talk with a lawyer who is familiar with public records work before you start offering this kind of research.

What Does a Public Records Researcher Do?

Public records research involves getting documents and other information from official sources. Those sources include:

- Courts: For information on court cases, tax liens, divorce filings, and other legal matters

- Government agencies: For documents that companies must file with regulatory agencies, reports and studies prepared by agencies, and documents generated by the agency that are available through the Freedom of Information Act or similar public-access requests

- Government records: For real estate deeds and property assessments; aircraft, car, and boat registrations; birth and death records; marriage licenses; and driver's license and occupational license information

- Government archives: For both published and unpublished material from government agencies

Some of this information is available online, through government websites or specialized online vendors. But much of it exists only in printed form and/or must be searched on-site at the courthouse or government agency office. Public records research is definitely hands-on research.

You might be surprised by the questions that can be answered using public records. Some of the more common types of research projects include:

- Pre-employment screening: Checking to see if a job applicant has a criminal record that she is not disclosing, whether any civil litigation or restraining orders have been filed against her, if she has made workers' compensation claims or filed for bankruptcy, whether she has the proper occupational licenses, and whether she really did graduate from the university she claims to have a degree from.

- Asset searching: Finding out what a person owns—real estate and other major assets such as cars, boats, and aircraft—as well as company owner-ship or significant stock holdings so that a divorced spouse or the victor in a court case can collect money owed.

- Environmental research: Tracking down which companies conducted operations at a particular site. When toxic waste sites must be cleaned up, there is a search for all the "potentially responsible parties" or PRPs. That means digging through archives and government records to discover all the companies that occupied the site—sometimes going back 100 years or more—in order to see which ones might be held responsible for the toxic waste.

- Executive due diligence: Verifying whether an executive is who he claims to be. This involves discovering whether a potential director or executive has been involved in any litigation; whether he has a criminal record; whether he is living within his means; the value of any property he owns; and what he has said in interviews, articles, and even in the social web.

- Corporate due diligence: Looking into a company that may be acquired or that a venture capitalist wants to fund to determine the company's assets, whether it has been sued, if there are any outstanding tax liens against it, and whether it is in good standing with the state or regional agencies that regulate corporations and industries.

- Competitive intelligence: Finding out about a corporate competitor. For example, to research how a particular manufacturing plant is configured, you might find an evacuation plan at the local fire department or filings with the government agency that regulates environmental safety and health. This may also involve tracking down former employees—through searches of online resumes, social networks, or online discussion forums— and interviewing them about their experience with the company.

- Labor union campaigns: Discovering financial information about a company and its management in order to determine executive compensation plans, company profitability, political campaign donations the company has made, who is accountable for corporate decisions, and so on.

- Opposition research: Investigating a political candidate, tracking down contributors to his campaign, learning his positions on issues over the years, confirming that the biographical information provided by the campaign is accurate, finding out his community activities, and so forth.

Is a Public Records Researcher a PI?

There are important distinctions between a public records researcher and a private investigator (PI). Many public records researchers also have PI licenses, and some PIs also do public records research. To further complicate the matter, not all jurisdictions define a PI the same way. In some U.S. states, for example, public records research is considered to be PI work; you can search public records databases, but you cannot tell your client about the results of your research without a PI license. Before you set yourself up as a public records researcher, check with your state or local licensing board to find out what is permitted.

The process for getting a PI license also varies from one jurisdiction to another. You may have to take a test or show that you have a certain number of years working under the supervision of a licensed PI or that you have attended continuing education courses. In some areas, you have to be bonded. Unfortunately, reciprocity among jurisdictions is the exception rather than the rule so you must check with every state or province in which you plan to conduct research to see what regulations apply.

Learning How to Research Public Records

As I mentioned earlier in this chapter, there are not any comprehensive user manuals or step-by-step guides to conducting public records research. That is because every government agency and courthouse has its own system for organizing its records and making them available. Unlike online researching or telephone interview skills, one region's system is not necessarily similar to that of another. You can learn the general concepts involved in public records research, but after that, it is a matter of discovering how each agency or court operates, how its information is organized, and how its online system, if any, works. Learning the craft of public records research also means knowing what the actual documents look like and contain. If you simply rely on online information sources, you only know about documents in the abstract. Digging around in the files themselves is the only way you will learn what you can expect, what to look for, and where the pitfalls lie in public records research.

Curiously, even the vocabulary is different from one jurisdiction to another. In most courts, you consult with the clerk of the court. But in Pennsylvania, this position is called Prothonotary. If you are looking for information on real estate, you might have to ask the clerk for grantor/grantee files, mortgager/mortgagee information, real property files, or land records, depending on where you are. Likewise, information on court cases might be listed on a docket sheet, a file folder, or the table of contents to a case file. Asking for a case file index in a court that uses the term docket sheets may get you nothing but a blank look from the person behind the desk.

Although more and more indexes of public records are being made available electronically, either through the originating government entity or a fee-based online service, an online public records search is by no means complete. It is a great way to develop leads—which must be verified by a hard copy of the original record—but you still have to go to the source for additional information and to search through files that were not included in the online source. And many jurisdictions load current records onto their databases but not information from five or 10 years ago, which in many cases can be just as useful as the more recent information.

More than in most types of research, it is critical to identify the gaps in coverage of the public records you are searching, especially when using online sources. Part of this comes with experience; you use the sources at a particular courthouse often enough, and you will remember that its indexes may only go back two years, for example. You also have to be persistent and verify every assumption you make. Ask the clerk how far back the information goes, ask whether there are other records stored elsewhere, and ask if there are other ways a record might be filed. This is another reason why public records research is primarily conducted on-site rather than over the phone or online; you have to verify the results and comprehensiveness of every search and that is very difficult to do if you are not there in person.

It might appear that public records research is one type of independent info pro business that you can learn on the job. It is true that, unlike telephone research in which you only have one chance to conduct a successful interview, you can go back to the same public records source several times if you don't find what you are looking for at first. And unlike the professional online services, public records searching does not require extensive training in Boolean logic, cascaded thesauri, and arcane search commands. However, you may incur significant out-of-pocket expenses such as photocopying charges and per-search fees for online public records databases, not to mention the wear and tear of driving 50 or 100 miles to an out-of-town courthouse, multiple times if necessary, to complete your work.

Challenges of Public Records Research

Public records research is one of the more challenging areas of specialization for independent info pros. It is not an exact science; you do the best you can and make sure that your clients do not have unrealistic expectations about how comprehensive a public records search can be. There is potential for errors throughout the research process, and you have to watch for and recognize gaps in coverage and errors in the indexes and databases. A clerk might tell you that records are not available when they are, information may be missing from a database, or the letters in a name may have been transposed by a data entry clerk. You try to think of all the possible ways you might locate what you are looking for, but the points of entry are limited. You are at the mercy of the way the index was set up for use, and the quality control imposed on the data by the court or government agency.

Public records research also involves a high level of client expectation management. You must help your clients understand that some things just cannot be done: You cannot get current personal bank account information, you cannot unseal a court file that has been sealed by a judge's order, and you cannot get a clerk to go to an off-site records storage facility to dig up a file for you just because your client needs it today. Clients who believe that "it's all on the web for free" have to be educated about the realities of finding public records, the vast majority of which are not on the web at all.

As a public records researcher, much of your work involves dealing with gatekeepers—the civil servants who staff the desks and who you must ask for help in locating documents or for copies. They all have rules to follow and, like you, they have good days and bad days. You will be dealing with them repeatedly so you must be courteous and professional. But you also have a client who wanted results today—and the clerk tells you that it will take three days to copy the file. If you maintain a good rapport, they will usually do what they can for you.

You have to watch carefully for name variations as well as outright errors. Jane Smith-Klein might be listed as Smith-Klein, Jane; Smith, Jane; Klein, Jane Smith; or Smithklein, Jane. Joe St. James could be indexed under St. James or Saint James or simply James. In most public records systems, each of these alternative names has to be searched separately. Some public records researchers charge by the total number of names searched rather than by the hour. If you are searching a printed index, or in a small town where there just are not that many places to look, the by-name approach can be reasonably cost-effective. But that kind of pricing also encourages the client (and the researcher) to skimp on the number of alternative names that might be checked. And that may leave your results incomplete and compromise your research efforts.

Sometimes, the information you want can only be released after you have made a request under the Freedom of Information Act or a local public records access law. That means that it could take months to get the information … or to be turned down. These types of projects require persistence; you might be able to get the information if you ask again, or reword the request, or appeal the decision. And during the entire process, your client may be tapping her fingers on her desk, wondering why it is taking you so long to find one simple document.

Public records researchers have to be very detail-oriented because it is all about following leads, making sure you do not miss anything. It can be tedious. You also have to be efficient because the public offices are only open certain hours, and your client is paying you to travel there. You need to get as much done as you can during a single trip.

Making your added value visible to your clients is at least as important in public records research as in other types of information services. You need to distinguish yourself from court records retrievers or court runners, relatively low-paid workers—essentially clerical support—who go to courthouses, copy docket sheets, and deliver them to a professional to review and decide which individual files to order. Lynn Peterson, owner of PFC Information Services, makes the distinction this way:

> I rarely go to the courthouse myself; I rely on a network of runners to go out to the various courthouses. I direct them, I tell them what I need, or I may make them go out several times—obtaining the docket sheet on the first trip, so that I can determine which documents I want copies of for my review. There is a world of difference between a court runner who goes out and grabs copies or checks the case index, and a public records researcher. It is similar to the distinction between a low-level clerk who shelves books at the library and a research librarian.

It is important to write up your report detailing the research you did, all the name variations you tried, the techniques you used, and what you found and didn't find. Documenting your efforts is even more important than with other types of research. Not only must you distinguish your services from those of a court runner, but, because what you deliver might contain very little actual material in relation to what you are charging, your client has to know all you did on his behalf.

Your search strategies may not be obvious by looking at the deliverable, particularly because in public records work you deliver only exact matches. In regular online research, you are often looking for information on a subject or industry. That means that even if you do not find anything exactly on point, you can include information that is close to what your client wants. For example, if you are researching the market for ice-cream parlors, you are bound to find relevant data. On the other hand, if your client needs information specifically on Joe's Scoop Shop in Missoula, Montana—who owns it, whether there are any outstanding liens, what other companies Joe owns—you cannot send her information on related companies; you either find information on Joe's or you don't.

Ethical and Legal Issues

Public records researching involves some unique ethical and legal concerns. For starters, as I mentioned at the beginning of this chapter, you must check with your local government to find out what aspects of public records research, if any, might be regulated or restricted to licensed private investigators.

One area of research that has been getting attention from law enforcement is what is called "pretext calling"—using deception to get information on an individual's bank account balance, stock portfolio, or other personal data. This type of information, unless disclosed in a divorce settlement or other legal filing, is considered off-limits; any independent info pro who promises to provide such information is waving a red flag in front of law enforcement.

Beyond the legal restrictions, there are types of research that some independent info pros simply do not want to tackle. The research itself is not illegal; public records are "pure" information in the sense that they are available to anyone who looks for them. But some public records researchers choose not to do certain kinds of research, such as domestic cases (divorces, child custody, tracking down an old boyfriend), identifying birth parents for an adopted child, finding out the identify of that so-and-so who cut in front of you on the road last week, getting information on celebrities and other people in the news, and so on. Decide which types of research fall beyond your own comfort level, and be prepared to refer those jobs to other experienced public records researchers.

You have to be careful to protect the confidentiality of both your client and the subject of your research; simply knowing that someone is researching an individual may tip off the opposing side in a court case to your client's legal strategy. If you need help conducting a search in a courthouse database, do not ask a clerk how to search for a specific name; ask, generically, how to conduct a search on an individual's name.

Although all independent info pros should carry general liability insurance, public records researchers usually carry errors-and-omissions (E&O) insurance as well. E&O insurance protects you from lawsuits in which a client claims that you failed to find information that you should have turned up. As Alex Kramer, owner of Kramer Research, noted, "Public records research is not an exact science. If something is written wrong, if something is misfiled, forget it. There are just too many variables out there. You do the best you can. That is all you can guarantee to your clients."

You may also want to use a more formal disclaimer notice, as discussed in Chapter 17, Ethics and Legalities. This could say, for example, "The information provided was compiled from public records and from third parties with authorization, when required. {your company} has exercised its best efforts to provide accurate information, but does not guarantee the accuracy of the data reported. {your company} hereby expressly disclaims any liability for consequential, incidental, or punitive damages resulting from errors, partial data, or inaccuracies in the data provided." Be sure to consult with your lawyer about an appropriate disclaimer to include with your research results, and remember that disclaiming liability does not by itself prevent a client from suing you.

Getting Started as a Public Records Researcher

Like other independent info pros, public records researchers get most of their business through networking and word of mouth. Much of your business will be local, but some jobs will be subcontracts from other info pros or from private investigation firms. A number of networks of public records researchers and private investigators exist that you can market to and that you can use when your clients need out-of-town research. Some public record research groups in the U.S. include:

- Public Record Retriever Network (PRRN; www.brbpub.com/PRRN), an online directory of public records researchers maintained by BRB Publications, Inc.

- National Association of Legal Investigators (www.nalionline.org)

- State associations or registries of licensed investigators that may also provide public records research. You will have to drill down from the state's main website to find a registry of investigators; some states do not make this information available online, but they will give you contact information for the regulatory board if you request it. You can also use a search engine and include the words *investigator*, *association*, and the state you are interested in.

Don't forget the Association of Independent Information Professionals (AIIP; www.aiip.org), which includes not only public records researchers but a wide variety of other info pros.

In order to build a public records research business, you have to recognize and create your own market opportunities. Figure out what unique local resources you have access to and who would need this type of information.

What if you live in a small town? Public records work does not necessarily have to be done in a big city. Law firms, the major market for public records searches, often require local research. If you specialize in title searches, you can market to real estate companies. In fact, you can often market informally as you are out in the field doing research. If you notice a lawyer or paralegal struggling to figure out how to look up a case file or frustrated at not being able to find anything on an individual, offer to help. It is a powerful marketing moment—you are face-to-face with a prospective client and demonstrating your proficiency at something that person realizes is difficult to do. Although I usually counsel against spending much time on one-to-one marketing, it makes sense to seize the opportunity when it presents itself; personal interaction can be very powerful in this type of setting.

Public Records Databases

As I said earlier in this chapter, no online public records database is complete or comprehensive. There is a lot of overlap, but there are gaps as well so you usually have to search more than one database for any given project.

Several specialized databases provide information from U.S. government sources, including:

- ChoicePoint (www.choicepoint.com), also searchable through AutoTrackXP (www.autotrackxp.com)

- KnowX (www.knowx.com)

- CourtLink (courtlink.lexisnexis.com)

These online services offer access to legally available information such as individuals' current and prior addresses, assets, real estate transactions, judgments or liens, professional and driver's licenses, and so on. Some public records information is also available through professional online services such as LexisNexis (www.lexisnexis.com), Westlaw (www.westlaw.com), and Factiva (www.factiva.com). In addition, PACER (pacer.psc.uscourts.gov) is the U.S. federal court system's collection of databases covering cases in district, circuit, and bankruptcy courts. Keep in mind that not all federal courts make their case information available on PACER and that the system does not include state or municipal court dockets. Also, PACER is not a single aggregated index but rather a collection of systems maintained by each court system. That means that you will have to search multiple systems if you are doing a comprehensive search, and you will have to budget the time to learn how to use each court's online system.

Many local jurisdictions maintain their own online indexes to public records. No comprehensive list exists of sites where you can search these indexes, but the following sites provide links to a number of government websites where you can check to see if such indexes are available for a particular jurisdiction (note that most focus on U.S. jurisdictions):

- SearchSystems.net (www.searchsystems.net)

- BRB Publications (www.brbpub.com/pubrecsites.asp)

- State and Local Government on the Net (www.statelocalgov.net)

- PublicRecordFinder.com (www.publicrecordfinder.com)

Many of the records in the local jurisdiction indexes include only cursory information on each case: the parties, the date the case was filed, the case number, maybe the attorneys of record, and perhaps a one- or two-word description of the type of case—divorce or contracts, for example. You still have to obtain the actual documents from the case file to find out what was really involved. Most jurisdictions will not take telephone requests so you have to go in person to request the file you want, review it, and photocopy whatever material your client needs. Many files are kept off-site in storage facilities, which often means requesting the file one day and returning another day to review the material once it has been retrieved from storage and sent to the public research room.

To complicate matters, if you are researching an individual with a common name, you may have trouble determining whether the cases you have turned up involve your Henry J. Smith or another Henry J. Smith. Often, nothing in the court documents uniquely identifies the participants—they do not include Social Security numbers, addresses, or other identification—so you will have to do additional research to figure out whether each case you identify actually involves your target.

As part of a public records job, you will often want to search newspapers and other periodicals as well to find any mentions of your target. That phase of the project might turn up issues in local jurisdictions you may not have thought of. See Chapter 33, Specialized Web Databases, and Chapter 34, Professional Online Services, for descriptions of some additional online sources that public records researchers either search themselves or subcontract to other independent info pros who specialize in searching these services.

Lessons for Public Records Researchers

- ✦ There is no single aggregated index to public records resources, despite various websites' extravagant claims.

- ✦ No online resource for public records is comprehensive or complete.

- ✦ Be sure you know the laws in your jurisdiction regarding access to and use of public records.

- ✦ Successful public records researchers are detail-oriented, persistent, and resourceful. If one approach doesn't work, they know how to pivot and try another strategy.

- ✦ Most public records work entails going on-site to conduct research, sometimes multiple times.

Chapter 37

Deliverables

We often spend so much time focusing on determining our clients' needs, managing our clients' expectations, and doing the research itself that we forget what might be the most important part of any project—the information we actually send to the client. We know how much work went into that final package, but unless we make it obvious, our client may not appreciate everything that was involved. You probably don't want to give your client a blow-by-blow description; indeed, your client almost certainly does not expect or need to hear all the gruesome details. But you do have to make sure that when you present your invoice, your client will pay it knowing how much value he received. When you provide analysis, synthesis, and a summary of the key elements of your research, you are providing tremendous added value. Be sure to surface that value so your client sees what you have contributed.

No Added Value = No Perceived Value

Every independent info pro knows that it is the content that matters, not the packaging, right? Well, yes and no. We are experts at finding information because we look past the hype and focus on whether the source is authoritative, accurate, and up-to-date. Our clients come to us because they know we are good at finding information efficiently; that is a given. What sets us apart from the competition—and by that I mean other info pros, our clients' internal information sources, and do-it-yourself searching—is that we add tangible value after the research, and we package the material in a way that makes it accessible and user-friendly.

As the research aspect of a project draws to a conclusion, look at the information you have gathered and think about how you can make it more digestible and more easily absorbed by someone who is looking at it for the first time. That is harder than it sounds; you have been immersed in this project and, in a sense, swimming in the data. You are probably perfectly clear on what all this material is and what it tells you. But try to step back and think about what it looks like to your client—someone who no doubt understands the concepts covered in the information you are sending, but who does not see the context until you make that clear. Your client did not spend the last three days doing the research, digging around in various resources, and sorting through an array of documents, websites, spreadsheets, and other information. Your job is to put the retrieved information in context.

Basic Data Massage

There are various levels of post-processing, from simply cleaning up and reformatting the output of an online search to sophisticated analysis and distillation of the information. If you are planning to send a set of electronic documents (articles, reports, patents, websites, and so on), I assume that you will at least insert page breaks at the end of each document and delete any extraneous material such as indexing terms. If you include plain text material in a tabular format, make sure that it is in a nonproportional font such as Courier, which will retain the proper spacing.

If you are including information from webpages, include the full URL and, if appropriate, the date it was accessed. Extract the key material so that your client does not have to go to the website in order to read the content.

Packaging Your Results

Even if you are providing very little polishing of the information, you can always generate a table of contents that helps guide your client through the material you are delivering. Other simple ways to enhance the usability of your work include:

- Highlighting, underlining, or bolding the key sentences or paragraphs in each item so that your client can easily locate the most useful information

- Summarizing the results in your cover letter, telling the client what you found and extracting the key points from your research results

- Providing a list of the resources you used, including hyperlinked website URLs, names of databases or files searched on the professional online services, contact information for the individuals you interviewed, and so on

I also always add a footer at the bottom of every page consisting of my company name, address, phone number, and email address. This ensures that, even if the package of material is taken apart and distributed within my client's organization or beyond, readers will know who provided the information.

Familiar Faces and Road Maps

Be aware of how your clients are accustomed to looking at information. Chances are they do not conduct research themselves on a regular basis, but they are probably comfortable reading newspapers or wire stories on the web, checking sports scores online, and so on. The more you make your work product look similar to what your clients see elsewhere, the more user-friendly and accessible your work becomes. For example, look at Figure 37.1—the beginning of an article from the *New York Times'* website—and Figure 37.2—the same article, downloaded from Dialog. Which one is easier to read? Which one will look more familiar to a client? For many clients, the unadorned Dialog format may be just fine, but for the CEO, you might want to make the extra effort of providing a more user-friendly and familiar-looking version.

In addition to formatting your material, find out if your client has any specific needs and preferences. Does she like to see bullet points of the key issues? Does she work extensively with charts, graphs, and spreadsheets? If so, would she like you to extract data from your results and create graphics that illustrate the information you found? And make sure your word processing software and delivery defaults are compatible with the ones your clients have. Some clients' organizations upgrade their software regularly, but some, especially smaller businesses, do not. Also, be sensitive to the fact that formatting features that work beautifully for you and most of your clients may be more of a hindrance than a help for clients with a different computer setup.

Regardless of what type of material you have pulled together, you want to make it easy for your client to navigate through the content. An alternative to a hyperlinked table of contents, for example, is a collection of article summaries with a link to click for the full text. Figure 37.3 is an example of one way to provide the client with a quick overview along with an easy way to read more.

Better Vision, With a Telescope Inside the Eye

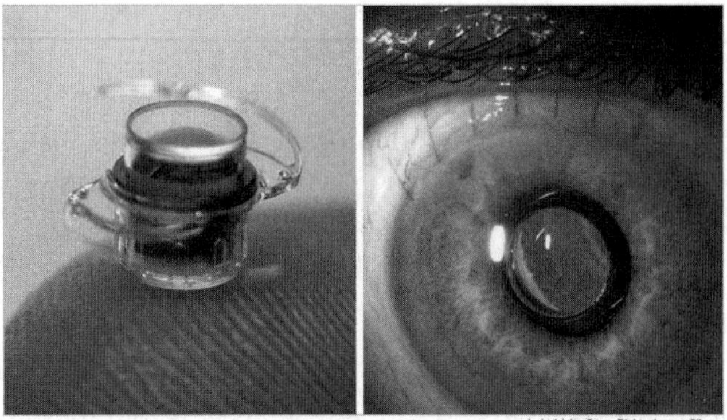

Left, VisionCare; Right, James Gilman

A tiny telescope, already approved for use in Europe, can be implanted in one eye to help people with an advanced form of macular degeneration. The device takes the place of the natural lens.

By ANNE EISENBERG
Published: July 18, 2009

A TINY glass telescope, the size of a pea, has been successfully implanted in the eyes of people with severely damaged retinas, helping them to read, watch television and better see familiar faces.

The new device is for people with an irreversible, advanced form of macular degeneration in which a blind spot develops in the central vision of both eyes.

SIGN IN TO RECOMMEND
E-MAIL
SEND TO PHONE
PRINT
REPRINTS
SHARE

Figure 37.1 Example of article in web version of the *New York Times*

1/9/1
04947877 885460090719
NOVELTIES; Better Vision, With a Telescope Inside the Eye
ANNE EISENBERG
New York Times , Late Edition - Final ED , Col 0 , p 4
Sunday July 19 2009
Document Type: Newspaper **Journal Code:** NYT **Language:** English
Record Type: Fulltext **Section Heading:** SECTBU
Word Count: 951

Text:
A TINY glass telescope, the size of a pea, has been successfully implanted in the eyes of people with severely damaged retinas, helping them to read, watch television and better see familiar faces.
The new device is for people with an irreversible, advanced form of macular degeneration in which a blind spot develops in the central vision of both eyes.

Figure 37.2 Example of article on Dialog

Consumers' Attitudes Toward Credit

The Last Temptation of Plastic
The New York Times, 7 December 7 2008

"Lenders will ultimately choose to provide fewer credit lines to fewer customers," Meredith A. Whitney, a banking analyst, said recently. By her projections, consumers could lose access to $2 trillion in credit in the next 18 months. This would force many Americans to radically change their behavior—saving for what they can afford rather than financing what they covet.

Shift to thrift could stick: Personal savings rate jumps, ideas on money change
Chicago Tribune, 16 November 2008

Americans' attitudes about debt and savings appear to be fundamentally changing, according to economists and market research experts. Weaving a financial safety net is becoming more important than having the largest plasma-screen TV on the block or the season's hottest handbag. "We think this is going to become part of a new way of life," said Madelyn Hochstein, president of DYG, a marketing firm that conducts social research.

Will downturn uproot nation's attitudes toward personal finances?
The Miami Herald, 19 October 2008

Beliefs woven into the fabric of American life—from the idea that a home is a rock-solid retirement asset to the adage that stocks always make money in the long run to the notion that markets should be left unfettered—all have been thrown into doubt. We may see a big shift in consumer behavior from wanting to take on debt and wanting to have a big house to a simpler lifestyle.

Figure 37.3   Example of hyperlinked summaries of articles

Moving Beyond Research Results

In addition to simply providing your research results, as pleasingly formatted as they are, develop added-value analysis that your client might find useful. I was taken aback the first time a client asked me for a PowerPoint presentation of the results of my work. How could I reduce all the information I found to five slides, I thought? Then I realized that he was accustomed to seeing information delivered that way and that presenting my results in the same familiar format was the most efficient way to let him see the key points before he dug deeper into the material. Your job is not only to find the most useful information you can but also to make that information as easy to use as possible. If your client is developing a PowerPoint slide show and needs information to insert into the presentation, provide the results in that format. If your client is accustomed to receiving reports from his staff in the form of one-page bulleted memos, use that format.

Another feature that you may want to make part of your cover letter or summary report is what I call an "information topography" report. We info pros sometimes forget that we learn a lot in the process of doing research, most of which is not obvious in the results we send. For example, here are some snippets of information I gleaned during a recent online research project:

- Contrary to the client's expectations, the topic was not being discussed in consumer publications.

- There seems to be a lot of interest in this topic in Europe, based on the number of articles I found from European sources.

- An industry only tangentially related to my client's is tracking this topic closely. This may indicate possible synergies that my client had not previously thought of.

What I related to my client in this case was essentially information *about* information—what I found as I was doing my research that would not have been surfaced simply by delivering the research results. As we conduct research, we see the lay of the information landscape; we see where deep pockets of information reside and where little information exists. We get a sense of what kinds of publications, groups, and industries care about the topic we are researching. All of this can be tremendously useful to our clients, but we have to spell it out for our client to see the information topography that we have mapped out.

Less Is More

It is difficult for new info pros to figure out what not to include in the final report to a client. You have found all this great information—pages and pages and pages of it—and since you will be charging the client for the cost of obtaining it all, shouldn't you include every single page? The answer is no—unless you have previously discussed the issue with your client, and he has said that he really, truly does want everything you can find. In most situations, your client is using you because he doesn't want everything—he wants the key information, the best of what is out there.

Clients will often pay more for five pages of information than they will for 105 pages. I will never forget a project I did for a client who wanted to know what people were saying about a specific aspect of color printers for home use. She authorized a budget that included 30 hours of my time, and I gathered information from all over—articles from consumer publications, photography and digital printing magazines, and newspapers; postings from web discussion forums on digital cameras and printing; email discussion list messages; blog postings; social network groups; and market research studies. My client told me that she wanted just a three-page summary of my findings, but I just did not believe that, for such a big budget, she would settle for so little material. So I sent her a 10-page report on what I found along with a separate file of all the material I had gathered. She called and said she was happy with the report, but she was still waiting for my three-page summary. Sure enough, once I managed to distill all I had found down to three pages, she was completely happy with the results. What she was paying me for was not just my ability to gather the information but to make sense out of it and provide distillation of what I had found into just the key elements.

When I first started my business, I did a good deal of subcontracted research work for Linda Cooper, an information consultant in Pennsylvania. In addition to doing the research, she had me send her a memo explaining in a sentence or two why I was including each article in the package. So, for example, I'd write something like, "Article 1 includes a useful chart on the company's market share in the women's apparel industry, and a discussion (which I highlighted) on its strategic plans. Article 2 is an interview with the leading women's apparel designer, discussing trends in the industry. I am including Article 3 because …" If I had decided to eliminate any article from the package I sent her, she asked to have it enclosed at the end as supplemental material.

What surprised me as I did this was how many articles I moved to the "supplemental" category. Once I had to articulate why I was including an article, I often realized that it wasn't really that useful, or it covered a tangential topic, or it duplicated what another article provided. After a while, Linda stopped asking for the article annotations since I had learned how to weed out the extraneous material. But, almost two decades later, I still conduct the Linda Cooper Exercise in my head each time I prepare a package of material for a client, ensuring that I am highlighting the most relevant and useful information rather than just dumping a big file of stuff in his email inbox.

Are You Professional or Strategic?

There is a difference between a professional researcher and a strategic information consultant. The former probably knows her way through every fee-based database, can generate the best-looking search results ever seen, and can do it without breaking a sweat or having a hair out of place. A strategic consultant, on the other hand, looks at the results of research as simply the first step. After gathering and organizing the information, she will look at the results and think about what this tells her. What connections does she see between disparate parts of an industry? What are the trends her client should know about? What does all the information she has gathered tell her?

Providing analysis and answers rather than just information—no matter how well-formatted—is what sets you apart from any competition and ensures client loyalty. Our clients already have access to far more information than they can ever absorb; what they often value the most is our ability to synthesize what we have gathered and to provide intelligence and perspective in addition to the best information available.

Of course, there are exceptions to this principle of providing analysis as well as information. In general, lawyers, clinicians, engineers, and other professionals who specialize in providing analysis need to draw their own conclusions from the information you provide. (As a side note, that is one reason why these professional groups are more difficult to market to, as they may have less use for or need of our value-added services.)

Working the Online Services

Dialog and DataStar are known for their powerful data-mining tools, some of which can be tremendously useful for info-entrepreneurs. (See Chapter 34, Professional Online Services, for more about the fee-based online services.) They both, for example, have the ability to sort your results a number of ways, depending on the database. If you are using a database of company information, you can sort the results to find out which companies that meet your search criteria have the highest price/earnings ratio. You can search a literature database and determine in which medical journals an author has been most frequently published. You can chart the number of articles mentioning a new technology over time, showing graphically, for example, that the peak interest in titanium widgets was four years ago, when the Widgelator company rolled out its latest product, and that discussion of titanium widgets has dropped off dramatically in the last two years.

Making Things Graphical

Keep an eye out for tools you can use to turn your results into a visual display that tells a story. For example, some search engines will display the frequency of search queries over time; you can see how often people looked for titanium widgets in Google over the past two years compared to how often they looked for any kind of widget or when people started blogging about the widgets. You can review which companies have been awarded the most patents in the last five years on a particular technology, which may indicate which companies are cutting-edge in that area or which may be moving into your client's arena.

How you highlight key facts or insights will depend on the project, the information you are working with, and your client's needs. There is no standard format—create whatever best conveys the information you need to highlight. See Figures 37.4 and 37.5 for examples in which I took results from my research and turned the information into a format that my clients could use immediately.

Key Messages of XYZ Competitors

	Honest Beverages	American Beverage Corp.	White Rock Distilleries	Proximo Spirits	Luctor Intl.
URL	honesttea.com	ambev.com	whiterock distilleries.com	proximospirits. com	luctor.com
Key products	Honest Tea, Honest Ade, Honest Kids	Daily Juice, Sunburst Fruit Juices, Twin Mountain	Orloff vodka, Barbarossa rum, Pinnacle gin, Tortilla tequila, Canadian Reserve whisky	Three Olives vodka, Centenario tequila, Matusalem rum, 1800 tequila	Van Gogh vodka, Esprexxo Ultimo vodka, Van Gogh gin
Key message	B2C messages, appeal to customers' social consciousness	B2B messages, targeted to suppliers and distributors, re: enhancing profitability	B2B messages, targeted to its distribution network, re: low cost, family-run business	Appeal to young, hip sophisticated consumers	High-end alcoholic beverages, sophisticated taste
Methods for communicating with customers	Co-owners have blogs showing hip customers with Honest Tea	Emphasis is on marketing to its "extensive network of brokers and distributors"	Emphasis is on marketing to its network of distributors	"Design your own bottle" contest, music, dance steps, postcards, recipes, ecards	Blog, recipes, "events," webcams at bars

Sources: company websites

Figure 37.4 Example of table created from company websites

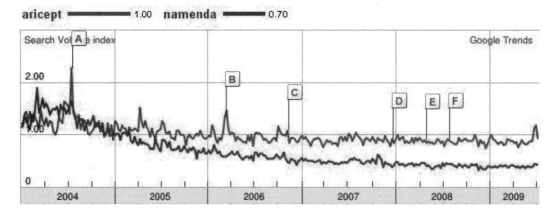

Figure 37.5   Example of table showing frequency of searches for two drugs, Aricept and Namenda

Branding and "Sealing" Your Results

I have suggested some ways to highlight the added value you bring to the research process by packaging your results in a manner that your clients will find easy and convenient to use. But it is also important to think about the format of your deliverable and about making that package look as professional as possible.

If I am concerned about maintaining the appearance and format of a report, I will often convert it to a PDF before sending it to the client. This ensures that when my client prints the report or looks at it on the screen, it will appear the same as when I sent it. Some word processing software packages come with a feature that lets you convert a file to PDF. If you buy the Adobe Acrobat software (www.adobe.com), you also have the ability to "lock" a PDF report so that the recipient cannot change it. If your report includes separate PDFs, your client may find it most useful if you create a single PDF file of your report with all the other PDF files inserted directly into your report.

Archiving Search Results

What do you do with the results of your research after you have sent your report to the client? You should probably save a copy of your search, although some professional online services impose restrictions on how long you can maintain such a file on your computer. I usually keep search results for six months, as permitted by my service agreements with the various online vendors. The only reason to keep a copy is in case a client loses the report you sent and you need to send a replacement, sometimes months after you completed the project. Of course, you will never send the results of a search to another client, especially if it includes material from any of the fee-based online services; when you download content from an online service, you are buying it for a single client only.

Another reason to save a copy of your search results is in case a client or someone else questions your search strategy. Although I only save the report itself for a few months, I retain a printout of all my search strategies as well as any webpages I relied on, the social networks I checked, the blogs I went to, the databases searched, the cover letter, and all other correspondence with the client regarding the extent and limitations of the research. Webpages can change at any time so you may want to use software that lets you save the original page—as opposed to just the URL—including all formatting, frames, links, and graphics.

Top Tips for Preparing Deliverables

◆ Format your report to look attractive and familiar to your client; plain text often appears too "dense."

◆ Highlight the key information in the text and/or include bullet points for important findings in your cover letter.

◆ Offer to provide analysis and synthesis of the information.

◆ Include an "information topography" report as part of your summary to the client.

◆ Less is more. Weed your search results ruthlessly; do not overwhelm your client with data.

◆ Consider "sealing" your results in PDFs to maintain their professional appearance.

Chapter 38

Other Services You Can Offer

The focus of this book has been on information businesses that provide some type of research and analysis service. However, many independent info pros also offer services that go beyond providing information and analysis. Some give workshops and seminars. Some write user manuals and training material for information companies or marketing copy for websites. Some provide consulting services to the information industry—to information providers who need help developing or improving their user interface, for example, and to libraries and information centers that require assistance in resolving a management problem or improving their service. And finally, some independent info pros offer out-sourcing—that is, personnel services such as library-staffing-in-a-box, temporary help, or specialized staff for specific library jobs such as cataloging or intranet website development.

All these services require a fair amount of marketing, particularly if you are offer-ing them as a sideline to your main focus. However, if you present your various serv-ices in a way that highlights your background and experience, your clients will see the synergies that come from hiring someone with a broad range of skills. When I am invited to teach workshops on advanced web research techniques, I often hear the comment, "It's great to find someone who doesn't just teach this kind of research but actually does it for a living." As long as the various services that you provide tie together somehow, you will benefit by reminding clients of all the information serv-ices you can provide. Just do not include a blurb for your sideline selling Tupperware; that's a fine business, but it does not relate to your skills as an infor-mation professional and merely dilutes your message.

Training, Workshops, and Seminars

Chapter 26, Marketing by Writing and Speaking, talks about using conference presentations to market your business. But more in-depth speaking opportunities can be a source of revenue as well. Some independent info pros offer customized or one-on-one training in areas such as searching the web, effective telephone research, or advanced search techniques on the professional online services—essentially, teaching clients about what you do every day. These personalized training sessions require a good deal of preparation because the focus is the needs, interests, and skills of the clients you are teaching. On the other hand, you can charge a premium for the customization, and it is rewarding to see your client's eyes light up as he finally realizes how to do something he did not think possible.

Other training possibilities include half- or full-day workshops or seminars on specific types of research or information skills. The advantage of developing a workshop or seminar is that, unlike the personalized training, creating the course content and handouts is a one-time investment; after that, you need only do minor updating and some customization each time you give the workshop. You might arrange to teach such workshops in conjunction with professional conferences or trade shows, usually on the days just before or after the main program. You can also organize and market your own workshop, but the amount of marketing required is generally beyond the scope of an independent info pro unless you intend to do this kind of work full time. Promoting a workshop usually requires a very large mailing list of people potentially willing to pay several hundred dollars for training. Purchasing a specialized list like this is expensive and is an ongoing expense; building your own high-quality list of likely customers can take months or years. It also requires administrative backup to handle registrations and credit card payments as well as access to an appropriate training facility and the required audiovisual equipment. Renting a room, renting or purchasing a digital projector, and lining up an internet connection alone can run several thousand dollars and that does not include the cost of your handouts or the coffee and snacks that workshop attendees expect. Until you know that you will be able to attract enough people to pay your overhead and make a profit, it is usually wiser to focus on offering workshops or seminars through the professional associations you belong to or other professional conferences or trade shows.

If you are contemplating doing a substantial amount of professional speaking, I recommend the National Speakers Association (NSA; www.nsaspeaker.org).

Membership is limited to people who, within the preceding 12 months, have given at least 20 paid presentations or made at least $25,000 in speaking fees. However, NSA also has local chapters, many of which offer "apprentice" membership for anyone interested in professional speaking. They usually have monthly meetings that focus on topics such as how to improve your delivery or presence, how to involve an audience, how to keep up with technology, and so on. NSA members are collegial and supportive of each other, and the association has a number of programs for new and aspiring speakers.

Podcasts, Webinars, and Other Web-Based Products

In both Chapter 24, Marketing on the Web, and Chapter 26, Marketing by Writing and Speaking, I allude briefly to developing web-based presentations, tutorials, and other learning material you can sell through your website. If you are willing to invest the time in learning how to produce professional-quality podcasts and to buy the equipment needed for high-quality recording, this can be a nice source of income.

Info-entrepreneurs have found a number of avenues for marketing their podcasts, webinars, and other web content. These include:

- Developing continuing education courses for specific professional groups. Becoming accredited for an association's certification or licensing is time-consuming and requires a clear demonstration that you understand the group's profession and learning needs. Once in the system, however, this can become steady revenue stream.

- Providing live webinars and then selling the recordings to attendees and those who missed the event. These are simple to produce as they generally require no more than a quick edit after the recording. As a result, the price point for these recordings will probably have to be lower than for a more polished production.

- Producing training programs, either customized for a client or designed for public sale. These products require high-quality recording, editing, and packaging, and may need to be updated regularly. The advantage of these products is that you can sell them from the back of the room during a presentation you give; what better group to market to than the people who just heard your brilliant, informative presentation?

One of the challenges in providing any downloadable content is that you have to troubleshoot customers who are trying to bring your files past their enterprise firewall, get a podcast to run on an older operating system, or distribute your webinar within an organization. Since you will be dealing with a wide variety of customers with a wide range of skills and expertise, expect to spend time handholding and walking people through the technical aspects of getting and using your product. Assume that whatever can go wrong will go wrong with at least one cranky customer.

Outsourced Library Services

Although most independent info pros focus on research services, a subset within the profession offers more direct library-related services. These are info pros who take over some or all of the functions of private libraries or information centers themselves. Their clients tend to be corporations, nonprofits, government agencies, or other types of organizations, rather than public or academic libraries.

Some libraries outsource functions beyond their core competencies so that they do not have to find or develop internal expertise. Specific tasks that are often outsourced include:

- Handling requests for photocopies or original documents and providing interlibrary loan services

- Cataloging

- Developing and maintaining intranet websites

- Managing subscriptions, checking in periodical issues, and routing periodicals

- Providing support and training services around the library's services and products

Most of these jobs require at least minimal information-professional skills but are relatively generic. So, unlike a library's reference and research services, for example, they can be outsourced fairly easily.

Some libraries outsource in order to address specific problems—a sudden upsurge in research requests, moving the library, or covering the workload of a library professional out on extended leave. Some of this kind of work borders on consulting, particularly if you are brought in not only to manage a library automation project but to make recommendations regarding which system to select and to train staff in how to use the system most effectively. And some libraries outsource some or most of their research work on an as-needed or ongoing basis.

Most libraries serve remote office locations by putting information on an intranet and offering telephone and email reference services. But some libraries need to maintain a physical presence in branch offices that are not adequately served by the main library. Rather than hire and supervise a remote staff, some library managers simply contract with a library outsourcing company to handle the management of the remote library. Similarly, some libraries in multinational companies (as well as companies with round-the-clock employees) need to provide reference and research services 24 hours a day, seven days a week. Rather than struggle to find staff willing to work the graveyard shift, they may opt to outsource that coverage to someone who is willing to work such hours. Alternatively, some libraries have arrangements with outsourcers in other parts of the world; they simply hand off the phone calls to the outsourcer when the library's workday ends, and the outsourcer's day is just beginning.

Sometimes libraries are outsourced entirely; the existing library employees are reassigned or let go, and all the library functions are handed over to an outsourcing firm. The contractor is responsible for hiring and managing staff who usually work on the client's premises and, as far as most employees can tell, are just like any other employees. This type of situation can be difficult and involves a delicate balance. Specialized libraries often rely on the support and cooperation of other local libraries for borrowing and lending materials, sharing resources, brainstorming, and so on. However, librarians in other organizations may harbor some ill will toward the staff of an outsourced library, who are perceived as having taken over the "real" library and prompting the decision to fire the staff. Obviously, this perception isn't based on reality because the decision to outsource a library is almost always made before any consideration of who or what entity will be hired to provide the services that employees still need. But the feelings are still there, and as a result, it can be difficult to hire and retain staff for an outsourced library.

In most outsourcing situations, the independent info pro has to find a way to provide the same level of service as an in-house info pro, while costing the client less and still making a profit. For short-term outsourced projects, the cost savings are obvious; it is almost always cheaper to pay a contractor for the duration rather than bring a new employee on board. And for jobs that involve specialized skill such as network management or training, the client may be willing to pay a premium to avoid having to build the expertise in-house. Outsourcing a branch library or the entire library function is the most difficult situation of all. The contractor wants to hire and retain good employees but is under pressure to keep costs down.

Consulting Services

Consulting—to information vendors, to libraries, or to groups or companies that need help organizing, managing or using information—is a service that a number of independent info pros provide either as a sideline or as the major focus of their business.

Running a consulting practice has much in common with running a research business, but it presents its own set of challenges as well. Projects are usually much larger in terms of scope, budget, and duration. You are selling your expertise and your opinions as opposed to information created by others; that is difficult for some info pros.

Types of consulting that info pros provide include:

- Library consulting: Conducting information audits, providing guidance in selecting a new online library system, developing a marketing program for the library, and providing strategic planning and other development services

- Enterprise information consulting: Working with a group or organization that needs to create and develop a library or information center or otherwise organize and manage their information

- Information industry consulting: Providing advice regarding the usability, functionality, and content of an existing or proposed online system or product; advising on training and marketing issues

Consulting can be a way to keep you fresh; you have a chance to go into an organization, ask lots of questions, see how things are done, and come up with recommendations on how things could be done better. Consulting can also be immensely frustrating. Often, you are dealing with many personalities, not all of whom see eye to eye on the problem at hand and how to resolve it, and you may feel pressured to come to a conclusion that your client wants but that you do not feel is the best solution for the organization.

The skills required to succeed as a consultant include the same ones needed by any independent info pro—the ability to run a small business, manage cash flow, market yourself and your company, manage your time, and so on. The unique demands of consulting require a special set of skills. These include the ability to:

- "Read" a situation and sort out the personalities, agendas, and concerns of all the players

- Evenhandedly assess the needs and priorities of the organization

- Build relationships of trust with the key players

- Evaluate alternatives, thinking beyond the options your clients perceive

You also need good writing skills because your deliverable usually consists of a report and set of recommendations. If you cannot clearly and persuasively articulate the problem, the alternative solutions, and your recommendation, your clients are not going to be happy with your work. And although it may seem obvious, you do have to have some experience as an information expert before you can provide consulting services; this is not service you can learn on the job. In order to successfully market yourself as a consultant, you need contacts and references, and a solid reputation in the information community. You may not be able to provide consulting services when you first start your information business, but later on, it can be a great way to take advantage of all the contacts and experience you have built up. My first few consulting jobs all came from existing clients who said, "I know you specialize in doing online research for us, but we really need some help in evaluating our in-house online resources. Can you help?" It is gratifying to be able to sell not only your expertise in finding information but also your knowledge and broad perspective on the information industry.

Checklist of Other Information Services Independent Info Pros Can Offer

✦ Personalized, one-on-one training

✦ Packaged workshops and seminars

✦ Webinars, podcasts, and other web-based products

✦ One-time or permanent outsourced staffing for libraries

✦ Consulting to libraries

✦ Needs analysis and information management consulting to organizations

✦ Consulting on product design and content and other issues to information providers

The Association of Independent Information Professionals

The Association of Independent Information Professionals (AIIP; www.aiip.org) was established in 1987 by 26 info pros, who met at the invitation of Dr. Marilyn Levine, a professor of Library and Information Science at the University of Wisconsin and the owner of Information Express. The composition of AIIP has changed over the years, as has the information industry itself and the expectations of our clients.

Today, AIIP has more than 600 members throughout the world, about 80 percent of whom are based in North America. There are five classes of membership:

- Full members: Those who own a business that provides information services

- Associate members: Those who are interested in the profession but don't own an information business

- Student members: Those who are interested in the profession and are currently enrolled in an accredited college or university (student members pay a discounted membership fee)

- Supporting members: Individuals or organizations that support the objectives of AIIP (and are willing to show their support by paying a significantly higher membership fee)

- Retired/emeritus members: Individuals who have retired from having owned an information business and who want to remain connected to AIIP

I joined AIIP before I started my information business, and it was one of the best investments I made. I was able to read and participate in AIIP's lively members-only electronic discussion forum, which gave me a good sense of the daily concerns of independent info pros. I also saved up money and airline frequent flier miles in order to attend the annual AIIP conference—again, before I launched my business. The conference was an extraordinary experience. Everyone there was serious about his or her business, and it seemed that all the conversations revolved around research, information, or being an entrepreneur. It also appeared that everyone knew everyone else, and, in fact, they did; the private discussion forum kept people in touch during the year. I remember taking detailed notes during the conference sessions and being astonished at how willing people were to share their experiences. One session was titled something like "My Biggest Marketing Mistakes." It consisted of a panel of four independent info pros telling all their colleagues what did and didn't work. I was amazed at the willingness of every member to share their expertise and knowledge with newcomers.

Obviously, one of the key benefits of AIIP membership is the ability to tap into the expertise of a network of longtime independent info pros, both in person at the annual conference and virtually on the private email discussion list. You will meet people with a wide range of backgrounds and experiences, you will find people you can subcontract work to and who will subcontract work to you, and you will develop a network of friends you can bounce ideas off who understand what it is like to run an information business.

The more tangible benefits of AIIP membership include:

- Significant discounts from a number of information vendors including waiver of monthly minimums or annual fees (some vendor benefits are limited to full members)

- Access to the members-only email discussion list, AIIP-L

- A listing in the AIIP directory, along with a description of your services and background

- Access to the free volunteer mentoring program, which connects new members with more experienced independent info pros

- A wide collection of electronic resources, including frequently discussed topics, white papers, and free webinars on topics ranging from "First-Year

Questions" to tips on conducting telephone research and how to market on a shoestring budget

- Sample subcontracting and nondisclosure agreements

- Subscription to AIIP's quarterly newsletter with practical articles on various aspects of the independent info pro business

You can join AIIP through its website. A searchable membership directory is also available on the website, along with material describing the independent info profession, an online store where you can purchase AIIP white papers, and other professional development resources.

Given the importance of maintaining the trust of clients, vendors, colleagues, and the public, AIIP has a code of ethics that all members are required to sign when they join the association and every year as they renew their membership. Once in a while, there is a flurry of news coverage when an unscrupulous company tries to sell access to information obtained illegally, and this makes a strong code of ethics even more crucial for our profession. We independent info pros must ensure that we not only comply with this code but that we avoid even the appearance of impropriety. Here is the current version of AIIP's *Code of Ethical Business Practice*:

An independent information professional is an information entrepreneur who has demonstrated continuing expertise in the art of finding and organizing information. The independent information professional provides information services on a contractual basis. Information professionals serve as objective intermediaries between the client and the information world. They bear the following responsibilities:

1. Uphold the profession's reputation for honesty, competence, and confidentiality.

2. Give clients current and accurate information within the budget and the time frames provided by the clients.

3. Help clients understand the sources of information used, and the degree of reliability which can be expected from those sources.

4. Accept only those projects which are legal and are not detrimental to our profession.

5. Respect client confidentiality.

6. Recognize intellectual property rights. Respect licensing agreements and other contracts. Explain to clients what their obligations might be with regard to intellectual property rights and licensing agreements.

7. Maintain a professional relationship with libraries, and comply with all their rules of access.

8. Assume responsibility for employees' compliance with this code.

Websites Mentioned in This Book

About the Author

Mary Ellen's website, www.BatesInfo.com

Info on Mary Ellen's strategic business coaching, www.BatesInfo.com/coaching

Mary Ellen's blog, www.LibrarianofFortune.com

AIIP

Association of Independent Information Professionals, www.aiip.org

Chapter 1: What's an Independent Info Pro?

Society of Competitive Intelligence Professionals (SCIP), www.scip.org

Special Libraries Association (SLA), www.sla.org

Chapter 2: A Day in the Life of an Independent Info Pro

Factiva, global.factiva.com

Dialog, www.dialogweb.com

Chapter 4: Are You a Potential Independent Info Pro?

U.S. Small Business Administration (SBA), www.sba.gov

Service Corps of Retired Executives (SCORE), www.score.org

American Library Association (ALA), www.ala.org

Chapter 7: Structuring Your Business

U.S. SBA, www.sba.gov

SBA, Small Business Planner: Managing Your Business From Start to Finish, www.sba.gov/smallbusinessplanner

HM Revenue & Customs, "Starting in Business," www.hmrc.gov.uk/startingup

Canada Revenue Agency, www.cra-arc.gc.ca

U.S. Internal Revenue Service (IRS), www.irs.gov

Companies House, www.companieshouse.gov.uk

Chapter 8: Before You Launch

U.S. SBA, www.sba.gov

SCORE, www.score.org

Center for Business Planning, www.businessplans.org

Ewing Marion Kauffman Foundation, www.entrepreneurship.org

Chapter 9: Setting Up Your Business

Network Solutions, www.networksolutions.com

DomainTools, www.domaintools.com

U.S. Patent and Trademark Office, www.uspto.gov

Companies House, www.companieshouse.gov.uk

Canada Business, Starting a Business, www.canadabusiness.ca/eng/125

Yellow Pages, www.yellowpages.com

Global Yellow Pages, www.globalyp.net

U.S. Internal Revenue Service, www.irs.gov

HM Revenue & Customs, www.hmrc.gov.uk

Canada Revenue Agency, www.cra-arc.gc.ca

U.S. SBA, Financial Assistance, www.sba.gov/financing

Google Voice, www.google.com/voice

Chapter 10: You.com

DomainTools, www.domaintools.com

Network Solutions, www.networksolutions.com

Search Engine Guide, www.searchengineguide.com

Google Webmaster Central, www.google.com/webmasters

Chapter 11: Business Apps for Info-Entrepreneurs

Zoho, www.zoho.com

Adobe Acrobat, www.adobe.com

Chapter 13: Managing Your Clients

U.S. SBA, www.sba.gov

U.S. SBA, Government Contracting, www.sba.gov/GC

Canada Business, www.canadabusiness.ca

Supply2.gov.uk, supply2.gov.uk

Chapter 14: Money, Money, Money

U.S. SBA, www.sba.gov

Canada Business, www.canadabusiness.ca

Business Link, www.businesslink.gov.uk

QuickBooks, quickbooks.intuit.com

U.S. IRS, www.irs.gov

Canada Revenue Agency, www.cra-arc.gov.ca

American Express, www.americanexpress.com

Chapter 17: Ethics and Legalities

Copyright Clearance Center, www.copyright.com

Chapter 18: Professional Development

SLA, www.sla.org

Public Record Retriever Network, www.brbpub.com/prrn

Chartered Institute of Library and Information Professionals, www.cilip.org.uk

American Association of Law Libraries, www.aallnet.org

Medical Library Association, www.mlahq.org

North American Sport Library Network, www.naslin.org

Patent Information Users Group, Inc., www.piug.org

Public Relations Society of America, www.prsa.org

Bates InfoTip, www.BatesInfo.com/tips

Chapter 19: Strategic Planning

SCORE, www.score.org

Chapter 23: Your Business Image

Paper Direct, www.paperdirect.com

Elance, www.elance.com

Guru, www.guru.com

craigslist, www.craigslist.org

Chapter 24: Marketing on the Web

Link Sleuth, home.snafu.de/tilman/xenulink.html

Librarian of Fortune, www.librarianoffortune.com

Chapter 25: Print and Eprint Marketing

How Stuff Works, www.howstuffworks.com

Did You Know, www.didyouknow.org

Paper Direct, www.paperdirect.com

Chapter 26: Marketing by Writing and Speaking

National Writers Union, www.nwu.org

WritersMarket.com, www.writersmarket.com

Toastmasters International, www.toastmasters.org

Chapter 27: Starting the Word of Mouth

Meetup, www.meetup.com

Chapter 28: Public Relations

BizJournals.com, www.bizjournals.com

Bacon's Media Database, www.cision.com

Gale Directory of Publications and Broadcast Media, www.gale.cengage.com

All-in-One Media Directory, www.gebbieinc.com

Media Contacts, www.burrellesluce.com.com

Yearbook of Experts, www.expertclick.com

Help A Reporter Out, www.helpareporter.com

Chapter 30: Thinking Like a Researcher

Stanford's Key to Information Literacy, skil.stanford.edu

21st Century Information Fluency, www.21cif.com

Chapter 32: Web Research 101

Search Engine Watch, www.searchenginewatch.com

University of California at Berkeley Library, "Finding Information on the Internet" tutorial, www.lib.berkeley.edu

Yahoo! Directory, dir.yahoo.com

IPL2, www.ipl.org

WWW Virtual Library, vlib.org

Scirus, www.scirus.com

BizToolkit, www.biztoolkit.org

Wikipedia, en.wikipedia.org

Yahoo! Groups, groups.yahoo.com

CataList, www.lsoft.com

BoardTracker, www.boardtracker.com

BoardReader, www.boardreader.com

Free Pint, www.freepint.com

ResourceShelf, www.resourceshelf.com

Chapter 33: Specialized Web Databases

Dialog, www.dialogweb.com

Factiva, global.factiva.com

Google Scholar, scholar.google.com

Public Library of Science, www.plos.org

PubMed Central, www.pubmedcentral.nih.gov

Directory of Open Access Journals, www.doaj.org

Open Access Directory wiki, oad.simmons.edu

U.S. Securities and Exchange Commission EDGAR files, edgar.sec.gov

STAT-USA, www.stat-usa.gov

Europa, www.europa.eu

Chapter 34: Professional Online Services

Dialog main corporate site, www.dialog.com

DialogWeb, www.dialogweb.com

DialogLink, support.dialog.com/dialoglink

Dialog1, www.dialog1.com

Dialog, Successful Searching on Dialog Command Language,
    support.dialog.com/searchaids/success

Dialog Training Programs, support.dialog.com/training

Dialog Quantum^2 Program, quantum.dialog.com

Factiva, www.factiva.com

Factiva InfoPro Alliance, www.factiva.com/infopro

LexisNexis, www.lexisnexis.com

LexisNexis InfoPro, law.lexisnexis.com/infopro

DataStar, www.datastarweb.com

Questel, www.questel.orbit.com

Westlaw, www.westlaw.com

Chapter 36: Public Records Research

Public Record Retriever Network, www.brbpub.com/PRRN

National Association of Legal Investigators, www.nalionline.org

ChoicePoint, www.choicepoint.com

AutoTrackXP, www.autotrackxp.com

KnowX, www.knowx.com

CourtLink, courtlink.lexisnexis.com

LexisNexis, www.lexisnexis.com

Westlaw, www.westlaw.com

Factiva, www.factiva.com

PACER, pacer.psc.uscourts.gov

SearchSystems.net, www.searchsystems.net

BRB Publications Free Resource Center, www.brbpub.com/pubrecsites.asp

State and Local Government on the Net, www.statelocalgov.net

PublicRecordFinder.com, www.publicrecordfinder.com

Chapter 37: Deliverables

Adobe Acrobat, www.adobe.com

Chapter 38: Other Services You Can Offer

National Speakers Association, www.nsaspeaker.org

People Quoted in This Book

Here is the contact information for the independent info pros and consultants I quote directly in this book. I am grateful to all of them for their assistance and contributions.

Michele Bate
Archer Van den Broeck Limited
mbate@archervandenbroeck.com

Andrea C. Carrero
Word Technologies Inc.
www.wordtex.com
Black Ink Marketing
www.blackinkmarketing.net
andrea@wordtex.com

Jan Davis
JT Research LLC
www.jtresearch.com
jt@jtresearch.com

Lorna Dean
Bedford Research Consultants
Lorna@BedfordResearch.com

Marjorie Desgrosseilliers
SmartyPants Research Services, LLC
www.smartypantsresearch.com
marjorie@smartypantsresearch.com

Kim Dority
G. K. Dority & Associates, Inc.
www.dorityassociates.com
kimdority@gkdority.com

Mary McCarty Earley
MME Research
www.mmeresearch.com
mary@mmeresearch.com

Michelle Fennimore
Competitive Insights
www.competitive-insights.com
m.fennimore@competitive-insights.com

Valerie Forrestal
Reference and Research Services Librarian
Stevens Institute of Technology
vforrestal.info

Liga M. Greenfield
BioMedPharmIS
www.biomedpharmis.com
lmgreenfield@biomedpharmis.com

Christine Hamilton-Pennell
Growing Local Economies, Inc.
www.growinglocaleconomies.com
christine@growinglocaleconomies.com

Jane John
On Point Research
www.onpointresearch.com
jjohn@onpointresearch.com

Amelia Kassel
MarketingBase
www.marketingbase.com
amelia@marketingbase.com

Margaret King
InfoRich Group, Inc.
www.inforichgroup.com
mking@inforichgroup.com

Jan Knight
Bancroft Information Services
www.bancroftinfo.com

Judy Koren
ResearchWise Associates
www.research-wise.com
judith@research-wise.com

Alex Kramer
Kramer Research
kramer@kramerresearch.com

Carol Lee-Roark, PhD
Hyalite Environmental, LLP
www.hyaliteenvironmental.com
carol@hyaliteenviornmetal.com

Chris Olson
Chris Olson & Associates
www.chrisolson.com
chris@chrisolson.com

Lynn Peterson
PFC Information Services, Inc.
www.pfcinformation.com
lpeterson@pfcinformation.com

Marcy Phelps
Phelps Research
www.phelpsresearch.com
www.MarcyPhelps.com
mphelps@phelpsresearch.com

Risa Sacks
Risa Sacks Information Services
www.risasacks.com
risa@risasacks.com

Cynthia Shamel
Shamel Information Services
www.shamelinfo.com
cshamel@shamelinfo.com

Ruth M. Shipley, MS, MLIS
SMR Information Solutions
www.smrinfosolutions.com
ruth@smrinfosolutions.com

Debbie Wynot
Library Consultants, LLC
www.libraryconsultants.com
debbie@libraryconsultants.com

About the Author

Mary Ellen Bates is the owner of Bates Information Services, Inc., now near its third decade of operation. She helps her clients make better strategic decisions, providing business research and analysis to business professionals and info pros. She also conducts webinars, workshops, and seminars for information professionals. The aspect of her business she enjoys the most is strategic business coaching for fellow info-entrepreneurs (www.BatesInfo.com/coaching). Prior to starting her own business in 1991, she worked in corporate and law libraries for 15 years. She received her master's in library and information science from the University of California at Berkeley and has been an online researcher since the late 1970s.

She is the author of five other books: *Super Searchers Cover the World* (Information Today, Inc., 2001), *Mining for Gold on the Internet* (McGraw-Hill, 2000), *Researching Online for Dummies*, 2nd edition, co-authored with Reva Basch (IDG Books Worldwide, 2000), *Super Searchers Do Business* (Information Today, Inc., 1999), and *The Online Deskbook* (Information Today, Inc., 1996). She writes for *EContent, ONLINE,* and *Searcher* and is the contributing editor of *The Information Advisor*. She is a frequent keynote speaker and has given presentations at information industry conferences around the world. She is a two-time past president and now a supporting member of the Association of Independent Information Professionals (AIIP) and is active in the Special Libraries Association (SLA).

She received AIIP's first annual Sue Rugge Memorial Award, created to recognize an AIIP member who, through mentoring, has significantly helped others establish their businesses. She also received the 2002 Professional Award from SLA and was named member of the year by the Communications Division and the Washington, DC Chapter of SLA.

Mary Ellen lives outside Boulder, Colorado, with her beloved partner and their two dogs.

You can find her at:
    email :: mbates@BatesInfo.com
    web :: www.BatesInfo.com
    blog :: www.LibrarianofFortune.com

Index

N

O

S

T

More Great Books from Information Today, Inc.

Point, Click, and Save
Mashup Mom's Guide to Saving and Making Money Online

By Rachel Singer Gordon

This immensely practical book and its supporting website provide clear, tech-savvy advice designed to reassure readers who are new to the world of saving and earning money online, while providing an array of innovative ideas, strategies, and resources for those who have been clipping coupons (online *or* off) for years. Rachel Singer Gordon is "Mashup Mom"—a widely read blogger who combines high- and low-tech strategies to help her readers achieve financial objectives. Here, she helps money-conscious web users gain immediate relief from the pain of rising prices, find fabulous freebies, engage the whole family in the fun of using the web to create income, and much more!

296 pp/softbound/ISBN 978-0-910965-86-6 $19.95

The Extreme Searcher's Internet Handbook, 3rd Ed.
A Guide for the Serious Searcher

By Randolph Hock

The Extreme Searcher's Internet Handbook is the essential guide for anyone who uses the internet for research—librarians, teachers, students, writers, business professionals, and others who need to search the web proficiently. In this fully updated third edition, award-winning writer and internet trainer Ran Hock covers strategies and tools (including search engines, directories, portals, and social networks) for all major areas of internet content. Readers with little to moderate searching experience will appreciate Hock's helpful, easy-to-follow advice, while experienced searchers will discover a wealth of new ideas, techniques, and resources.

368 pp/softbound/ISBN 978-0-910965-84-2 $24.95

The Mobile Marketing Handbook
A Step-by-Step Guide to Creating Dynamic Mobile Marketing Campaigns

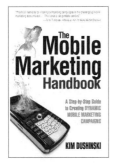

By Kim Dushinski

In this practical handbook, Kim Dushinski offers easy-to-follow advice for firms that want to interact with mobile users, build stronger customer relationships, reach a virtually unlimited number of prospects, and gain competitive advantage by making the move to mobile device users. *The Mobile Marketing Handbook* will help you put your message in the palms of their hands.

256 pp/softbound/ISBN 978-0-910965-82-8 $29.95

Business Cases for Info Pros
Here's Why, Here's How

By Ulla de Stricker

This practical guide explains why, when, and how a formal business case can be used as an effective tool for gaining support for information-based projects. Ulla de Stricker discusses the psychology of decision-making involving human and financial investments and demonstrates a logically sequenced progression for structuring a business case—from identifying the "problem, need, or opportunity" to proposing viable solutions and ensuring the presentation is delivered with impact. She then provides and comments on three case studies illustrating different approaches to creating successful business case documents.

120 pp/softbound/ISBN 978-1-57387-335-2 $39.50

What's the Alternative?
Career Options for Librarians and Info Pros

By Rachel Singer Gordon

In this book, Rachel Singer Gordon explains the dynamics of the shifting market for information-based work, reveals a range of nontraditional employment opportunities for librarians, and encourages info pros to utilize their skills in new and exciting ways by mixing practical advice with real-life stories of librarians working in various fields. Whether you're a recent library school grad facing a tight job market, a working librarian seeking improved work/life balance, or an info pro with an entrepreneurial streak, *What's the Alternative?* will help you explore your options and maximize your career potential.

288 pp/softbound/ISBN 978-1-57387-333-8 $35.00

Designing the Digital Experience
How to Use Experience Design Tools and Techniques to Build
Web Sites Customers Love

By David Lee King

As website design and functionality take a mighty leap forward, today's marketers and site designers can harness the power of "experience design" to help customers quickly find information, make purchases, or participate. Here, David Lee King explains the concepts behind designing digital experiences, describes a range of new tools and techniques, and shares experience design best practices. King demonstrates that digital experience design is all about giving web users what they want and shows how organizations can use it to distinguish themselves from the competition and uncork the viral marketing genie.

200 pp/softbound/ISBN 978-0-910965-83-5 $24.95